Handbook of Behavior Therapy with Sexual Problems

Volume I — General Procedures

(pp. i-liii, 1-258)

PGPS-64

PERGAMON GENERAL PSYCHOLOGY SERIES

Editors: Arnold P. Goldstein, *Syracuse University*
Leonard Krasner, *SUNY, Stony Brook*

TITLES IN THE PERGAMON GENERAL PSYCHOLOGY SERIES
(Added Titles in Back of Volume)

The terms of our inspection copy service apply to all the above books. A complete catalogue of all books in the Pergamon International Library is available on request.

The Publisher will be pleased to receive suggestions for revised editions and new titles.

Handbook of Behavior Therapy with Sexual Problems

Volume I — General Procedures

Joel Fischer, D.S.W.
and
Harvey L. Gochros, D.S.W.
University of Hawaii
Honolulu, Hawaii

Foreword by Leonard P. Ullmann

PERGAMON PRESS
New York / Toronto / Oxford / Sydney / Frankfurt / Paris

Pergamon Press Offices:

U.S.A.	Pergamon Press Inc., Maxwell House, Fairview Park, Elmsford, New York 10523, U.S.A.
U.K.	Pergamon Press Ltd., Headington Hill Hall, Oxford OX3, OBW, England
CANADA	Pergamon of Canada, Ltd., 75 The East Mall, Toronto, Ontario M8Z 5WR, Canada
AUSTRALIA	Pergamon Press (Aust) Pty. Ltd., 19a Boundary Street, Rushcutters Bay, N.S.W. 2011, Australia
FRANCE	Pergamon Press SARL, 24 rue des Ecoles, 75240 Paris, Cedex 05, France
WEST GERMANY	Pergamon Press GmbH, 6242 Kronberg/Taunus, Frankfurt-am-Main, West Germany

Library of Congress Cataloging in Publication Data

Main entry under title:

Handbook of behavior therapy with sexual problems.

(Pergamon general psychology series; 64)
Includes bibliographies and index.
1. Sexual disorders. 2. Sexual deviations.
3. Behavior therapy. I. Fischer, Joel. II. Gochros,
Harvey L. (DNLM: 1. Sex deviation—Therapy. 2. Sexual
disorders—Therapy. 3. Behavior therapy. WM610 F529b
RC556.B37 1976   616.6   75-34411
ISBN 0-08-020373-6 Vol. I
ISBN 0-08-020374-4 Vol. II

Printed in the United States of America

This book is dedicated to the new breed of clinical scientists in the helping professions: the practitioner who is open to new ideas and practice methods, who carefully monitors his client's progress and evaluates outcome, and who takes the risk of critical analysis of his work by others through publication of his results in professional journals. All of our work — and the outcome for our clients — is enhanced by these efforts.

Contents

VOLUME I

VOLUME II

Foreword

More than any other subject, sex brings behavioral, social and biological scientists face to face with human interactions and human values. Here physical pleasure and species survival are constrained and modified by custom and personal feeling. Theoreticians may test their models and clinicians their practices in an area that is changing, vital, exciting and complex. Because sex is important and interesting to all people, nowhere else is the amount of dogmatically asserted misinformation greater, just as nowhere else is the pain caused by such misinformation greater.

It is in this context that it is such a pleasure to give an Aloha of welcome to the present two volumes by Professors Fischer and Gochros. They have brought together many articles about behavior-change procedures for diverse target behaviors. The result is an impressive body of data and clinical alternatives which providers of therapeutic services should have not only on their library shelves, but also firmly mastered and in mind. This information supplements and adds crucially to the excellent presentations of integrated approaches such as those by Annon (1974, 1975) and Masters and Johnson (1970). The clinician should know not only procedures, but also the professional literature and thinking that underlie his or her daily efforts. Without such additional study and thought, the practitioner becomes a technician rather than an open, flexible, creative professional. Repetition of new procedures without understanding leads to dogmatism, ritual and a conservatism as damaging as the ones they replace.

The present volumes should therefore be treated as far more than a how-to-do-it manual. The variety of procedures should alert the clinician to the duty of the professional to choose among options. Here is a good sample of options—a chance to increase one's choices among meaningful alternatives: that is one definition of freedom. But with freedom comes responsibility to read, to learn, to study and to think. These volumes are a growth opportunity for those who will make the effort.

But, because of the very ease of communication of procedures and documentation of efficacy when used by the expert clinicians who developed them, these procedures may lead to an unfortunate effect: an unthinking application that was not the context of their development. Effort is required on the part of practitioners lest there be an inappropriate generalization of procedures and data from the skilled and thoughtful developers to the dogmatic and intellectually lazy application by "technicians." Examples of misapplied, over-simplified behaviorism that are used to justify brutal and incompetent activity are already appearing, and this author is far more concerned about "converts" to behaviorism than he is about thoughtful critics of the behavioral approach. Blind adherence to technique rather than to principle is a method of decreasing responsibility and gaining distance from the client whether it occurs in the context of a psychoanalytic, Rogerian, existential or behavioral framework. This problem becomes all the more critical in the area of sexual behavior where the therapist's dogmatism may lead to a new specialized morality that is as inhumane and constricting as the one replaced. The therapist must think before he applies. The very certainty of eighteenth- and nineteenth-century "scientific" statements such as those dealing with masturbation stand as examples. Our current "truths" must be constantly reviewed lest they lead us into error, and we are at our best as scientists and practitioners when we evaluate ourselves critically. *The very strength of behavioral techniques increases rather than decreases responsibility.*

Beyond improving service to clients, the present book stems from a model of human behavior that is different from theological-moralistic, medical, mystical, legislative or psychoanalytic ones. *Sexual behavior is a human interchange in a social context. Sexual activity does not start in the bedroom and does not end with orgasm.* It is a learned social activity that is expressive of a person's role within a culture.

The very variety of techniques that may be effective indicates that we are not dealing with "diseases" that have specific etiologies and cures, but rather with behaviors that have been learned directly and, as with other social behaviors, that may be changed through direct interventions of many different types.

The role-expressive nature of sexual behavior has major implications for therapists. First, therapists must present their treatment in a manner that is congruent with the client's values and expectations. No longer is it possible to say one form of behavior is "good" because it is "healthy" or "natural," and another should be changed because it is "bad," "sick" or "unusual." Rather, the client has a choice, and the therapist makes alternatives available. The therapist must investigate the meanings and consequences of various sexual activities within the context of the client's social system and personal life.

A problem with presentation of innovative approaches, such as those in this volume, is that they focus on what is novel and what is added to existing skills. They presume well-trained competent therapists trained in the fundamentals of interviewing and rapport-building. Technique supplements basic interpersonal skill; it does not replace such skills.

Because treatment goals are set in the context of social values and personal goals, *treatment must be tailored to the individual client.* Just as there is no one best sexual adjustment, so there is not one set procedure for any, much less every, sexual reaction. In fact, poor results will ensue when all people with the same behavior are treated in the same way. Such a procedure may be justified for researches which determine the relative effectiveness and cost of different treatments or which determine the cues indicating who will benefit most from what specific treatment. In research, the goal is to develop general statements that will guide many future therapists working with clients. In practice, these general statements are applied to individual cases. The process is reversed. In short, many of the articles in the behavioral literature must be taken in the context of exploration rather than practice. The articles are communications among scholars and must be considered as such rather than unchangeable clinical directions. Of particular importance is that a research worker, with his goal of general statements, will rule out alternative explanations by holding constant factors that may affect success. A research worker may indeed seem "cold," because he wishes to hold this factor constant across conditions and therapists. This does not mean that the working clinician should be "cold." Again, the research context is not the same as the context of application, and there are some behaviors in one that are not appropriate in the other. The reader should keep this in mind when studying the articles in these two volumes.

Behavioral approaches lend themselves to specification, teaching and evaluation. To the extent that procedures account for differences in treatment outcome, emphasis on therapist "personality" is reduced. It is not that therapists must be "good people" in all aspects of their lives before they can be effective therapists. This does not mean that demands on the therapist are decreased; quite the contrary, for no longer is it enough to "just be oneself" or to "be therapeutic" without stipulation of what being therapeutic is. Rather than being warm, genuine and empathic, or uniformly positive, the therapist must now be able to discriminate when to be warm and when not. The therapist becomes far more disciplined and accepts the constraint of service to clients rather than the pleasure of "letting it all hang out." The effect of the behavioral approach is a public accountability that is external to the therapist's personal feelings. Service becomes professional, that is, based on specialized knowledge which is not affected by personal whim. Put differently, therapists working within the behavioral framework must be able to think through what to do, when to do it, for what results and for what reasons. Again, more is required of the therapist, not less.

In addition, the behavioral therapist should consider a number of points. First, if there were a disease within the individual, as is the view of the psychoanalytic theory, the therapist might think of himself as "curing." But if there is a learned interaction, that is, reactions to situations created and labeled by others or the person himself, then the therapist is in the role of teacher or coach. Teachers help their students to master new material, but it is not the teachers who pass exams or apply information in the pay-off situations. Coaches show new ways and devise strategies, but they are not the people who score. Our clients and their significant others are the ultimate change agents. We must teach, and, like all teachers, we must be modest and realize that accomplishments belongs to the client and student.

When there is pleasure and expression of pleasurable roles through changed sexual activity, there is likely to be generalization of feelings of competence and worth in place of feelings of inadequacy and helplessness. On the one hand, sexual activity is role expressive—it has meaning for individuals as a demonstration of the sort of people they are. On the other hand, insight most often follows changed behavior, for people can then see where they were from the vantage of new positions. People can discover not only that change is possible, but also that change is a result of their own efforts. Such experiences engender further feelings of increased competence and worth. Such feelings are role expressive and not the result of any particular sexual adjustment.

This leads to the next point. Behavior therapy not only does not preclude sensitivity to others, it demands that the client be treated as an individual and not as a member of a category. The client is a person who under certain circumstances acts in a particular way. The person is not to be thought of, much less labeled, in terms of the limited sample of behavior of the sexual situation. Only after a careful analysis of the situation is a treatment plan devised. This analysis will focus on the present, but case-history material plays a crucial role because we must know who our client is so that we may present treatment in a manner that is consistent with that person's social role and goals. A case history also provides material to help the client develop a rationale for the present activity. Finally, historical material not infrequently leads us to find that a sexual difficulty that is the presenting complaint may stem from difficulties of a nonsexual nature. Forcing a person to change in the manner desired by some significant other may make the therapist and the treatment *examples* of the pressures by "others" against the client.

When we think of reactions to situations, we focus on observable behaviors and cues. We not only treat a whole person in a social context, we make the client our active partner in a problem-solving process. This leads to respect for our client and helps establish genuine adult rapport.

Therapists who deal only with reactions and not the situations in which the reactions occur are doing only part of their job. Aversive conditioning may indeed rapidly reduce a behavior and should be thought of if and when there is an act that severely threatens the individual's life or social adjustment, that is, when there is clear harm to the person or others. But the goal is the making of new, alternative, effective social responses that are welcome to both the client and other people. We should not think of responses, much less diseases, but of *social reactions to situations,* and the increase of new behaviors that will be more consistent with the goals of the client and society.

Still another feature of the behavioral approach is that of responsibility. We have touched on this a number of times. With a social-learning approach, the therapist must evaluate behavior and cannot merely label it as sick or healthy per se. Further, the role of teacher fostering specific new reactions to situations is different from therapist as a provider of a general "climate" in which the client can "grow." Behavior therapists must take responsibility for the client's progress and can no longer hide behind words such as "resistance."

In similar fashion, as we move to the social learning or behavioral model, our clients increase in responsibility. As noted above, our clients and their significant others are the ultimate change agents. Our clients must choose their goals and whether they will apply what they have learned or not. Our clients are also responsible to their significant others. For example, what choices are opened to the wife of an impotent man? The behavior therapist may not let his contact with the man become an excuse for the man to make no further efforts and leave the woman waiting. Therapists are responsible to wives as well as husbands, and they must make this clear.

Finally, I have been talking about the clinical consequences of the behavioral framework in the area of work with sexual activity. It should be clear that what I have been saying applies to all behavior therapy. Sexual activity is an example, not a special case.

Many of the points I have made in this introduction are touched on throughout these two volumes. I can only urge the reader to remember that research, teaching and treatment arise in social contexts in the same way as sexual reactions to situations. The theory is one of human behavior, and what we say of clients and students should apply equally to teachers and therapists. We are not apart; we are one in our humanness. Sexual behavior is part of and expressive of larger social roles, just as are the acts of teaching and treating. Just as the specific sexual act should not blind us to the social context, so we must not let a therapy procedure or technique become a dogmatic practice. Behavior therapy is not defined by gimmicks, but by how human behavior is formulated. It is a mode of action, not a set of responses taken out of the context of the situations to which they are reactions. We want what is most useful to specific people in particular situations who have varying goals. The beginning of behavior therapy is not technique, but learning about an individual, welcoming that unique person and context, and searching for what will best serve that one person. Such an orientation moves behavior therapy beyond designated techniques, just as such an orientation moves a physiological release from a sexual act to one of love.

Leonard P. Ullmann, Ph.D.
Professor, University of Hawaii
Department of Psychology
Honolulu, Hawaii

REFERENCES

Annon, J.S. *The behavioral treatment of sexual problems: Volume 1, Brief therapy.* Honolulu: Enabling Systems, 1974.

Annon, J.S. *The behavioral treatment of sexual problems: Volume 2, Intensive therapy.* Honolulu: Enabling Systems, 1975.

Masters, W.H. & Johnson, V.E. *Human sexual inadequacy.* Boston: Little, Brown, 1970.

Preface

The basic purpose of this Handbook is to make available to practitioners and educators of every theoretical orientation and in all of the several helping professions a practical and demonstrably effective system of procedures for implementation with their clients who suffer from sexual problems. This focus on practicality leads to several emphases in the book: 1) a focus on intervention rather than on philosophical issues or attempts to describe the "etiology" of sexual problems; 2) descriptions of all the major techniques that behaviorists have developed for dealing with sexual problems; 3) illustrations of the application of those techniques with the entire range of sexual problems which practitioners encounter in their everyday practice.

Behavior therapy has been found to be particularly adaptable to sexual problems. Since most sexual behavior, whether functional or dysfunctional, is learned, it is amenable to change through the directed learning experiences which are the core of behavior therapy. These behavioral procedures for dealing with sexual problems have been found to be quicker, more effective and accompanied by fewer undesired side effects than any other approach to these problems. Further, the use of behavior therapy procedures can be more easily taught and more easily implemented than the procedures advocated by other theoretical orientations. Thus, behavioral procedures have a wide appeal to practitioners of various backgrounds. Unfortunately, however, clinicians have had to forage for information about behavior therapy of sexual problems from diverse sources rather than having access to such information in one anthology, an apparent lack which led to the development of these volumes.

As mentioned above, this book was developed to be useful to practitioners from all the helping professions—physicians, psychologists, social workers, counselors, nurses, psychiatrists and clergy. All of these groups have considerable contact with individuals suffering from sexual problems, and the need for a sourcebook on behavior therapy that is intended to transcend professional boundaries seems obvious.

Further, we do not believe it necessary for the reader to adhere to a behavior therapy theoretical orientation to find this book useful. The procedures described in this book can be applied by persons of diverse theoretical orientations. On the other hand, these procedures should not be applied in some arbitrary or purely "cookbook" fashion—in a vacuum of knowledge about the basic principles underlying them or without knowledge of the careful assessment considerations of each client and problem that must take place before procedures are implemented. Since this volume is not intended as a beginning book on the basic principles of behavior therapy (or behavior modification—the terms will be considered synonymous in this book), for gaining such knowledge we would recommend some basic texts such as Bandura (1969), Kanfer and Phillips (1970), Yates (1970), as well as several new comprehensive treatises on the subject: Fischer and Gochros (1975), O'Leary and Wilson (1975), Rimm and Masters (1974), Staats (1975), and Ullmann and Krasner (1975).

A comprehensive review of all available articles on behavioral approaches to sexual problems has led to the selection of articles included in this book. Selections were made in line with the purposes of the book: focus on practicality, effectiveness, innovativeness, clarity and lucidity and, when possible, brevity. Additional Selected Readings for each section reference all the articles not included in the book.

This book is organized into two volumes. Volume I, General Procedures, contains articles that focus on the specific behavioral techniques that have been devised or adapted for use with sexual problems. The emphasis in Volume I is on descriptions of the techniques, per se, plus indications for their use. Also included in Volume I of the book are articles describing the context for use of those techniques, including the special knowledge and skills needed by practitioners to enhance their success, development of rapport and relationship with clients, interviewing skills and so on. The intention, of course, is to convey the idea that use of behavioral techniques does not preclude a sensitivity to interpersonal and human concerns.

Volume II of the book, Approaches to Specific Problems, covers the range of sexual problems to which behavior therapy procedures have been applied. As we note in the Introduction to Volume II, sexual problems are defined in this book as specific behaviors in which people engage, which, because they are undesired, need to be decreased or, because they are desired, need to be increased. The attempt is to avoid labels and inferences about disease entities. The articles in Volume II include reviews of research dealing with specific problem areas, descriptive articles, empirical articles and case studies. All of the articles, however, illustrate use of specific techniques with specific problems. There is a focus on innovative practice since more than one technique may be presented for dealing with each problem.

Each volume is organized into two parts, the first part dealing with techniques and problems involved in heterosexual couple relationships, and the second part dealing with techniques and problems involved in undesired sexual object choices, i.e., those the client wishes to alter. We hope this organization adds to the consistency and integration of the two volumes.

We would like to express our appreciation to the authors whose work is reprinted here. The stimulation we received from their collective work has been very reinforcing to us. We hope the reader will find this material equally reinforcing, and, of paramount importance, of value in enhancing the lives of their clients.

We are also particularly indebted to Dr. Leonard P. Ullmann for taking the time and energy to write a Foreword for this book. Dr. Ullmann is a pioneer in the field of behavior therapy, and in its application to sexual dysfunction, and we are honored by his Foreword. Indeed, his contribution is more than "just" a Foreword, but is an important position statement on the relationships between ethics and technology. This is a position to which both of us subscribe, and we hope it will both set the tone for critically examining the work included in this book and provide a frame of reference against which the reader might test out his own thoughts and values.

J.F.
H.L.G.
University of Hawaii
Honolulu, Hawaii

REFERENCES

Bandura, A. *Principles of behavior modification.* New York: Holt, Rinehart and Winston, 1969.

Fischer, J. & Gochros, H.L. *Planned behavior change: Behavior modification in social work.* New York: The Free Press, 1975.

Kanfer, F.H. & Phillips, J.S. *Learning foundations of behavior therapy.* New York: Wiley, 1970.

O'Leary, K.D. & Wilson, G.T. *Behavior therapy: Application and outcome.* Englewood Cliffs, N.J.: Prentice-Hall, 1975.

Rimm, D.C. & Masters, J.C. *Behavior therapy: Techniques and empirical findings.* New York: Academic Press, 1974.

Staats, A.W. *Social behaviorism.* Homewood, Illinois: Dorsey Press, 1975.

Ullmann, L.P. & Krasner, L. *A psychological approach to abnormal behavior* (2nd Ed.). Englewood Cliffs, N.J.: Prentice-Hall, 1975.

Yates, A.J. *Behavior therapy.* New York: Wiley, 1970.

Acknowledgments—Volume I

The editors are grateful to the authors and publishers of the articles included in this book for permission to reprint them. Following are the sources and publishers of the articles according to their chapters in this volume.

Chapter
1 "New Methods in the Behavioral Treatment of Sexual Dysfunction." *Journal of Behavior Therapy and Experimental Psychiatry,* 1972, **3**, 265-271. Copyright 1972 by Pergamon Press.
2 "Taking a Sexual History." In R. Green (Ed.), *Human Sexuality: A Health Practitioner's Text.* Baltimore: The Williams and Wilkins Co. Copyright 1975. Reproduced by permission.
3 "Treatment of Common Marital Sexual Problems." In Gochros, H.L. and Schultz, L. (Eds.), *Human Sexuality and Social Work.* New York: Association Press, 1971, 126-137.
4 "Counseling with Sexually Incompatible Marriage Partners." In R.H. Clemer (Ed.), *Counseling in Marital and Sexual Problems.* Baltimore: Williams and Wilkins, 1965, Copyright 1965. The Williams and Wilkins Co. Reprinted by permission.
5 "A Modification of Masters and Johnson Sex Therapy Model in a Clinical Setting." *Psychotherapy: Theory, Reserach and Practice,* 1973, **10**, 290-293. Copyright 1973.
6 "The Treatment of Inhibited Sexual Responses." *The Practice of Behavior Therapy* (2nd ed.). New York: Pergamon Press, 1973, 163-180.
7 "Systematic Desensitization in Sexual Disorders." *Journal of Behavior Therapy and Experimental Psychiatry,* 1973, **4**, 93-101. Copyright 1973 by Pergamon Press.
8 "The PLISSIT Model: A Proposed Conceptual Scheme for the Behavioral Treatment of Sexual Problems." *Journal of Sex Education and Therapy*

(in press), 1976. Reprinted by permission of the American Association of Sex Educators and Counselors.

9 "The Mechanotherapy of Sexual Disorders." *The Journal of Sex Research,* 1971, **7**, 1-12.

10 "Aversion Therapy Applied to Taped Sequences of Deviant Behavior in Exhibitionism and other Sexual Deviations: A Preliminary Report." *Journal of Behavior Therapy and Experimental Psychiatry,"* 1970, **1**, 59-66. Copyright 1970 by Pergamon Press.

11 "An Automated Technique for Aversive Conditioning in Sexual Deviations." In Rubin, R.D. and Franks, C.M. (Eds.), *Advances in Behavior Therapy, 1968.* New York: Academic Press, 1969, 25-30.

12 "Positive Control as an Alternative to Aversion Therapy." *Journal of Behavior Therapy and Experimental Psychiatry,* 1970, **1**, 291-294. Copyright 1970 by Pergamon Press.

13 "Orgasmic Reconditioning: Changing Sexual Object Choice through Controlling Masturbation Fantasies." *Journal of Behavior Therapy and Experimental Psychiatry,* 1970, **1**, 263-271. Copyright 1970 by Pergamon Press.

14 "The Therapeutic Use of Masturbation in the Treatment of Sexual Disorders." In Rubin, R.D., Brady, J.P. and Henderson, J.D. (Eds.), *Advances in Behavior Therapy, Vol. 4.* New York: Academic Press, 1973, 199-215.

15 "The Modification of Sexual Fantasies: A Combined Treatment Approach to the Reduction of Deviant Sexual Behavior." *Behaviour Research and Therapy,* 1973, **11**, 557-564. Copyright 1973 by Pergamon Press.

16 "Shame Aversion Therapy." *Journal of Behavior Therapy and Experimental Psychiatry,* 1970, **1**, 213-215. Copyright 1970 by Pergamon Press.

17 "Covert Sensitization for the Treatment of Sexual Deviations." *The Psychological Record,* 1971, **21**, 37-48.

18 " 'Assisted' Covert Sensitization: A Preliminary Report." *Behavior Therapy,* 1973, **4**, 117-119. Copyright 1973 by Academic Press.

19 "Aversion Therapy for Sexual Deviation: Contingent Shock and Covert Sensitization." *Journal of Abnormal Psychology,* 1973, **81**, 60-73. Copyright 1973 by the American Psychological Association.

20 "Increasing Heterosexual Responsiveness in the Treatment of Sexual Deviation: A Review of the Clinical and Experimental Evidence." *Behavior Therapy,* 1973, **4**, 655-671. Copyright 1973 by Academic Press.

21 "A Forward-Fading Technique for Increasing Heterosexual Responsiveness in Male Homosexuals." *Journal of Behavior Therapy and Experimental Psychiatry,* 1973, **4**, 257-261. Copyright 1973 by Pergamon Press.

22 "An Experimental Analysis of Exposure to 'Explicit' Heterosexual Stimuli as an Effective Variable in Changing Arousal Patterns of Homosexuals." *Behaviour Research and Therapy,* 1974, **13**, 335-345. Copyright 1974 by Pergamon Press.

23 "An Experimental Analysis of Feedback to Increase Sexual Arousal." *Journal of Behavior Therapy and Experimental Psychiatry,* 1974, **5,** 271-274. Copyright 1974 by Pergamon Press.

24 "Basic and Applied Research in Human Sexuality: Current Limitations and Future Directions in Sex Therapy." Original manuscript prepared especially for this book.

Appendix A.   "Sexual Response Inventory." Copyright 1975 by Enabling Systems, Inc.

Contributors—Volume I

ABEL, GENE G., M.D., Department of Psychiatry, University of Tennessee Medical School, Memphis, Tennessee.

AGRAS, W. STEWART, M.D., Department of Psychiatry and Behavioral Sciences, Stanford University Medical School, Stanford, California.

ANNON, JACK S., Ph.D., Senior Consultant, Sexual Counseling Service, Department of Obstetrics and Gynecology, School of Medicine and Adjunct Graduate Faculty, Department of Psychology, University of Hawaii.

APPEL, JAMES B., Ph.D., Department of Psychiatry, University of Chicago, Chicago, Illinois.

BARLOW, DAVID H., Ph.D., Professor of Psychiatry, Brown University and Butler Hospital, Providence, Rhode Island.

CALLAHAN, EDWARD J., Ph.D., Camarillo State Hospital, Camarillo, California.

CAUTELA, JOSEPH R., Ph.D., Professor of Psychology, Boston College, Chestnut Hill, Massachusetts.

CLANCY, JOHN, M.D., F.R.C.P.(C), Professor of Psychiatry, University of Iowa, Iowa City, Iowa.

DENGROVE, EDWARD, M.D., West Allenhurst, New Jersey.

FARKAS, GARY M., Clinical Studies Program, Department of Psychology, University of Hawaii, Honolulu, Hawaii.

FEINGOLD, LEONARD, Haverford State Hospital, Haverford, Pennsylvania.

GOCHROS, HARVEY L., D.S.W., Professor and Director of the Center for the Study of Sex Education in Social Work, University of Hawaii, Honolulu, Hawaii.

GREEN, RICHARD, M.D., Professor in Departments of Psychiatry and Behavior Science and Psychology, State University of New York, Stony Brook, New York.

HERMAN, STEVEN H., Ph.D., Psychology Service, Miami Veterans Administration Hospital, Miami, Florida.

HIGGINBOTHAM, HOWARD N., M.A., Clinical Studies Program, Department of Psychology, University of Hawaii, Honolulu, Hawaii and Degree Scholar, East-West Center Culture Learning Institute, Honolulu, Hawaii.

JOHNSON, VIRGINIA E., Co-director, Reproductive Biology Research Foundation, St. Louis, Missouri.

LEITENBERG, HAROLD, Ph.D., Professor of Psychology, University of Vermont, Montpelier, Vermont.

LEVIS, DONALD J., Ph.D., Department of Psychology, State University of New York at Binghamton, Binghamton, New York.

LOBITZ, W. CHARLES, Ph.D., Psychology Clinic, University of Oregon, Eugene, Oregon.

LOPICCOLO, JOSEPH, Ph.D., Associate Professor of Psychiatry, School of Medicine, State University of New York, Stony Brook, New York.

MALETZKY, BARRY M., M.D., Director of Research, Woodland Park Mental Health Center, Portland, Oregon and Assistant Clinical Professor, University of Oregon Medical School.

MARQUIS, JOHN H., Ph.D., Veteran's Administration Hospital, Palo Alto, California.

MARSHALL, W.L., Ph.D., Queen's University, Kingston, Ontario, Canada.

MASTERS, WILLIAM H., M.D., Co-director, Reproductive Biology Research Foundation, St. Louis, Missouri.

McCARTHY, BARRY W., Ph.D., Associate Professor of Psychology, American University, Washington, D.C.

McCRADY, RICHARD E., Ph.D., Private Practice, Pomona, California.

MOSS, GENE R., M.D., Assistant Professor in Psychiatry (Adjunct), University of California at Irvine, Irvine, California.

OBLER, MARTIN, Ph.D., Professor, Brooklyn College, Private Practice, Brooklyn, New York.

PION, RONALD J., M.D., Professor, School of Public Health, University of Hawaii, Director of Family Planning, Kapiolani Hospital, Honolulu, Hawaii.

PREWETT, MICHAEL, Ph.D., Psychology Department, Western Carolina University, Cullowhee, North Carolina.

RADA, RICHARD T., Department of Psychiatry, University of California at Davis, Davis, California.

SERBER, MICHAEL, M.D., Clinical Director, Atascadero State Hospital, Atascadero, California.

WISOCKI, PATRICIA A., Ph.D., Department of Psychology, University of Massachusetts, Amherst, Massachusetts.

WOLPE, JOSEPH, M.D., Professor of Psychiatry, Temple University, School of Medicine and Eastern Pennsylvania Psychiatric Institute, Philadelphia, Pennsylvania.

Introduction *all*

In the years since the end of the Second World War, Americans have increasingly displayed a pervasive interest, fascination and open preoccupation with the problems and potentials in sexual behavior. There are many interrelated factors which have led to this "sexual revolution." Perhaps of greatest significance has been the growing emphasis on individual rights and freedom. Among other changes, this has led to the women's liberation movement, with a concomitant reduction in sexism, and the recognition and acceptance of the expression of female sexuality. The revolution in the perception and rights of women has been closely linked with the development and improved acceptance and access to safe and effective contraception, as well as the decriminalization of abortion.

The emphasis on individual freedom has also led to changing attitudes toward formerly unacceptable sexual behaviors. An increasing number of states have decriminalized homosexual behavior along with most other forms of consensual adult sexual behaviors. Indeed, the American Psychiatric Association has decided, by a vote of its members, to declassify homosexuality as a "disease." Professionals in all fields, as well as the lay public, are increasingly recognizing that sexual expression is not the prerogative of just the young and the physically sound. More and more attention is being addressed to the sexual needs and problems of the adolescent, the old, the retarded and the handicapped (Gochros and Gochros, 1976).

All these changes are both products of and contributions to the growing willingness to break down old taboos of silence about sexual behavior and to openly explore the problems and possibilities of human sexuality.

Many men and women in all social and economic classes are critically evaluating their sexual lives and attempting to more fully express and enjoy their sexuality. They have been exposed to social expectations that they not only can but should be meeting their own and their partners' sexual needs. Masters and Johnson (1970), for example, have estimated that over 50 percent of all married couples experience problems in their sexual relationships. Even those who are not experiencing any particular sexual problems seem intent on enhancing their sexual "performance," as attested to by the wide circulation of such books as *The Sensuous Woman* ("J," 1969) and *The Joy of Sex* (Comfort, 1972).

Certainly many of those caught up in the search for the perfect orgasm have had to pay a price for their quest. Some have become so preoccupied with "performing" adequately and becoming truly sensuous that they have, paradoxically, prevented themselves and, often, their partners from enjoying their sexual activities. Ellis (1972) has pointed out the hazards of some of the cookbook approaches to sex and sensuality. Such preoccupation with sexual performance leads to what Masters and Johnson (1970) have described as the "spectator role" in sexual behavior. That is, the individuals look upon themselves as actors in a performance with their partners and are so preoccupied with how they are doing as competent, up-to-date, uninhibited lovers that they cannot relax and spontaneously enjoy their sexuality.

Nevertheless, whatever their motivation, an increasing number of people are expressing dissatisfaction with aspects of their sex lives and are seeking professional help for their problems. Indeed, it has been estimated recently that there are from 3500 to 5000 professionals, clinics and agencies offering treatment for sexual dysfunctioning *(The New York Times,* May 5, 1974, p. 71).

This explosion of interest in sex and the demands upon professionals to treat sexual problems are just beginning to be reflected in the education of professional helpers. For example, in 1964, there were less than 10 medical schools that offered even a single lecture on sexual behavior and problems. Less than ten years later, more than half of the 82 medical schools in the United States were offering courses on human sexuality. (*See* Lief, H. "New Developments in the Sex Education of the Physician." *Journal of the AMA,* June 15, 1970, and Buckley, T. "All They Talk About is Sex." *The New York Times Magazine,* April 20, 1969, 98.) Similarly, in 1965, only one course in human sexual problems was offered in one graduate school of social work. Ten years later, there were over 35 schools offering such courses (Gochros, 1976).

Unfortunately the existence of such courses does not guarantee effective practice for the future professionals taking them. Often, these courses focus on the physiology and character of "normal" sexuality along with a categorization of "deviance." Little direction for effective intervention may be offered.

Even when the student or practitioner seeks out information about treatment approaches to sexual problems, he may be overwhelmed with the current plethora of novel interventive approaches of dubious effectiveness and questionable ethics. Current sex-treatment literature, for example, includes suggestions for group and office nudism often with bodily contact, recommendations for bisexual relationships, therapeutic infidelity, training with sexual surrogates, prostitutes as co-therapists, and therapeutic sexual intercourse between therapist and client (Bindrim, 1972; Coons, 1972;

Dahlberg, 1973; English, 1971; Hartman & Fithian, 1973; Kovacs, 1965; Lobitz & LoPiccolo, 1972; McCartney, 1966; and Yoell, 1971).

Many of these direct and sometimes sensational interventive strategies were developed in reaction to the notable lack of success of traditional psycho-dynamically-based talk therapies. Indeed, the psychoanalytic model supported ideas about sexual behavior—such as the concept of sexual "perversions" and the superiority of the vaginal over the clitoral orgasm—which probably did more harm than good.

The very positive reception to Masters and Johnson's (1970) book describing a two-week treatment program for sexual "inadequacy" reflected the desire of both the public and the helping professions to cut through traditional, indirect, slow and expensive approaches to sexual problems and instead treat them more rapidly as reversible dysfunctional learned behaviors.

There are, however, difficulties inherent in the nature of many sexual problems which can prevent rapid "cures." Sexual problems often are a product of many factors—social, legal, psychological, genetic and physiological—which combine to produce complex behaviors. Some of these problems can appear insurmountable, especially since there are few catagories of behavior which are either so powerfully reinforced or powerfully punished (and sometimes both) as sexual behavior. However, behavioral procedures have been developed which have been demonstrated to be effective with a number of specific sex-related problems; these are the subject of this book.

Advantages of Behavior Therapy

There are several characteristics of sexual behavior which lend themselves to behavior therapy approaches: First, since most sexual behaviors, whether dysfunctional or functional, are learned, they are amenable to change through the directed learning experiences which are the core of behavior therapy. Many of these behavioral procedures for dealing with sexual problems have been found to work more quickly, are more effective and are accompanied by fewer undesired side effects than any other approach.

Second, sexual behaviors are also reinforced by a wide variety of social stimuli, such as peer and spouse approval. The behavior modifier, therefore, has available the potential of these significant reinforcements to motivate client cooperation to bring about the desired behavior.

Third, many desired sexual behaviors such as orgasm, erection, ejaculation and even subjective pleasurable experiences are fairly easily pinpointed and counted. Fourth, society has already built in—for better or worse—powerful aversive stimuli for undesired sexual behavior. These, again, negatively reinforce participation in programs specifically aimed at decreasing undesired sexual responses. Finally, the use of behavior therapy procedures is easily taught and is more easily implemented than the procedures advocated by other theoretical orientations.

SOCIAL CONTROL OF SEXUAL BEHAVIOR

Society generally wields considerable influence over sexual expression. The sexual response is a powerful one, and one of its products, reproduction, is of prime concern to the survival of any group. Indeed, there are few areas of behavior which are more carefully regulated (Marshall & Suggs, 1971). Until very recently, the strength of any group very much covaried with its ability to reproduce itself. This reproductive imperative, along with other factors, led to strong societal reinforcement for sexual behaviors resulting in reproduction, as well as permitting the reinforcement intrinsic to sexual behavior to be enjoyed by those engaging in certain prescribed sexual behaviors. These behaviors had to be compatible with the maintenance of semi-permanent, monogamous, heterosexual relationships in which children would be conceived, born, cared for and socialized. Thus, through a complex system of learning experiences provided by parents, peers, teachers, media and others, certain behaviors are shaped, varying somewhat from culture to culture, place to place and time to time.

For example, those sexual behaviors which potentially bring about socially approved pregnancies are reinforced. Thus, most men who are taught to work toward achieving and maintaining firm erections seek more or less responsive women who will accept the penis into the vagina, where in due time they will ejaculate. Such behaviors are certainly conducive to pregnancy, and are considered by most reinforcing agents as the ideal, natural, normal and mentally healthy activities associated with sexuality. Other sexual behaviors which can potentially provide physical and/or psychological pleasure but cannot lead to pregnancy, such as homosexual behavior, self-stimulation, or manual, oral or anal stimulation of a partner's genitals have often been met with aversive social consequences ranging from feelings of guilt to peer ridicule and even legal sanctions.

The societal reinforcement for reproduction and the acceptance of the separation of reproduction and sexuality has somewhat diminished among the 15 percent of college-educated Americans who, because they produce most of our educators and writers, influence sexual attitudes of most Americans. Further, the relatively new awareness of the hazards of over-population has tended to diminish the focusing of the sexual drive exclusively into traditionally acceptable sexual behaviors. Thus, recent studies (Hunt, 1974) show that nonreproductive behaviors such as self-stimulation and oral-genital contact are gaining greater acceptance. However, powerful long-established patterns of societal reinforcement and punishment—and even sex-related laws—change slowly, and conflicting attitudes about desirable sexual expression coexist in many individuals as well as society as a whole.

BEHAVIORAL PERSPECTIVE ON SEXUAL PROBLEMS

Behaviorists today generally concur that any individual's sexual behavior is the product of complex learning experiences. Such writers as Bandura (1969), Staats (1968), Staats and Staats (1963) and Ullmann and Krasner (1975) have presented empirical data to support the point of view that this learning conforms to generally accepted learning principles. These learning experiences generally derive from the individual's numerous experiences of the consequences resulting from sexual activities, including responses of significant others to sexual ideas and behaviors as well as the physical reinforcements—particularly sexual arousal and orgasm—accompanying a variety of sexual activities.

It follows that if sexual behavior is essentially the product of such learning experiences, changes in sexual behavior can also be learned. The numerous cases of successful change in sexual behavior brought about through behavioral strategies, as reported in this book, tend to confirm this conviction.

Behaviorally oriented therapists generally assume that the same learning principles explain both dysfunctional or undesired (often labeled as "abnormal") and functional or desired (often labeled as "normal") sexual behavior. They perceive the differences between these two classes of behavior as subject to changing definitions, client perceptions and value systems. This point of view differs considerably from those who espouse the "disease" model which assumes that different principles explain the acquisition of "normal" and "abnormal" sexual behavior. The "disease" model implies a static "normal" or "healthy" mode of sexual maturation which may be inhibited or distorted by a "mental disease" process which results in abnormal sexual expression. This model of healthy sexual development has tended to be influenced by the social class, education and sexism of those who have created it.

In contrast, the behavioral model suggests that while people learn their behaviors—including sexual behaviors—as a result of common learning principles, there are a tremendous variety of learning experiences to which individuals are exposed. As a result, a range of sexual behaviors are learned, resulting in a richness of human differences. These differences need not be divided into "normal" or "abnormal," conforming to some preset value system, which may vary considerably from culture to culture, society to society, religion to religion, and within individuals, from time to time. A factual assessment of the effects of the behavior on the individual and those in his environment is a far more effective guide to intervention goals. The behaviorist, therefore, sees behaviors as either adaptive or maladaptive for the individuals performing them, not "normal" or "abnormal."

Just as the general labels of "normal" and "abnormal" are irrelevant in the behavioral approach, so, too, are the specific "disease" labels—such as impotence, homosexuality, frigidity, premature ejaculation—which so frequently are applied to sexual behaviors both by professionals and the lay public. This prevalent practice is not only unsupported by our understanding of human behavior but also can be harmful to those so labeled.

There are several hazards inherent in labeling people as a reflection of their sexual problems:

Labeling is not behaviorally specific. It describes a general category of behavior but not the specific behavioral difficulties encountered by a particular client. For example, "premature ejaculation" may be defined and perceived as ejaculation prior to vaginal penetration for one man, ejaculation after five minutes of thrusting by another, and ejaculation as a result of being close to an attractive woman by still another.

Labels bias practitioners in terms of attitudes and treatments (Fischer & Miller, 1973). Once a woman is labeled as "frigid," a cluster of attitudes and expectations are created in herself and in those having contact with her. Such pigeonholing of people into labeled categories obscures the major behaviors, and, of more importance, many routes away from these behaviors.

Labels also imply that the problem condition pervades the individual experiencing the problem. Thus, "the homosexual" is totally under the influence of his "sickness," and all his thoughts and behaviors are perceived as being colored by it. Those working with him are likely to make assumptions about his behavior and attitudes as a product of the label and overlook problems or behavioral patterns unrelated to his sexual orientation.

Labels suggest that the set of problem behaviors is reified within the individual. If clients are "homosexual," "impotent" or "frigid," they are that way at all times and in all kinds of situations. This is rarely true. A man may have trouble achieving or maintaining erections under certain conditions, but not under others. An individual may seek out homosexual experiences at certain times, but reject them at others. Only clear descriptions of the unique patterns of the problem behavior over time can direct the practitioner to useful interventions.

Not only does labeling bias the helping practitioner so that he may see little beyond the "pathology," but labeling may have an even more damaging effect on the client. Labels can have a devastating effect on one's image of oneself. Once an individual pictures himself in the role prescribed by the label, he tends to act out the role. Thus, the anxiety generated by a man who thinks he *is* impotent may well prevent him from having an erection. Once a person thinks he *is* a "homosexual," he may conform to his own or others' stereotypes of how "a homosexual" should act. It is generally more accurate and useful for both the individual experiencing a sex-related problem and the practitioner working with him to view a person as occasionally or frequently, in certain circumstances, being unable to achieve erection or orgasm in the way he—or his partner—wishes, or engaging or wishing to engage in certain sexual activities with one of his own sex. Certainly, labeling oneself as anything limits one's behavioral options and impairs subsequent efforts to modify that behavior. Further, it may blind both the therapist and the client to other significant behaviors of the client. For instance, overlooking major problems in a couple's relationship because the focus has been placed on overcoming the wife's "frigidity" can be, at best, counterproductive (Kaplan & Kohl, 1972).

In view of the hazards associated with labeling, hazards which behaviorists have long cautioned about, it is saddening to observe how frequently behaviorists themselves use these very labels (there are several examples in the chapters in these two volumes). Even behaviorists are often victims of the "disease" model of sexuality which so pervades our helping professions. Nevertheless, such labels are more than mythical (Szasz, 1961); they are potentially destructive to the individuals so labeled and do violence to our understanding of human behavior.

BEHAVIORAL ASSESSMENT

Because of the complexity of many sexual problems, a careful behavioral assessment is essential. Generally, both the search for historical "causes" and any efforts to place the client into a traditional diagnostic classification are avoided. (As noted above, however, many behaviorists—including some whose works are included in this book—often lapse unnecessarily and, perhaps, dysfunctionally into traditional labeling.)

The behaviorist recognizes that there are many routes to more or less similar behaviors, as there are many routes away from these behaviors. Knowing patterns of behavior as well as some data about past contingencies on the behavior may be helpful. However, such information may be of limited accuracy, and of limited utility for treatment planning.

Instead of focusing on historical causes and psychiatric labeling, behavioral assessment focuses on individualized precise descriptions of the problem behaviors and the factors which either maintain or prevent their occurrence. The only purpose of such an assessment is to collect enough information about the problem behavior to design a focused intervention plan to change it.

Since direct observation of sexual behavior by the therapist would not usually be acceptable or practical, the therapist must generally rely on helping the clients themselves to provide a clear description of, and, if possible, accurate data on the problem behaviors and environmental factors associated with these behaviors. A number of the following questions may be useful in eliciting this information:

1. What is the behavioral description of the problem?

2. Who is upset about it, and how are they involved in the problem?

3. Since when has the problem existed? What were the circumstances surrounding its onset?

4. Does the problem only occur at certain times and under certain contingencies, such as when the individual is drunk, tired, angry or away from home? What are the effects of performing or not performing the problematic behavior; i.e., are there specific consequences that may be maintaining or strengthening the problem?

5. What are the individual's (and the partner's) expectations for sexual behavior? How do they hope the behaviors will change as a result of intervention? Are these goals realistic? For example, ejaculation after a half-hour of intra-vaginal thrusting may not be realistically considered "premature," even if the partner labels it so.

6. How has the individual's sexual behavior changed over time in frequency and in pleasure? For example, if the problem occurs in the context of a pair relationship, have other aspects of the relationship covaried over time?

7. What does the individual consider to be the environmental contingencies which affect the sexual relationship, such as the individual's health, the setting in which the sexual behavior occurs, the proximity of children and others.

8. What specifically have the individuals attempted to do to resolve the problem, such as use of medications, psychotherapy, and variations in the sexual behavior?

9. Is there a suspicion of a physical source for the sexual problem (such as diabetes in the case of impotence)? Medical consultation may be advisable. However, the therapist should carefully select a medical consultant. Until recently, medical schools did little to prepare their students for working with sex-related problems (Vincent, 1968). Destructive attitudes of, and perhaps misinformation given by, biased physicians (see, for example, Reuben, 1972) could well set back treatment programs and create additional problems for clients.

10. How does the individual (and the therapist) perceive societal attitudes toward the behavior? Do such attitudes tend to reinforce or punish its occurrence?

Such questions can be augmented by having clients complete checklists describing their sexual behavior. A sexual response profile has been developed by Pion, which is reprinted as an Appendix in this book, and a variety of instruments by Annon (1975), which provide an opportunity for people with sex-related problems to indicate the degree to which they either fear or enjoy a wide range of sexual stimuli, such as parts of the body (vagina, testicles, pubic hair), specific sexual activities (caressing a female's breasts, caressing the buttocks and thighs of a male) and interpersonal situations (asking a woman for a date, sitting in a car in a remote location with a male's arm around one). This type of survey allows many clients to supply information about their sexual feelings more readily than they could in face-to-face interviews, especially if they consider their feelings "abnormal"; all they have to do is choose among printed options. (See also the instruments developed by LoPiccolo and Steger, 1974, and Harbison et al., 1974). For a detailed discussion of the process of behavioral assessment of sexual problems, the work of Annon (1974, 1975) is highly recommended.

BEHAVIORAL INTERVENTION

In essence, the main purpose of behavioral assessment is to lead to the selection of an interventive strategy and specific behavioral procedures to alter the problem/situation. This is facilitated in the assessment process by classification of problems as those which are deficits and need to be increased (e.g., inability to achieve firm erections) and those that are excesses and need to be decreased (e.g., undesired fetishistic behavior). An analysis such as this would thus lead to selection of the appropriate behavioral procedures which, in turn, can be categorized as follows:

1. Increasing desired sexual responses (such as achieving and maintaining erection at appropriate times, achieving orgasm with reasonable frequency and at a desirable point in sexual activity, and obtaining and giving enjoyment from sexual activities); and

2. Decreasing undesired sexual responses (that is, eliminating sexual responses to stimuli if the responses are considered inappropriate or undesired by the individual experiencing them, or if the responses are clearly harmful to others; this category might include such responses as fetishistic, transvestite, exhibitionistic, pedophiliac, and homosexual behavior).

This categorization tends to overshadow the fact that several techniques can be used to either increase or decrease behavior. For example, systematic desensitization can be used to increase desired behavior—say, heterosexual behavior—by decreasing the anxiety associated with it, or can be used simply to decrease anxiety without a concomitant increase in desired behavior. Similarly, some of these techniques can be used to increase desired behavior and decrease undesired behavior at the same time. For example, "aversion relief" has been used to decrease undesired homosexual behavior at the same time as desired heterosexual behavior is increased.

Further, in many behavioral programs, as can be noted from many of the chapters in these volumes, more than one behavioral technique is used. Indeed, as desired and undesired behaviors are identified in the behavioral assessment, the job of the therapist is to select the specific procedures that would appear to be the best approaches for changing the target behaviors. Thus, at times, several procedures may be used simultaneously or concurrently to change a behavior that is particularly refractory to intervention while, at other times, several procedures may be used to change several problem behaviors that can be identified as part of a general configuration of maladaptive behaviors.

Increasing Desired Sexual Responses

The specific pattern in which an individual behaves sexually is to a great extent the product of his specific learning history, involving, among other dimensions, the reinforcement and punishment which have followed particular sexual thoughts and overt behaviors. An individual may have learned that sexual behavior with a partner can be reinforced both from the physical pleasure experienced and from the reinforcement of the partner who communicates pleasure from the sexual activities.

On the other hand, unsatisfying sexual experiences can be highly aversive not only because of the unpleasant physical sensations, such as tension, congestion and irritation experienced by one or both partners, but also because of the considerable emphasis and premium placed on "normalcy" and competent sexual performance, or at least "adequacy," by many contemporary Western societies. Thus, a woman who has rarely experienced orgasm, or whose vagina has tightened in anticipation of penile penetration, or the man who has had occasional difficulty in maintaining erection or delaying ejaculation may well begin to associate sexual behavior with failure, embarrassment and pain. It is possible they will subsequently avoid sexual contact which could have aversive consequences.

But sexual abstinence may involve too much of a cost. More likely, such individuals as a result of respondent learning begin to approach sexual activities with anxiety, yet continue to seek or engage in sexual activities in the hope that next time it will be better. However, the conditioned anxiety is likely to preclude satisfaction in these attempts and, thus, only compound the problem. Therefore, while many sexual problems manifest themselves in obvious physiological malfunctions, the undesired behaviors are often conditioned responses, such as anxiety which prevents "natural" responses (e.g., receptive lubricated vaginas, erect penises and orgasms).

A number of procedures have been found useful in reducing anxiety and performance expectations which can inhibit desirable intrinsically reinforceable sexual behavior. The procedures include those which work directly to increase desired behavior (e.g., shaping, modeling) and those which increase desired behavior by decreasing the anxiety associated with it (e.g., systematic desensitization). Since these procedures are described in depth in this book, only a brief overview of some of the most commonly used procedures will be described here.

Provision of Information
Many sex-related problems have their origin in misinformation or lack of accurate information. For example, a man may approach sexual relationships with considerable anxiety (or not approach them at all) out of concern his penis is not large enough. Realistic reassurance can be provided by pointing out that only the outside inch or two of the vagina along with the clitoris provide the most physiological stimulation to the woman. Thus, even a reasonably "small" penis can stimulate a woman to orgasm. Accurate direct information about basic sexual anatomy, physiology and common behavior patterns, as summarized by such books as McCary (1975) or Katchadourian and Lunde (1975), when clearly and comfortably presented, can eliminate dysfunctional sexual myths.

Modification of Dysfunctional Self-Regulation and Cognitive Restructuring

Closely related to the provision of information is the debunking of the dysfunctional "shoulds" and "musts" which often rigidly regulate many individuals' sexual behavior, and prevent satisfying sexual experience. Typical "shoulds" are: the woman should experience orgasm through her vagina, not her clitoris, and only while a penis is in it; all sexual contact should culminate in genital intercourse, and the man should be above the woman in intercourse; married people should never masturbate. The informed, empathic therapist can modify such conceptions and help the client get reinforcement from a wider range of satisfying sexual behaviors which may have been proscribed prior to intervention.

Stimulus Change

The pain, embarrassment and anxiety related to sexual problems can become paired with stimuli associated with the time and place of the sexual activities. For example, the couple's bed and even the bedroom, late at night, may provide cues to sexual anxiety and failure. To reduce the impact of such stimuli, Masters and Johnson (1970) bring a couple to St. Louis. While in residence in the program, the couple stays in a new environment, free from their home distractions (children, phone calls, etc.) and reminders of their sexual disappointments. A less-extensive stimulus change is described by Gochros (in Chapter 3) as "motel therapy," in which couples spend a weekend early in the intervention process at a motel or hotel, where they carry out several homework assignments, such as learning about what each partner enjoys in sexual activities, and trying out new modes of sexual activities, avoiding demands for sexual performance.

Positive Reinforcement and Shaping Desired Sexual Behavior

Much of the anxiety experienced by those with sexual problems is a product of anticipating each planned sexual contact as an upcoming major test of their sexual competence, a case of "do or die." Such expectations of performance mitigate against successful sexual behavior: the participants can become spectators of their own sexual test in which the bed becomes the arena for their contest with their bodies. Since anxiety coupled with performance expectations is a breeding ground for sexual disaster, such an orientation is inevitably self-defeating. The clinician can help the couple approach the desired sexual activity by shaping the end goal rather than meeting it head-on. The therapist can suggest to the couple, for example, that they explore each other's body, stimulating each other, but not making any demands for genital satisfactions. As the partners feel comfortable with each step along the way, they can both discover and more closely approximate the desired sexual behaviors. (Several specific procedures using these basic principles are described in Volume I and illustrated in Volume II.)

Systematic Desensitization

Anxiety is one of the major barriers to satisfying sexual relationships. Systematic desensitization is a widely used approach (described in several chapters in this book) designed to dissipate anxiety which impedes desired, functional behavior through the use of a structured, sequential process. It involves teaching the client to relax in situations which would usually elicit anxiety. The client is first helped to achieve a state of physiological relaxation, and is then exposed either through imagination or *in vivo* (in the real world) to a stimulus which would usually arouse some weak anxiety. The presentation is repeated while relaxation is maintained until the stimulus no longer elicits anxiety. Subsequently, progressively more anxiety-provoking stimuli are presented in a similar way. For example, in the case of a woman who fears and rejects sexual overtures from her husband, the therapist might help the woman construct a hierarchy of stimuli which evoke anxiety in her, from the least ("husband touching my knee") to the most anxiety-producing situation ("husband inserts penis in my vagina") and experience deep relaxation, or other emotional states incompatible with anxiety. Eventually, as the anxiety is dissipated, the client resumes the desired—and usually well-reinforced—behavior (Wolpe, 1973).

Retraining: Modeling, Role-Playing and Instructions

In these procedures, the clinician presents specific ideas and literally trains his clients in new modes of sexual behavior. Some therapists (Lobitz and LoPiccolo, Chapter 1, Volume I, for example) have found that helping women to role-play the experiences associated with orgasm will indeed facilitate their having orgasms. The viewing of videotapes and films of explicit sexual activities leading to sexual satisfaction can provide models for individuals or couples whose own sexual models for effective sexual functioning have been limited or non-existent. Finally, specific instructions, such as the "squeeze" technique recommended by Masters and Johnson and Wolpe to treat individuals who ejaculate before they want to, can quickly facilitate behavioral change.

Guided Masturbation

Masturbation is by far the most common form of sexual outlet. The fantasies accompanying the intense and repeated pleasure of masturbation reflect and, at the same time, have a profound effect on sexual desires and behavior. Further, especially in women, masturbation facilitates an awareness of physiological responses to effective genital manipulation which can be transmitted to sexual activities with partners. Guided masturbation takes advantage of these facts to deliberately alter habitual arousal responses.

Guided masturbation has been used for two very different purposes:

1) to familiarize women with their own genital responses, particularly in reference to what specific patterns of stimulation will most likely lead to orgasm. Such knowledge can then be applied to enhancing the probability that the behaviors of both the woman and her partner will lead to orgasm in intercourse.

2) A very different use of guided masturbation is to develop sexual responses to socially approved and desirable objects for men who have encountered difficulty in their sexual orientation. (There are several

examples of use of guided masturbation with several forms of undesired behavior in both Volumes I and II.) Thus, a man is trained to masturbate while fantasizing the desired object or activity (e.g., an attractive woman) in place of habitual images (e.g., children, or other men). If the individual experiences difficulty in becoming aroused while fantasizing the "desired" activity, he may be instructed, at least initially, to fantasize his regular activities and "switch" to the "new" fantasy at a point close to ejaculation. This procedure seems to work well if the new desired object had been, previously at least, neutral. If, however, the client perceives the object as aversive, then a shaping procedure may be called for.

Decreasing Undesired Sexual Responses

Certain sexual behaviors are considered "problems" because they deviate from norms of acceptable sexual behavior. Various aversive social consequences (ridicule, legal penalties) as well as emotional respondents (guilt, anxiety) often accompany any reinforcement which maintains these behaviors, thus producing considerable conflict.

The practitioner who works with individuals whose sexual responses are considered unacceptable by themselves and/or others is confronted with several value issues, which are detailed in a subsequent section. Such cases call for the clinician to be able to objectively evaluate the behavior in the light of the individual's total life situation and changing community standards. The clinician will likely accept the individual's own choices, while understanding the factors which maintain the behavior as well as the consequences of the behavior. If tension or anxiety is high, the problem focus may not be on the sexual behavior itself but on altering the contingencies which bring about the anxiety. Further, the anxiety and guilt which often accompanies a typical sexual behavior can be reduced if the factors which reinforce these respondents are weakened.

However, if an individual clearly chooses to decrease a sexual response he finds undesirable, there are several procedures which have proven useful in bringing these changes about.

Trained Avoidance/Discrimination Training

One approach is to train the individual to avoid those situations which are likely to lead to the undesirable behavior. Bergin (1969) reports on a procedure which focuses on determining those specific stimulus and response links which form a behavior chain leading to the unwanted behavior. Once these sequences are identified, the client is taught to watch for the onset of such a chain, to interrupt the sequence quickly by deliberately attending to other stimuli or engaging in unrelated activities before the intensity of the situation gets out of hand. After several attempts, the client in the Bergin report was increasingly successful in avoiding involvement in the undesired sexual activities, and continued to be successful in regulating his behavior through a two-year follow-up. It should be noted, however, that Bergin used other procedures in his approach to the problem, and it is therefore difficult to evaluate which specific procedure brought about the change.

Covert Sensitization

A procedure which more directly attacks unwanted sexual responses is based on the technique called "covert sensitization" developed by Cautela (see Chapter 17, Volume I). In this procedure, the individual is trained to relax and then is instructed to vividly imagine a series of scenes leading up to the unwanted sexual behavior. As the scenes begin to arouse the individual, the scene is turned into a powerfully aversive one. The individual is then instructed to visualize turning away from the sexual object and, as a result, he escapes the aversive stimuli and finds himself feeling better. To be most effective, the scenes used in the procedure should incorporate situations which could exist in the individual's natural environment and both arousing and aversive stimuli known to have a strong effect on the individual.

Guided Masturbation

In Chapter 64, Volume II, Davison describes the use of guided masturbation to help eliminate sadistic fantasies. The client was instructed to replace his sadistic fantasies, which usually accompanied his masturbation, with fantasies of non-sadistic relations. Only if the man lost his erection was he to revert to his former fantasies, but just long enough to restore his erection. Such replacement of lost fantasies—or, any other unwanted sexual stimuli— are important in any program which aims at removing unwanted sexual responses. People will more likely decrease behaviors which have been strongly reinforced if they learn to respond to acceptable alternate behaviors. Reinforcement for such new behaviors even can be covertly self-administered, as in a case reported by Cautela (1970) in which heterosexual approach behaviors were shaped in a man whose behaviors had previously been exclusively homosexual. The man was taught to covertly reinforce himself for each step toward heterosexual relations by vividly visualizing a scene which was very reinforcing to him—"swimming on a hot day, feeling the refreshing water and feeling wonderful."

Systematic Desensitization

As described earlier, systematic desensitization accomplishes two reciprocal behavioral goals simultaneously: it eliminates or reduces painful dysfunctional anxiety, and by doing so frees the individual to engage in those reinforcing behaviors which had previously been impeded by the anxiety. The procedures used in systematic desensitization aimed specifically at reducing sex-related anxiety are described in a number of chapters related to painful or difficult intercourse. orgasmic, erectile and ejaculatory problems.

Aversive Conditioning

It is often difficult to alter undesired sexual patterns which have been exhibited and reinforced over extended periods of time. Aversive conditioning frequently has been effective in altering such behaviors as undesired homosexual responses and fetishistic, exhibitionistic and pedophiliac responses which have generally been unresponsive to other approaches.

In aversive conditioning, an aversive stimulus (in the past, often a chemical substance, but more recently a mild but painful electric shock) is presented by the therapist or the client himself either concurrently with the presentation of an undesired stimuli (such as, with undesired homosexual responses, a slide of an attractive male), thus bringing about a classical (respondent) conditioning process, or, in operant punishment, subsequent to an indication of sexual arousal in response to the undesired stimulus. An innovation in aversive conditioning is the use of aversive social stimuli, particularly shame from illustrating the socially undesirable behavior in front of a group of peers, to eliminate the undesired behavior (*see* Chapter 16, Volume I).

Another application of aversive conditioning is called aversion-relief therapy. In this approach, aversive stimuli are presented along with the undesired sexual stimuli, and removed when an acceptable sexual stimuli is substituted. This procedure, therefore, both decreases the undesired response, and increases the desired responses. This takes into account a general dictum about the use of aversive procedures: If an undesired sexual response is to be removed, an alternate and acceptable sexual response should be taught or made available. Thus, one or more of the various procedures to increase sexual responses described earlier should be paired with aversive conditioning. A number of case illustrations presented in both volumes reflect such dual procedures.

ETHICAL ISSUES

The potential power of behavior therapy procedures in altering sexual behavior makes it necessary to consider such questions as: Who should evaluate the goals of those who are trying to influence others? Under what circumstances should we agree to influence the sexual behavior of those who may or may not want to change their behavior? Do we have any models of a functional sexual life style for our clients to guide our interventions, or do we go along with any model they choose? There is always a danger of using any therapeutic approach to force an individual (or class of individuals) to engage in behaviors that conform with our standards rather than to help him behave in a way that is consistent with his own goals. There is an increasing conviction within the helping professions that individuals must be encouraged to enjoy their individuality, rather than be molded into any prevailing "norm."

Beyond the questions of the individual practitioner's and his profession's values about sexual behavior, there is the question of values implicit in the behavior therapy approach itself. Although based to a large extent on objective studies of behavior, behavior therapy does appear to have certain values that are connected to its use. The following list is proposed as guidelines for the practice of behavior therapy with sexual problems. There is some overlap between values (beliefs) and knowledge (empirically testable propositions) in the list; however, it covers some of the basic precepts involved in the use of behavior therapy. All have clear relevance for the treatment of sexual problems (Fischer & Gochros, 1975). Values that appear basic to the use of behavior therapy include the following:

1. Human suffering should be reduced by the most effective, efficient, and harmless methods that can be found.

2. The scientific method is the best available method of ordering knowledge; it can, and should be, applied to studying human behavior.

3. Scientific, objective knowledge about human behavior is available, and should be utilized by practitioners to bring about greater satisfaction for those who lack appropriate behaviors or exhibit dysfunctional behaviors.

4. Labels of "mental illness," "sexual deviance" or concepts of intrinsically bad behavior often do more harm than good. All behaviors, including sexual behavior, must be evaluated in their environmental contexts. Thus, the practitioner must evaluate a behavior in terms of its effects both on the persons who emit it and on their social environment. Similarly, any change in behavior must be considered in terms of both its positive and its negative effects on the individual and his environment. Psychiatric labels related to the disease model (such as "latent homosexual") are both conceptually unsound and potentially harmful, since they can create a chain of responses that reinforce expected patterns of dysfunctional behavior.

5. Much of human behavior is modifiable; hence, a sense of optimism pervades the use of behavior therapy. Since a great deal of sexual behavior is a product of interaction with the environment, maladaptive sexual behaviors can be altered by modifying such interactions.

6. A focus on inferred inner states (such as "autonomous ego," or "unfulfilled dependency needs") or assumptions about interpersonal relations (such as "transference" or "unresolved Oedipals") obfuscate problems, since their existence can neither be proved nor disproved. Therefore, there are advantages in basing interventions on observable behavior. While much goes on with regard to ideas and feelings about sex that is unobservable, there is also much that is observable in behavior that can be modified to bring about greater reinforcement and pain reduction for people.

7. The goals of intervention are those of the client as long as they do not conflict with the rights of others. Exploration of the client's own perceptions of his problem and his goals for his sexual behavior is essential before intervention.

8. The relationship between practitioner and client must be open and honest. Goals, strategies and techniques used to modify the client's sexual behavior should be clearly explicated. No hidden agendas or secret labels should be used.

9. The value of any intervention plan is determined by whether it works (i.e., whether it changes behavior in a desirable direction), not whether it somehow sounds good or feels good.

10. Interventions should be focused on the client's sexual behavior in his everyday life. The intervention process should focus on the client's reactions to, and activities in, his natural environment. The practitioner should attempt to bring about changes in the client's sexual behavior through the regular relationships existing in the client's natural environment.

11. Interventions should focus on environmental events as they relate to specific behaviors rather than only on extensive talk and conceptualization between the person experiencing stress and a professional talker (therapist).

12. Interventions should be applicable with individuals from all social classes, rather than limited largely to upper- and middle-class clients. People from all social classes, educational levels and ethnic backgrounds experience sexual difficulties. Behavior therapy is widely applicable to people from all social class backgrounds. Furthermore, the behavior therapy approach does not require that clients be very intelligent, sophisticated or verbal to be "treatable."

13. The client should be a full and active participant in the intervention process. However, the practitioner should take responsibility for the successful application of his knowledge to each case.

14. The practitioner should be honest, open, direct and human in his relations with clients and others involved in the sexual problem. There should not be a focus on mystical elements in these relationships. The treatment relationship consists of one or more persons with a problem working with another person who has both special skills and an interest in helping people. Although the relationship should be mutually reinforcing, it should not be a replacement for the relationships in the client's—or therapist's—natural environment.

15. The practitioner is accountable, in each case, for developing a system for ascertaining the success or failure of an intervention on the basis of objective criteria and data. These data should be shared with the client, who has a right to participate both in goal selection and in the evaluation of the outcomes of intervention.

Ethical Issues when Working with Undesired Sexual Behavior

Certain sexual behaviors are considered "problems" because they deviate from norms of acceptable sexual behavior. Various aversive social consequences (ridicule, legal penalties) as well as emotional responses (guilt, anxiety) often accompany any reinforcements that maintain these behaviors, thus producing considerable conflict.

The practitioner encountering individuals whose sexual responses are considered undesired by themselves or others (or both) is confronted with several value issues. Does society—through the practitioner—have the right to proscribe sexual behaviors that are not intrinsically harmful to the individual or society? How should the practitioner respond when a person asks to change his sexual patterns primarily in order to avoid both the subtle and the overt oppression he experiences (such as harassment, ridicule, discrimination, etc.)? What should the practitioner do when a client is ambivalent about his sexual behavior: decrease his anxiety and guilt about the socially undesirable behavior, or initiate behavior-change procedures to reinforce socially approved sexual patterns?

Certainly such cases call for a careful evaluation of the behavior as objectively as possible in the light of both the individual's total life situation and of changing community standards. The therapist might be of considerable help by presenting to and exploring with the client alternative behavioral goals he might strive toward and the necessary tasks associated with each option in the context of his present wishes and environment. For example, if a married man is bothered by sexual attraction to men as well as women, the therapist might present the following intervention options:

1. Stay married and undertake behavioral procedures to reduce his sexual attraction to men and increase his enjoyment of heterosexual activities.

2. Get a divorce and engage in homosexual activities at will.

3. Stay married, but either secretly or openly engage in homosexual relationships while he, and perhaps his wife, are helped to adjust to his bisexual orientation.

If the practitioner understands the factors that maintain his client's behavior as well as the consequences of the behavior, he will probably accept the individual's own choices. If the individual's tension or anxiety associated with his chosen behavior is high, the focus may not be on the alteration of the sexual behavior itself but on the modification of those factors that bring about the anxiety. Furthermore, the anxiety and guilt which often accompany an atypical sexual behavior can be reduced if the factors that reinforce these responses are weakened. Discussions with empathic therapists who approach such behavior without criticism or disapproval can significantly reduce anxiety and the resulting pressure for major changes in the individual's sexual choices (Dittes, 1957).

The ethical problems associated with attempts to influence the sexual behavior of institutionalized clients, children and involuntary clients, who are under the potentially coercive control of social agencies, correctional programs, child-welfare organizations and so on, are more serious. Complex issues of professional ethics and civil rights are often raised by the use of any interventive approach with people who are not specifically asking for behavioral change.

The practitioner obviously should avoid using his influence to alter his client's behavior if such intervention clearly violates the rights of his client. But the balance of individual rights and social expectations is sometimes difficult to establish. The process of making the ethical decision of who, indeed, the therapist represents in such situations, and who should control those who modify others' behaviors is, of course, a difficult problem. It is perhaps significant, however, that the potential strength of behavior therapy technology as well as the clarity and explicitness of its procedures bring the ethical issues involved in its utilization into sharp focus, whereas the use of less-explicit technologies may permit the illusion of self-determination for involuntary clients when, in fact, such self-determination does not exist (Morrow & Gochros, 1970).

Special concern is often expressed about the use of aversive procedures to eliminate sexual behaviors that are perceived by the client or significant others as self-destructive, such as abusive sexual behavior or exhibitionistic behavior. The ethical dilemmas in such situations include determining who defines these problems as dysfunctional. Is the client forced into behavioral change because the behavior is truly dysfunctional, or because others in his environment have made him believe so? Can aversive techniques be avoided by positively reinforcing competing desirable behavior or by using other non-aversive procedures? If the client participates voluntarily—and is not in any way coerced into the process—if there is no known non-aversive procedure that would bring about the same desired terminal goal, and if he fully understands and accepts the procedures that are to be followed, including their rationale and the probabilities that the intervention will be successful, then the temporary discomfort of aversive procedures may be as legitimate in terminating the client's suffering as surgery is for relieving a physical disorder. Fortunately, as experience in the use of, and knowledge about, behavior therapy technology increases, it is likely that aversive techniques will be applied with even more precision and with clearer indications of their potential success than we now have.

Many professionals who use behavior therapy believe any use of aversive control to be undesirable. Sometimes, however, aversive procedures may be the only effective strategy for intervention into grossly damaging behaviors, or those behaviors that are not responsive to other procedures or, simply, when no other interventive strategy is available. Then the task becomes one of balancing the potential positive effects of the use of aversive procedures with the potential negative effects such as pain and discomfort. In such situations the choice must be the client's.

The emphasis, so far, has been on the ethical issues involved in the modification of dysfunctional sexual behaviors. A broader ethical issue for the helping professions is their commitment to preventing sexual dysfunctions from occurring in the first place. The helping professions—medicine, psychology, social work, clergy, education—should more aggressively offer relevant positive sexual education not only to children but also to adults, including those within their own professions. Such education should stress contemporary knowledge about the wide range of sexual behavior and the range of consequences, positive and negative, for these behaviors. It should stress the right and need for each person to develop his own sexuality rather than conforming to some arbitrary or even dysfunctional concept of "normalcy," or even a stereotyped "performance" ideal. Such education could lead to the realization of the hope expressed by LoPiccolo and Lobitz (1973, p. 356) "... that eventually our society will have such positive attitudes toward sexuality and will so effectively teach people the elements of effective sexual technique that sex therapists will become extinct."

Or, if they do not become extinct, perhaps they can begin to address themselves to the enhancement of human sexuality and the companion joys of intimacy.

REFERENCES

Annon, J.S. *The behavioral treatment of sexual problems: Volume I, Brief therapy.* Honolulu: Enabling Systems, 1974.

Annon, J.S. *The behavioral treatment of sexual problems: Volume 2, Intensive therapy.* Honolulu, Enabling Systems, 1975.

Bandura, A. *Principles of behavior modification.* New York: Holt, Rinehart and Winston, 1969.

Bergin, A.E. A self-regulation technique for impulse control disorders. *Psychotherapy: Theory, Research and Practice,* 1969, **6**, 113-118.

Bindrim, P. A report on a nude marathon. In H. Gochros and L. Schultz (Eds.)., *Human sexuality and social work.* New York: Association Press, 1972, 205-220.

Buckley, T. All they talk about is sex. *The New York Times Magazine,* April 20, 1969.

Cautela, J.R. Covert reinforcement. *Behavior Therapy,* 1970, **1**, 33-50.

Comfort, A. (Ed.). *The joy of sex: A gourmet guide to lovemaking.* New York: Crown Publishers, 1972.

Coons, F. Ambisexuality as an alternative adaptation. *American Journal of College Health Association.* December 1972, **21**, 142-144.

Dahlberg, C. Sexual contact between patient and therapist.. In M. Curtin, (Ed.), *Symposium on Love.* New York: Behavioral Publications, 1973, 143-174.

Dittes, J.E. Extinction during psychotherapy of G.S.R. accompanying "embarrassing" statements. *Journal of Abnormal and Social Psychology,* 1957, **54**, 265-271.

Ellis, A. *The sensuous person: Critique and corrections.* Secaucus, New Jersey: Lyle Stuart, 1972.

English, O.S. Positive values in the affairs. In H. Otto (Ed.), *The New Sexuality.* Palo Alto, California: Science and Behavior Books, 1971, 173-192.

Fischer, J. & Gochros, H.L. *Planned behavior change: Behavior modification in social work.* New York: Free Press, 1975.

Fischer, J. & Miller, H. The effect of race and social class on clinical judgments. *Clinical Social Work Journal,* 1973, **I**,(2), 100-109.

Gochros, H. Courses in sex-related problems in American schools of social work. Paper presented at the Annual Program Meeting, Council of Social Work Education, Philadelphia, Pa., 1976.

Gochros, H.L. & Gochros, J. *The sexually oppressed.* New York: Association Press, 1976.

Harbison, J.M., Graham, P.J., Quinn, J.T., McAllister, H. & Woodward, R. A question-naire measure of sexual interest. *Archives of Sexual Behavior,* 1974, **3**, 357-366.

Hartman, W. & Fithian, M.A. *Treatment of sexual dysfunction.* Long Beach, California: Center for Marital and Sexual Studies, 1973.

Hunt, M. *Sexual behavior in the 1970's.* Chicago: Playboy Press, 1974.

"J." *The sensuous woman.* New York: Lyle Stuart, 1969.

Kaplan, H. & Kohl, R. Adverse reactions to the rapid treatment of sexual problems. *Psychosomatics.* 1972, **13**, 185-190.

Katchadourian, H.A. & D.T. Lunde. *Fundamentals of human sexuality.* New York: Holt, Rinehart and Winston, 1975.

Kovaks, A. The intimate relationship: A therapeutic paradox. *Psychotherapy: Theory, Research and Practice,* October 1965, **2**, 97-103.

Lief, H. New developments in the sex education of the physician. *Journal of the AMA,* June, 1970.

Lobitz, W. & LoPiccolo, J. New methods in the behavioral treatment of sexual dysfunc-tion. *Journal of Behavior Therapy and Experimental Psychiatry,* 1972, **3**, 265-271.

LoPiccolo, J. & Lobitz, W.C. Behavior therapy of sexual dysfunction. In L.A. Hamer-lynck, L.C. Handy, & E.J. Mash, (Eds.), *Behavior Change, Methodology, Concepts, and Practice.* Champaign, Ill.: Research Press, 1973.

LoPiccolo, J. & Steger, J.C. The sexual interaction inventory: A new instrument for assessment of sexual dysfunction. *Archives of Sexual Behavior,* 1974, **3**, 585-595.

Marshall, D.S. & Suggs, R.C. *Human sexual behavior.* New York: Basic Books, 1971.

Masters, W.H. & Johnson, V.E. *Human sexual inadequacy.* Boston: Little, Brown and Co., 1970.

McCartney, J. Overt transference. *Journal of Sex Research,* October, 1966, **2**, 227-237.

McCary, J.L. *Human sexuality* (2nd ed.). New York: Van Nostrand, 1975.

Morrow, W.R. & Gochros, H.L. Misconceptions regarding behavior modification. *Social Service Review.* 1970, **44**, 293-307.

Reuben, D. *Everything you always wanted to know about sex.* New York: David McKay Co., 1969.

Staats, A.W. *Social behaviorism and human motivation: Principles of the attitude-reinforcer-discriminative system.* In A.G. Greenwald, T.C. Brook and T.M. Ostrom (Eds.), *Psychological Foundations of Attitudes.* New York: Academic Press, 1968, 33-66.

Staats, A.W. & Staats, C.K. *Complex human behavior: A systematic extension of learning principles.* New York: Holt, Rinehart and Winston, 1963.

Szasz, T. *The myth of mental illness: Foundation of a theory of personal contact.* New York: Hoeber-Harper, 1961.

Ullmann, L.P. & Krasner, L. *A psychological approach to abnormal behavior.* Englewood Cliffs, New Jersey: Prentice Hall, 1975.

Vincent, C.E. *Human sexuality in medical education and practice.* Springfield, Ill.: Charles C Thomas, 1968.

Wolpe, J. *The practice of behavior therapy.* New York: Pergamon Press, 1973.

Yoell, W., *et. al.* Marriage, morals and therapeutic goals. *Journal of Behavior Therapy and Experimental Psychiatry.* 1971, **2**, 127-132.

Introduction to Volume I

In recent years, practitioners and researchers in behavior therapy have built up an armamentarium of procedures to alter a wide range of human behaviors. Many of the procedures have been effective in helping to increase desired sexual behaviors, such as increased frequency of orgasm and achieving and maintaining erections, and to decrease undesired sexual responses such as fantasizing about or engaging in sexual behaviors with undesired or inappropriate sexual objects. The articles in Volume I describe these specific behavioral procedures. Some of these procedures, although based on already existing models of behavioral intervention, have been developed for specific application to sexual problems (e.g., sensate focus, *see* Chapters 3 and 4), and some have been adopted virtually unchanged from other applications (e.g., systematic desensitization, *see* Chapter 7).

The purpose of this volume is to present descriptions of these basic procedures as they have been applied to and differentially used with sexual problems. Volume II then presents in detail specific categories of problem situations to which these general procedures have been applied. Thus, Volume II largely consists of case illustrations of the procedures described in this volume.

However, behavioral procedures are not carried out in a vacuum, nor necessarily used exclusive of other relevant interventions. Therefore this part of the book also includes articles which provide a background and format for the use of these procedures. Thus, Chapters 2, 3, 4, 5 and 8 all provide models for and guidelines to the process of behavioral intervention with sexual problems. These chapters reinforce the premise that behavioral techniques—particularly when applied to sexual problems—must be carried out in the context of a sensitive, empathic therapist-client relationship.

This volume is divided into two parts. The first part describes a range of procedures which have been used primarily for dealing with the common problems experienced by men and women in heterosexual intercourse. A parallel section in Volume II focuses more specifically on the particular problems and provides case illustrations of the procedures described in Volume I. This section, however, provides some of the basic models applicable to heterosexual pair problems (*see*, for example, Lobitz & LoPiccolo's review in Chapter 1 of a variety of emerging methods used to approach sexual dysfunctioning, Masters and Johnson's presentation in Chapter 4 of their widely discussed program, and Annon's very practical model in Chapter 8 for the use of various levels of behavioral intervention based on the specific characteristics of each case). In addition, specific behavioral tools applicable to a wide range of problems are presented, such as an approach to sexual history-taking (Chapter 2) and procedures for carrying out the widely applicable systematic desensitization procedure.

Part 2 presents several chapters describing procedures which have been found useful for a wide variety of sexual problems, especially those described in greater detail in the corresponding second part of Volume II. Most of these chapters relate to the modification or elimination of undesired response patterns. That is, these procedures, particularly the aversive techniques described in Chapters 10, 11, 15, 16 and 19 help the individual terminate his sexual arousal to inappropriate sexual objects as determined by the individual, or help in cases in which the behavior stimulated by the sexual response is potentially harmful to others. Accompanying these techniques—and often supplanting them—are procedures which condition such individuals to respond sexually to more desired stimuli. Such techniques as the controlled use of masturbation and often fantasies (*see* Chapters 13 and 14) effectively reinforce these new desired responses.

Actually, many of the articles presented in this book, particularly in Volume II, consist of case studies. This is for two reasons. The first is that a major purpose of the book is to illustrate for the clinician the way others have successfully treated a variety of common sexual problems, so that the clinician's efforts in dealing with those problems will be cummulative —informed to the extent possible by the best the literature has to offer.

The second reason is that, except for a few of the articles included in this book involving experimental research, plus several studies dealing mainly with homosexual behavior (*see* Volume II), there are very few group experimental studies with rigorous controls in the area of behavior therapy with sexual problems. Of course, some of these procedures (e.g., systematic desensitization) have received extensive research validation in slightly different contexts, thereby suggesting their priority for consideration. But on the whole, very few rigorous empirical guidelines exist for the selection of procedures to treat sexual problems. Typically, the clinician is left with the problem of considering: 1) what research is available on a given technique with a given problem? 2) what techniques have been developed (or modified) to deal with the specific problems with which he is faced? 3) what does the case study literature suggest about given procedures with given problems? 4) and what biases does he have *vis-à-vis* techniques (e.g., for or against physically aversive methods)?

The problems with all of these is they are less than perfect guidelines (the "art" of behavior therapy?); all allow for a certain degree of distortion in selecting techniques; and few if any of these guidelines allow a definitive decision. Indeed, the problem is compounded even further by the fact that in many of the case studies, several techniques were used, so that, strictly speaking, it is impossible to determine which procedure had optimal effect or whether the combination of procedures—*in toto*— was responsible for the observed changes (or for that matter, whether any of these factors were).

But perhaps these are the problems with which any new field is beset. Lest that be taken as an apology, the key point is that these problems need not remain. Future research it is hoped will disentangle some of the knotty problems involved in selecting with a greater degree of certainty the optimal techniques to deal with a given problem. This is not to say that the "art" of behavior therapy is valueless. But it is to say that it is likely that the greater the degree of scientifically validated input into practice, the better off will be our clients.

Part 1

Part I

Procedures Focused on Problems in Heterosexual Couple Relationships

The most common, or at least, most obvious sexual problems that come to the attention of clinicians are those that involve heterosexual couple relationships, such as in marriage. As noted in the Introduction, there have been estimates that over 50 percent of marriages involve some degree of sexual dysfunction which is encapsulated as an isolated problem and/or is a result of other difficulties in the marital relationship. Such problems generally revolve around problems in achieving satisfying intercourse: for men, problems associated with achieving or maintaining erections (commonly called "impotence") and problems associated with ejaculation; for women, problems associated with orgasmic functioning (traditionally labeled as "frigidity") and problems of difficult or painful intercourse (termed "vaginismus" in the first instance and "dyspareunia" in the second).

The first article in this section, "New Methods in the Behavioral Treatment of Sexual Dysfunction" by Lobitz and LoPiccolo, describes a program for treating couples for a variety of sexual dysfunctions including orgasmic dysfunctioning in women and problems associated with ejaculation and achieving or maintaining erections in men. The authors describe how an "orthodox" behavioral treatment program emphasizing *in vivo* desensitization has been supplemented by several other methods either adapted from other approaches or newly developed. They use a systematic masturbation procedure in combination with erotic fantasy and literature to enhance sexual responding. Role-playing orgasmic responses is used to disinhibit sexual responses. Therapist self-disclosure is used to reduce client inhibition and anxiety and to model an open acceptance of sexuality. These clinicians also use daily client records to provide data on ongoing sexual behavior. The program also features a refundable penalty deposit to heighten client motivation to continue in treatment, and client involvement in planning "homework" assignments for later sessions and follow-up maintenance of gains. The outcome report at the end of the article suggests very positive

3

results for most of the problems with which this program has dealt. The one exception, involving "secondary orgasmic dysfunctioning," showed a failure rate of six out of the first six cases. Based on data from these cases, however, the authors revised their program and claimed to achieve success in all of the subsequent three cases.

The Lobitz and LoPiccolo article presents a brief overview of a comprehensive program that is based on the combined use of several different procedures, many of which are described in more depth in the following chapters. For example, a most basic element of therapeutic intervention with sexual problems involves gaining an understanding of the problem through the clinician's sensitive exploration and discussion of the problem with the client(s). In the next article, Green describes some of the key features involved in "Taking a Sexual History." Although this article was originally written as a guide for nonpsychiatric physicians, it contains sound guidelines for any clinician working with sexual dysfunction. Green divides the bulk of his article into suggestions regarding interviewing in eleven areas: 1) sexual dysfunction; 2) teenage sexuality; 3) the unmarried client not living with a sexual partner; 4) sexual myths; 5) masturbation; 6) the homosexual client; 7) "unusual" sexual interest; 8) old age; 9) miscellaneous situations; 10) "up front" sexual problems; and 11) the close of history-taking.

In the next article, Gochros presents a discussion of "Treatment of Common Marital Sexual Problems." As with the preceding article, the emphasis here is less on specific behavioral techniques than on the *context* of intervention with sexual problems. Obviously, the use of behavior therapy does not preclude a sensitivity to interpersonal and human concerns, nor does it preclude the use of information that, strictly speaking, is not derived from the field of behavior therapy, per se. Thus, in this article, Gochros reviews some of the basic sources of sexual problems in marriages and some approaches for dealing with them. Gochros describes two common models of sexual expression—the romantic model and the sexual athlete—which in their extreme form often contribute to marital sexual dysfunctioning. He then describes four common, often overlapping, sources for many of the sexual problems in marriage and some methods for dealing with them. These areas are: 1) lack of sexual knowledge; 2) lack of communication; 3) lack of consensus on sexual activities; and 4) problems in sexual ability.

Several references in the preceding articles were made to the pioneering work of Masters and Johnson. And, indeed, no book on the treatment of sexual dysfunction would be complete without some discussion of their methods. In the following article, "Counseling with Sexually Incompatible Marriage Partners," Masters and Johnson describe their program. Again, though not a behavior therapy program, per se, the Masters and Johnson approach—in focusing on specific target behaviors, use of empirically derived principles of intervention and development of specific techniques to deal with specific problems—is highly compatible with behavior therapy.

The first part of their program involves the necessity for recognition of when the sexual problem is a primary problem and when it is more a result of marital incompatibility. The next phase involves the taking of a sexual history (*see also* Chapter 2), which involves (for both assessment and intervention) a male-female therapy team. They then describe the therapeutic processes for dealing with "impotence" (including failed erection, inadequate erection and nonemissive erection) with particular emphasis on the procedure involving controlled manual penile stimulation in a relaxed atmosphere. The final part of their article discusses in detail strategies for dealing with "frigidity," or female orgasmic dysfunction, based on a five-point framework for their therapeutic approach.

In the following article, McCarthy discusses "A Modification of the Masters and Johnson Sex Therapy Model in a Clinical Setting." The basic modification involves time, efficiency and expense. Instead of a two-week residential, dual therapist (including a physician) model, McCarthy describes use of one therapist (not necessarily a physician), with once-a-week sessions (usually 10-15 following assessment), in a manner that more clearly fits into most clinic and agency operating patterns. McCarthy also presents a detailed case history illustrating the general process plus some of the specific techniques such as "sensate focus" which are used in the process.

In the next article, reprinted from his book *The Practice of Behavior Therapy* (2d. ed.), Wolpe describes in detail "The Treatment of Inhibited Sexual Responses." Working largely within a respondent framework, Wolpe hypothesizes that anxiety (or other emotions such as shame or disgust) have become conditioned to the stimuli associated with sexual responding; since they are incompatible responses, the anxiety inhibits the sexual responses. The prescription for change, based on Wolpe's principle of reciprocal inhibition: arrange for the use of sexual responses that are strong enough to inhibit and eventually overcome the anxiety responses. (Of course, the principle of reciprocal inhibition also underlies Wolpe's conceptualization of other techniques such as systematic desensitization and assertive training.)

Wolpe's chapter provides an excellent overview of behavior therapy (and associated procedures) with two kinds of problems—"impotence" and "frigidity." Wolpe not only describes the key techniques in detail but also presents several case examples illustrating their use. With regard to "impotence" (which Wolpe considers to include both inadequacy of penile erection and/or premature ejaculation), Wolpe presents the basic techniques—graduated manual penile stimulation plus the Masters and Johnson "squeeze" variation, and then presents a detailed case illustration. He notes the need for therapist flexibility in dealing with each case individually. For example, at times, systematic desensitization to the stages of the sexual approach may be indicated when anxiety levels preclude moving to practice in the actual sexual situations.

Wolpe then describes several procedures for dealing with, first, "essential frigidity," lack of sexual response to males in general, and second, "situational frigidity," lack of response to a particular male (often, unfortunately, the client's husband). Treatment may involve provision of information, systematic desensitization and/or assertive training, based upon the assessment of the individual case. Wolpe also describes in detail a procedure for inducing a "clinical orgasm" by suggestion which has been used with apparent success with women who have never experienced a full coital orgasm.

The Masters and Johnson model and its variations are obviously crucial components of the clinician's repertoire for dealing with sexual problems. But their effectiveness should not rule out use of other techniques. For example, Wolpe, in his chapter, implies that systematic desensitization is an adjunct to the Masters and Johnson type treatment. Indeed, systematic desensitization is perhaps the most widely used, widely researched and experimentally validated procedure of behavior therapy. And, as Obler illustrates in the next article, "Systematic Desensitization in Sexual Disorders," desensitization still should be a basic technique in the clinician's armamentarium when sexual problems are involved, both to directly treat the sexual dysfunction and to treat related anxieties. Obler describes a modified version of systematic desensitization therapy using *in vivo* stimuli and incorporating assertive confidence training as applied to persons suffering from severe sexual disorders ("premature ejaculation, ejaculatory incompetence and secondary impotence in males and primary and secondary orgasmic dysfunction in females"). This therapy was compared with a conventional psychoanalytically-oriented group treatment and an untreated control group. Effectiveness was evaluated on the basis of physiological and subjective reports of change. The results of this program showed that the modified desensitization technique used in this program was significantly more successful in eliminating sexual dysfunctions and reducing associated sexual and social anxieties than the comparison conditions.

In the next article, Annon describes his "PLISSIT Model: A Proposed Conceptual Scheme for the Behavioral Treatment of Sexual Problems." The model deals with four levels of approach, with each letter or pair of letters designating a suggested method for handling presenting sexual concerns. The four levels are arranged on the basis of increasing complexity of the problem and intensity of the treatment. The four levels (the first three of which are "brief therapy") are: 1) Permission; 2) Limited Information; 3) Specific Suggestions (including many of the behavioral and other procedures described to this point in Part I of this book); and 4) Intensive Therapy. Annon's scheme provides a consistent, sound and, perhaps most important, useful framework for organizing and implementing a variety of procedures to treat common sexual problems.

The final article in Part 1 is Dengrove's, "The Mechanotherapy of Sexual Disorders." As Dengrove points out, mechanotherapy has a place in the treatment of several sexual problems, and knowledge about available devices should be part of the interventive repertoire of every clinician working with sexual dysfunction. Dengrove reviews the use of the artificial penis, a constricting device for the penis, the vibrator and the Kegel perineometer. All of these devices have been useful in the treatment of such problems as those associated with erections and ejaculation in men and with orgasmic dysfunction in women (although the article tends to suggest an undocumented distinction between clitoral and vaginal orgasm). Although these devices are not necessarily the primary therapeutic instrument, they should be available for use either as supplementary methods, or in cases where the dysfunction is refractory to such other methods as described in Part 1 of this volume.

1
New Methods in the Behavioral Treatment of Sexual Dysfunction*

W. CHARLES LOBITZ and JOSEPH LoPICCOLO

Since 1969 the Sex Research Program at the University of Oregon Psychology Clinic has been treating couples for a variety of sexual dysfunctions. This program, directed by Joseph LoPiccolo, is part of a doctoral training program in clinical psychology and has involved the treatment of approximately 25 couples per year by a total of 16 different male—female co-therapy teams over the last 3 years. The program has had good success in treating sexual dysfunction by a behavioral approach. Within this approach we have developed or adapted from others a number of new techniques for the treatment of sexual dysfunction. This paper describes some of these techniques and presents clinical examples and outcome statistics to document their effectiveness.

BACKGROUND

The general behavioral model used is based on the procedures developed by Wolpe (1969), Hastings (1963), and Masters and Johnson (1970). In the absence of any physical pathology, sexual dysfunction is viewed as a learned phenomenon, maintained internally by performance anxiety and externally by a nonreinforcing environment, principally the partner. In addition, a lack of sexual skill, knowledge and communication on the part of one or both partners contributes to the dysfunction.

Within this social learning model, the dysfunction is treated through training changes in the couple's sexual behavior. Both partners are involved in the therapy process. Treatment consists of 15 sessions in which a male-female co-therapy team plans tasks ("homework") to be carried out by the dysfunctioning couple between sessions. Performance anxiety in either the totally inorgasmic female or in the male with erectile

* Preparation of this manuscript was supported in part by a grant from the University of Oregon Office of Scientific and Scholarly Research. Portions of this paper were presented at the Fourth Annual International Conference on Behavior Modification, Banff, Alberta, Canada, March 1972, and at the annual meeting of the Western Psychological Association, Portland, Oregon, April 1972.

failure is treated through *in vivo* graded exposure tasks following the systematic desensitization format developed by Wolpe (1969) and refined by Masters and Johnson (1970). Premature ejaculation is treated through a retraining program advocated by Semans (1956), as modified by the use of the "squeeze" technique (Masters & Johnson, 1970). In the case of all dysfunctions, intercourse is temporarily prohibited while the couple's repertoire of sexual behavior is rebuilt.

On the above framework, the Sex Research Program has developed several clinical innovations designed to facilitate changes in sexual behavior. These innovations fall into one of five classes: 1) Procedures designed to allow the therapists to obtain regular data on the clients' sexual behavior and to ensure that the clients carry out the "homework" assignments. 2) Procedures which enhance the clients' desire and arousal toward his or her partner. 3) Procedures which teach interpersonal sexual skills. 4) Procedures which disinhibit clients toward displaying their own sexual arousal and responsiveness. 5) Procedures designed to maintain treatment gains after therapy has ended.

DATA ON CLIENTS' SEXUAL BEHAVIOR

A hallmark of behavioral approaches to treatment has been the reliance on observable, quantifiable client behavior. Most problems which lend themselves to a behavioral approach (e.g., phobic or aggressive responses) are readily observable. Home observations of client behavior have become commonplace in behavioral assessment and intervention (e.g., Lewinsohn & Shafer, 1971; Patterson, Ray & Shaw, 1968). However, for both ethical and practical reasons neither home nor laboratory observations of client behavior is possible when treating sexual dysfunction. Yet, for our program, therapists must know exactly what the clients are doing and whether they are following the treatment procedures at home. Our clients are asked to be their own data collectors. On each day on which any sexual activity occurs, clients fill out a *daily record form* detailing their sexual behavior. For each activity, the client specifies its duration, numerical ratings of the pleasure and arousal that he obtained, and subjective comments about the activity. In addition, he specifies numerical ratings of the degree of pleasure and arousal which he perceived his partner to have obtained. Throughout treatment these daily records provide therapists with feedback. Using this data they tailor the program to the client's progress.

CLIENT MOTIVATION

While clients are generally motivated to carry out the program, including filling out daily record forms, at times they may find it difficult to follow the prescriptions. For example, they may be tired or busy with other activities and thus avoid engaging in the prescribed number of "homework" sessions. They may be tempted to break the prohibition on intercourse or to resist trying new sexual activities that the therapists prescribe. A *refundable penalty deposit* provides an incentive for following the program. At the beginning of treatment, the clients pay their full 15-session fee plus an equal amount as a penalty deposit. If the client does not violate any of the treatment rules, his deposit is refunded in full at the end of treatment. However, should a violation occur, 1/15th of the deposit is not refunded. On a second violation, another 2/15ths is forfeited, i.e., 3/15ths altogether. The progression continues arithmetically, so that for the fifth violation 5/15ths of the deposit is forfeited, using up the entire deposit. A sixth violation would cause the therapists to terminate treatment. Treatment rules are specified in a "penalty contract" which the clients sign at the beginning of therapy. Basically, the rules are that the clients must keep appointments, turn in the daily record forms prior to their appointment, and engage in only those sexual behaviors programmed for them by the therapists.

Although this procedure has not been systematically evaluated, the fact that more than one violation rarely occurs attests to its effectiveness in motivating the clients to follow the program rules. Over the last 19 cases treated, couples were fined an average of 0·7 times. No couple has been penalized more than three times. For some clients, the penalty deposit is a more effective motivator than for others. Younger couples, especially those in the counterculture for whom money is not a powerful reinforcer, are less apt to be influenced by the threat of losing their deposit. However, for older, middle-class couples, the penalty deposit provides a powerful motivation. For example, a successful certified public accountant resisted completing his assigned "homework" sessions with his wife, complaining that he had too much office work to do. Instead of cajoling her husband, the wife quietly reminded him of the penalty fee. A quick mental calculation convinced him that it was financially worthwhile to forego his office work in favor of the session with his wife.

ENHANCING CLIENTS' AROUSAL

A frequent aspect of sexual dysfunction is the inability of one or both clients to become sexually aroused by the partner. In cases of sexual deviations, other therapists (Davison, 1968; Marquis, 1970) have used a *classical conditioning* procedure during masturbation to condition arousal to appropriate sexual objects. We have adapted this to raise arousal levels in dysfunctional couples. The conditioning is accomplished either through masturbation or in sexual activity with the partner.

In masturbation, the client is instructed to focus on any erotic stimuli that are currently arousing. These stimuli may consist of literature, pictures, and/or fantasy. Within our program, stimulus materials have ranged from heterosexual erotic materials to homosexual fantasies. Once aroused, the client masturbates to orgasm. Just prior to orgasm, he switches his focus to fantasies of sexual activity with his partner. The unconditioned stimuli of previously arousing fantasies and materials and the unconditioned responses of sexual arousal and orgasm are, thus, paired with the presently neutral stimulus of sexual activity with the partner. On subsequent occasions, the client is instructed to switch to fantasies of the partner at earlier points in time, until fantasies of the partner become a conditioned stimulus for sexual arousal and the artificial stimuli previously used are no longer necessary. For clients who have difficulty in fantasizing their partner we have supplied a Polaroid camera and instructed them to photograph their partner in sexual activity. They use these photographs in lieu of fantasy.

The same conditioning procedure is used in sexual activity with the partner as well as in masturbation. The client first fantasizes erotic scenes to become aroused and then switches his focus to the present reality of sexual activity with his partner. A case study detailing this procedure has been reported elsewhere (LoPiccolo, Stewart & Watkins, 1972).

In the case of women who have never experienced orgasm from any source of physical stimulation, fantasy and erotic materials alone do not enhance the arousal level enough to produce orgasm. In such cases, *a nine-step masturbation program* has proven highly successful in producing the clients' first orgasm. The use of masturbation in treating frigidity has been reported previously (Ellis, 1960; Hastings, 1963). We have incorporated it as a systematic part of our treatment for primary orgasmic dysfunction. This program is based on evidence that more women can reach orgasm through masturbation than through any other means (Kinsey et al., 1953), and that masturbation produces the most intense orgasms (Masters & Johnson, 1966). The nine steps follow a graduated approach model (Wolpe, 1969) to desensitize the client to masturbation. The details of the program have been described elsewhere (LoPiccolo & Lobitz, 1972, in press) but can be summarized as follows:

Step 1: The client is given the assignment to increase her self-awareness by examining her nude body and appreciating its beauty. She uses a hand mirror to examine her genitals and identify the various areas with the aid of diagrams in Hastings' book *Sexual Expression in Marriage* (1966). In addition she is started on a program of Kegel's (1952) exercises for increasing tone and vascularity of the pelvic musculature.

Step 2: The client is instructed to explore her genitals tactually as well as visually. To avoid performance anxiety, she is not given any expectation to become aroused at this point.

Step 3: Tactual and visual exploration are focused on locating sensitive areas that produce feelings of pleasure when stimulated.

Step 4: The client is told to concentrate on manual stimulation of identified pleasurable areas. At this point the female therapist discusses techniques of masturbation, including the use of a lubricant.

Step 5: If orgasm does not occur during Step 4, the client is told to increase the intensity and duration of masturbation. She is told to masturbate until "something happens" or until she becomes tired or sore.

Step 6: If orgasm is not reached during Step 5, we instruct the client to purchase a vibrator of the type sold in pharmacies for facial or body massage. In our most difficult case to date, three weeks of daily 45-minute vibrator sessions were required to produce orgasm.

Step 7: Once the client has achieved orgasm through masturbation, we introduce the husband to the procedure by having him observe her. This desensitizes her to displaying arousal and orgasm in his presence and also functions as an excellent learning experience for him.

Step 8: The husband manipulates his wife in the manner she has demonstrated in Step 7.

Step 9: Once orgasm has occured in Step 8, we instruct the couple to engage in intercourse while the husband stimulates his wife's genitals, either manually or with a vibrator.

We currently also use heterosexual erotic pictures or literature to supplement the nine-step masturbation program. The efficacy of this combination was demonstrated fortuitously when three different women in the masturbation program saw a sexually explicit film at a local x-rated cinema. They each reported masturbating to their first orgasm shortly after having viewed the film.

TEACHING INTERPERSONAL SEXUAL SKILLS

Most couples who seek treatment for sexual dysfunction have behavioral skill deficits. They may feel deep affection for each other, but have difficulty expressing their emotions, initiating and refusing sexual contact, and assertively communicating their likes and dislikes. We view these deficits not as emotional inhibitions, but primarily as a lack of social skill. These deficits are overcome in therapy sessions through therapist *modeling* and client *role-playing*. These techniques have achieved considerable efficacy in the treatment of social avoidance and other phobias (e.g., Bandura, 1971). We have directly adapted them to cases of sexual dysfunction.

In the Sex Research Program these techniques are used to demonstrate appropriate initiation, refusal, and emotional assertion responses, and to allow the couple to practice these in a protected environment. They are then instructed to practice these skills at home as part of their intersession "homework" assignment. For example, a female client might complain that her husband initiates sexual activity in a crude, alienating manner, that he never displays his love for her, and that he does not engage in sexual behaviors that she finds arousing. In this case a mutual failure is involved—the wife has not taught her husband what she desires. The therapy team models verbal initiation of sexual activity and verbal expression of tender emotions and has the clients practice these behaviors in the therapy session, while giving each other feedback about their performances.

DISINHIBITION OF SEXUALITY

Role-playing is useful not only in skill training, but also as a disinhibitor of sexual responses. Hilliard (1960) has instructed inorgasmic women to feign orgasm to satisfy their partners. She reported that in many cases this pretense became a reality. Therapists in our own program have instructed inorgasmic women to role-play an orgasm, not to deceive their partner, but to disinhibit themselves about losing control and showing intense sexual arousal. Since the male partner is present when these instructions are given, deceit is avoided. This particular use of role-playing is analogous to Kelly's (1955) fixed-role therapy in which the client is asked to enact the role of someone different from himself. In sex therapy, the role is a different sexual response rather than an entire personality change.

Orgasmic role-playing is useful at two points in therapy: first, for the woman who is highly aroused by masturbation but becomes apprehensive at the approaching orgasm and thus loses sexual arousal as stimulation continues; second, for the woman who masturbates to orgasm when alone but cannot achieve it if her partner is present. In either case, we instruct the couple to engage in the following procedure. During sexual activity at home the woman is to role-play not just an orgasm, but a gross exaggeration of orgasm with violent convulsions and inarticulate screaming. Knowing that this orgasm is not real, the couple is free to make a game, even a parody of the response. We instruct them to repeat this until they pass from their initial anxiety and embarrassment to amusement and finally boredom with the procedure.

Orgasmic role-playing has been especially useful with intellectual, controlled clients who are ashamed and embarrassed about the muscular contractions and involuntary noises which accompany orgasm. In three cases where the women had been unable to reach orgasm despite the use of all our other treatment procedures, this technique led to their first orgasm.

Our most common stratagem for disinhibiting clients to sexual responses is *therapist self-disclosure.* In advocating self-disclosure, Jourard (1964) has emphasized therapist spontaneity during the session but has stated that one need not tell the client about one's life outside the therapy hour (p. 71). In the Sex Research Program therapists do not only answer clients' questions, but also volunteer information about their own sexual behavior. Because the therapist has a respected position of authority in our culture, the therapists unashamedly discussing their own enjoyment of sexual activity is an acceptable and seemingly effective way of disinhibiting clients about their own sexuality. In particular, self-disclosure about masturbation and oral-genital sex facilitates change in the client's attitude toward these behaviors. However self-disclosure should be withheld until the client has gotten to know the therapist. Premature self-disclosure may alienate some clients.

Another use of therapist self-disclosure has been in reducing clients' anxiety about their "abnormality" or "inadequacy" in having a sexual dysfunction. For example, one premature ejaculator, who had made considerable progress in therapy, was concerned that he would always have to rely on the squeeze technique as part of his lovemaking. The male therapist reassured him by saying that he also used the squeeze on occasion. The female therapist, who, in this instance was the male therapist's wife, reinforced the point by stating that she encouraged the squeeze as part of their sexual repertoire because it prolonged their lovemaking.

MAINTAINING TREATMENT GAINS

Regardless of a treatment program's initial success, the proof of its efficacy is the degree to which clients can maintain their gains once therapy has ended. Our follow-up assessment 6 months after termination indicated that treatment gains have generally persisted.

This maintenance is due, in part, to *client participation in planning treatment* in the final therapy sessions. After 12 or 13 sessions of therapy, the clients have a good idea of the strategy behind their treatment. With the therapists' guidance, they now plan their own "homework" assignments for the next sessions. This prepares them to handle any problems which may arise after therapy has terminated. At the end of therapy the clients write out a maintenance program of specific behaviors for the months following. At this time, they also make a list of the behaviors that contributed to their problem before treatment, how these have changed, and what they plan to do should the problems recur. The clients keep these lists.

RESULTS

Over the past three years the Sex Research Program has experienced generally good results in the treatment of sexual dysfunction. Applying Masters and Johnson's (1970) criterion that the female partner be satisfied "in at least 50 percent of their coital connections (p.92)," our success rate is as follows: 13 out of 13 treated cases of female primary orgasmic dysfunction, six out of six premature ejaculation cases, four out of six erectile failure cases, and three out of nine cases of secondary orgasmic dysfunction. However, with regard to the secondary orgasmic dysfunction cases, it should be noted that our three most recently treated cases are our three successes. These followed a major revision of our program for secondary orgasmic dysfunction, based on data from the first six cases. The data and the revisions are reported elsewhere (McGovern & Stewart, 1972).

To supplement Masters and Johnson's (1970) criterion for success, we have developed a measurement instrument, the Oregon Sex Inventory (LoPiccolo, 1972; Steger, 1972), for assessing pre-post treatment changes in a couple's sexual functioning. Our success rate as reflected by the scales of this inventory equals or exceeds the rate on Masters and Johnson's (1970) criterion.

We think our success is due, in part, to the clinical innovations with which we supplement a "traditional" behavioral-treatment program. Daily client records provide data on ongoing sexual behavior. A refundable penalty deposit heightens motivation. Fantasy and pornography, in combination with a nine-step masturbation program, enhance sexual responsiveness. Role-playing serves to impart social-sexual skills and to disinhibit female orgasm. Therapist self-disclosure reduces client inhibition and anxiety, and models an open acceptance of sexuality. To ensure the maintenance of therapy gains, clients plan their own treatment for the final stages and for the months following therapy.

Despite our generally good success rate, the separate effectiveness of each procedure needs to be investigated. In all of the cases treated, a combination of procedures has been used, thus precluding an evaluation of any particular technique's contribution. We are currently engaged in research to evaluate the components of our program.

REFERENCES

Bandura, A. Vicarious and self-reinforcement processes. *The nature of reinforcement* (Ed. by Glaser). New York: Academic Press, 1971.

Davison, G.S. Elimination of a sadistic fantasy by a client-controlled counter-conditioning technique. *J. abnorm. Psychol.* 1968, 77, 84-90.

Ellis, A. *The art and science of love.* New York: Lyle Stuart, 1960.

Hastings, D.W. *Impotence and frigidity.* Boston: Little Brown, 1963.

Hastings, D.W. *Sexual expression in marriage.* New York: Bantam, 1966.

Hilliard, M. *A woman doctor looks at love and life.* New York: Permabook, 1960.

Jourard, S.M. *The transparent self.* Princeton, N.J.: D.Van Nostrand, 1964.

Kelly, G.A. *The psychology of personal constructs.* New York: Norton, 1955.

Kegel, A.H. Sexual functions of the pubococcygens muscle. *West. J. Sang. Obstet. Gynol.* 1952, 60, 521.

Kinsey, A.C., Pomeroy, W.B., Martin, C.E. & Gebhard, P.H. *Sexual behavior in the human female.* Philadelphia: W.B. Saunders, 1953.

Lewinsohn, P.M. & Shafer, M. Use of home observations as an integral part of the treatment of depression: Preliminary report and case studies. *J. consult. clin. Psychol.,* 1971, 37, 87-94.

LoPiccolo, J. Scoring and interpretation manual for the Oregon sex inventory. Unpublished manuscript. University of Oregon.

LoPiccolo, J. & Lobitz, W.C. The role of masturbation in the treatment of sexual dysfunction. *Arch. Sexual Behav.* (in press).

LoPiccolo, J., Stewart, R. & Watkins, B. Case study: Treatment of erectile failure and ejaculatory incompetence of homosexual etiology. *J. Behav. Ther. & Exp. Psychiat.* 1972, 3, 233-236.

Marquis, J.N.   Orgasmic reconditioning: Changing sexual object choice through controlling masturbation fantasies. *J. Behav. Ther. & Exp. Psychiat.* 1970, 1, 263-271.

Masters, W.H. & Johnson, V.E. *Human sexual response.* Boston: Little, Brown, 1966.

Masters, W.H. & Johnson, V.E. *Human sexual inadequacy.* Boston: Little, Brown, 1970.

McGovern, K.B. & Stewart, R.C. The secondary orgasmic dysfunctional female: A critical analysis and strategies for treatment. Paper presented at the annual meeting of the Western Psychological Association, Portland, Oregon, April 1972.

Patterson, G.R., Ray, R.S. & Shaw, D.A. Direct intervention in the families of deviant children. *Oregon Research Institute Research Bulletin* 1968, 8, No. 9.

Semans, J. Premature ejaculation: A new approach. *Sth med. J.* 1956, 46, 353-357.

Steger, J. The assessment of sexual function and dysfunction. Paper presented at the annual meeting of the Western Psychological Association, Portland, Oregon, April 1972.

Wolpe, J. *The practice of behavior therapy.* New York: Pergamon Press, 1969.

2
Taking a Sexual History

RICHARD GREEN

Emotional health and physical health are so interwoven that to neglect the emotional is inadequate coverage of the physical. Sexual health is so integral to both that to ignore the sexual is poor patient care. Thus, medical history-taking is incomplete without a comprehensive sex history. Conflicts over sexuality can result in depression, anxiety and alcoholism. Depression, anxiety and alcohol abuse lead to reduced sex drive and inadequate sexual functioning. Diabetes can lead to male impotence; postoperative surgical adhesions can result in painful female intercourse; Klinefelter syndrome males may have an organic base for low sex drive and impotence. Half of married couples have an area of sexual incompatibility which may manifest as vague somatic symptoms and general disease.

Taking a sexual history requires even greater skill than with other systems. Significant obstacles stand between the clinician's capacity to ask a question and the patient's capacity to respond. While comprehensive knowledge is required of the cardiovascular system to cover all the symptom bases, these are typically asked without anxiety or inhibition once the questions are memorized and their rationale understood. Similarly, the patient experiences little or no hesitancy in responding truthfully to the paths of inquiry. Hardly the same exists with sexual history-taking. Memorizing a series of questions pertaining to masturbation does not guarantee that the clinician considers the area worthy of time expenditure and hardly eliminates embarrassment when reciting the questions to a middle-aged patient of the opposite sex. Reciprocally, the patient may never have discussed masturbation, may harbor considerable conflict, embarrassment and guilt over the subject and not see where it is especially relevant to his or her medical history.

An eye-opening exercise in revealing sex history-taking distress is the following: First, choose a medical colleague of the same sex. Ask questions about his or her sexual practices and areas of conflict. Audio record, or better yet, videotape record the interview. Play it back. Listen and watch for hesitancies, vocal tone changes and facial hints of interviewer distress such as eye-contact deflection. Next, role-play a specific sexual problem, for example (if male) a young man with impotency or poor ejaculatory

15

control, or a young father whose child is asking questions about where babies come from. If female, role-play a woman with painful intercourse or a mother whose child asks about babies. Reverse patient-physician roles. Then, choose a colleague of the other sex and repeat. Finally, role-play again, this time as a person of the other sex. This exercise, beyond displaying the unique problems in taking a sex history, is also an effective practice device for learning to interview in specific areas.

The interviewer ill at ease in discussing sexuality communicates a metamessage to the patient which belies the content of the questioning. The metamessage says: "I would really rather *not* hear the answers to your question and hope you have none." Further, the interviewer who conveys a bias regarding the "appropriateness" of certain behaviors shapes patient responses and inhibits elements of patient communication which might elicit physician disapproval.

A patient's initial visit prompted by influenza, complicated by otitis media and bronchitis, is hardly the optimal time for a detailed inquiry into sexual attitudes, habits and possible difficulties. Nor is the appropriate time the third anniversary of the physician-patient relationship. The sexual history should be taken when the initial full medical history is taken. Its inclusion early in the relationship communicates to the patient the physician's appreciation of the importance of sexual health and the physician's comfort in meeting those health needs. Delay in approaching the topic communicates discomfort. The effect when "the subject" is finally broached is comparable to the painfully familiar scene of a father finally initiating discussion of the "facts of life" with his son on his 13th birthday.

Whether or not the initial sexual history elicits significant problem areas may have little primary significance. Perhaps none exist. Perhaps it will take a period of incubation for the patient to experience the necessary degree of trust and comfort to confide a long-standing secret. Or, the early investment may pay off if and when a problem does evolve in a patient who appreciates that the physician is emotionally available for counsel.

The opening statement can be: "As I am going to be your physician, I will be responsible for helping maintain your health in all areas. Where your needs may call for more specialized care, I am prepared to refer you to a specialist colleague. One area of health which has been relatively neglected by physicians in the past has been sexual health. It has become increasingly apparent that if we are to fulfill all our responsibilities to patients, this important part of our lives must also receive attention. Therefore, I am going to ask you a number of questions in the area of sexuality. Typically, there are certain issues which most frequently raise questions or cause concerns. These include our sexual functioning, the types of sexual experiences we have, our sexual preferences, our sexual adjustment within marriage or outside marriage, the sexual education of our children, the meaning of childhood sex play, teenage sexuality, and so forth. You should know that what we discuss is medically confidential, in the same way as the other areas of your health care." Each interviewer should utilize an opening statement that is personally comfortable. The above has been offered as one model.

An axiom of interviewing style is the "ubiquity" question. Topics are introduced with the assumption that most people have experienced the phenomenon to be introduced. Then the person's own experience in this area is explored. We ask: "*When* or *how* did you first learn about. . .' (rather than "*Did* you learn about. . .?"). "*When* or *how* did you first experience. . ." (rather than "*Did* you ever experience. . ."). Or after the preliminary statement: "Many people experience. . ." the interviewer follows with "What has been your *own* experience with. . .?"

Another axiom is proceeding from less "sensitive" to more "sensitive" areas. Those areas of sexual behavior which are more acceptable and comfortable for discussion are addressed earlier. Topics more likely to elicit anxiety or embarrassment, such as unusual sexual practices, are discussed after greater rapport has been established.

The interviewer's language must be geared to that of the patient. "Fellatio" and "cunnilingus" may be terms familiar to the interviewer and suitable for some patients, whereas "mouth-genital sex," "sucking," "blowing" and "going down" may communicate more effectively with others.

1. *Sexual Dysfunction.* Consider first sexual dysfunction (impotency and premature ejaculation in the male, non-orgasmia or painful intercourse in the female). This topic can be introduced: "Much has been written and discussed during the past few years about sexual incompatibilities within marriage. The work of Masters and Johnson has received much attention with their *successes* (the interviewer promotes optimism) with couples in which the male has difficulty obtaining an erection, or is unable to delay sexual climax, or the female has difficulty in reaching orgasm or has unpleasant intercourse. Most people experience one or more of these difficulties at some time during their sexual relationships. What have your own experiences been?" Or "Most people experience some disappointments, sometimes minor, sometimes major, in the sexual part of their lives. Can you tell me what disappointments you have met?" (No relationship is 100 percent satisfactory and professional permission to report shortcomings facilitates the revealing of problem areas.) Another facilitating statement is: "Frequently, one member of a married couple will desire a variety of sexual activity in which the other person may not be as interested. What has been your own experience in this regard?"

2. *Teenage Sexuality.* For parents with teenagers, the history-taking can continue: "When children reach teenage, parents typically have new concerns about their child's sexuality. They worry about sexual experimentation, pregnancy, venereal disease, and so on. *Which* of these areas has been of *most* concern to you?"

Education can be an integral part of the interview. "Statistics show us that about one in four girls by the end of high school are engaging in sexual intercourse. Parents then must face the dilemma of teenage pregnancy or contraception. In the past, parents of teenage girls had only limited control (as did their daughters) in preventing unwanted pregnancies. Some parents feel that if they talk with their daughters about pregnancy and perhaps help them with contraceptive control they are endorsing sexual activity (which the parent may find undesirable). Other parents have been impressed by the fact that the vast majority of unwanted teenage pregnancies were the products of intercourse without contraception. Clearly the absence of contraception did not *prevent* intercourse, but did have the effect of yielding a more painful consequence. What have been your own views on this?"

Trans-generational differences in sexual values are frequent. Where problems in communication exist between teenager and parent, both generations should be seen separately and then conjointly. "Empathy" statements are useful: "It's often very difficult for those of us who grew up in different generations which held different perspectives on sexuality to feel comfortable with the views of those younger or older." (Then the specific conflict areas are brought into focus.)

Questions and concerns about the physiological changes of puberty are common. They can be acknowledged:

"Many girls growing up receive either no information or hear rumors about the body changes which will occur sometime between 11 and 14. One area in particular is the beginning of monthly bleeding or menstruation. What do you know about what to expect and what this sign of growing up means?" Information provided should stress the unique, positive aspects of becoming a mature woman and the variety in menstrual patterns experienced by young women.

"Many boys during teenage, as their body matures, find that they have dreams with sex in them. They may wake up to find their pajama bottoms wet or that the sheet is wet or stained. They may be confused as to what this means. What has been your experience in this regard?"

3. *The Unmarried Patient Not Living with a Sexual Partner.* The unmarried person's sexuality can be simply explored with this opening statement: "The degree to which unmarried persons have sexual outlets of one or another type varies considerably. Some persons have several partners, others prefer one, others provide themselves release through masturbation, and still others experience no outlet at all. What pattern are you currently following? . . . Has this always been your pattern? . . . Is this your preferred pattern or would you find an alternative preferable? . . . Some unmarried persons find it difficult meeting other persons with whom they might experience a satisfying relationship. To what extent has this been a problem for you?" Then specific questions relating to *sexual dysfunction* can be asked.

4. *Sexual Myths. Seventy* sexual myths and fallacies have been described by McCary (1971). Many plague patients. More common ones may be explored: "Most of us growing up are exposed to many sexual myths, or half-truths which continue to trouble or puzzle us. Are there any which come to mind?" (For males) "One of these are the frequent stories about the importance of penis size. What concerns have you had in this regard?" (For females) "There is much discussion about sexual climax or orgasm. There is talk as to whether women are supposed to have one or several, whether they are supposed to be like inner 'explosions,' whether they are supposed to be 'clitoral' or 'vaginal' and so on. What questions have you had in this regard?"

5. *Masturbation.* Some interview statements here can be: "Many of us growing up hear a variety of stories about the meaning and implications of masturbation. Some may be upsetting and remain with us well into adulthood. Do you recall when you first learned anything about masturbation? . . . What did you hear? . . . For many of us, these childhood tales continue to exert an influence over us regarding whether we should or should not masturbate. What role do you feel this continues to play in your own life?"

The topic of masturbation is continued if the patient has a child: "Many of us in childhood felt that masturbation was a taboo subject for discussion at home. Most of us practiced it in secret believing our parents would disapprove. Then when we get to be parents ourselves, many of us discover that we're not so sure just *how* to best manage these things with our *own* children. What have been your own thoughts on this?"

Again, history-taking can also be a time to provide information: "Many parents acknowledge that all children *will* masturbate whether parents like it or not. Therefore, what they decide is to limit it to the private sphere of the child's life in the way that their own adult sexuality is private. Therefore, they do not attempt to prevent masturbation by 'forbidding' it or threatening the child with punishment. Rather they inform the child that it is something to be done alone in the privacy of their room, and not in the classroom, or in the middle of the living room with neighbors visiting." This advice is designed to promote sexual health and reduce conflict within the family regarding an ubiquitous sexual function.

6. *The Homosexual Patient.* If the patient is homosexual, empathy for the uniquely controversial problems of the homosexual can be underscored: "Some say homosexuality is a mental disorder, others an emotional block, others a crime, others a sin. What is your attitude toward your own homosexual orientation? How has the public view of homosexuality affected your own life?" Questioning is designed to find out whether homosexuality is a source of conflict—in the same way that aspects of heterosexuality can be a source of conflict. Keep in mind that homosexuals may have the same sexual dysfunctions as heterosexuals. The interviewer should also know the incidence of homosexuality and treatment results via various approaches for those who wish change (4 percent of males may be exclusively homosexual, another 6 percent primarily so; for females the rate appears to be about half (Kinsey, et al., 1948; 1953); about one-third of highly motivated homosexuals reorient with psychodynamic or behavioral modification techniques (Bieber, et al., 1962; Hatterer, 1970; MacCulloch & Feldman, 1967).

7. *"Unusual" Sex Interests.* "One man's meat is another man's passion." The variety of sexual fantasies may not be finite. Patients can be troubled by their private pornography. Trouble areas can be explored: "Most of us at times experience what we consider to be unusual sexual thoughts, or wish to perform sexual acts which we or others may consider strange. Sometimes we are bothered by these thoughts or impulses. What has been your own experience in this regard?"

8. *Old Age.* Sexual problems during the advanced years result from misinformation or personal mismanagement of various sorts: 1) the false belief that the physiology of old age inevitably leads to radical diminution and cessation of sexual functioning; 2) the misinterpretation of a lessening of sexual drive and incidental sexual dysfunction (e.g., an occasion of male impotency) as the "beginning of the end," with subsequent reluctance to initiate sexual attempts; 3) painful intercourse for the female due to atrophy of the vaginal mucosa and painful uterine contractions during the orgasm, secondary to inadequate sex steroid maintenance; and 4) waning physical attractiveness of one or both partners with significant weight gain and poor cosmetic care reducing the sexual interest of the other partner.

Studies of male sexuality in older years indicate that the capacity for erection can be maintained throughout life. Kinsey, et al. (1948) found that three-quarters of their sample of 70-year-old males were potent and that at 75, nearly one-half were still potent. Females in the same age group retain the capacity for multiorgastic response (Masters & Johnson, 1966). For those couples still sexually active at 65, the mean frequency of intercourse has been reported as one per week and at 75, about one per month (Kinsey, et al., 1948). Pfeiffer, et al. (1968) reported that 15 percent of their sample aged 78 and older were still sexually active.

Some physiological changes do occur with age. For the male the degree of erotic stimulation required for erection becomes greater, the force of ejaculation less, and the refractory period after orgasm, during which the man does not either desire or have the capacity for erection, becomes longer (Masters & Johnson, 1966). For the aging female the length of time required for vaginal lubrication becomes longer and the degree of lubrication less, especially in the sex-steroid starved woman (Masters & Johnson, 1966).

An additional problem for the aging male can be the effects of prostatectomy. Psychological trauma from this procedure can lead to impotency. However, the surgical trauma from transurethral prostatectomy should not affect the capacity for erection. In addition to this reassuring note, the patient should be advised that ejaculation may be retrograde into the bladder, rather than via the penis.

Forearmed with these data and dependent on the circumstances of the patient, questions can be individually tailored and rational counsel provided. With patients in their fifties and beyond, the subject can be approached:

"Many people, as they enter the advanced years in life, believe or are worried that this signals the end of their sex life. Much misinformation has been popularized to perpetuate this myth. What is your understanding about sexuality during the later years? How has the passage of years affected your sexuality?"

9. *Miscellaneous: An Interview Pattern.* "Frequently people have questions about venereal disease (V.D.). What questions do you have?" or "Frequently people have questions about methods of contraception. What would you like to know about the various methods?" etc.

10. *"Up Front" Sexual Problems.* The above interviewing strategies presume that problems relating to sexuality will be cryptic. What if the "chief complaint" is sexual? In that case, general principles of history-taking apply. These include the nature and duration of the complaint, the circumstance under which it occurs, and, in the sexual system, the patient's understanding of the cause of the problem and previous efforts at obtaining help. Having covered the chief complaint, the remainder of the sexual history should not be ignored. Just as the remainder of the health systems are covered when the problem is restricted to one system, inquiry into other areas of sexuality can yield important clues as to how to best serve the whole patient.

11. *The Close.* Having exhausted the salient areas of human sexuality, the history-taking can be completed: "Is there anything further in the area of sexuality which you would like to bring up now? . . . I hope that as questions *do* arise over the course of time we will be able to discuss them here."

PHYSICIAN JUDGMENTALISM

Our language reveals our personalized attitudes and communicates them to patients. Consider the word "promiscuous" to describe multiple sexual experiences with varied partners. Consider the term "unfaithful" to describe extramarital sexual experiences. In place of moralizing we must be able to integrate and provide objective data regarding what people do and feel, and what evidence exists regarding such experiences. Our language must be nonjudgmental and must permit patients to make decisions based on these facts. The decision must be *theirs,* no matter how repugnant it may be to *our* inner censor.

For a parent who feels masturbation to be a mortal sin, we can only provide a perspective that other equally knowledgeable and well-intentioned parents feel differently. We can point out the data documenting the ubiquity of the behavior and other data associating early-life prohibitions with subsequent sexual inhibitions and dysfunctions. If parents remain adamantly opposed to masturbation, they should state to the child their specific reasons for their opposition. They should assert that it is their religious belief that such behavior is wrong, that not everyone agrees with this belief, and further that masturbation does not cause great harm such as making one go crazy or some tragic consequence. Parents should realize that the child will know in the course of time the facts about masturbation, and that earlier statements which may frighten the child and are not truthful, may be the basis for later resentment.

For the teenager engaged in repetitive sexual experiences with transient partners, we can counsel on effective methods of contraception and the symptoms and prophylaxis of the venereal diseases. For the adolescent homosexual, we can point out that many homosexuals lead satisfying lives with good emotional and sexual fulfillment but that others are plagued by societal oppression, feel guilty over their orientation, and desire the greater degree of interpersonal stability usually associated with heterosexual marriage and children. We can describe various reorientation techniques for those who are interested.

It is not easy to be nonjudgmental. Who among us has grown up without strong value feelings about sexual behavior? Many of us are comfortable in what we have settled upon as fitting our life style. Correctness of fit is idiosyncratic. Most of us come from middle-class family systems which may not correspond with our patient's. Were our childhoods uniquely comfortable and sexually aconflictual? How many of us had our own sexual questions comfortably answered and did not feel embarrassed talking with our parents about sex? How many of us were not at least temporarily victimized by peer group misinformation and confused by bathroom graffiti and locker-room gossip? Whose parents did not impart their value systems of a generation earlier about masturbation, "sex deviants," intercourse, and marriage? Can we expect these value systems to concur with those of each patient?

Is it our professional responsibility to meet patient needs or our own? Where many medical diseases are concerned, facts abound, and collective research/treatment wisdom and patient-activated guidelines exist. With sexual conduct symptoms of disease exist. The individual who "hurts" because of "too little" sexual conduct or "too much" sexual conduct has a different reason for disease. Our private attitudes may favor the life style of one person over the other; however, that attitude does not belong in the clinical interview or in responsible patient management. It is as inappropriate as if stock ownership in a company producing an orally administered anti-hyperglycemic drug entered into the decision-making process of carbohydrate regulation in a diabetic. One's private belief about abortion or marital monogamy is irrelevant in meeting the immediate disease of the unmarried teenager or married woman pregnant out-of-wedlock.

Fielding wrote in *Tom Jones:* "Every physician almost hath his favorite disease." Sexual disease will not be each physician's favorite. But, "ease" is as contagious as "disease." Learning to take a sexual history will be both a professional and personal growth experience. It also carries the potential for "spreading" sexual health.

REFERENCES

Bieber, I. & Colleagues. *Homosexuality: A psychoanalytic study*. New York: Basic Books, 1962.

Hatterer, L. *Changing homosexuality in the male*. New York: McGraw Hill, 1970.

Kinsey, A., Pomeroy, W., Martin, C. *Sexual behavior in the human male*. Philadelphia: Saunders, 1948.

Kinsey, A., Pomeroy, W., Martin, C. & Gebhard, P. *Sexual behavior in the human female*. Philadelphia: Saunders, 1953.

MacCulloch, M. & Feldman, P.M.   Averson therapy in management of 43 homosexuals. *Br. Med. J.,* 1967, **2**, 594-97.

Masters, W. & Johnson, V. *Human sexual response*. Boston: Little, Brown, 1966.

McCary, J. *Sexual myths and fallacies,* Princeton: Van Nostrand and Reinhold, 1971.

Pfeiffer, E., Verwoerdt, A. & Wang, H. Sexual behavior in aged men and women. *Arch. Gen. Psychiat.* 1968, **19**, 753-58.

3
Treatment of Common Marital Sexual Problems

HARVEY L. GOCHROS

Over twenty years ago Margaret Mead (1949, p. 7) said of American marriage: "It is one of the most difficult marriage forms that the human race has ever attempted." Since then, it has not become any simpler. Greater premarital sexual freedom, more tolerance of difference, changing attitudes toward sexual expression and improved birth control methods have added greater complexity and potential for sexual satisfaction in marriage.

Women are succeeding in their revolution, leading not only to economic and social justice, but also to equal sexual rights and pleasure ("J," 1969). At the same time, men are increasingly under social and personal pressure to become sexperts, achieving a combination of romantic, choreographic and athletic competence in bed, in order to maintain their own self-esteem and the acceptance and respect of others—especially their spouses. These pressures seem to be leading to a preoccupation with the skilled accomplishment of the sex act with an unending quest for the perfect orgasm. Such pressure has led to the development as well as uncovering of a high incidence of sexual problems in marriage. "A conservative estimate," according to Masters and Johnson (1970), who have revolutionized both the understanding and the treatment of sexual problems, "would indicate half the marriages in America as either presently sexually dysfunctional or imminently so in the future." Much contemporary laboratory and clinical sexual research is oriented toward helping to reduce these problems.

It would seem likely, therefore, that in an age of concern, if not preoccupation, with sexual fulfillment, the number of people seeking help for explicit sexual problems in their marriage will continue to increase. This paper will concentrate on some of the basic sources of these problems and some approaches for dealing with them.

A major determinant of the type of sexual adjustment developed in the marriage is the learning each partner has had regarding expectations for their sexual performance. There currently are two common models of sexual expression which in their extreme form often contribute to marital sexual dysfunctioning. One is the romantic ideal and the other is the model of the sexual athlete.

ROMANTIC LOVE

The sexual component of American marriage has been greatly influenced by the concept of romantic love (Ellis, 1970). Indeed, while love itself may be defined as an intense emotional attraction to and a feeling of interdependence with another human being, our concept of love has been greatly influenced by the tradition of *romantic* love. "Real" romantic love implies a state of intense passion toward a perfect partner and the probability of a permanent state of bliss in the relationship. This tradition leads one to perceive a potential spouse in an unrealistically idealized, highly esthetic, worshipful way. It presumes that there is the possibility of true love with only one object, who is "meant" to be the only one for the lover. If there is a sexual component in romance, it is usually perceived as being idyllic and almost nonphysical. Yet, only in romantic love, so the myth goes, is sexuality legitimate and fully realized. Without it, sex is reduced to an animalistic level and becomes worthy only of contempt.

It is this view of love and sex which is still widely portrayed in fictionalized accounts of marriage in books, magazines, on television and even in teenage romance comic books. As such, it provides the role model and ideal for many marital relationships and has taken its toll in sexual dysfunctioning in marriage. Few couples can maintain a romantic fiction for any extended period without devastating interpersonal results. The facts of life, marriage and intimacy preclude maintaining such an unrealistic perception of the marital relationship. Indeed, a sound marriage is based on honest benevolent acceptance of each other and not on attempts to maintain an idealized fantasy.

Because romantic love is frequently dissipated by the facts of life, the ideal of romance often pulls people out of potentially rewarding, honest interpersonal relationships to seek new romantic experiences outside of the marriage.

Clearly the role of a therapist, in relation to romantic love, is to help couples enunciate and evaluate their mutual expectations, accept each other and themselves as "just" human beings, find joy and pleasure with each other as they are and accept the honest give-and-take satisfactions of their sexual relationship.

THE IDEAL OF THE SEXUAL ATHLETE

Whereas the romantic ideal relegates sex to an idealized spiritual experience and intellectual fantasy, the other common model is epitomized by marriage-manual technocracy which portrays sex as a purely physical activity. The sexual manual, generally written by people who are 1) men, 2) past 40 and 3) physicians, antiseptically emphasizes the technical skills related to sexuality and general physiological reactions. While they provide needed information and often endorse sexual flexibility,[1] they also emphasize skill, dexterity, and orgasmic competence.

Preoccupation with the mechanical aspects of sexuality as depicted in many manuals can be threatening and do more harm than good. The athletic approach glorifies the

---

[1] Recently sex books have begun to emerge which do indeed encourage the joy of individual sex styles. A notable example is the significant impact of a very popular book written by a woman entitled "J." *The Sensuous Woman* (New York: Lyle Stuart, 1969).

perfectly functioning body. It is noteworthy that those books which are illustrated almost always use models who are young, well endowed and attractive, while many of their readers are not, further encouraging feelings of inadequacy. They tend to be preoccupied with techniques, positions and orgasms rather than general tactile and emotional satisfactions. They encourage modeling of the sexual behavior described in the book, with promised exquisite results rather than encouraging spontaneity in the sexual act as determined by the unique personalities, needs, capacities and desires of a particular couple at a particular time.

The sex-athlete model contributes to one of the main inhibitions of sexual satisfaction: the quest for normalcy. This preoccupation encourages what Masters and Johnson have described as the "spectator role" in sexual behavior. That is, an individual finds that he cannot totally immerse himself in sexual behavior, but looks upon himself as an actor in a performance with his partner, preoccupied with how well he is doing as a lover, how long it will last and how well it will end.

The presence of these two diverse models of sexual behavior and the relative absence of other more functional models for the sex relation create many of the common problems in sexual adaptation in marriage seen by therapists. Indeed, most of the problems in sexuality are bio-emotional consequences of inadequate or faulty learning regarding sexuality maintained by the sexual attitudes of peers, sexual partners and the social environment. The therapist's function is to help correct this learning.

APPROACH TO TREATMENT

The therapist who treats marital sexual problems must first come to terms with his own sexuality and own marriage (or nonmarriage) style. Obviously, the clinician need not be a paragon of marital and sexual success . . . whatever that is . . . in order to qualify as a competent sexual counselor. But he cannot let his own needs, biases and anxieties interfere with his role as sexual counselor without potential harmful effects on his clients.

The next task in the process is to determine the place of the sexual problem in a client's total marital relationship. The sexual problem may well be a direct result of other basic problems that the couple is facing: an unemployed man, whose efforts to find employment have been thwarted, may seek reaffirmation of his masculinity through activities such as extramarital affairs or aggressive sexual attacks on his wife. These problems could conceivably change or be eradicated once the man's employment and masculine security is restored.

Sometimes the sexual problem is just one of a constellation of difficulties in a marriage — ranging from economic to in-law difficulties — and may be unrelated to these other problems but coexistent with them. If this is the case, the therapist must determine and then contract his priorities for problem resolution with the client. He may conclude that treatment of the general marital relationship should come first and anticipate that improvement in the general relationship and communication will naturally lead to an improved sexual relationship. If the therapist chooses this option, he should check out this hypothesis as treatment progresses. It is not unusual for sexual problems to precipitate other problems which may obscure—possibly purposefully—their sexual genesis. In any event, the therapist must put the sexual problem in each marriage into perspective. He should acknowledge the need and, to the extent possible, help his clients achieve adequate sexual functioning and satisfaction, but recognize, as does much sexual research, the interdependence of sexual behavior and interpersonal marital complementarity in achieving physical and consequent emotional satisfaction from the sexual relationship.

Whether the therapist feels that a sexual problem is coexistent with other problems in the marriage or is a repercussion of them, he must still be prepared to deal directly with it and not minimize its importance as a result of his own discomfort in working with sexual problems and, as often happens, react by referral to another disinterested or incompetent professional. Conversely, the therapist's sexual interests and curiosity should not lead him to choose sex as the focus for intervention out of his own needs, when the sexual conflict is not a logical priority.

Masters and Johnson have largely sidestepped the issue of the relation of sexual problems to general marital interaction in their work and have approached sexual problems as a learned phenomenon which can be isolated from other elements of the marital relation but can have a profound effect on the rest of the marriage. "If you can't communicate in bed," says Dr. Masters, "you probably can't communicate in a marriage." With this orientation, the Masters-Johnson team have had more than a 75 percent success rate with the problems with which they deal.[2]

Sexual problems are as diverse as the people who experience them—ranging from primary "impotence" to conflict over extramarital relations. Their origins often lie in the past experiences and self-image of each partner as well as in the couple's current reciprocally contingent marital relationship. Attempts to resolve marital sexual problems through increased "self-awareness" and insight into past experiences have had uninspiring results and will not be explored in this paper. Rather, the effects of current attitudes and behaviors on the sexual relationship and their modification will be reviewed.

The majority of sexual problems in marriage presented to clinicians can be attributed to four sources: lack of adequate sexual knowledge; lack of clear, explicit communication and expectations between spouses regarding sexual matters; lack of consensus on sexual activities; and the lack of sexual ability. While these problems are often interrelated and stem from similar causes, they will be treated separately here.

LACK OF SEXUAL KNOWLEDGE

Perhaps the greatest component of what many consider a copulation explosion is the recent increase in the presentation of explicit sexual material in everyday life. "Sex pervades this world of ours, dominating advertisements, fashion, plays, novels, poetry. Never have painting and literature been more outspoken. Couples copulate across the canvas; homosexuals woo each other before the footlights; lesbians hammer each other through 400 pages of prose. Sadism is almost old hat, and fetishism scarcely raises an eyebrow. Pornography is printed by the ton or shot on miles of film. Everyone knows we are in the middle of a sexual revolution. . . . Ignorance is sin and sexual instruction begins in the cradle" (Plumb, 1968, p. 23). It is this seeming saturation of sexual material—often even

[2] However, it is noteworthy that in many of the "successfully" treated couples (in terms of sexual problems) other marital problems continued which not infrequently resulted in divorce. This does not negate, however, the improved sexual competence.

in our daily conversation—which leads practitioners to the mistaken idea that everyone knows everything he needs to know about sexuality. Yet, despite recent advances, there still remains much that not even our sex researchers know, and lay knowledge of sexuality is distorted by biases, personal needs and firmly entrenched attitudes. Indeed, it is disturbing to perceive the same misconceptions and lack of knowledge in our helping professions, such as medicine, psychology and social work. In 1959 a study of Philadelphia area medical students from five medical schools revealed that half of the students, after three or four years of medical education, thought that masturbation is a frequent cause of mental illness. Still more frightening was the finding that one-fifth of their faculty agreed (Lief, 1966)!

The lack of sexual knowledge (or even worse, distorted knowledge) in marriage is compounded by the inordinate need of many people to perform "normally" in sex. While most people could not care less how many slices of white bread people consume each day or what the average length of the male right index finger is, many *are* preoccupied with frequencies of sexual contact and the average length of the phallus. The fact that these vary considerably and that they tend to be irrelevant to sexual fulfillment is perhaps more significant than the knowledge of the statistics themselves.

Many marriages are blighted by false perceptions of what does or "should" go on in the marriage bed. Since sexual ideas are deeply rooted in the value system of each individual, they become harder to modify.

Sometimes sexual information given dispassionately by a therapist—ideally of the same sex as the holder of the false ideas—can make significant changes in a marital relationship. Many of our clients suffer needless problems because they do not know, for instance, that men, as well as women, have sexual anxieties and cannot always perform on command despite socially reinforced pretenses of super-masculinity, that masturbation by men does not cause "insanity" and by women is not only harmless but may enhance general sexual response, that women who enjoy clitoral as well as vaginal stimulation are not neurotic, that penis size is correlated with neither masculinity nor capacity for giving and receiving sexual satisfaction, that sexual activity need not terminate at 50, and that many mentally competent, law-abiding citizens juxtapose their mouths to their partner's genitals in sexual contacts.

An often overlooked area in which lack of knowledge can impede mutual sexual satisfaction in marriage is contraception practices (Rainwater, 1964). It can be important for the therapist to determine whether the contraception practices in a marriage cause sexual problems or mask some more basic conflict. For example, a wife might avoid intercourse, allegedly because of fear of pregnancy but actually dislike the sex act and fear to discuss this with her husband.

Sometimes the particular birth control procedure can have a significant effect on the marital sexual adjustment. The use of withdrawal, for instance, one of the most common forms of contraception, especially among lower-income groups, is often the result of lack of knowledge of or biases regarding other contraceptive alternatives, as well as problems of access to them. This procedure not only limits sexual pleasure, but has questionable efficacy as a birth control measure. Other contraceptive methods are often avoided by couples out of the false idea that they would negatively affect sexual satisfaction, or are a threat to masculinity. It is not unusual for a woman to avoid many contraceptives because of discomfort about touching her own body or resistance to acknowledging premeditated sex activity even when she might want to limit the size of her family.

LACK OF COMMUNICATION

Many people of all ages find it difficult to talk directly with their marital partners about their own sexual desires, reactions and problems. Even where communication is satisfactory in most areas in a marriage, sexual communication can be a problem, especially for those couples who have gone through their adolescence and young adulthood before the social and sexual revolution following the Second World War. They have been conditioned to perceive discussion about sex as being so private, so embarrassing and so revealing that they hesitate to talk about their own feelings and wishes even with the person they have been married to for years. Often this communication difficulty is a result of inability to know which words to use, or fear of revealing some inadequacy and looking ridiculous in the eyes of their spouse. They may be concerned that breaking a tacit contract of noncommunication will bring to light sexual problems or inadequacies that have been hidden by mutual consent and create a threat to the balance of a marriage. Such a void of communication prevents the establishment of reasonable mutual expectations between sexual partners and diminishes the opportunity for each partner to meet the other's needs. As the couple reaches or passes middle age, there is the additional stress of physiological and psychological changes affecting the sexual relationship. If no groundwork of communication regarding sex has been laid, then the problems of modifying the sexual relationship become even more difficult.

Such a simple problem as how to indicate explicitly the desire to have sexual intercourse is a problem for some couples. The request from one partner and an equally concise acceptance or rejection from the other partner are sometimes very difficult to get, perhaps out of sense of "nothing ventured, nothing lost!" Nonverbal cues in sex are frequently used, and can be a functional form of communication, if they are clearly understood by each partner.

Seeking help for marital and sexual problems can be the first step to enhancing communication. But it cannot be assumed that, simply because a couple has sought a therapist's help, they have adequately discussed their sexual problems themselves. One of the major contributions of the therapist—whenever possible in a compatible two-sex team—is to have the couple explicitly discuss their sexual adjustment, first alone, and then with each other.

A useful procedure used by this writer in working with couples experiencing sexual problems is to have them stay overnight in a motel during the course of treatment, even if they have a home in the same city. Here the emphasis is easily placed on relaxation and mutual enjoyment. A similar procedure is reported by Masters and Johnson during their intensive two-week therapy program. Couples live in rented apartments for the duration of their treatment well away from family and business pressures. (It is noted that couples who came to the Masters & Johnson program from out of town had more success than those who were residents of St. Louis, and were still affected by local pressures.)

The new setting, plus the somewhat erotic atmosphere of a motel, provides stimuli which encourage new modes of communication as well as new patterns of sexual interaction. Couples can be encouraged to discuss honestly with each other what tactile experiences and sexual activities or approaches they enjoy or don't enjoy, what wishes and reactions they have never before expressed to each other regarding sex, and then subsequently try out the results of this new communication, step-by-step. With clients who cannot afford the expense of a motel, sometimes such a simple matter as rearranging their bedroom furniture and arranging for a night away from their children will provide the stimulus for change in behavioral and communication habits.

LACK OF CONSENSUS ON SEXUAL ACTIVITIES

This problem is complicated by the ones mentioned above—the lack of knowledge and the problems in communicating sexual wishes. There is no doubt that there has been increasing acceptance and knowledge that man is capable of taking many avenues to sexual pleasure; however, this freedom is unevenly accepted by many marital couples. Religious teachings that often dwell on what limited sexual behavior falls within the range of the acceptable can exacerbate sexual confusion in a marriage, particularly when such ideas are not shared equally by the partners. The therapist can initiate and facilitate a negotiation process with the couple, perhaps assisted by a cooperative clergyman, when there is this problem. The almost trite information that what is acceptable to both partners is by definition acceptable often puts concerns about "normalcy" to rest.

PROBLEMS IN SEXUAL ABILITY

Frequently, the problems of inadequate knowledge, faulty communication and lack of consensus on sexual activity plus faulty learning combine to produce obstacles to satisfying sexual activity in the form of temporary or permanent "impotence," inability to relax, or other physical sexual reactions of psychogenic origin. Many clinicians hesitate to work with these problems, feeling that the body is the exclusive province of the medical profession. This is unfortunate. Generally speaking, there is usually not a purely physical source to these problems. Further, there is nothing to prevent a therapist from having a medical consultation on clients experiencing these problems. In the work of Masters and Johnson, the vast majority of their clients were responsive to purely relearning, nonmedical, interpersonal procedures.

All sound approaches to sexual problems require the participation of both husband and wife, regardless of which partner is experiencing the specific or most obvious sexual problem. The therapist should avoid the trap of seeing the marital partner with the sexual "symptom" as the sole target of intervention. In all cases of sexual dysfunction, it is the relationship of the couple which is the subject of attention and the milieu of successful treatment. "There is no such thing as an uninvolved partner in any marriage in which there is some form of sexual inadequacy," according to Masters and Johnson (1970).

Many of the principles of the Masters and Johnson approach, a concentrated two-week (seven days a week) process of exploration and relearning of sexual behavior, are readily adaptable to clinical practice. Already mentioned were the value of a compatible male-female therapy team—providing husband and wife with empathic "friends in court," focus on the relationship rather than either partner, and the elimination of the spectator role in which fear of inadequate performance inhibits spontaneous behavior. The therapist helps the couple to accept the naturalness of sex and assures them that once irrational obstacles are removed, sexual fulfillment becomes inevitable. As part of this philosophy, there is no pressure on performance. Rather the couple is helped to proceed step-by-step, learning to enjoy each other's bodies without a preoccupation with ultimate genital and orgasmic response.

Often anxiety over coital competence can be decreased for either spouse if the therapist can convince them that there are many avenues to achieve sexual satisfaction besides genital intromission, such as oral and manual stimulation. Wolpe and Lazarus (1966) have advocated that couples experiencing problems in coital competence develop competence in those techniques which not only provide "powerful sources of sexual arousal, but also lead to distracting attention from the sufferer's genital problem through focusing on pleasures being bestowed on his partner. The primary sexual difficulty is overcome without further formal treatment when a couple learns to accept the fact that sexual satisfaction does not necessarily depend on coitus" (pp. 105-6).

Often, of course, adequacy can also be enhanced by encouraging sexual variation and experimentation, based on mutual exploration, compatible with mutual wishes.

In essence, the approach of the therapist is to determine and then clear away the obstacles to the couple's learning the joys of each other's bodies by "pleasuring" one another. The couple soon discovers or rediscovers the two sources of sexual satisfaction: that of giving pleasure to a partner and receiving pleasure in return.

CONCLUSION

Major emphasis in this paper has been placed on the common obstacles to achieving a spontaneous, "natural" sexual relationship. Several references have been made to the pioneering and successful work of Masters and Johnson. Their approach is in many ways novel. It may be criticized for isolating sex from other aspects of marital interaction; it has created controversy for using partner surrogates for unmarried men; so far it has been applied largely to a fairly well-motivated, sophisticated client group, and has required intensive involvement by expensive, highly skilled, well-qualified and compatible practitioners. However, its substantial relevance to marital counseling should not be minimized. Their approach is based on generally responsible laboratory (as reported in their earlier book; 1966), as well as clinical, research. Its success is substantiated by considerable follow-up work. It enables couples to discover the nature and source of their problems, to communicate effectively about their sexual relationship, and thereby discard dysfunctional prior learning and develop a new, mutually satisfying form of sexual interaction.

Certainly these approaches must be modified according to the resources available to the clinician as well as the particular needs perceived in each case. Dr. Masters himself anticipated this but commented: "Sure, people will bastardize, but even then what they do has an excellent chance of being better than what's gone before."[3]

Marital sexual problems, which affect and are affected by general marital complementarity, are a legitimate focus of clinical intervention and are amenable to change using procedures from social work practice as well as the work of such sexual clinicians as Masters and Johnson. Clinical practice that avoids pathologic labeling and focuses on the mutual learning that affects sexual relations can make a marked impact on other aspects of the marital relationship as well as contribute to greater joy in the marriage bed.

---

[3]Quoted by Will Bradbury from interview reported in *Life*, May 1, 1970, 46.

REFERENCES

Ellis, Albert. "Romantic love." In *Sex and human relationships,* Cecil E. Johnson, Ed. Columbus: Charles E. Merrill Books, 1970.

Leif, Harold. Teaching doctors about sex. In R. Brecher and E. Brecher, *An analysis of human sexual response.* Boston: Little, Brown and Company, 1966.

"J." *The sensuous woman.* New York: Lyle Stuart, 1969.

Masters, William & Johnson, Virginia. *Human sexual response.* Boston: Little, Brown and Company, 1966.

Masters, William & Johnson, Virginia. *Human sexual inadequacy.* Boston: Little, Brown and Company, 1970.

Mead, Margaret. *Male and female.* New York: William Morrow and Company, 1949.

Plumb, J.H. Perspective. *Saturday Review,* July 27, 1968.

Rainwater, Lee. Attitudes of patients affecting contraceptive practice. In *Manual of Contraceptive Practice,* ed. M.S. Calderone. Baltimore: The Williams & Wilkins Company, 1964.

Wolpe, J. & Lazarus, A.A. *Behavior therapy techniques.* London, England: Pergamon Press, 1966.

4
Counseling with Sexually Incompatible Marriage Partners

WILLIAM H. MASTERS and VIRGINIA E. JOHNSON

At least one result of the cultural relaxation of sexual taboos has been of major consequence. Today, more—many more—marital partners are seeking professional assistance when sexual incompatibility threatens their marriage. Anyone exposed professionally to the emotional anguish and disrupted marriage caused by such clinical problems as impotence and frigidity will look upon this help-seeking trend with considerable satisfaction.

Most of the sexually distressed people are bringing their problems to their family physicians. Although the individual or combined efforts of psychiatrists, psychologists, marriage counselors, social workers, and/or clergymen may be needed in addition to those of the chosen physician to solve some problems of sexual inadequacy, it is the family physician, taking advantage of initial rapport and established confidence, who ordinarily overcomes any patient reluctance or embarrassment and builds motivation for further treatment.

Unfortunately, until recently the physician has been hampered in treatment by three major stumbling blocks:

First, there has been a long-standing and widespread medical misconception that a patient will not reveal sex history background with sufficient accuracy and in adequate detail for effective therapy.

Second, in the past the physician has been provided with very little basic information in sexual physiology upon which to develop any effective treatment of sexual inadequacy.

Third, many physicians have been convinced that since most sexual problems are psychogenic in origin, only a specialized psychopathologist can treat them effectively.

Increasingly large numbers of physicians are demonstrating clinically that none of these obstacles now has much substance in fact.

Almost ten years of investigation in the broad areas of human sexual response has brought conviction to the writers that if the interviewing physician can project sincere interest in the patient's problem and, even more important, exhibit no personal embarrassment in an open sexual discussion, almost any individual's sexual history will be reported with sufficient accuracy and in adequate detail for treatment purposes. Others, such as Eisenbud (1948), who have worked with human sexual problems, also believe that patients are usually very ready to talk freely about their disturbed sexual behavior patterns once they have gathered their courage to a degree sufficient to seek professional guidance.

While it is true that the amount of research in sexual physiology has in the past been meager indeed, this situation is rapidly being corrected (Masters & Johnson, 1959, 1960, 1961, 1962, 1963). Some of this recent material is synthesized in the latter part of this chapter and quite possibly may provide a minimal baseline for the more adequate clinical treatment of frigidity or impotence.

With regard to the third stumbling block—that of requisite referral to the psychopathologist of problems of sexual incompatibility—two things should be noted. First, there is ample clinical evidence for the observation that sexual imbalance or inadequacy is not confined to individuals who have been identified with major psychoses or even severe neuroses. Secondly, long-maintained individually oriented psychotherapy for sexual inadequacy frequently places irreversible strains on the marital state. While the psychopathologist is working with one marriage partner or the other toward the resolution of his or her individual sexual inadequacy, the marriage itself may be deteriorating. One or two years of therapy directed specifically toward the impotent male or frigid female frequently leaves the unsupported marital partner in a state of severe frustration. Not only are unresolved sexual tensions of the nontreated spouse of major moment, but frequently no significant attempt is made by the therapist to keep the supposedly adequate partner apprised of his or her mate's fundamental problems and/or the specifics of therapeutic progress. Such situations of spouse neglect not only are sure to increase the performance pressures on the sexually inadequate partner, but obviously may lead to many other areas of marital strife and, for that matter, stimulate extramarital interests.

As the result of these observations, the conviction has grown that the most effective treatment of sexual incompatibility involves the technique of working with both members of the family unit. The major factor in effective diagnosis and subsequent productive counseling in sexual problems lies in gaining access to and rapport with both members of the family unit. This approach not only provides direct therapy for the sexually inadequate partner, but provides something more. An indirect therapeutic gain results from enlisting the complete cooperation and active participation of the adequate spouse (the husband of the frigid woman or the wife of the impotent male). It is virtually impossible for the mate of the sexually distressed partner to remain isolated from or uninvolved in his or her partner's concern for adequate sexual performance. Therefore, most of these individuals can and will be most cooperative in absorbing the necessary material of both physiologic and psychologic background necessary to convert them into active members of the therapy team.

As in so many other areas of medical practice, treating sexual incompatibility involves, first, recognizing the nature of the patient's problem, second, determining the type and degree of the incompatibility and third, developing and activating the therapeutic approaches applicable to the particular clinical involvement.

RECOGNIZING THE SEXUAL PROBLEM

The patient with sexual distress defines the problem directly with increasing frequency during this era of marked change in our cultural attitudes toward sexual material. However, many women initially may discuss such symptoms as fatigue, "nerves," pelvic pain, headaches or any other complaint for which specific pathology cannot be established. The physician-interviewer must anticipate conscious vocal misdirection when Victorian concepts of sexual taboos still exist, or where there is a personal demand to fix blame on the marital partner.

If, for example, the female is the partner experiencing major dissatisfaction with her marriage, for any one of a number of reasons, she purposely may obscure her basic personal antipathies by describing gross sexual irregularities on the part of her marital partner. Sometimes when it is the husband who wishes to end the marriage, he often employs the pressure of partial sexual withdrawal, or even complete sexual refusal. At this point, medical consultation is sought solely to justify condemnation of what is termed the mate's unfair, inadequate or perverted sexual behavior.

Actually, the marital incompatibility that brings the couple to the physician usually is not primarily of sexual origin. Sexual incompatibility may well be the secondary result of marital disagreement over such problems as money, relatives or child care. Such areas of dispute easily may undermine any poorly established pattern of sexual adjustment. Frequently, withholding of sexual privileges is used as punishment in retaliation for true or fancied misdeeds in other areas. If the preliminary history reveals such a situation of secondary sexual incompatibility, the physician must decide whether he wishes to carry the full, time-consuming burden of total marriage counseling or if referral is in order. In the latter case, he still may wish to retain an active clinical role in the psychosexual aspects of the problems involved.

However, once the problem is established as primarily sexual in nature and as the cause and not the effect of the marital incompatibility, the complaint should be attacked directly and with the same sense of medical urgency with which clinical complaints of either a medical or a surgical background are investigated. Otherwise, permanent impairment of the marital relationship may be inevitable.

THE SEXUAL HISTORY

The need to acquire accurate and detailed sexual histories is basic to determining the type and the degree of the incompatibility of the members of the distressed family unit.

Sex histories must reflect accurately details of early sexual training and experience, family attitudes toward sex, the degree of the family's demonstrated affection, personal attitude toward sex and its significance within the marriage and the degree of personal regard for the marital partner. While the actual nature of the existing sex difficulty may be revealed during an early stage of history-taking, the total history, as it discloses causation and subsequent effect, provides the basis for the most effective means of therapy.

The first step in the team approach to diagnosis and treatment has been to see the husband and wife together as a complaining unit during the initial interview (Johnson & Masters, 1961, 1964). Procedures and philosophies are explained to them. If the couple desires to continue after the investigative concepts have been outlined, they are separated for individual interrogation but only after each partner is assured that similar background material will be covered simultaneously by the two interviewers.

The knowledge that both unit members are undergoing similar interrogative procedures, that essentially the same background material will be investigated, and that all areas of professed concern will be probed in depth, produces an atmosphere that encourages honest reporting and an unusual amount of patient attention to detail.

Finite details of past and present sexual behavior may be obtained during the initial interview with the facility and integrity anticipated for the recording of a detailed medical history. Encouraged by a receptive climate, controlled, brief questioning, and a nonjudgmental attitude, the patient is just as free to discuss the multiple facets of, for example, a homosexual background, as he might be to present the specific details of a chronic illness in a medical history.

It should be noted particularly that in the process of acquiring a detailed sexual history, the usual basic physical and social histories of medical and behavioral significance also are recorded.

For the rapid diagnosis and treatment of sexual incompatibility, a male-female therapy team approach has been developed as reported elsewhere (Johnson & Masters, 1964). This approach involves the male marriage partner being interviewed first by the male member of the therapy team. Simultaneously, material from the female partner of the involved marital unit is acquired by the female member of the therapy team. Prior to the second investigative session, members of the therapy team exchange pertinent details of the marital unit's reported sexual distress. During the second session the female partner of the complaining couple is reinterviewed by the male member of the therapy team. Meanwhile, the husband is evaluated by the female therapist. At the third interview, the therapy team and the marital couple meet to review the positive features of the earlier interrogative sessions and to discuss in detail the active degree of the sexual incompatibility.

While the male-female therapy approach has been found to be eminently satisfactory, obviously this technique usually is not possible in the typical physician's practice. However, the broad general steps toward diagnosis and evaluation that are outlined here can be adapted by the individual physician. For instance, the advantage of honest reporting obtained by simultaneous interviews of members of the marital unit can be retained by interrogating them consecutively.

THE THERAPEUTIC PROCESS

Once the background of the individual couple's sexual imbalance has been defined, and the clinical picture explained to their satisfaction and understanding, a discussion of therapeutic procedure takes place.

In general terms, the psychotherapeutic concepts and physiologic techniques employed to attack the problems of frigidity and impotence are explained without reservation. Specific plans are outlined for the therapeutic immediacies and a pattern for long-range support is described. With this specific information available, a decision must be reached as to whether the couple has sufficient need or interest for active participation in the therapeutic program. The decision obviously is based not only on a joint evaluation of the quality of the marriage and the severity of the sexual distress, but also on a review of the individual abilities to cooperate fully with the program. If doubt exists, on the part of either member of the investigative team or either partner of the sexually incompatible marital unit, as to real interest in remedial techniques or ability to cooperate fully as a unit, the couple is directed toward other sources of clinical support.

Since the two major sexual incompatibilities are frigidity and impotence, treatment for these problems will be discussed in detail.

IMPOTENCE

Three major types of impotence ordinarily are encountered in the human male. They are:

1. *Failed erection.* Penile erection cannot be achieved.
2. *Inadequate erection.* Full penile erection either cannot be achieved or, if accomplished, is maintained fleetingly and lost, usually without ejaculation.
3. *Nonemissive erection.* Full penile erection is achieved, but ejaculation cannot be accomplished with the penis contained within the vagina.

   Note. Premature ejaculation—ejaculation before, during, or immediately after mounting is accomplished—while not considered a form of impotence, is discussed in this chapter due to the similarity of therapeutic approach.

Impotence is rarely, if ever, the result of lesions of the posterior urethra. Once the possibility of spinal cord disease or certain endocrinopathies, such as hypogonadism or diabetes insipidus, has been eliminated, the total history should be scrutinized for the omnipresent signs of psychogenic origin for the specific type of male impotence reported.

In the case of the male with failed or inadequate erection, history-taking should stress the timetable of symptom onset. Has there always been difficulty, or is loss of erective power of recent origin? If recent in origin, what specific events inside or outside the marriage have been associated with onset of symptoms? Are there any masturbatory difficulties? Is there a homosexual background of significance?

Further questioning should define the male's attitude toward his sexual partner. Is there rejection not only of the marriage partner, but also of other women? Are the female partner's sexual demands in excess of his levels of sexual interest or ability to comply? Is there a sexual disinterest that may have resulted from the partner's physical or personal traits, such as excessive body odor or chronic alcoholism?

In the case of a patient with premature ejaculation, questions should be concentrated in a different area. Does this rapid ejaculatory pattern date from the beginning of his sexual activity? Has he been exposed to prostitute demand for rapid performance during his teenage years? Does he come from a level of society where the female sexual role is considered to be purely one of service to male demand?

When working with the male with a nonemissive erection still other questions are more appropriate. Has the male always been unable to ejaculate during intercourse or has this difficulty been confined to exposure to his marital partner? Are nocturnal emissions frequent, especially after heterosexual encounters? Is there an active homosexual history?

Actually, the fundamental therapeutic approach to all problems of impotence is one of creating and sustaining self-confidence in the patient. This factor emphasizes the great advantage in training the wife to be an active member of the therapeutic team. All pertinent details of the anatomy, physiology and psychology of male impotence should be explained to her satisfaction. The rationale of treatment, together with an explanation of the specific stimulative techniques most effective in dealing with the specific type of impotence distressing her husband must be made clear to her.

In the early stages of treating failed or nonerective impotence, it is wise to avoid emphasizing the demand that intercourse be the end of all sexual play. Frequently, the male's inability to meet just such a repetitive female demand is already one of the primary factors in his impotence. Some males find release from fear of performance when they are given to understand that sexual play need not necessarily terminate in intercourse. They are then able to relax, enjoy and participate freely in the sexually stimulative situations created by their clinically oriented wives to a point where erection does occur. After several such occasions of demand-free spontaneous erections, the males may even initiate the mounting procedure and complete the sexual act. This casual mating may well be the beginning of release from their chronic or acute failed or nonerective impotence.

In most cases, manual penile manipulation varying in degree of intensity and duration probably will be necessary. This controlled penile stimulation must be provided by his previously trained female partner. The male with inadequate erection syndrome should be exposed to long and regularly recurrent periods of manual stimulation in a sensitive, sexually restrained, but firmly demanding fashion.

In the opposite vein, the male with the difficult problem of premature ejaculation should be manually stimulated for short, controlled periods with stimulation withheld at his own direction as he feels ejaculation is imminent. The shaft of the penis should be well lubricated to reduce cutaneous sensation. This technique will fail frequently and ejaculation will occur. However, the couple should be encouraged to return to the technique repetitively until the male's obviously improved control leads to the next therapeutic step. This will be a female superior mounting, which can later be converted to a nondemanding lateral resting position. These progressive control techniques emphasize the unit approach to the problem of sexual inadequacy and from here on psychogenic support and the cooperation of the wife certainly will reclaim many of those males who were formerly inadequate sexually.

The problem of the male with nonemissive erection is somewhat different. His is largely an infertility problem rather than one of sexual incompatibility. In these cases, reassuring both husband and wife that the problem is of little clinical consequence provides the basic therapy. Sometimes the infertility concern connected with this variant can be overcome by artifically inseminating the wife with her husband's seminal fluid obtained by manipulation. Since psychotherapy has produced so few positive results with this type of impotence, providing clinical reassurance and conceptive information may have to suffice in these cases.

FRIGIDITY

There is a great deal of misunderstanding over the connotation of the word "frigidity." It is often used in a context that presumes an irrevocable lack of sexuality on the part of a female sexual partner. Misconceptions are likely to occur when this word is used too freely as a diagnostic term.

From a therapeutic point of view, the maximal meaning of the word should indicate no more than a prevailing inability or subconscious refusal to respond sexually to effective stimulation. A woman is not necessarily lacking in sexual responsiveness when she does not experience an orgasm. Therefore, the achievement of orgasmic response should not be considered the end-all of sexual gratification for the responding female. Unhappily, many women, unable to achieve an orgasmic level of sexual response in the past, have been labeled frigid not only by their marital partner but also by the physician they may have consulted.

The free use of this term frequently does great psychologic damage. Frigidity is a term that should rarely be employed in the presence of the sexually inadequate female for it may well add shame, and/or fear of inadequate performance to whatever other psychologic problems she may have.

It is true that there are a number of women who experience a persistently high degree of sexual tension, but, for unidentified reasons, are not able to achieve a satisfactory means of tension release. In evaluating this problem, initial exploration should be concentrated in two areas of psychosexual withdrawal. The first is to determine the presence or absence of psychologic inability to respond to effective sexual stimulation. The second is to define the possible existence of sexual incompatibility caused by misunderstandings resulting from a difference in the sex tension demands of the marital partners.

As described elsewhere (Masters, 1959), three positive indications of female psychosexual inadequacy can be developed by careful history-taking:

1. Attitude toward sex and its significance within the marriage.
2. Degree of personal regard for the marital partner.
3. Fear of pregnancy.

In investigating the attitude toward sex, existing negative concepts should be pursued by careful interrogation. Questioning should explore early sexual training and experience, exposure to lack of demonstrated parental affection, history of homosexual experience, if any, and/or any traumatic sex-oriented incidents that might have affected natural sexual responsiveness.

When exploring the area of personal regard for the marital partner, the female partner's disinterest or lack of cooperation with the consulting physician may be an interesting clinical symptom of itself. When essential indifference toward a marital partner has been exposed, the existence of a basically unwanted marriage or marriage undertaken without intelligent preparation or emotional maturity is a real possibility. Perhaps, in these cases, referral to a marriage counselor or undertaking marriage counseling in the more general frame of reference is in order, rather than concentrating on the sexual aspects of the problem.

When there is any indication of fear of pregnancy the therapeutic approach is obvious to the counseling physician. Actually, satisfactory results are ordinarily more easily achieved in pregnancy-phobia situations than in either of the other two areas of psychosexual withdrawal.

After the background of the female's sexual unresponsiveness has been established, and the marital unit has accepted the conclusions presented during the diagnostic sessions, therapy may begin. Female sexual responsiveness may well depend upon the successful orientation to the following framework of therapeutic approach:

1. The possibility of anatomic or physiologic abnormalities that can contribute to varying shades of discomfort during intercourse should be eliminated. Orientation to male and female sexual anatomy, directly if necessary, should be accomplished.
2. Affirmation that sexual expression represents an integral basis for sharing within the marriage should be emphasized.
3. A mutually stimulative sexual pattern should be developed and adapted to the individual psychosocial backgrounds of the marriage partners.
4. Gentleness, sensitivity and technical effectiveness in the male partner's approach to sexual encounter should be encouraged.
5. Emphasis should be placed on the fact that female orgasm is not necessarily the end-all of every sexual encounter.

With regard to pelvic abnormalities, it might be noted that a history indicating actual pain or any other physical displeasure during sex play or coition certainly suggests the need for an adequate physical examination. If physiologic variants, such as pelvic endometriosis, causing severe, recurrent discomfort during intercourse with deep penile penetration are revealed, subsequent medical and/or surgical adjustments may be indicated. However, it should be noted that sometimes the simple clinical expedient of teaching the couple proper positioning for coital activity may remove the female partner's distress despite existing pelvic pathology.

A high percentage of psychologically based problems of inadequate female response begin as the result of rejection of, or ignorance of effective sex techniques by either or both marital partners. The physician may also be called upon to provide reassurance as to the propriety of variants of stimulative sexual behavior. Although the number of patients who are sexually incompatible as the result of the wife's or husband's total lack of sexual experience before marriage may well be declining, patients with this type of problem are seen occasionally. Moreover, many women have been taught that only certain specifics of sexual stimulation or certain coital positions are acceptable. These women do not readily accept any deviation from what they consider "right and proper," regardless of the interests of their marital partners. Victorianism, although vanishing from the American social scene, left a residual influence that may well require attention for at least another fifty years.

Teaching the sexually inadequate woman and her partner the basic rudiments of sexual anatomy may be extremely important. Many males, however experienced in coition, are unaware of the importance of adequate techniques for clitoral area stimulation. Few are aware that it is the gentle friction of the mons area or of the clitoral shaft rather than the clitoral glans that provides the most effective stimulation for the female partner. Moreover, many females as well as males are not aware of the basic physiology of sexual response and of the fact that physiologic orgasm takes place within the vagina and in the clitoris, regardless of where sensation is perceived by the female or initiated by the male.

In the development of a mutually stimulative sexual pattern it is important that the marital unit's move toward maximal female sexual responsiveness should be accompanied by the female's vocalizing such things as: specific sexual preferences, desired zones of erogenous stimulation, choice of coital positioning and, particularly, the fact of her approaching orgasm. The couple must be taught to consider moments of individual preference for sexual encounter. Experimentation with varieties of time, place, and sexual techniques should be made in order to achieve the necessary mood conducive to the female's successful sexual response. It is well to bear in mind that the two basic deterrents to female sexual responsiveness are *fatigue* and *preoccupation.*

The item in the therapeutic framework emphasizing gentleness and sensitivity needs little elaboration. But it should be noted that the male's approach—his ability to project both security and affection to the female—may be an absolute essential to any improvement in the female's sexual responsiveness. A re-evaluation of the male's attitudes toward sex and toward women may be as important to the progress of therapy as the attention paid to his education in specific sexual techniques.

The second major area to be explored with the couple is the possible difference in the degree of basic sexual tension demonstrated by the wife as opposed to that indicated by her husband. In analyzing this area, it should be emphasized that an impression of low-level female sexual demand should only be established in relative comparison to a higher-tension partner. A lower level of demand does not necessarily connote either inability to respond adequately to effective heterosexual stimulation or homosexual tendency. Yet, when such a divergence in sexual interest is encountered, there are inevitable misunderstandings between the marital partners. In some cases there may be a conscious sexual withdrawing by the lower-response partner, developing from a sense of personal inadequacy or from a wish to punish what is considered as excessive demand. Conscious sexual withdrawal also may develop from a deep resentment or a sense of rejection felt by the partner wishing a higher degree of sexual participation.

The marital unit's understanding and acceptance of a difference in sexual tension demand is far more important than its causation and the determination of a specific spouse role-playing. A higher level of demand may well belong to either partner. This is evident in marriages between younger partners as well as in many marriages between older individuals. Feelings of sexual inadequacy, distrust or withdrawal may be corrected by education of each mate to the other partner's individual, highly personal, sexual requirements. Thereafter, the problem becomes one of adjusting acknowledged differences in sexual tension to a mutually accepted plan for effective release of the higher level of demand. It has been noted frequently that the relief of inhibitions of the lower-tension partner (once the marital unit problem is understood) may be marked by a more receptive, or even increased willingness to participate in sexual activity, even though there is no permanent elevation of the lower-level partner's own sexual tensions (Johnson & Masters, 1964).

As emphasized many times previously, the individual or combined interests of psychiatrists, psychologists, medical specialists, marriage counselors, social workers and clergymen may be needed to solve severe problems of sexual incompatibility. However, the advice of the initially consulted family physician frequently will be the most important step in relief of marital sexual maladjustments. The physician's forthright guidance and initial reassurance, whether he refers his patients to other professionals or treats them himself, provide the best foundation for the solution of problems of sexually incompatible marriages.

REFERENCES

Eisenbud, J. A Psychiatrist looks at the report. *Problems of social behavior.* New York: Social Hygiene Association, 1948, 20-27.

Masters, W.H. The sexual response cycle of the human female: II. Vaginal lubrication. *Ann. New York Acad. Sc.,* 1959, **83**, 301-317.

Masters, W.H. The sexual response cycle of the human female: I. Gross anatomic considerations. *West. J. Surg.* 1960, **68**, 57-72.

Masters, W.H. & Johnson, V.E. The physiology of vaginal reproductive function. *West. J. Surg.,* 1961, **69**, 105-120.

Masters, W.H. & Johnson, V.E. The sexual response cycle of the human female: III. The clitoris: Anatomic and clinical considerations. *West. J. Surg.,* 1962, **70**, 248-257.

Masters, W.H. & Johnson, V.E. The sexual response cycle of the human male: I. Gross anatomic considerations. *West. J. Surg.,* 1963, **75**, 85-95.

Johnson, V.E. & Masters, W.H. A team approach to the rapid diagnosis and treatment of sexual incompatibility. *Pac. Med. & Surg.* (formerly *West. J. Surg.*), 1964, **72**, 371-375.

Johnson, V.E. & Masters, W.H. Sexual incompatibility: Diagnosis and treatment. Lloyd, Charles W., Ed. *Human reproduction and sexual behavior.* Philadelphia: Lea & Febiger, 1964, 474-489.

Johnson, V.E. & Masters, W.H. Treatment of the sexually incompatible family unit. *Minnesota Med.,* 1961, **44**, 466-471.

5
A Modification of Masters and Johnson Sex Therapy Model in a Clinical Setting

BARRY W. McCARTHY

sexual misconceptions
use one therapist
the sessions

The publication of the book *Human Sexual Response* in 1966 by the research team of Masters and Johnson was a major breakthrough in the area of sexual knowledge. Physicians and therapists at last had a base of information from which to evaluate the many sexual problems brought to them by patients. Even more exciting was the publication in 1970 of the clinical sequel to their research, *Human Sexual Inadequacy*. In this book they proposed, described, and evaluated a radically different model to clinically treat the most common marital sexual dysfunctions. The major aspects of their therapy model were: 1) Any individual sex problem was a problem of the couple, and both partners had to be involved in the treatment procedures; 2) Use of a dual sex therapy team with a physician and a behavioral scientist; and, 3) An intensive two-week structured therapy program with an emphasis on reeducation. Masters and Johnson did a five-year follow-up on their program, and their success rate was generally quite high (average was 81 percent), with some treatments remarkably successful. i.e., success rate with premature ejaculation was 97 percent. Undoubtedly, these techniques have caused a revolution in the conceptualization and treatment of sexual disorders. At present, Masters and Johnson have set up a program to train dual-sex therapy teams in the techniques that they have developed. Approximately one team a month is being trained in St. Louis, which is not nearly enough to meet the need for competent sex therapists in this country.

Although this is an extremely exciting research and clinical breakthrough in sexual knowledge, there are some evident problems in applying this model to "typical" therapeutic practice. Chief among these is the issue of time and expense, especially in a public mental-health facility. The usual practice is for clients to be seen on a once-a-week, 50-minute basis by one therapist—the Masters and Johnson model calls for a much more concentrated and much greater time commitment on the part of two therapists. Very few mental health clinics, university counseling centers, or other public agencies can afford that kind of time expenditure by two staff members. A rough estimate for the "average" case is that each therapist devotes approximately 40 to 50 hours of therapy time to the couple during a two-week period. Another major difficulty with the model is the need for a physician to be involved as one of the therapists. In fact, there is some question whether

41

the typical practicing psychiatrist would be able to function as a physician in the Masters and Johnson approach, since generally the psychiatrist does not do extended physical examination or laboratory work. Again, the typical mental health facility or private practitioner does not have available to him this kind of medical resource.

This paper will describe an alternative to the Masters-Johnson model of sex therapy which is more relevant to a typical clinical setting. The author has utilized this alternative approach with approximately 14 couples seen either at a university counseling center, a community mental-health center, or in private practice. Generally, the success rate with this small sample has been equivalent to that reported by Masters and Johnson—marked improvement in 12 of the 14 couples seen. Many of the ideas for these alterations come from Dr. E. Lee Doyle, the first female sex therapist trained by Masters and Johnson, who does private practice in Dallas, works alone, and sees couples on a once- or twice-a-week basis.

The proposed modifications which I have labeled "Clinical Sex Therapy" accept the first premise of the Masters-Johnson model that the sex problem is a couple problem and that both partners must be involved, but does not utilize a dual-sex therapy team nor the two-week program. Instead, the couple is seen by a single therapist and on a once-a-week basis. The typical therapy sequence is that the couple is seen first together, usually for about half an hour to discuss the problem, to see if sex therapy is appropriate, and if so to define the goals of the therapy and establish the therapeutic contract. Then one partner (usually the one with the sexual problem) is seen alone to begin the sex history. Typically, sex histories take approximately one and one-half hours per person, and an attempt is made to put two sessions together or see them twice in the week so that the history is completed within a week. The couple is asked not to discuss the history-taking until the "roundtable," although they are permitted to have sex as usual unless the sex has become so aversive that continuing sex activity would be antitherapeutic. Also, the clients are told to visit their own physicians to determine if there might be any physiological reason for the sexual dysfunction.

During the next week there is another two-hour appointment to do the "roundtable" and begin programming the "pleasuring" or "sensate focus" exercises. Thereafter, weekly appointments of one hour are scheduled. The clients are informed that if any difficulty does arise in doing their "homework" they should call the therapist. Since monitoring progress is more difficult on the once-a-week as opposed to daily-therapy basis, the telephone serves as a very convenient way to ensure that if the clients misunderstand the instructions or have difficulty with a procedure, that it does not have to be a wasted or negative week. In the author's experience the typical sex therapy contract is between 10 and 15 sessions after the assessment phase. The history-taking, roundtable concept, and sex therapy techniques utilized are all substantially based in the Masters and Johnson program.

Perhaps at this point a case illustration from the author's private practice would be appropriate. The referring problem was the woman's complaint of nonorgasmic responding during her five years of marriage. She had seen her minister, two gynecologists and one psychiatrist for brief periods of time. Interestingly, none had suggested sex therapy. She was referred to the author by her neighbor who was a student in the author's university psychology course, "Human Sexual Behavior." When the client called for an appointment, she was asked to bring her husband for the initial interview. Mr. and Mrs. F. were a lower middle-class, nonpsychologically minded couple, but after a half-hour interview, they agreed there was a sexual problem which was causing them and their marriage a good deal of unhappiness, and that a direct sex therapy approach to the problem seemed most relevant. A history was begun with Mrs. F., and although she was anxious and embarrassed, she did attempt to respond directly during the interview. The next week, a two-hour appointment was arranged, and the husband was interviewed first and then the wife. This couple seemed to fit very well the clinical sex therapy model; neither had major psychological problems, and both had major sexual misconceptions and were very uncommunicative about sex with each other. Mr. F. had no specific sex dysfunction, but was grossly lacking in knowledge of sexual technique and during childhood and adolescence had gotten the message that sex was "fun but dirty, and not to be talked about." Mrs. F. had a great deal of guilt about masturbation (in fact, she was situationally nonorgasmic rather than primarily nonorgasmic as she had said at first. She was too embarrassed to say she had masturbated to orgasm). She had experienced rape, and was very unsure of her sexuality. Sexual intercourse was attempted usually once every two weeks, and Mrs. F. found it very negative. In this case the couple was instructed not to have intercourse until the therapist told them. Before the roundtable, each was seen individually to get their permission to reveal "secrets" they had first said they did not want their spouse to know. Both spouses had the same secrets—both masturbated and both had considered having an extramarital affair. The meaning of the sexual problem and the need for a psychoeducational approach to learn to accept and respond to their sexuality and give feedback to each other on what was pleasurable was clearly related to the couple by the therapist. The roundtable was the key to the treatment process. Rather than sex being placed in the context of guilt and a threat to masculinity or femininity, it was redefined as an area of their lives that they had to learn about and then learn as a couple to respond to each other. The pleasuring or sensate focus procedures were introduced as a primary means of beginning this process. They were told that a reasonable schedule was to try sensate focus three days, one day off, and then three more days. Since there was a week between appointments, the programming was done explicitly and in sequence—first day was sensate focus, eyes closed, no genital touch; second day was sensate focus with spouses guiding each other, eyes closed, no genital touch; third day eyes open, guiding each other, no genital touch; fourth day off; fifth day eyes open, sensate focus with lotion, no genital touch; sixth day eyes closed, sensate focus with genital touch; seventh day eyes open, guided sensate focus with genital touch. However, the couple is told they need not view this as a rigid program, but rather as a guideline. The first few exercises are carefully and fully programmed, but as the sex therapy proceeds, the structure of the programming gradually decreases and the couple are encouraged to be spontaneous and experiment. Mr. and Mrs. F. moved through these procedures at a slower pace than most couples, but this seemed important for them in that they needed a solid base of reawakened bodily feelings before they could move on. In fact, it took them into the third week before they got to the exercises listed as appropriate for day six. In addition to these exercises, Mrs. F. was told to do self-pleasuring (i.e., masturbation) activity. She had only masturbated rubbing her knees together, had never manually stimulated her vulva area. Generally, the self-pleasuring sequence which parallels the sensate focus is a process the author uses with most nonorgasmic women so that they may learn what turns them on sexually. She did this at a different time than the sensate focus exercises.

After this, appointments were made on a once-a-week basis. Each hour would begin with a recap on how the previous week's "homework" went, general concerns and feedback between the spouses with the therapist encouraging them to be more open and specific in their feelings and sexual needs, and finally programming next steps in the sex program. After the third session, Mrs. F. was regularly orgasmic during manual masturbation and feeling good about this responding. Both Mr. and Mrs. F. had a better understanding of both their own and their spouse's sexual responses. The fourth session saw the nondemand position introduced, but two days later the therapist received a call saying Mrs. F. did not understand the position. The position was re-explained over the phone; they were told to try it again and if it still felt uncomfortable to discontinue it for the week and return to the genital sensate focus exercises. However, after the telephone consultation the problem was resolved. It should be noted at this point that the sex therapy program is a block-building model, that each new technique is supplemental rather than eliminating a previous one, i.e., the couple would do the sensate focus and then the nondemand position. The eventual goal is that these techniques gradually become a regular and natural part of sexual foreplay. The fifth session introduced oral-genital stimulatory techniques. There was some reluctance on Mrs. F.'s part to attempt this. She was told that this was something which could be tried, that many couples enjoy it and that she could not know her reactions until it was attempted. She was told that if she started to become anxious, she could move back to manual genital touch. During the next two sessions reactions to various stimulatory techniques were discussed, and by the end of the eighth week she was orgasmic with both manual and oral stimulation. During this time they were not having intercourse, but the husband was ejaculating regularly either by masturbation or Mrs. F.'s manual stimulation. The ninth week was spent discussing changes in the couple's marital relationship and communication pattern. At this point it should be mentioned that with this couple, as with most, even though the major focus is on a psycho-educational model of relearning sexual response, other marital and personal factors do come into play. Often a major factor in the success of sex therapy is the couple's having really improved their communication-feedback skills.

At the tenth week, intercourse was initiated using the female superior position. By the 12th week, Mrs. F. was functioning orgasmically during both foreplay and intercourse. At this point the last procedure was introduced—the lateral coital position which both Mr. and Mrs. F. responded very favorably to. Two sessions were used to integrate and complete the therapy contract, and we terminated at the 14th session. On a three-month follow-up, they reported that not only had the orgasmic response continued, but that their entire relationship had continued to improve.

In terms of the modifications of the Masters-Johnson model, several things deserve mention. The elongated therapy period was beneficial to this couple in that it allowed them to pace themselves in terms of acceptance of their sexual responses. They were also able to integrate their sexual lives into the mainstream of their lifestyle; it is almost a "honeymoon" effect to have no responsibilities for two weeks except sex and then when the couple return to their regular lifestyle, there can be a letdown and new adjustments. Mrs. F. had gone to her gynecologist for a medical check, and he was very straightforward in ruling out any organic pathology. With this type of medical support, there is no doubt in the author's mind that a qualified nonmedical psychotherapist is quite competent to do clinical sex therapy. Undoubtedly, some data and help is lost by not having a co-therapist. However, the therapist was aware of the needs of the female client and of the data available about female sexual response. It would appear that as long as the therapist is aware of both male and female physical and psychological responses, as well as the power and communication aspects of the triadic therapeutic relationship, then he or she can function in a therapeutic way. Also, it must be remembered that co-therapy is expensive both in terms of time and resources as well as requiring the co-therapists to work out any problems they might have in working with each other in the difficult areas of sex therapy.

REFERENCES

Masters, W.H. & Johnson, V.E. *Human sexual response.* Boston: Little, Brown, & Co., 1966.

Masters, W.H. & Johnson, V.E. *Human sexual inadequacy.* Boston: Little, Brown & Co., 1970.

6

The Treatment of Inhibited Sexual Responses

JOSEPH WOLPE

Uninhibited sexual responding is correlated with intense pleasurable arousal during sexual intercourse. While some cases of chronic sexual inhibition are due to failure of physical development or to physical pathology, the great majority are the result of conditioning. Usually anxiety responses have become conditioned to the stimuli associated with sexual responding, and, being incompatible with the latter, inhibit it. The same inhibitory effect may be due to other conditioned emotions, like shame or disgust. Temporary inhibitions may, of course, result from intercurrent stresses or interfering stimuli of all kinds.

Anxiety inhibits sexual responding in a particular direct way, because it involves some of the very autonomic functions concerned in the sexual response. Pre-orgasmic sexual arousal is predominantly parasympathetic in character (Langley & Anderson, 1895; Masters & Johnson, 1966), while anxiety is essentially a sympathetic function. Therefore, the more intensely anxiety is aroused, the more inhibition there will be of the sexual response (Wolpe, 1958). Reciprocally, sexual responses may be used for overcoming the anxiety habits that inhibit them. As always such utilization depends upon arranging for the sexual response to be strong enough to dominate the anxiety response so that it may inhibit it; for thus it will diminish the anxiety habit. Napalkov and Karas (1957) have shown that experimental neuroses in dogs can be overcome by counterposing sexual excitation to neurotic anxiety. Clinical neuroses have been successfully treated on the same basis—as will be described below. Of course, other inhibitors of anxiety can also be used to treat the anxiety that affects sexual responding.

As might be expected, it is usually in connection with anxieties related to sexual stimuli that sexual arousal has therapeutic application. But its potential is not confined to these stimuli. The neurotic reactions of the dogs treated by Napalkov and Karas were conditioned to nonsexual stimuli. Similarly, sexual emotions can be instrumental in overcoming human nonsexual neuroses. Quite frequently, such therapeutic effects occur fortuitously in life. A fortunate twist in a person's life may provide him with an exciting new sexual relationship that has therapeutic consequences. The emotion then involved is often not purely sexual excitation—but a broad-based arousal that can be called love. A case in point was an exceptionally intelligent young woman who felt herself disparaged by all intelligent people whom she encountered, especially at social gatherings, where she became exceedingly anxious. Then she married a man with whom she had fallen deeply in love. Now, suffused with amorous feelings, constantly reinforced by reciprocation, she found that she no longer had anxiety in social contexts. Years later, when the phase of high romance was long past, she was still free from her original anxiety. The anxiety had presumably undergone conditioned inhibition due to its reciprocal inhibition in social situations when love was on the wing.

As a matter of fact, many other nonanxious emotions can also produce therapeutic changes without the intervention of a therapist. It is probable that the majority of neuroses that people acquire are mild, and that most of them are in time overcome by the competition of the intercurrent emotions aroused by life events (Wolpe, 1958, p. 198).

THE TREATMENT OF IMPOTENCE

The most common deliberate use of the anxiety-inhibiting effects of erotic arousal is in the treatment of inhibited sexual responding in the male, called impotence, which is generally manifested as inadequacy of penile erection or premature ejaculation or both. Penile erection is a parasympathetic function. The sympathetic discharges that charac- terize anxiety tend both to inhibit erection and to facilitate ejaculation, which is subserved by the sympathetic (Langley & Anderson, 1895). Thus, the key to the problem — of impaired sexual performance is the subtraction of anxiety from the sexual encounter. Sometimes the anxiety has nonsexual antecedents, e.g., a fear of traumatization of human flesh (Wolpe, 1958, p. 152), but in the great majority of cases its stimuli are to be found within the sexual situation.

In using the sexual response as an anxiety-inhibitor, the first requirement is to ascertain at what point in the approach anxiety begins and what factors control it. Perhaps the man begins to feel anxiety the moment he enters the bedroom, or perhaps it is when he is lying in bed in the nude with his wife. The basic idea of the treatment is explained to him—that the sexual response, being antagonistic to anxiety, can weaken his habitual anxiety if it can be consistently counterposed to anxiety that is relatively weak. He can arrange for this by limiting his sexual approaches always to the point where anxiety begins. He obviously has to obtain the cooperation of his wife since she would certainly regard his behavior as odd if he were to institute it without explanation. She has to know that a treatment program is under way. The essence of her role is to avoid making her husband tense and anxious. She must not mock him or goad or press him to achieve any particular level of performance. Though this may mean her enduring a good deal of frustration, she may expect to reap the reward of her helpfulness eventually. Actually, many women obtain a reasonable degree of relief from digitally induced orgasms during this treatment. In the case of the man who begins to feel anxiety when just lying next to his wife in bed, he must do nothing more active until he no longer has anxiety in that situation. Usually after 2 or 3 occasions he will be able to say: "I feel perfectly comfortable, now—only sexually excited." Then, he can go on to the next stage—perhaps to turn toward her and lie facing her on his side and fondle her breasts while she remains on her back. When this can be done without anxiety, he again advances—this time perhaps to lying on top of her, but not attempting intromission. At the next step, the penis may be approximated to the clitoris or other parts of the vulva, but still without intromission. After this he is permitted a small degree of entry, and later greater degrees, followed by small amounts of movement and then greater movement. The precondition for advancing beyond a stage is the disappearance from it of all anxiety.

The details of the treatment, naturally, must be decided from case to case. A procedure that is frequently of great value was suggested by Semans (1956). The wife manipulates her husband's penis to a point just short of ejaculation and then stops. After an interval, she does the same again. The procedure may be repeated several times during a session, and over several sessions. Its effect is to increase the latency to ejaculation— sometimes from a few seconds to half an hour or more. It is easy to see how helpful this may be for prolonging intercourse when the time comes. Semans describes his technique, which case 1 in part illustrates, as follows.

If fatigue is present in either partner, he or she should sleep for a brief period of time. After this love play is begun and progresses to mutual stimulation of the penis and clitoris. Each is instructed to inform the other of the stage of sexual excitement being experienced. When the husband feels a sensation which is, for him, premonitory to ejaculation, he informs his wife and removes her hand until the sensation disappears. Stimulation is begun again and interrupted by the husband when the premonitory sensation returns. . . . By continuing the technique described above ejaculation can eventually be postponed indefinitely. Both husband and wife are advised that if erection subsides more than temporarily, a brief sleep or postponement of further stimulation is to be preferred to continuing their efforts at that time. Next, each is told separately, and later together, that ejaculation occurs more rapidly with the penis wet than dry. It is necessary, therefore, to use a bland cream or other means to lubricate the penis while the procedure is repeated.

Masters and Johnson (1970) describe a maneuver that can facilitate this technique. They state that when ejaculation seems inevitable it can be inhibited by the woman applying gentle pressure on the penis at the coronal sulcus, one finger pressing on the urethra and another on the dorsum.

Case 1

Mr. I., a 36-year-old realtor had suffered from premature ejaculation ever since the beginning of his coital life at the age of 16. Ejaculation generally occurred within 15 seconds of intromission. He had married at 24. His wife, though deriving some satisfaction from digital orgasms, had become increasingly conscious of her incomplete fulfillment, and had in the past two years been showing interest in other men. About 18 months previously, Mr. I. had had about 25 consultations with a "dynamic" psychiatrist. Though he had found the probing type of approach irritating, his general confidence had been improved by the treatment, but his sexual performance had remained unchanged. In three short-lived extramarital affairs, his sexual performance had been no better than with his wife. He usually felt that he was doing the "chasing," and was being accepted to some extent on sufferance.

Mr. I.'s Willoughby score was 30, with highest loadings for humiliation, stage fright and being hurt. He lacked assertiveness in relation to people close to him, but not at all in business affairs. A program of assertive training was seen as a secondary, but very relevant therapeutic requirement.

Mrs. I., briefly interviewed, expressed great willingness to take part in a behavior therapy program. She stated that digital orgasms satisfied her physically, but not emotionally. She felt that even a relatively small degree of prolongation of intromission would enable her to have coital orgasms. She regarded her marriage as very satisfactory in all other respects.

Therapy of the sexual inadequacy based upon use of sexual responses made combined use of two lines of approach: 1) Graded penile stimulation by the technique of Semans (*see* above), and 2) Gradual advances toward coitus. Mr. I. kept a detailed record of his performances, which he timed as accurately as possible with a bedside clock. The data of the early and middle stages of his record are reproduced below. Each figure refers to the *number of minutes of manual stimulation of the penis by his wife that brought him just short of ejaculation* for each successive sequence of stimulations.

First occasion (Saturday) 8, 6, 6, 6 and 3 minutes.
Second occasion (Saturday) 11, 7, 3, 4 and 4 minutes.
Third occasion (Sunday) 8, 6, 5 and 18 minutes.
Fourth occasion (Sunday) 17 minutes.
Fifth occasion (Monday) 33 minutes. At this juncture he felt confident enough to have Mrs. I. stimulate him as he sat astride her. The time to "pre-ejaculation" on two successive sequences was 2 minutes and 3 minutes.
Sixth occasion (Monday) lying face to face sideways the pre-ejaculatory point was reached in 10 minutes and was maintained for 20 more minutes, when Mrs. I. desisted because of fatigue.

After this occasion, Mr. I. declared that he had never before been able to reach and maintain so high a level of excitement, but this became the norm subsequently.

Seventh occasion (Monday) Same as sixth occasion, but "pre-ejaculation" was reached in 14 minutes and again maintained to a total of thirty minutes.
Eighth occasion (Tuesday) Same as sixth occasion, but "pre-ejaculation" was reached in 12 minutes and maintained to 30 minutes.
Ninth occasion (Wednesday) Penile stimulation while astride: 5, 12+ and 9+ minutes.
Tenth occasion (Wednesday) Penile stimulation while astride: 12 and 11 minutes.
Eleventh occasion (Tuesday) Penile stimulation while astride: 12½, 12 and 23 minutes. After the last, Mr. I. inserted just the glans of his penis into the vagina, maintaining it there for 5 minutes. In the course of this time Mrs. I. became excited. Thereupon he withdrew, and they both had orgasms digitally.
Twelfth occasion (Friday) Partial insertion (glans penis) for 20 minutes during which Mrs. I. alone moved and in this way gradually manipulated the penis deeper. At the end of the period Mr. I. withdrew as he felt ejaculation imminent.

Mr. I. now reported with satisfaction that he was feeling very much less anxious than before at partial insertion of his penis. He was finding that his stimulation of his wife was the greatest factor increasing his own excitation. The next objective was to increase both depth and duration of insertion, and thereafter to add small amounts of movement. In the meantime at each meeting with the therapist the patient was receiving training in progressive relaxation.

Thirteenth occasion (Friday evening after meeting with therapist) Partial intercourse lasted 30 minutes—partial insertion 80 percent of the time and full insertion about 20 percent, for about a minute at a time. During this minute Mr. I. would move constantly, without feeling any danger of ejaculation, but when Mrs. I. moved 5-10 times ejaculation would become imminent.

Fourteenth occasion (Saturday) Partial intercourse as above, 23 minutes and then Mr. I. ejaculated during an attempt to reverse positions.

Fifteenth occasion (Saturday) Fifteen minutes, much the same as the thirteenth occasion.

Sixteenth occasion (Sunday) Ejaculation after four minutes.

Seventeenth occasion (Monday) Forty minutes, varying between one-quarter to half insertion of penis. Ejaculation was several times imminent, but Mr. I. averted it by relaxing each time.

Now the therapist directed Mr. I. to concentrate first on prolonging full intromission, and then gradually to introduce movement, but preventing excessive excitation by avoiding stimulation of Mrs. I. He was told always to keep well within his capacity to control. After a few minutes of this, it would be permissible to go on to orgasm, concentrating then on clitoral pressure by the penis.

Eighteenth occasion (Monday) Orgasm after 15 minutes of complete insertion with small movements.

Nineteenth occasion Orgasm after 29 minutes of small movements. Mrs. I. said that she too had been on the point of orgasm.

Further sexual occasions enabled gradually increasing excursions of movement, and finally a major breakthrough occurred after the thirteenth therapeutic interview. While Mr. I. retained his erection, Mrs. I. had four orgasms, and he ejaculated during the last of them. From this time onward there was mutually satisfactory sexual performance that gradually improved. There were 14 therapeutic interviews in all, over 5 weeks. Mr. I.'s Willoughby score at the last interview was 13.

The course that events took in the treatment of Case 1 is typical. Some patients do not make this kind of progress because they cannot maintain the low levels of anxiety essential to success in the real sexual situations, even though these are delimited. Usually, the imagination of these patients takes them beyond the reality to the eventual "threat" of actual coitus. Systematic desensitization to the stages of the sexual approach is then indicated; or the use of tranquilizing drugs may be considered.

In occasional cases of premature ejaculation, recovery may be obtained in a much more simple way. The couple are told to have coitus as frequently as possible. The husband is instructed to try to enjoy himself as much as possible, just letting himself go and not caring how soon he ejaculates. The wife is asked to endure the situation if she can, and, of course, some cannot. It is quite helpful in cases like this to encourage the procural of orgasm in the wife by noncoital means—by manual and oral manipulations. A method that Semans (1962) has found effective is for the woman to move her clitoris rhythmically against the husband's thigh.

In general, patients who complain of erectile failure or insufficiency are more difficult to treat than those with premature ejaculation, for theirs is a more profound inhibition of response. In some of them, there is clearly a biological factor involved. The onset of biologically based impotence is insidious, with erectile power diminishing over a period of months or years. The history usually reveals a lifelong low level of sexual function. If there is no evidence of anxiety or other reactive source of sexual inhibition, a biological causation is highly probable. The diagnosis may be settled by laboratory estimation of urinary testosterone (Cooper et al., 1970). Less directly relevant, but more easily available, is the estimation of urinary 17-ketosteroid excretion. A distinctly low testosterone assay is a strong indication for hormone therapy; but even with a moderately high reading the patient need not be denied the possible benefits of testosterone treatment although most of those so treated fail to respond (Cooper et al., 1970).

For some of those who do not respond to the relatively simple methods described above, a two-week spell with spouse in St. Louis, Mo., at The Reproductive Biology Research Foundation (Masters & Johnson, 1971) should be considered. This is, in essence, a highly structured opportunity for reconditioning sexual responses, although the principals are not very explicitly cognizant of the conditioning principles involved.

It was mentioned in the opening paragraph of this chapter that various intercurrent stresses may cause temporary inhibition of sexual responding. Chronic stress that has nothing to do with the sexual relationship as such may in parallel fashion cause chronic sexual inhibition. Prolonged stress may come from an enduring real misery, such as an incurable illness in the wife. Most often it is bound up with disharmonies in the relationship of a nonsexual kind. A program for mutual readjustment should then be undertaken. Sometimes two or three joint sessions with the couple on a "commonsense" basis are all that is needed. Other cases require more formal arrangements involving "contracts," score cards and a token economy, as described by Stuart (1969).

A less common form of male sexual inadequacy is ejaculatory incompetence. One case was successfully treated by desensitization to the idea of the penis in the vagina (Razani, 1972).

Problems of Female Collaboration

A cooperative sexual partner is indispensable to the success of most of the techniques described above. Many patients have a partner readily available. Others are less fortunate. Sometimes one has to wait months before the patient finds somebody sufficiently interested in him to be willing to make the effort and bear the discomforts required for his treatment. Sometimes, although the patient has a wife or paramour, she is unable to participate as needed, either because she is contemptuous of her mate's impotence, or, more often, because a long history of disappointment and frustration has quenched her amorous responses. If the woman is unmoved by her husband's prefiguration of the behavior therapy program, the therapist should arrange to speak to her himself. If she can be persuaded to take the first steps, and if she is encouraged by early advances, the rest can be plain sailing.

When all feasible efforts have failed to extract from the wife the affectional behavior needed for the therapeutic program, it seems entirely reasonable to encourage the husband to seek out another woman who may be more responsive to him. If moral justification is required, it may be said that if the man's sexual potency should be established through his relationship with the other woman, it may lead to reconstruction of the marriage; and even if it does not, the man is better off biologically and psychologically to be able to have outside satisfactions than to be doomed to lifelong chastity.

Provided that reasonable safeguards are observed, it is best for a therapeutic extramarital relationship to be conducted with somebody in whom there is some wider personal interest, but, when this is not possible, paid help has to be sought. The casual "pick up" will not do, as she is likely to be interested only in her own immediate pleasure. Perhaps there will some day be a "pool" of accredited women who will sell their services to men with sexual problems. At present there seems to be no other recourse than to seek out a regular prostitute—and it is usually no easy matter to find one who is both personally appealing and able to muster enough sympathetic interest to participate in the therapeutic program. One patient, with a 16-year history of impotence, tried about 10 prostitutes before he found a warm-hearted and considerate one with whose help his sexual anxiety was overcome and his potency restored. Others have found help more easily.

The Results of Behavior Therapy of Inhibited Male Sexual Responses

Among 18 cases I surveyed retrospectively in 1966, 14 (78 percent) recovered to the extent of achieving entirely satisfactory sexual performance. Another 3 cases (17 percent) attained a level that was acceptable to their partners. The mean span of time required was 11.3 weeks and the median 8.0 weeks. Table 1 gives some details of these cases.

THE TREATMENT OF FRIGIDITY

Frigidity is an unfortunate term inasmuch as it seems to suggest emotional coldness—a total lack of sexual response, but it is too late to do away with it now. The best we can do is to recognize that there are all grades of inhibition of sexual response in women, from absolute frigidity (no response whatever of a sexual kind) to the inability to achieve coital orgasm in spite of very high sexual arousal.

Two kinds of cases must be distinguished. In "essential frigidity," the lack of response is in relation to males in general, while in "situational frigidity" it is relative to a particular male who in many cases is, unfortunately, the patient's husband. The solutions required are of very different kinds.

Essential Frigidity

Essential frigidity may be either absolute or relative. Some cases of absolute essential frigidity have an organic basis. Occasionally, one encounters a woman whose sexual response system seems somehow to have failed to develop. She does not recall ever having known sexual arousal and gives no history of distressing sexual experiences that might have led to conditioned inhibition. It must be supposed that her deficiency is constitutional; and there seems to be no available solution to the problem. In organically-based relative frigidity, the woman is erotically arousable to at least some degree, but coitus is

Table 1. Results of Behavior Therapy in Eighteen Cases of Impotence

Patient Number	Age	Therapeutic Time Span	Outcome and Remarks
1	31	1 week	Recovered
2	40	8 weeks	Recovered
3	46	10 weeks	Recovered
4	46	20 weeks	Recovered
5	40	4 weeks	Recovered
6	41	12 weeks (intermittent and furtive)	Much Improved
7	50	6 weeks	Recovered but no transfer to wife.
8	49	2 weeks	Recovered (major factor was removal of anxiety through wife taking contraceptive pills).
9	20	6 weeks	Recovered (major factor was resolution of fears about masculinity from psychoanalytic reading).
10	49	10 weeks	Improved from almost complete erectile failure to functionally sufficient erections to make marriage possible and to satisfy and impregnate wife.
11	35	6 weeks	Markedly improved when therapist left country. Appropriate assertion toward wife major factor.
12	36	5 weeks	Recovered (Case 2)
13	44	16 weeks (infrequent opportunities)	Unimproved. No apparent sexual anxiety. Hypersensitivity of glans penis.
14	40	9 weeks	Recovered (See Case 10, Wolpe, 1960)
15	35	8 weeks (preceded by 12 weeks of overcoming interpersonal fears)	Improved from no erection to strong one. Coitus improving when therapist left country.
16	18	66 weeks (very irregular opportunities at first)	Recovered
17	53	3 weeks	Recovered with new consort. Previously no benefit in 12 weeks with uncooperative consort.
18	39	12 weeks	Recovered. At first, erections occurred only after testosterone injections.

precluded, usually by some painful pathological condition of the vagina—usually either a zone of scar tissue or an inflammatory lesion. I once saw a woman who had been psychoanalyzed for the whole 4 years of her marriage for vaginal spasm that was really due to a painful ulcer. A gynecological examination should be advised in every case of frigidity in which there is the slightest possibility of physical pathology.

In the great bulk of cases, essential frigidity is a matter of conditioned inhibition. Some women are absolutely or relatively frigid due to early experiences that have attached negative, and usually anxious, feelings to sexual stimuli. Sometimes, the relevant experiences have consisted of anti-sexual indoctrination that may have had a religious basis, or may have come from a mother who herself had unhappy or fearful sexual experiences. The patient may have been told that sex is filthy and disgusting and permissible only for the purpose of having children. The emotions customarily attached to these adjectives would have been evoked in the little girl and thus conditioned to the sexual stimuli, so that later, when she grows up, they inhibit any sexual response that tends to be evoked. In other cases that originate in early life, the frigidity is the direct result of traumatic experiences related to sex. Sometimes, the inhibition originates from having been punished or frightened in the context of masturbation.

Frigidity that develops after puberty may follow attempted rape or other sexual trauma, or may be a consequence of sexual arousal having repeatedly been frustrated in one way or another. Often the patient relates that she has rarely or never achieved a satisfactory coital orgasm; and repeated frustration has created a growing revulsion toward sexual activity. Frigidity sometimes develops out of the very goodness of a relationship—a satire of circumstance—as in Case 2.

The treatment of essential frigidity depends upon what the stimulus-response analysis of the case reveals. Where there has been faulty indoctrination, it is necessary to remove misconceptions about sex and sexual activity and to re-educate the patient. Having done this, one is almost always still left with a negative emotional attitude to sex, bound up with anxiety toward various aspects of the sexual situation. The treatment is generally then systematic desensitization whose details are determined by the identified stimulus antecedents of the anxiety. In yet other cases, frigidity is a byproduct of an endless stream of simmering resentments at the spouse's "failings" which would be corrected if she were able to make her wishes known, and here the cure may lie in assertive training.

Case 2

A woman who had for years had a very good relationship with her husband in all respects developed a vaginitis which made intercourse painful. However, because of her great affection for her husband she had gone on permitting intercourse; but it was very aversive so that she had become completely frigid, developing marked vaginismus. Even after the vaginitis had been treated and intercourse was no longer painful, the vaginismus had persisted, so that it was impossible for her husband to gain entry. When I first saw her this state of affairs had been going on for 3 years.

In the case of vaginismus that afflicted Case 2, the spasm was found to be part of an anxiety reaction to the entry of any object into the vagina. Treatment consisted of a combination of standard desensitization and *in vivo* desensitization. I instructed the patient to relax and to imagine, at first, a very thin rod (about 1/8 inch in diameter) being inserted a depth of 1/2 inch into her vagina. This produced anxiety. I continued repeating the scene until the anxiety disappeared. I then gradually increased the length of the rod's insertion, and subsequently repeated the sequence with progressively wider rods. When the width of the imaginary rod had reached 1/2 inch, I arranged for the construction of a set of wax rods (bougies) that varied in diameter from 1/8 inch to 1-1/2 inch, that the patient was to use at home, starting with the insertion of the 1/8 inch bougie into her vagina, slowly, inch by inch. Thereafter, *in vivo* "shadowing" a few widths behind the imaginary diameter was continued. When we reached about 3/4 inch diameter in imagination, movement such as would occur during coitus was introduced. This was a new source of anxiety which required repeated scene presentations for its desensitization. Then, movement with the bougie was started. Increasingly rapid movement came to be comfortably tolerated. At this point, I began to encourage careful experimentation with actual coitus, which became possible very soon, without producing vaginismus or any other manifestation of anxiety.

Case 3

The following is a case of a much more common kind. Because of a fearful experience at puberty, a woman of 32 had a revulsion against sex. She had, nevertheless, married. She had borne 4 children in 6 years, because being pregnant was a defense against sex. She had been treated by various methods, drugs and electro-convulsive therapy, all without benefit. Her psychiatrist, not a behavior therapist, had then decided to try systematic desensitization. This had been a fiasco. The weakest item on his hierachy was the sight of naked female breasts. When the psychiatrist presented this image to the patient it had produced such a severe anxiety reaction that it was impossible to go on. Then he referred her to me. I added to the weak end of the hierarchy several items that were quite remote from the bedroom. The first scene was at a swimming pool where there was only one male present, 50 yards away, with his bare chest exposed. This man was later brought progressively closer. Next, we utilized, first at a distance of 50 yards and then closer, a completely nude male statue in a park. A later item in the hierarchy was seeing a little nude boy of four gamboling in a paddling pool. Eventually, after many steps, she was successfully desensitized to such images as dogs fornicating, French pictures of nude males, four-letter words and finally, personal coital contingencies. It became possible for her to indulge in and enjoy sexual intercourse with her husband.

Case 4

A somewhat similar case was the subject of a week-to-week demonstration to a group of psychiatric residents some years ago. The patient was a 27-year-old woman with several interpersonal neurotic problems in addition to frigidity. Her interpersonal anxieties called for teaching her to assert herself. She caught on to the idea very quickly and soon began to implement it. After the fifth session, the main thrust of therapy was turned to the frigidity. Though she had worked as an actress, and actresses are by repute rather free and easy sexually, this lady had been extremely reticent. She had often been darkly warned by her mother about the evils of sex. Those warnings had been vindicated by an attempted sexual assault by a much older man about the time of puberty. After her marriage, she had found sex unpleasant and tried as much as possible to avoid it. The essence of her problem was a tense abhorrence of the male sex organ. In treating this by desensitization, I started by having her imagine looking at a nude male statue in a park, from a distance of 30 feet. After coming progressively closer to the statue, she eventually imagined herself handling the stone penis with equanimity. The next series of scenes began with her imagining herself at one end of her bedroom and seeing her nude husband's penis 15 feet away. As desensitization proceeded, he was brought closer and closer. Then she imagined that she quickly touched the penis. With repetition this gradually stopped arousing anxiety. I then gradually increased the duration of contact. By about the 20th therapeutic session, she was enjoying sexual relations and having coital orgasms on about 50 percent of occasions.

It is quite often helpful to employ tranquilizing drugs in deconditioning the neurotic anxieties on which frigidity is based. Brady (1966), who treated frigidity by desensitization, but used intravenous Brevital as an adjuvant to relaxation, gained the impression that his cases improved more quickly than if he had used relaxation alone. If this impression is confirmed, its relevance is not likely to be confined to the special field of fridigity.

A technique has recently been described that seems to be especially applicable to subjects who are sexually arousable to a considerable and often marked extent, but who have never experienced full coital orgasm. Many of these women are easily able to have frictional clitoral orgasms—some of them even during coitus when special efforts are made to continue clitoral stimulation then. Even so, the experience is unsatisfactory because this kind of orgasm has a restricted sensory locus in contrast with the widespread excitation that characterizes a full orgasm.

An effective solution to this kind of problem seems to lie in the induction of a "clinical orgasm" by suggestion (MacVaugh, 1972). A similar procedure has been described by Rubin (1972). Rubin's schedule is considerably the simpler. The following is a summary of MacVaugh's procedure, which has the advantage of the availability of a detailed written account.

First, the patient is shown that it is possible, in general, to induce emotions—to turn on, modify and erase hate, jealousy and love by the presentation of appropriate cues. It is pointed out that an orgasm involves a kind of control of emotions. Then, some general facts about sex are discussed to combat any idea that it is unclean or sinful, and to convey that it is a mature and desirable activity which a woman should not feel ashamed to initiate. The next step consists of drawing attention to the anatomical features of the female sex organs—the sensory zones and the controlling muscles. She is made to practice contracting and relaxing these muscles. The typical sensations in the build-up of the orgasms are then described, and the comparative male and female excitation curves shown. After this, the patient is shown a list of the common colloquial words for the male and female organs, and for coitus, and is asked to read out the words until it becomes comfortable to do so, and then to put as much feeling as possible into their enunciation.

MacVaugh then goes on to show a series of slides portraying the stages in lovemaking of a Japanese couple, from their getting out of a car, through their entrance into a pagoda and bathing together, up to lying together on a Japanese floor mattress. What is emphasized throughout is that the woman initiates and controls every stage: she takes off his shoes; she does the washing in the bath. This may be of importance because of its marked differences from the female passivity which is the mode in European lovemaking, and especially notable in frigid women. MacVaugh states (1972) that his success rate has risen from 25 to 90 percent since he introduced this Japanese sequence.

After obtaining evidence of responsiveness to suggestion, MacVaugh goes on to suggest the successive steps of an imaginal lovemaking with a stimulating partner previously chosen, giving a good deal of attention to pelvic sensations, and later, when appropriate, suggesting pelvic movements. He builds upon these finally to elicit a full orgasm. The tape recordings I have heard are utterly convincing. The whole procedure takes up to about 3 hours. Once the clinical orgasm has been induced, orgasmic behavior is in the women's repertoire, available for elicitation in her real sex life. The whole of this schedule is unlikely to be always necessary, and a behavioral analysis beforehand should indicate what parts might be omitted.

Situational Frigidity

Behavior analysis often reveals that a woman who complains of frigidity is not negatively conditioned to sexual stimuli in general, but unresponsive to the particular man with whom she consorts. The question then is why she does not respond to him. In many cases, one finds that she simply does not care for him as a person. Perhaps she did once, but no longer does. One patient had fallen in love with her husband for his wisdom and erudition, only to discover after marriage that she had been misled. When his image slumped, so did her ability to respond to him erotically. But sometimes the deficiencies are not easy to define. There may be a general lack of communion. I know of nothing that can be done about this. Perhaps one day we shall have ways of making people like things that they do not like, but we do not have them now.

However, one should make every effort to identify sources of inhibition and to see whether change is possible. As a rule, one discovers something potentially changeable in the husband's behavior. It may be that he does not show his wife reasonable consideration. Perhaps he comes home from work at irregular hours without ever telling her in advance or phoning her. Such behavior can be extremely disturbing, and, if persistent, may transform a woman's attitude from affection to revulsion, and her sexual pattern from passion to frigidity. One patient in whom this has happened has a husband who is an "empire builder," busy establishing branches of his business all over the United States. He is usually out of town. When he gets home, he gives his wife scant attention, rushes out to play golf and watches baseball or football on television. Though he protests that he loves his wife (who is, in fact, very attractive) all efforts to change his behavior have failed. He has a paternalistic attitude toward her and regards her demands as childish. It is Ibsen's *A Doll's House* in the flesh. But since, for practical reasons, she cannot leave him, nobody can blame her if she takes a lover.

Fortunately, few husbands are as immovable as this one. Quite often, if the wife learns to behave with well-tempered assertiveness, the husband's behavior will also change favorably. In one case of situational frigidity, the husband, deeply involved in international affairs, treated his spouse essentially as a servant and caterer. He would bring home many visitors, often without notice, requiring her to prepare countless dinners and entertainments. Her behavior was extremely passive and compliant. In the context of assertive training I had her start structuring activities in such a way as to follow the principle: "If you will do things for me, I will do things for you." This almost at once made his attitude toward her more pleasant. The next step was for her to make a stand regarding their way of life: "This kind of living does not suit me. I cannot have people here every night. I need some personal life, and I would like you to do something about it." He acceded to this, a much closer relationship progressively developed, and a sex life gratifying to both of them.

This unilateral approach to readjustment of marriages is not always appropriate. Discord is often a matter of spiraling resentments on both sides. One partner's feelings are hurt, and he withdraws affection or retaliates against his spouse in some other way, provoking further negative behavior from the latter. It is necessary to break a vicious circle which, sometimes, has gone on for a very long while. This can only be done by some kind of contractual arrangement involving both partners. Stuart (1969) has devised a detailed program that includes a "marital contract," a written undertaking by each person to do things that the other desires, and score cards. In effect each partner is given the opportunity to learn that if he positively reinforces the other he will be compensated commensurately.

REFERENCES

Cooper, A.J., Ismail, A., Smith, C.G., and Loraine, J. Androgen function in 'psychogenic' and 'constitutional' types of impotence. *Brit. Med. J.,* 1970, July 4.

Langley, J.N. and Anderson, H.K. The innvervation of the pelvic and adjoining viscera, *J. Physiol.,* 1895, **19**:71.

MacVaugh, G. *Frigidity: Successful Treatment in One Hypnotic Imprint Session with the Oriental Relaxation Technique.* New York, Medcon Inc., 1972.

Masters, W.H. and Johnson, V.E. *Human Sexual Response.* Boston, Little, Brown, 1966.

Masters, W.H. and Johnson, V.E. *Human Sexual Inadequacy.* Boston, Little, Brown, 1970.

Napalkov, A.V. and Karas, A.Y. Elimination of pathological conditioned reflex connections in experimental hypertensive states. *Zh. Vyssh. Nerv. Deiat.,* 1957, **7**:402.

Razani, J. Ejaculatory incompetence treated by deconditioning anxiety. *J. Behav. Ther. Exp. Psychiat.,* 1972, **3**:65.

Rubin, M. Verbally suggested responses as reciprocal inhibition of anxiety. *J. Behav. Ther. Exp. Psychiat.,* 1972, **3**:273.

Semans, J.H. Premature ejaculation, a new approach. *South Med. J.,* 1956, **49**:353.

Semans, J.H. Personal communication, 1962.

Stuart, R.B. Operant-interpersonal treatment for marital discord. *J. Consult. Clin. Psychol.,* 1969, **33**:675.

Wolpe, J. *Psychotherapy by Reciprocal Inhibition.* Stanford, Stanford University Press, 1958.

7
Systematic Desensitization in Sexual Disorders*

MARTIN OBLER

Systematic desensitization has recently been extended to the treatment of sexual disorders in two ways: a) to attack directly the symptomatic dysfunction: and b) to desensitize indirectly anxiety related to social and sexual activity (Garfield et al., 1969; Kraft, 1967; Lazarus, 1965). Both of the above approaches are based on Wolpe's (1958) reciprocal inhibition theory and use muscle relaxation (Jacobson, 1932) or drug-induced relaxation (Brady, 1966) as the major counteracting response to social and sexual anxieties, with high rates of reported success (Wolpe, 1969).

Masters and Johnson's (1969) success can also be interpreted within the framework of reciprocal inhibition theory. Their patients are taught to experience sexually arousing responses and muscle relaxation through the use of body creams, massages and the establishment of a relaxed environment during coital experiences, producing effects similar to those of relaxation exercises. The major therapeutic focus is relaxation during sexual activity to counteract inappropriately learned responses.

Despite the rather formidable literature on systematic desensitization with sexual disorders (Wolpe, 1969), few studies have used adequate control conditions, sufficient sample size or objective physiological and cognitive measures of dependent variable change to determine the efficacy of the intervention. Frank (1959) and Paul (1966) have suggested that these methodological deficiences are characteristic of most psychotherapeutic studies, the effects of interviewing (Goldstein, 1960), "experimenter demand characteristics" (Rosenthal, 1958) and "criterion problems" (Bergin, 1963) typically not even being considered. Further, Yates (1970) points out, these deficiencies are even more apparent in sexual research because of our inability to observe dependent variable change directly, due to the cultural stigma surrounding sexuality. Paul's (1966) model for measuring the efficacy of particular therapeutic interventions can be used to overcome these limitations in sexual anxiety research. His model emphasizes multi-dependent variable measures evaluated in conjunction with subjective patient and partner reports of

*This article is based on a dissertation submitted to the faculty of New School for Social Research in partial fulfillment of the requirement for the PH.D. degree.

therapeutic effectiveness, and comparison with control conditions comprising alternative interventions.

Accordingly, a behavior therapy study focusing on sexual anxiety was conducted with the following objectives: a) to investigate the efficacy of systematic desensitization in eliminating specific sexual dysfunctions, namely premature ejaculation, ejaculatory incompetence and secondary impotence in males and primary and secondary orgasmic dysfunction in females;[1] b) to refine and modify the technique through combining the indirect (assertive and confidence training in social situations) and direct approaches (hierarchy and relaxation training); c) to compare these modifications to comparable non-behavioristic treatment and control groups, while controlling for the effects of interviewing, testing and individual difference variables (i.e., extroversion-introversion, emotionality, age, motivation and educational status); and d) to apply the principle of multi-dependent variable agreement where direct observation is not possible.

METHOD

Subject Selection

Sixty-four subjects were selected from a population of 235 volunteers on the basis of their scores on the Taylor Manifest Anxiety Scale (TMAS)[2] and information obtained at an initial interview session pertaining to the etiology and development of their sexual dysfunction. The volunteers were directly referred by professional clinicians from community-based psychotherapeutic clinics and counseling services at major universities in the New York City area. In addition, personal referrals were made by the graduate faculty and student body at the New School for Social Research. In all instances the referral sources were familiar with the research criteria for acceptability to treatment. Two independent clinicians reviewed the initial interview reports and rated Ss according to the following criteria: a) presence of sexual dysfunction under study; b) absence of other related psychological (i.e., hysteria, schizophrenia) or physiological disorder (i.e., curvature of cervix, vaginismus); c) at least 1 year of college; d) high motivation for treatment; e) average or above intelligence. The ratings were based on information obtained from a standardized interview questionnaire which elicited information regarding patient and parental attitudes toward sex, conditions under which the dysfunction developed and related medical and psychological factors.[3] Ss meeting these criteria were then classified into three matched groups each containing equivalent classification of dysfunction, marital status and duration of symptom. Each group contained 22 matched subjects and received one of the following treatments: Systematic Desensitization Therapy (SD- 13F, 9M), Traditional Group Therapy (GT- 11F, 9M), and No-Treatment

---

[1] *See* Masters & Johnson (1969) for definitions of these disorders.

[2] Subjects were acceptable if scores fell below 34 on the TMAS (Taylor, 1958). Standardization has indicated a median score of 34 for psychotics and 13 for normals.

[3] Detailed information on the rating scales, and procedures used for subject selection are available on microfilm at the New School for Social Research library, 65 Fifth Avenue, N.Y.C., or by writing the author directly to the Department of Educational Services, Brooklyn College, Brooklyn, New York.

Control (NT- 13F, 9M). Two GT subjects elected to discontinue participation in the research when informed of their placement in group treatment.

Test Procedure

Ss were seen on two separate occasions prior to exposure to treatment. On the first occasion all Ss completed a pre-test battery consisting of the Pittsburgh Scale of Extroversion-Introversion and Emotionality (PSEI), Sexual Anxiety Scale (SAS), Anxiety Differential (ADS). In addition, SD and GT Ss received base level Galvanic Skin Response (GSR) and Heart Rate (HR) measures. The tests were administered to determine pretreatment levels of cognitively experienced sexual and social anxieties and their physiological correlates. On the second occasion Ss were instructed to keep a careful record of their successful and unsuccessful sexual experiences as defined by a success-experience form supplied to each subject (e.g., premature ejaculation—success defined as the ability to withhold ejaculation for a period of at least 2 minutes). This form was also mailed to S's sexual partner to corroborate the patient's reports. A second GSR-HR was administered during this occasion while Ss watched a sexual film specifically portraying their dysfunction (e.g., impotent males observing difficulty in erection during coitus).

A post-treatment battery was administered 15 weeks later consisting of all the above scales exclusive of the PSEI. During this time SD Ss were treated at 45-minute weekly sessions, GT Ss at 1½ hour weekly meetings for 10 weeks and NT controls had no further research involvement. Comparison of group changes on the pre-post measures in conjunction with changes in success-experience ratios were assumed to represent the differential effectiveness of the three experimental conditions. Further, these comparisons allowed for the isolation of testing and interview effects, time factors and experimenter demand.

[handwritten marginal notes: ① Systematic desensitization group therapy ② traditional ③ no treatment / 3 groups]

Description of Tests

PSEI (Bendig, 1962). Administered only during pre-treatment battery in modified form on a scale of 0-30, higher scores indicating greater emotionality and extroversion. Used for inter-correlation of personality variables with anxiety test scores and success in treatment.

SAS. Developed by the investigator to measure cognitively experienced social and sexual anxieties. The scale consists of 22 items in separate forms for males and females and has a 0.92 reliability coefficient and a 0.62 validity coefficient with intensity of sexual dysfunction. Items ranged from anxiety experienced during contact with a member of the opposite sex to intra-vaginal penetration.

ADS (Husek & Alexander, 1962). Used to measure situational anxiety to specific stimulus conditions causing momentary stress. Administered immediately after subjects were exposed to a new sexual film portraying instances of sexual stress (i.e., woman unable to achieve orgasm).

GSR. Recordings were taken on a B.S.R. Foringer 802 machine monitored at 8 V and calibrated in μA on a scale of 0-200. Ss were measured at the first session for base level without exposure to any external stimuli and at the 2nd, 4th and 15th sessions upon exposure to highly intense films portraying sexual failure situations (i.e., female unable to feel arousal). NT controls did not receive this measure during the pre-treatment testing but were exposed to a separate GSR percent change recording during post-testing administered under equivalent conditions. This measure was taken on a GSR 801 monitoring device at 1½ minutes intervals during exposure to a new 15-minute sexual film.[4] A mean of the 10 readings was computed to determine a final GSR level response after treatment intervention.

TREATMENT

The treatment was a modified version of systematic desensitization, (Wolpe, 1958). It was administered to individual subjects by the researcher under standardized conditions at 45-minute weekly sessions. During the first session S's sexual history was reviewed with special emphasis on experienced anxiety during social and sexual encounters. Ss were told that their dysfunctions were a direct result of previous anxiety learning in sexual situations and could be unlearned by working on the situations in which they experienced sexual anxiety. Hierarchy training was explained to Ss and related to their actual sexual exposure during the preceding week. Further, each S was instructed to refrain from any sexual encounter that had induced subjective anxiety during a therapy session. For example, if S experienced anxiety while imagining a member of the opposite sex naked, he was asked to refrain from this experience until no anxiety was felt under desensitization.

At the second session Ss were trained in muscle relaxation using Paul's (1966) abridged version of Jacobson's (1932) technique. Individual hierarchy items were presented for a duration of 30-60 seconds and repeated twice, at 1-minute intervals. The duration of presentation was increased from the usual standard procedure because many Ss were not successful in imagining the item during a shorter duration. Approximately 8-10 items were presented at each session from least to most disturbing. Hierarchy items initially averaged approximately 12 per subject with additional items added at later sessions whenever appropriate. The new items were drawn from the S's actual experienced sexual anxiety during the week. However, hierarchies never exceeded 25 items, and in every instance Ss avoided the actual sexual activity that induced anxiety until anxiety was no longer experienced under desensitization. A further modification consisted of using graphic aids (films or slides of sexual encounters) to portray the S's dysfunction. The aids were introduced at proper intervals in the hierarchy when S had difficulty imagining a particular item (i.e., male's failure to maintain an erection).[5] Further, specific aids were selected that portrayed sex difficulties consistent with an individual's actual experienced anxieties during a given week (i.e., actual inability to achieve vaginal penetration). The instruction to abstain from sexual experiences inducing anxiety resulted in Ss experiencing little or no anxiety during their actual sexual interaction, because participation was only allowed for those encounters already desensitized. (The absence of anxiety

[4] The monitoring device is designed by B.R.S. Foringer, Inc., Beltsville, Maryland, and is accurate at ±20 percent reading with an input resistance range of 20k-120k.

[5] A detailed description of the graphic aids and the procedures used for presentation are available at B.R.S. Foringer, Inc., Beltsville, Maryland.

provides optimum conditions for sexual performance and arousal. Since the turn of the century, biologists have sufficiently documented the implications of anxiety as a deterrent to sexual arousal.[6])

At the sixth session each S received assertive training (Salter, 1949) and confidence training (Susskind, 1970) to overcome anxiety related to social functioning with members of the opposite sex. The training was repeated at the 8th, 10th and 12th sessions with Ss role-playing and imagining successful achievement in actual social situations. For example, a female unable to establish social relations with males was trained to assert herself in conditions conducive to dating. Ss suffering from negative self-images or social inferiority received confidence training by inserting items of assertiveness and self confidence within the desensitization hierarchy until no anxiety was experienced in actual social situations. This was measured by weekly verbal reports concerning S's ability to more successfully confront previously experienced social situations without feeling withdrawn, dejected, or rejected. Further, items of assertiveness and self-confidence were role-played and imagined in sexual situations related to the dysfunction. For example, a female terrified of experiencing physical pain during vaginal penetration imagined and role-played facing this situation with confidence and ease.

The physiological measures—galvanic skin response and heart rate (GSR and HR)—were correlated with the Ss subjectively felt anxiety as a further indication of actual elimination of specific situational anxieties. Ss who reported experiencing no anxiety to specific items continued desensitization to them until the physiological correlates indicated its elimination. All Ss completed the 15 treatment sessions irrespective of earlier successful symptom reduction or elimination.

Group Therapy

Traditional group therapy was conducted by two trained psychotherapists who followed their typical approaches used in daily work with neurotically anxious patients.[7] Both therapists were unaware of the purposes of the research or the criteria used for selection of Ss. Throughout they remained independent of the behaviorial approach. Two groups were formed, each containing 10 subjects with the focus on fostering open discussion of Ss' sexual and social problems. In addition, emphasis was placed on analytical interpretations of etiology and recommendations for overcoming the dysfunc-tion. The therapists initially assumed a supportive, non-judgmental attitude, helping subjects gain greater insight and reduce misconceptions surrounding sexuality. As members became more active, the therapists switched to the roles of analyzer and interpreter of underlying dynamics and repressions. All sessions were tape-recorded and independently rated to insure procedural regularity. Both therapists rated their methods as Neo-Freudian (see Fenichel, 1945). During the 2nd, 4th and 10th sessions, the groups were shown the same films and slides as seen by SD Ss, and their reactions were

---

[6]See Langley & Anderson (1895) for a detailed discussion on anxiety as a sympathetic nervous system response which interferes with sexual arousal. Arousal is characterized by a parasympathetic function (involuntary response) and assumes a secondary role under stress conditions.

[7]The author is indebted to Dr. Robert Slotnick of Richmond College and Mr. Martin Becker of Brooklyn College for their participation.

incorporated into the therapy sessions. This procedure also served to insure equivalent adaptation and exposure to the sexual graphic aids. The conditions of exposure to all test and physiological measures were equivalent for all Ss.

RESULTS

Pre-post success/experience ratio changes for individual Ss provide the most direct and stringent measure of treatment effectiveness. Table 1 shows the success to experience sexual ratio for all Ss in both treatment and control groups over the treatment period. The individual S's ratio changes, as well as the group mean changes, indicate the differential effects of the treatment and control interventions. Inspection of Table 1 reveals that 42 percent of the female and 61 percent of the male SD sexual attempts were successful as compared to only 2/3 percent of the NT attempts (M and F) and 3 percent of the GT attempts. Significance differences for these comparisons on the Wilcoxon (1945) Sum of Ranks Test were at the 0·0005 level for females, 0·05 level for males (combines NT and GT ranks) and 0·0001 level for total group. Subject ratios correlated at a +0·89 level (N=117) with partner(s) reports.

Table 1. Success Experience Ratios for All Desensitization, Group Therapy and No-Treatment Control Subjects over Treatment Period (N=64)

Subject	Desensitization Females N = 13 Success	Experience	Ratio	Subject	Group Therapy Females N = 11 Success	Experience	Ratio	Subject	No-Treatment Control Females N = 13 Success	Experience	Ratio
D1	20	53	0·38	G1	0	28	—	C1	0	30	—
D2	0	14	—	G2	1	13	0·08	C3	0	0	—
D3	10	57	0·18	G3	0	34	—	C6	0	26	—
D4	12	33	0·36	G5	0	2	—	C7	0	15	—
D5	11	15	0·73	G6	0	41	—	C8	0	58	—
D6	2	8	0·25	G7	0	30	—	C9	1	17	0·06
D7	21	62	0·34	G8	0	0	—	C10	0	46	—
D8	25	31	0·81	G9	5	106	0·05	C11	0	30	—
D9	10	28	0·36	G10	0	20	—	C12	0	0	—
D10	32	42	0·76	G11	2	24	0·08	C13	3	58	0·05
D11	54	85	0·64	G12	1	13	0·08	C14	0	0	—
D12	18	41	0·40					C15	0	3	—
D13	0	52						C20	1	12	0·08
F	217	521	0·42(1)	F	9	311	0·03	F	5	291	0·02
Males N = 9				Males N = 9				Males N = 9			
D18	0	0	—	G17	0	35	—	C4	1	1	1·00
D19	14	30	0·47	G18	0	85	—	C5	0	45	—
D20	10	14	0·71	G19	0	4	—	C16	1	31	0·03
D21	12	29	0·41	G20	3	5	0·60	C17	0	0	—
D22	6	9	0·67	G21	0	1	—	C18	0	0	—
D23	16	16	1·00	G22	1	3	0·33	C19	0	0	—
D24	13	19	0·68	G23	0	72	—	C21	0	14	—
D25	6	11	0·55	G24	3	54	0·06	C22	0	30	—
D26	0	0	—	G25	0	5	—	C25	2	70	0·03
M	78	128	0·61(2)	M	7	264	0·03	M	4	191	0·03
Totals N = 22				Totals N = 20				Totals N = 22			
ET	295	649	0·45(3)	ET	16	575	0·03	ET	9	482	0·02

Note: (1) P=0·0005 level of significance for females on the Wilcoxon Sum of Ranks Test—for comparison between desensitization and control conditions. (2) P=0·10 for males; but for desensitization versus group and control combined=0·05 level. (3) P=0·0001 level of significance for the total groups.

Table 1 further reveals that female SD subjects attempted more sexual encounters (521-311 Female GT and 291 NT) with greater number of successes (217-9 and 5, respectively), as contrasted to their male counterparts who, although attempting fewer experiences (128-264 male GT and 191 NT) achieved greater success (78-7 and 4, respectively). An analysis of the week-to-week ratio changes revealed that although each group began at approximately the same ratio level early in treatment, by the 6th week SD's were consistently superior in overcoming their dysfunctions to either control condition. The ineffectiveness of group therapy in eliminating sexual dysfunctions is evident. Its success rate did not significantly differ from the NT control. Nonspecific attention during testing and interviewing (NT exposure) appears to result in an equivalent level of symptom elimination (two successes per condition).

Physiological Measures

Shifts in GSR-HR rates were consistent with SD and GT changes in success/ experience ratios. The mean scores for female, male and total group comparisons appear in Table 2 for measures 1-4. Although base and initial sexual stimuli exposure rates (GSR 2-HR 2) are essentially equivalent early in treatment, the reduction in anxiety level is much greater for SD Ss by the 4th (SDX=37; GTX=72) and final treatment session (SDX=25; GTX=60). HR changes correlated 0·96 with GSR 2-4 reductions and are therefore identical indices in reflecting anxiety level changes. In fact, GT Ss recorded a higher level HR measure at the end of treatment than when they began ($\bar{X}$ of 79-83). A Wilcoxon Significance test analysis indicated a 5 percent level ($P=0·05$) for GSR-GR female comparisons and a 1 percent level ($P=0·01$) for male comparisons.

GSR percentage change recordings for all experimental conditions at the end of treatment further reflects the greater effectiveness of desensitization in reducing sexual

Table 2. Means of Galvanic Skin Response and Heart-rate Scores for Measures I-IV; Means of Galvanic Skin Response Percentage Change at the Last Session of Treatment

Group	Sex	Size N	GSR 1 (Baseline) (recording)	GSR 2	GSR 3*	GSR 4*	HR 1 (Baseline) (recording)	HR 2*	HR 3*	HR 4*	GSR % Change
Systematic	Female	13	21·23	100·36	36·82	26·27	75	79	76	75	18·93
Desensitization	Male	9	22·37	89·30	37·81	25·30	75	81	74	72	20·53
	Total	22	21·70	95·83	37·22	25·86	75	80	75	74	19·57
Group	Female	11	21·90	85·55	73·94	60·27	76	81	80	79	36·72
Therapy	Male	9	21·96	77·52	71·15	61·22	83	87	88	87	43·83
	Total	20	24·63	81·93	72·68	60·53	79	84	84	83	39·92
No-Treatment	Female	13									
Control	Male	9									37·20
	Total	22									36·60

Note: GSR percent change indicates $\bar{X}$ for the groups at the last session—upon exposure to new stimulus conditions (new sexual film).

*Changes from GSR (and HR)2-3, 3-4 are significant at the 0·05 level for females and the 0·01 level for males; for comparison between systematic desensitization and group therapy subjects.

anxiety. SD female, male and total group means were consistently lower than the GT and NT conditions (F-$\overline{X}$=18 to 36-36; M-$\overline{X}$=20 to 43-37; total -$\overline{X}$=19 to 39-36, respectively) while GT Ss had a non-significantly higher rate than the NT control. If adaptation to experimental conditions (films and therapy) were a factor then it would be difficult to explain the higher GSR rate for GT Ss as compared to NT Ss who received less previous film exposure.

Cognitive Measures

The pre-treatment PSEI (Pittsburg Scale of Emotionality) mean for all groups ranged between 14 and 16, suggesting that the sexual dysfunctional Ss were not as introverted, shy or overemotional as anticipated. Individual PSEI scores did not significantly correlate with either elimination of dysfunction or changes in physiological or cognitive anxiety (coefficients – R=+0·05 success/experience, –0·02 ADS, +0·10 TMAS, +0·12 SAS, +0·01 GSR-HR). The only variable which correlated significantly was age of subject with introversion (R=+0·91) suggesting that Ss who are older have lived with the dysfunction for a longer period of time and thus are likely to be more withdrawn.

Mean changes on the pre-post anxiety scales appear in Table 3. Significance comparisons on the SAS scale indicate that female SD subjects significantly reduced their sexual anxiety as compared to NT controls (P=0·0005) but only approached significance with GT controls (P=0·05). Total group and male comparisons, however, indicate significantly reduced sexual anxiety for SD subjects as compared to either control condition. On the TMAS (manifest anxiety) female SD subjects again reduced general anxiety as compared to their NT counterparts (P=0·05) but not in comparison to GT subjects (P=40). Total group and male comparisons indicate no significant manifest

Table 3. Means and Mean Differences of Pre-Post Scores for Taylor Manifest Anxiety, Sexual Anxiety and Anxiety Differential Scales. Mean Scores for Extroversion-Introversion and Emotionality Scales

Group	N	Taylor Manifest Anxiety			Anxiety Differential			Sexual Anxiety Scale			PSEI E-I	PSEI Em
		Pre	Post	Δ	Pre	Post	Δ	Pre	Post	Δ	Pre	Pre
Systematic	F 13	21	19	2	102	88	14*	6	2	4*	15	18
Desensitization	M 9	23	19	4	·107	103	4*	10	6	4*	14	22
	T 22	22	19	3	106	94	12*	8	4	4*	15	20
Group Therapy	F 11	23	22	1	105	110	-5	6	6	0	15	20
	M 9	23	18	3	110	113	-3	9	8	1	14	20
	T 20	23	20	3	108	112	-4	7	6	1	14	20
No-Treatment control	F 13	20	21	-1	100	102	-2	6	7	-1	14	17
	M 9	24	23	1	106	105	1	10	10	0	12	22
	T 22	22	23	-1	102	103	-1	8	8	0	13	19

Note: Comparisons are given for male, female and total groups. Minus signs indicate an increase in Pre-Post Means.

*Difference in Pre-Post Means are significant on at least the 5 percent level (P<0·05) on the Wilcoxon Sum of Ranks Test for comparisons between systematic desensitization and group therapy or no-treatment control groups. The asterisk indicates significance in comparison to both control conditions.

anxiety reduction among all conditions. Apparently the modified SD method is equivalent to group therapy in reducing non-related sexual anxieties but more effective in reducing specifically sexual and social anxieties. Further, female subjects appear to receive similar benefits from both treatment interventions in reducing manifest anxiety. An analysis of the ADS scale significance results (specific sexual stress) further lends support to the above interpretation. Both male and female SD subjects significantly reduced specific sexual anxieties as compared to their GT and NT counterparts (GT-P=0·05 and 0·03 respectively; NT-P=0·02 and 0·01). It appears that the modified treatment is highly effective in attacking anxieties directly related to the dysfunction.

DISCUSSION

Systematic agreement among the multiple dependent variable measures lends support to the contention that modified SD is superior to group therapy or no treatment in eliminating sexual dysfunctions, reducing related situational and social anxieties and lowering physiological response (anxiety) to sexual stimulation. Over 80 percent (18 out of 22) of SD subjects became sexually functional; and a follow-up study conducted 1½ years later has indicated no regression. In contrast, GT subjects were equivalent to Ss receiving no formal therapy in sexual functioning (approximately a 0·025 success rate per group) and only slightly more successful in reducing sexual anxiety (see Table 3). This finding lends support to the position that the non-specific aspects of attention and interest shown during testing and interviewing with the no-treatment controls could actually be therapeutic and demonstrate similar rates of improvement as formal psychotherapy (Bergin, 1963; Eysenck, 1952; Frank, 1961; Rosenweig, 1954). A study comparing SD Ss exposed to both the modified method and testing (interviewing) with SD Ss not exposed to the latter could effectively isolate out the significance of this variable.

A most important finding of this study was the therapeutic effectiveness of combining the direct and indirect SD approaches with graphic aid hierarchy presentation. Eighty-two percent of the Ss improved in their sexual functioning in 15 or fewer treatment sessions using rigorously defined selection and success criteria procedures. Theoretically the assertion, confidence and graphic aid modifications were directed toward augmenting elicitation of inhibited sexual responses by encouraging participation in appropriate social and sexual encounters. Once elicited, these responses counteracted concurrently evoked conditioned anxiety responses in the same way as desensitization eliminates the autonomic effects that accompany anxiety through the counteracting effect of deep relaxation (Jacobson, 1938). The exact physiological relationship between anxiety and the inhibition of sexual arousal is not completely understood, but sufficient evidence exists to show that higher levels of anxiety lead to greater sexual impairment (Masters & Johnson, 1966).

Typically, formal desensitization is difficult to implement with individuals having problems in imagining highly anxious items or transferring imagined items into reality (Dengrove, 1968). The use of graphic aids accelerated the treatment process by eliminating the former problem while the assertion and confidence modification attacked the latter. Additionally, the use of physiological correlates of subjective anxiety overcame the problem of total dependency on patient reports during desensitization. Many Ss reported experiencing no anxiety to specific hierarchy items although the GSR recording indicated its continued presence. Recent clinical evidence has suggested that objective feedback information on patients' emotional and physical states is an invaluable source of therapeutic information (Budzynski & Stoyva, 1970).

Unanswered, however, is the question of what exactly is measured by the changes in GSR-HR recordings. The inferred construct of increased anxiety to sexual film exposure was based on logical considerations; but both sexual arousal and anxiety may have contributed to these measures. Further research is required to quantify the relative contributions of these components.

The small frequency of sexual attempts by male Ss during the study is comprehensible because males with sexual difficulties experience greater anxiety and social pressure than females with similar problems. The image of masculinity depends on an ability to satisfy sexual partners, and it is more difficult for men to hide difficulties in erection and ejaculation than for females to simulate an orgasm. This difference in sexual apprehension may be reflected in the greater number of attempts and successes for female Ss.

In conclusion, the current study appears to provide a useful model for investigating and improving the effects of systematic desensitization in eliminating sexual dysfunctions. The criteria measures and treatment methodology are sufficiently precise to allow for close replications to take into account the following limitations: a) administration of treatment by the researcher; b) absence of placebo control groups to isolate the effects of treatment from discrimination learning and modeling (Miller & Dollard, 1950; Bandura, 1968); and c) unequal treatment conditions for SD and GT groups—individual versus group treatment.

REFERENCES

Bandura, A., Blanchard, E.D. & Ritter, B. *The relative efficacy of desentitization and modeling approaches for inducing behavioral, affective and attitudinal changes.* Unpublished manuscript, Stanford University, 1968.

Bendig, A.W. The Pittsburgh scales of social extroversion-introversion and emotionality. *J. Psychol.,* 1962, **53**, 199-209.

Bergin, A.E. The effects of psychotherapy; Negative results revisited. *J. Counseling Psychol.,* 1963, **10**, 244-250.

Brady, J.P. Brevital-relaxation treatment of frigidity. *Behav. Res. & Therapy,* 1966, **4**, 71-77.

Budzynski, T. & Stoyva, J. *Biofeedback techniques in behavior therapy.* Unpublished thesis, University of Colorado Medical Center, 1970.

Dengrove, E. Personal communication to J. Wolpe. Cited in *Practice of Behavior Therapy.* New York: Pergamon Press, 1969.

Eysenck, H.J. The effects of psychotherapy: An evaluation. *J. consult. Psychol.,* 1952, **16**, 319-324.

Fenichel, O. *The psychoanalytic theory of neuroses.* New York: Morton, 1945.

Frank, J.D. The dynamics of the psychotherapeutic relationship; Determinants and effects of therapist's influence. *Psychiatry,* 1961, **22**, 17-40.

Frank, J.D. Problems of controls in psychotherapy. *Research in psychotherapy* (Ed. by Rubinstein, E.A. and Parloff, M.B.). Washington: D.C., American Psychological Association, 1959.

Garfield, Z.H., McBreaty, J.F. & Dichter, M. A case of impotence successfully treated with desensitization combined with *in vivo* operant training and thought substitution. *Advances in behavior therapy* (Ed. by Rubin, R. & Franks, C.M.). New Academic Press, 1969, 97-103.

Goldstein, A.P. Patient's expectancies and nonspecific therapy as a basis for un-spontaneous remission. *J. clin. Psychol.*, 1960, **16**, 399-403.

Jacobson, E. *Progressive relaxation.* Chicago: Chicago University Press, 1938.

Kraft, T.A. (1967) A case of homosexuality treated by systematic desensitization. *Am. J. Psychother.*, **21**, 815-821.

Kraft, T.A. & Al-Issa, I. Behavior therapy and the treatment of frigidity. *Am. J. Psychother.*, **21**, *1967, 116-120.*

Lazarus, A.A. The treatment of a sexually inadequate man. *Case studies in behavior Modification* (Ed. by Ullmann, L.P. & Krasner, L.). New York: Holt, Rinehart & Winston, 1965, 243-245.

Masters, W.H. & Johnson, V.E. *Human sexual response.* Boston: Little, Brown, 1966.

Masters, W.H. & Johnson, V.E. *Human sexual inadequacy.* Boston: Little, Brown, 1969.

Miller, N.E. & Dollard, J. *Personality and psychotherapy: An analysis in terms of learning, thinking and culture.* New York: McGraw-Hill, 1950.

Paul, G.L. *Insight vs desensitization in psychotherapy.* Stanford: Stanford University Press, 1966.

Rosenweig, S. A transvaluation of psychotherapy. A reply to Hans Eysenck. *J. abnorm. Social Psychol.*, 1954, **49**, 298-304.

Rosenthal, D. & Frank, J.D. Psychotherapy and the placebo effect. *Psychopathology: A source book* (Ed. by Reid, C.F., Alexander, I.E. & Tompkins, S.S.). Cambridge: Harvard University Press, 1958.

Salter, A. *Conditioned reflex therapy.* New York: Capricorn Books, 1949, 78.

Susskind, D.J. The idealized self-image: A new technique in confidence training. *Behav. Therapy,* 1970, **1**, 538-541.

Wilcoxon, F. *Biometrics Bulletin.* 1945, 80-85.

Wolpe, J. *Psychotherapy by reciprocal inhibition.* Stanford: Stanford University Press, 1958.

Wolpe, J. *The Practice of behavior therapy.* New York: Pergamon Press, 1969.

Yates, A.J. *Behavior Therapy.* New York: Wiley, 1970.

8
The PLISSIT Model: A Proposed Conceptual Scheme for the Behavioral Treatment of Sexual Problems*

JACK S. ANNON

The psychological treatment of sexual problems has been known to be costly and time-consuming, and, in the past, the prognosis for change was not very encouraging. With the advent of a learning oriented, or behavioral approach to treatment, more successful therapeutic results have been obtained in resolving such problems that have long been known to be resistant to other forms of therapy. Although this model has produced some promising results, its application to sexual disorders has been relatively recent, and there is a clear need for a broad spectrum approach which allows the clinician a wide range of therapeutic procedures for implementing his treatment strategy. On the other hand, use of a particular procedure just because it is available is obviously not therapeutically justified. Careful assessment of relevant factors in the client's life, history, and environment should dictate which treatment procedure to use for which aspect of the client's problem in a given social setting.

In other words, initial assessment should have a direct relationship to the treatment procedures used. Contrast this approach with that of many sex therapy clinics who do a comprehensive and exhaustive initial assessment only to have their clients all go through the exact same therapy program. In such standardized programs, it is difficult to see what purpose the initial intensive assessment serves.

It should also be made clear that the current stress by many behavior therapists on a broad spectrum approach to therapy has no virtue unless there is some theoretically based plan for the ordering and selection of appropriate treatment techniques from among the various therapeutic interventions now available. Without such a plan, broad spectrum treatment is just as much a shotgun approach as is using the same one or two procedures for all problems. As a step in this direction, and due to the prevalence of sexual problems and the difficulties associated with their resolution, it was considered of practical as well as theoretical value to design and carry out a study to investigate methods of assessment and treatment in this area.

*Revised from a paper presented at the annual meeting of the Society for the Scientific Study of Sex, Las Vegas, November, 1974.

RESEARCH BACKGROUND

Such research was carried out (Annon, 1971) with the goal of developing, testing and refining a conceptual scheme for the ordering of sexual problems and their treatment from within a learning theory framework. The major conclusion of the research was that an initial analysis of a client's sexual problem from within the A-R-D framwork advanced by Staats (1968, 1970, 1975) *followed* by a behavioral diagnosis of relevant behavioral repertoires, offered the most promising learning-based approach for the ordering of sexual concerns and the development of appropriate therapeutic strategies.

This conclusion was based on a number of considerations. The use of the scheme offered a plan for simultaneously considering the full range of circumstances that might be related to the client's problem. Such an approach also allowed for the ordering of priorities for intervention and provided guidance for the timing of multiple interventions. Finally, the use of such a conceptual scheme was not tied to any particular behavioral technique or procedure, but fostered the development of efficient procedures based upon theoretical analysis.

CLINICAL BACKGROUND

Use of the conceptual scheme in clinical practice provided additional evidence that the approach was highly effective in developing and ordering relevant interventions resulting in positive outcomes, particularly with those sexual problems of long-term duration (e.g., pedophiliac, transsexual, fetishistic, etc.). However, as others attempted to use the approach in different settings with different problems, it gradually became apparent that the scheme was not always appropriate, and there seemed to be three main reasons for this situation: a) use of the system was not suited to those settings where the client could not be seen on an ongoing, possibly long-term basis; b) effective use of the system was restricted to those who had a thorough knowledge of learning theory together with relevant training and experience in behavioral methods of treatment; and c) even those with suitable training and experience who worked in settings where they had sufficient time available reported that the use of the scheme was often unnnecessary for treating some of the more common problems such as those concerned with arousal, ejaculation, erection or orgasm.

In sum, the conceptual scheme was appropriate for those problems requiring intensive therapy, but not for those which could profit from a brief therapy approach. What was needed was a more flexible and comprehensive scheme that could be adapted to many settings and to whatever client time was available. To be most effective, such a plan should also be able to be used by a wide variety of people in the helping professions and allow for a range of treatment choices geared to the level of competence of the individual clinician. Ideally, the approach also needed to provide a framework for screening out and treating those problems that would be responsive to brief therapy approaches and those that would require intensive therapy.

After further experience in devising and testing a number of different plans in diverse settings with a variety of sexual problems, a conceptual scheme that looked promising was finally developed. This tentative scheme was then shared and taught to others, and, after further refinement, the final model emerged. Since that time this model has been passed on to others via lectures, courses, consultations, workshops and training programs. It appears that many in the helping professions have found it to be useful, as it is currently being employed by: health aides, clergymen, nurses, paraprofessionals in a range of disciplines, physicians from diverse specialties, practical nurses, psychiatrists, psychologists, school counselors and social workers.

THE PLISSIT MODEL

As an aid to memory, this conceptual scheme is referred to as the PLISSIT model or more accurately: P-LI-SS-IT. The model provides for four levels of approach, and each letter or pair of letters designates a suggested method for handling presenting sexual concerns. The four levels are: Permission — Limited Information — Specific Suggestions — Intensive Therapy. A visual presentation of the proposed model may help clarify how it may be applied in a variety of clinical settings. Let each line in Fig. 1 represent the different presenting sexual concerns that a particular clinician encounters over time. Depending upon his setting, profession and specialty, these problems may represent what he meets in one day, one month, one year or even one professional lifetime. For reasons previously discussed, it would obviously be inappropriate to attempt to assess and treat each presenting sexual concern in exactly the same way.

Figure 2 depicts the theoretical application of the P-LI-SS-IT model to these presenting sexual concerns. As Fig. 2 further illustrates, the first three levels can be viewed as *brief therapy* as contrasted with the fourth level, *intensive therapy.*

Utilization of this model has a number of distinct advantages. It may be used in a variety of settings and adapted to whatever client time is available. Theoretically, each descending level of approach requires increasing degrees of knowledge, training and skill on the part of the clinician. Because each level requires increasing professional experience, the model thus allows the individual to gear his approach to his own particular level of competence. This also means that the clinician now has a plan which aids him in determining when referral elsewhere is appropriate. Most important, the model provides a framework for discriminating between those problems which require intensive therapy and those which are responsive to brief therapy.

How many levels of approach a particular clinician will feel competent to use will directly depend upon the amount of interest and time he is willing to devote to expanding his knowledge, training and skill at each level. The remainder of this paper will be devoted to brief practical suggestions on how to apply the four levels of treatment.

The First Level of Treatment: Permission

Sometimes, all that people want to know is that they are normal, that they are okay, that they are not "perverted," "deviated" or "abnormal" and that there is nothing wrong with them. Mostly, they would like to find this out from someone with a professional background or from someone who is in a position of authority to know. Many times these people are not bothered by the specific behavior that they are engaging in, but they are bothered by the thought that there may be something "wrong" or "bad" with what they are doing. Frequently, clients just want an interested professional to act as a

A Proposed Conceptual Scheme

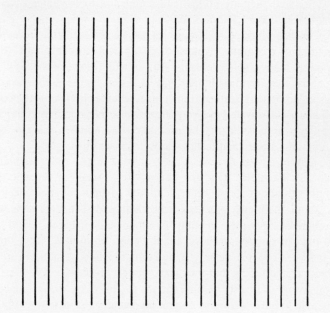

Fig. 1. Presenting Sexual Concerns Over Time

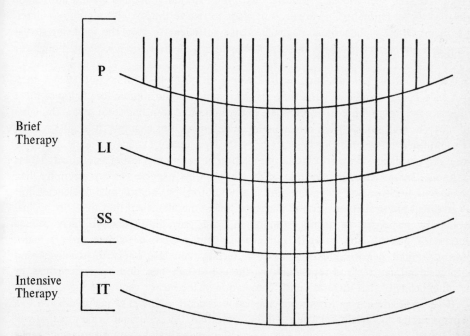

Fig. 2. Application of the P-LI-SS-IT Model

sounding board for checking out their concerns. In other cases, the clinician can let them know that they are not alone or unusual in their concerns and that many people share them. Reassurance that they are normal and permission to continue doing exactly what they have been doing is sufficient in some cases to resolve what might eventually become a very major problem. Thus, permission-giving can also be seen as a preventive measure as well as a treatment technique. Permission-giving will certainly not solve all sexual problems, or even many such problems, but it will resolve some as Fig. 2 suggests. Furthermore, it has the advantage in that, provided that there is some measure of privacy, it can be used in almost any setting at any time, whether it may be at a cocktail party, a business luncheon or a private-practice office. It also takes minimal preparation on the part of the clinician. Finally, it may be used to cover a number of areas of concern, such as thoughts, fantasies, dreams and feelings, as well as overt behaviors.

Thoughts, Fantasies and Dreams. Concerns over sexual thoughts and fantasies are very common. For example, it is not unusual for a man or woman to have sexual thoughts or fantasies about people other than their partners, or about people of the same sex, or even about their own parents, or brothers and sisters, or sons and daughters. Occasional thoughts such as these are quite common, and letting the client know this may relieve some anxiety or guilt feelings about being "abnormal." It is only when such thoughts or fantasies become persistent or begin to directly interfere in some manner with other areas of functioning that they may create a problem.

Permission-giving may also be appropriate for handling dream concerns. It is not unusual for people to have occasional dreams involving sexual activity with a wide variety of people other than their partners, such as friends, relatives, parents, brothers and sisters or even their own children. At times, the dreams may also involve sexual activity with the same sex, even though the dreamer may never have had such actual experiences. Reassurance that such dreams are entirely within the normal range and are not unusual or indicative of "abnormality" is usually sufficient to relieve the anxiety or guilt associated with them. Often such permission-giving is also sufficient to stop the recurring sexual dream that was associated with anxiety, just as it can alleviate the persistent thought or fantasy.

Feelings. It is not uncommon for people to respond with anxiety when they experience sexual arousal to what they consider inappropriate stimulation. Many of these concerns arise from failure to discriminate between arousal resulting from sexual thoughts and fantasies and arousal from direct tactile stimulation. For example, it is quite normal for a mother who is breastfeeding her baby to occasionally experience some degree of sexual arousal due to the direct tactile stimulation of her breasts rather than to any latent incestuous desire. Another example is the father who experiences an erection when playing with his little boy on his lap. This is not due to latent homosexual tendencies, but due to direct physical stimulation of his penis. Reassuring the client that these are normal involuntary responses to tactile stimulation, and are quite common, may reduce unnecessary anxiety and prevent a minor happening from developing into a major concern. Similar permission-giving for such feelings can also apply to horseback and motorcycle riding, tree and rope climbing, the use of tampons, douches and enemas, or any other behavior that involves tactile stimulation of the breast, genital or anal areas.

Behaviors. The degree to which a clinician feels comfortable in giving permission to a client to engage in certain behaviors will be determined by a number of factors that will be discussed shortly. Theoretically, such permission-giving may be applied to a wide range of sexual behaviors that the clinician recognizes as common and normal but that the client does not. For example, take the case of the couple who read in their favorite magazine that the average frequency of sexual intercourse for people of their age and education is approximately two-and-a-half times a week. Their personal frequency may be eights times a week or eight times a year, but now they begin to worry whether they are "normal," "oversexed" or "undersexed." A response by the clinician that in essence gives them permission to continue with their own preferred frequency may be all that is necessary to relieve their anxiety. There are other numerous examples, such as the man who really likes the "woman on top" position, but remembers reading somewhere that this was indicative of latent homosexual tendencies; or the young couple who "secretly" enjoy mutual oral-genital contact, but they have read or heard somewhere that this is considered "perverted" or "abnormal" or the symptoms of "homosexual tendencies." The list could go on indefinitely, but by now the major point should be clear: Many of these types of sexual concerns may be resolved by a permission-giving approach.

It should be further pointed out that many sexual concerns can also be handled by giving the client permission *not* to engage in certain sexual behaviors unless he or she chooses to. For example, the young woman who is receiving pressure from her partner to experience "multiple orgasms" or who has read or heard that it is every woman's right to "expect and demand them," yet is very satisfied with the one orgasm that she experiences with her partner and does not really care whether she is multi-orgasmic or not. Giving her permission *not* to experience multiple orgasms, unless she chooses to, may be very helpful to her. Conversely, in the case of the woman who would really like to experience multiple orgasms but is fearful or hesitant that she might then become a "nymphomaniac," permission to be multi-orgasmic, if she chooses to, might be the more helpful approach. Permission-giving is most appropriate and helpful when it is used in direct relation to the client's goals. Keeping this in mind will make it easier for the clinician to decide what form of permission-giving will be most beneficial for a particular client concern.

The use of the permission-giving approach has a number of advantages. It is adaptable to almost any setting and takes relatively little time or preparation on the part of the clinician. It can resolve a wide range of sexual concerns, and it may also prevent new ones from evolving. In addition, it may also be applied in conjunction with all other levels of approach in the P-LI-SS-IT model. However, there are also limitations to its application. As stated earlier, this approach will certainly not solve all sexual problems, or even many problems, but it may resolve some concerns for some people.

Limitations. On the surface, it may appear that the basic assumption underlying the permission-giving approach is that the clinician may sanction whatever sexual thought, fantasy or behavior that a consenting adult wishes to privately engage in, or engage in with other mutually consenting adults. In a very general sense this may be correct; however, there are some definite limitations to such an assumption. While it is ultimately up to the individual client to choose whatever behavior that he wishes to engage in, "blanket" permission-giving by the clinician may not be appropriate if the client is not making an *informed* choice. It is the author's definite belief that it is the clinician's responsibility to inform the unaware client of the possible adverse consequences that may result from engaging in certain thoughts, fantasies or behaviors. For example, a number of popular books have "given permission" by extolling the joys and harmless fun to be had for indiscriminate use of any sexual fantasy that a person may desire while engaging in masturbation or sexual behavior with a partner. Learning theory suggests, and clinical evidence substantiates (Annon, 1973), that systematically associating thoughts and fantasies with sexual activity is a very powerful means for conditioning arousal to almost any stimuli. This fact has been used to therapeutic advantage. However, in certain circumstances, engaging in such activity by the uninformed may have undesired results. For example, a woman who consistently uses fantasies of dogs while engaging in self-stimulation may eventually find that she is aroused by actual dogs in the environment. Fortunately, such conditioning does not usually take place unless the client systematically uses the same fantasy over an extended period of time. Informing clients of the possible consequences of their behavior and leaving the ultimate choice up to them seems more appropriate than "blanket" permission-giving in such cases.

While further limitations of the permission-giving approach are obviously set by legal considerations (e.g., sexual activity with children, rape, etc.), most likely the major limitations will be set by the clinician. The extent to which the clinician feels comfortable with and is willing to use the permission-giving approach will generally depend upon his breadth of sexual knowledge, his theoretical orientation and his value system.

The more knowledge that a clinician has of sexual behavior in his culture and in other cultures, the more comfortable he may feel in applying this level of treatment. The clinician's particular theoretical or professional orientation may also place limits on how appropriate permission-giving may be for a particular thought, fantasy, dream, feeling or behavior. For example, those clinicians with a psychoanalytic background may wish to withhold permission-giving for recurrent sexual dreams, preferring to work through such material with the client. Obviously, that is the individual clinician's choice. It is not the intention of this paper to persuade professionals of any one orientation to change their viewpoint to that of a learning oriented approach. It is assumed that the clinician will only use those suggestions that he feels appropriate to his frame of reference, but it is hoped that he may be willing to experiment a little.

Ideally, the clinician will try not to intentionally impose his personal value system on his clients. However, in practice, this is sometimes very difficult to achieve. This does not mean that the clinician gives up his own personal value system. There may be times when the client's goals come into direct conflict with the clinician's value system. When this happens it is the clinician's responsibility to clearly inform the client of this and refer him elsewhere where appropriate.

A final important point is self-permission. The clinician should also be able to give permission to himself not to be an expert. He must not be afraid to say that he does not know the answer when he does not. No one person is an expert in this field. Theory, research and practice in the sexual area are so far-ranging that no one individual or group of individuals can be expected to know or keep abreast of even a sizable fraction of the area. The clinician does what he can for his client, based on his own knowledge and experience. In some cases, the most important thing that a clinician has to offer is himself. Someone who will listen, who can communicate interest, understanding and respect, and who will not label or judge the client. If permission-giving is not sufficient to resolve the client's concern, and the clinician is not in the appropriate setting, or does not have sufficient time or relevant knowledge and skills, then this is the time to refer the client elsewhere. On the other hand, if the clinician does have the appropriate setting, knowledge and skills, then he can combine his permission-giving with the second level of treatment.

The Second Level of Treatment: Limited Information

In contrast to permission-giving, which is basically telling the client that it is all right to continue doing what he has been doing, limited information is seen as providing the client with specific factual information directly relevant to his particular sexual concern. It may result in his continuing to do what he has been doing, or it may result in his doing something different. For example, a young man was seen by the author whose major concern was a feeling of inadequacy because he considered his penis too small in comparison to other males. He had withdrawn from any social contact, was depressed over his situation and contemplating trying to obtain surgery to correct his "deficient" penis. He was provided with the usual information that can be given in such cases (e.g., the foreshortening effect of viewing his own penis compared to looking across at other males; no correlation between flaccid and erect penis size except the tendency for the smaller flaccid penis to become longer in the erect state than the longer flaccid penis; that the average length of the female vagina is usually three to four inches and that there are very few nerve endings inside the vagina, etc.). A few minutes of such relevant information giving was sufficient to change his outlook, and within two months he was socially popular and involved in a close sexual relationship with a young woman with whom he eventually became engaged. Of course, it is impossible to predict what might have happened had he not been given such relevant information, but it seems likely that his situation might have progressively deteriorated. Thus, as with permission-giving, providing limited information may also be seen as a preventative measure as well as a treatment technique. Also, in the situation described, the client was given permission to have his concern and to accept his own body, but he was not directly given permission to avoid or seek out sexual contact with women. By supplying relevant information, he was provided with an opportunity to change his behavior if he chose to do so.

It should be pointed out that limited information is usually given in conjunction with permission-giving. While each may be used as separate levels, there obviously may be considerable overlap between the two. Furthermore, both can also be used in conjunction with the remaining two levels of treatment. However, because each descending level of treatment usually requires more time, knowledge, experience and skill on the part of the clinician for most effective application, each level is presented and discussed separately.

In giving limited information, it is important for the clinician to do just that, provide "limited" information directly relevant to the client's concern. Robinson (1974a, 1974b) has provided evidence indicating that even presenting three hours of a broad range of sexual information has little direct influence on changing a client's attitude or behavior associated with a specific sexual problem; however, presenting limited information directly related to the client's problem can effect significant change in relevant attitudes and behavior.

Common Areas of Sexual Concern. Providing limited information is also an excellent method of dispelling sexual myths, whether they are specific ones such as those pertaining to genital size, or more general ones such as: on the average, men and women differ markedly in their capacity to want and to enjoy sexual relations and in their fundamental capacity for responsiveness to sexual stimulation.

General myths, such as the one mentioned above, are quite common in our culture, despite the fact that there is a great deal of evidence to indicate that men and women are far more similar in their capacity for, and experience of, sexual responsiveness than they are dissimilar. Numerous cross-cultural studies from such fields as anthropology and sociology consistently reveal that cultures which are free and encourage women to be free in sexual expression produce sexually responsive women who are as uninhibited and responsive as males. Cultures which encourage and expect women to experience orgasm yield women who do experience orgasm, and vice versa.

Other examples of common areas where limited information can be most helpful are sexual concerns related to: breast and genital shape, size, and configuration; masturbation; genital intercourse during menstruation; oral-genital contact; and sexual frequency and performance. It is not within the scope of this paper to provide extensive information for each of the many possible areas of sexual concern that may be handled by this level of treatment. Obtaining such knowledge is up to the individual clinician and how much interest, time and effort he is willing to devote to such readings which are available elsewhere (e.g., Annon, 1974).

Limitations. The extent to which the clinician is willing to use the limited information approach in handling sexual concerns will obviously depend upon his breadth of knowledge in the sexual area. *How* the clinician offers such information to his clients will depend upon the individual style that he feels most comfortable with and, hopefully, the manner of presentation that he feels will be most helpful to his client. For example, with a conservative-appearing, middle-aged couple who hesitantly ask if anal contact is "normal" or "perverted," he may reply: "Such activity is not considered unusual or abnormal. In fact, a recent national survey of married males and females under 35 indicated that half of them experienced manual anal foreplay, and more than 25 percent had experienced oral-anal foreplay." On the other hand, with a young couple who casually ask if it is possible to transfer germs through oral-genital contact, he may respond: "Yes, it is possible. The *mouth* has a very high bacteria count."

Whatever his style of approach, the clinician now has two strategies for approaching sexual concerns. As with permission-giving, the degree to which he feels comfortable with and is willing to use the second limited information-giving level will also generally depend upon his breadth of sexual knowledge, his theoretical orientation and his value system. The limitations imposed by these factors discussed in the first level of treatment apply here equally as well.

As suggested in Fig. 2, the additional use of this level of treatment may resolve some concerns that could not be handled by the application of the first level of treatment, permission, alone. If giving limited information is not sufficient to resolve the client's sexual concern, the clinician then has two options available to him at this point. He may refer the client for treatment elsewhere, or, if he has the appropriate setting, knowledge, skills and experience, he may proceed to the third level of treatment.

The Third Level of Treatment: Specific Suggestions

Before the clinician can give specific suggestions to a client, he must first obtain certain specific information. The assumption here is that it would not be therapeutically appropriate or helpful to the client to offer specific suggestions without first obtaining information about him and his unique set of circumstances. If the clinician were to immediately launch into a number of suggestions after hearing the client's initial description of his problem (not his "label" of the problem), he may not only waste the client's time (e.g., offering suggestions that the client has already tried), but also he may further compound the problem. By suggesting inappropriate and possibly useless treatment procedures based on insufficient data he may overlook other more necessary and appropriate treatment such as medical evaluation and therapy.

The Sexual Problem History. What the clinician needs is a sexual *problem* history. This is not to be confused with a sexual history. If the clinician begins to take a sexual history, then he is heading into intensive therapy, not brief therapy. It is an assumption of the model proposed here that a comprehensive sexual history is not relevant or necessary at this level. As suggested in Fig. 2, the application of the specific suggestion approach may resolve a number of problems that filtered through the first two levels of treatment; but, needless to say, it is not expected that it will successfully deal with all such problems. If the third level of approach is not helpful to the client, *then* a complete sexual history may be a necessary first step for intensive therapy.

Guidelines for taking a sexual problem history that is deemed necessary for a brief therapy approach to treatment are outlined below.

Sexual Problem History

1. Description of Current Problem.
2. Onset and Course of Problem.
   a. Onset. (Age, gradual or sudden, precipitating events, contingencies.)
   b. Course. (Changes over time: Increase, decrease, or fluctuation in severity, frequency, or intensity; functional relationships with other variables.)
3. Client's Concept of Cause and Maintenance of the Problem.
4. Past Treatment and Outcome:
   a. Medical Evaluation. (Specialty, date, form of treatment, results, currently on any medication for any reason.)
   b. Professional Help. (Specialty, date, form of treatment, results.)
   c. Self-Treatment. (Type and results.)
5. Current Expectancies and Goals of Treatment. (Concrete or ideal.)

The taking of such a problem history will necessarily have to be adapted to the clinician's setting and the amount of time he has available. The proposed problem history is easily adapted to five minutes or five hours. It may be helpful to the clinician to have a form made containing the sexual problem history guidelines. He may then use it as a general guide while interviewing, or he can write the client's responses directly on the form for future reference. Either method may help him to become comfortable and experienced with the guidelines until he no longer finds them necessary as an aid to memory.

It is not relevant to the purpose of this paper to provide further information on the sexual problem history. However, those interested in obtaining a more detailed explication of the taking of a such problem history along with illustrative case examples may refer to Annon (1974). Once the clinician is familiar with the guidelines and he feels comfortable and at ease in obtaining the problem history from the client, he is then ready to apply the third level of treatment.

Specific Suggestions. In contrast to permission and limited information-giving which generally do not require the client to take any active steps to change his behavior unless he chooses to, specific suggestions are direct attempts to help the client to change his behavior in order to reach his stated goals. This is done from within a brief therapy framework which means that the approach is time- and problem-limited. Most of the suggestions that may be given are those that can be used by a clinician who has only a relatively brief period, say ten to thirty minutes, for a client interview. Furthermore, they may also be used in those situations where the clinician is only able to see the client on one, or several, occasions at the most. Obviously, these are minimum time limits that may be expanded and adapted to whatever time that the clinician has available. However, this level of approach is mainly intended for use within the brief therapy framework proposed, and if the suggestions are not seen as helpful within a relatively brief period of time, then it is suggested that intensive therapy is probably more appropriate.

As with the previous levels of treatment, specific suggestions may also be seen as a preventive measure as well as a treatment technique. For example, suggesting to a woman specific ways to avoid experiencing pain associated with genital intercourse may prevent her from eventually experiencing vaginismus. Or, direct treatment of ejaculation concerns with a male may prevent the eventual occurrence of erection problems. Also, this level of treatment may easily and advantageously be combined with the previous two levels.

There are two common sayings that are often quite helpful in applying this particular level of approach. These sayings may be passed directly on to the clients depending upon their particular situation. One that is particularly beneficial for those clients with concerns about a particular feature of their body is: *It is what you do with what you have, rather than what you have that counts.* Use of this saying in conjunction with specific suggestions on "what they may do with what they have" can be very effective in promoting attitude and behavior change in a particular client's area of concern.

The second saying has even broader application. Many clients who come in with sexual concerns relating to failure in arousal, erection, orgasm or ejaculatory control tend to see each sexual contact with their partner as their "final test." If the man again ejaculates too soon, or again does not obtain an erection, he often feels as though he has lost his last chance. Similar concerns are reported by women in search of orgasms. Thoughts such as "Will it happen this time? It's got to happen this time or I'll die!" are not conducive to success in experiencing such goals. Helping the client to learn to say, and to believe *There is always another day;* or *There is always another time;* or *There is always another occasion;* can do a great deal to relieve some of the self-defeating, grim determination that many clients have in trying to overcome their particular sexual problem.

The application of this level of treatment is seen as providing clients with specific suggestions directly relevant to their particular sexual problem and designed to help them achieve their stated goals. This level of treatment is particularly effective for dealing with those heterosexual problems that are concerned with arousal, erection, ejaculation, orgasm or painful intercourse. The specific suggestions given (e.g., redirection of attention; graded sexual responses; sensate focus techniques; dating sessions, alternate sessions; interrupted stimulation; squeeze technique; vaginal muscle training, etc.) will, of course, depend upon the information obtained in the sexual problem history. In general, it might be helpful to consider such suggestions as falling into three categories: suggestions to the male alone, suggestions to the female alone and suggestions to the couple. Quite often the clinician is seen by a client with a heterosexual problem who has no immediate partner available. In such cases there are a number of suggestions that can be made using self-stimulation procedures (Annon, 1973) that may be helpful to the client until a partner is available. Often, too, the clinician may be faced with a situation where he is seen by a client who is in a relationship with a second person who has a problem, but the second person is not able, or willing, to come in for consultation. Assuming that the second person is looking for suggestions, it is important for the clinician to obtain as much of a problem history as he can in such a situation. Depending upon the information that he receives, he can then give whatever suggestions that he feels might be appropriate under the circumstances. However, the most helpful suggestions are usually those that can be made to both partners together. If at all possible, the client should be encouraged to have a partner come in. When the couple comes in together and they are willing to cooperate with the treatment suggestions, there is always a higher probability that they will achieve their goals than when one or the other comes in alone. It is always risky in working with one person on a problem that involves two people in such an intimate situation, and the clinician should definitely attempt to see both people involved if at all possible.

Limitations. Efficient use of this level of treatment will largely depend upon the clinician's breadth of knowledge in the behavioral and sexual area, his skill and experience and his awareness of relevant therapeutic suggestions. The limitations discussed previously apply here equally as well. It is not within the province of this paper to offer extensive specific suggestions covering all possible sexual problems. For the interested clinician a detailed description of the application of such suggestions to the more prevalent heterosexual problems encountered by males and females is available elsewhere (Annon, 1974).

Readings. Specific client readings may also be suggested by the clinician for a number of reasons. He may use them as another means of providing permission or limited information pertaining to a certain sexual area of client concern. Also, he may use them to supplement specific suggestions that he has made, or to promote new client-initiated procedures. Finally, because of time limitations, either on his or the client's part, he may suggest them in lieu of any other specific suggestions. It is assumed that the clinician will not suggest any readings to clients until he is first well acquainted with their content and feels comfortable with recommending them.

As Fig. 2 illustrates, this level of approach concludes the presentation of the brief therapy approach of the P-LI-SS-IT model. As Fig. 2 further implies, a number of sexual concerns may successfully be treated by such an approach, but, on the other hand, a number of problems that cannot be solved by this approach will also filter through. This is the point at which the clinician may refer the client for appropriate treatment elsewhere, or if he has the requisite time, knowledge, experience and skills, he may apply the fourth level of treatment.

The Fourth Level of Treatment: Intensive Therapy

It is not within the scope of this paper to describe, or even to attempt to outline, an intensive therapy approach to the treatment of sexual problems. For the clinician who has already received training within his particular discipline for intensive therapy, this is the appropriate time to initiate such treatment. For the clinician who is interested in a behavioral approach to the intensive treatment of sexual problems, refer to Annon (1975).

CONCLUSION

This concludes the presentation of the P-LI-SS-IT model. The possible advantages of employing this model have been described earlier and will not be repeated here. For those who are involved in teaching or training sexual therapists, this model may offer a framework for providing training that can be geared to the level of competence of the individual trainee. For the clinician, it is hoped that the model may provide a framework within which he can continue to develop and expand his knowledge, experience and skills.

The clinician will naturally have to adapt his use of the P-LI-SS-IT model to his particular setting, to the amount of time that he has available to him and to his particular level of competence. It is also important to emphasize that while the brief therapy part of the model is not intended to resolve all sexual problems, it may handle many. It is the author's firm opinion, based on an ever-increasing amount of clinical and research evidence, that it is now bordering on being unethical to involve a client in an expensive, long-term treatment program without first trying to resolve his problem from within a brief therapy approach. As the schematic presentation in Fig. 2 implies, a number of sexual concerns may successfully be treated by such an approach if the clinician is willing to apply it. On the other hand, as the model also indicates, a number of problems that cannot be solved by this approach will filter through. There will be times when the specific suggestions that may work for many others will not be effective for a particular client's problem, whether the clinician has suggested one or a dozen. There will also be times when interpersonal conflict may prevent many of the suggestions from being carried through. When this happens, and when the clinician feels that he has done as much as he can from within the brief therapy approach, *then* it is time for highly individualized intensive therapy.

Finally, it should be pointed out that in the model proposed here, intensive therapy does *not* mean an extended standardized program of treatment. By their very nature such standardized programs will not be of help to some people, or they may not even be necessary. It is the author's belief that many of the essential elements of some of the current standardized programs can be successfully utilized within a brief therapy approach. In the P-LI-SS-IT model, intensive therapy is seen as highly individualized treatment that is necessary *because* standardized treatment was not successful in helping the client to reach his goals. In the present framework, intensive therapy means that a careful initial assessment of the client's unique situation and experiences is necessary in order to devise a tailor-made therapeutic program that is unique to the particular individual and to his life circumstances. This is particularly important, because what is available to the client beyond the fourth level of treatment?

REFERENCES

Annon, J.S. *The extension of learning principles to the analysis and treatment of sexual problems.* (Doctoral dissertation, University of Hawaii, 1971.) *Dissertation Abstracts International.* 1971, **32**, (6-B), 3627. University Microfilms No. 72-290, 570.
Annon, J.S. The therapeutic use of masturbation in the treatment of sexual disorders. In Rubin, R.D. Brady, J.P. & Henderson, J.D. (Eds.). *Advances in behavior therapy, Vol. 4.* New York: Academic Press, 1973, 199-215.

Annon, J.S. *The behavioral treatment of sexual problems. Vol. 1. Brief therapy.* Honolulu: Enabling Systems, Inc., 444 Hobron Lane, 96815, 1974.

Annon, J.S. *The behavioral treatment of sexual problems. Vol. 2. Intensive therapy.* Honolulu: Enabling Systems, Inc., 444 Hobron Lane, 96815, 1975.

Robinson, C.H. *The effects of observational learning on sexual behaviors and attitudes in orgasmic dysfunctional women.* (Doctoral dissertation, University of Hawaii, 1974a.) *Dissertation Abstracts International.* 1975, 35 (9-B). University Microfilms No. 75-5040.

Robinson, C.H. The effects of observational learning on the masturbation patterns of preorgasmic females. Paper presented at the annual meeting of the Society for the Scientific Study of Sex, Las Vegas, November 1974.

Staats, A.W. Social behaviorism and human motivation: Principles of the attitude-reinforcer-discriminative system. In Greenwald, A.G. Brook, T.C. & Ostrom, T.M. (Eds.). *Psychological foundations of attitudes.* New York: Academic Press, 1968, 33-66.

Staats, A.W. Social behaviorism, human motivation, and the conditioning therapies. In B.A. Maher (Ed.). *Progress in experimental personality research, Vol. 5.* New York: Academic Press, 1970, 111-168.

Staats, A.W. *Social behaviorism.* Homewood, Ill.: Dorsey Press, 1975.

9
The Mechanotherapy of Sexual Disorders

EDWARD DENGROVE

Once one's name is added to the mailing lists of those companies which sell mechanical devices for sexual pleasure, a flood of mail may be expected which will be an education in itself. The devices are numerous and the variety has become a match for those commonly written of as having been availabe to the Japanese for years past.

The following discussion is limited, however, to the artificial penis, a constricting device, the vibrator, and the Kegel perineometer, all of which may be considered to be devices useful in the treatment of impotence and frigidity.

THE ARTIFICIAL PENIS

Under various names there has been a renaissance of the artificial penis. The latest models appear superior to the dildo or godemiche of old: made of a flexible, yet firm, plastic, manufactured in varied sizes, colored in flesh tones, easy to wear.

A patient of mine who purchased one is a divorcee, living alone, approaching middle age, and passionate. She had no sexual outlets other than masturbation and found the artificial phallus an adequate substitute. Adequate, that is, but not satisfactory. She longed for a male companion, a husband, but this the device could not replace.

The following case illustrates its use in the treatment of impotence. A 32-year-old housewife was seen in a depressed state. Her husband 25 years her senior, had lost his potency and precipitated her depression the year before. He loved her but found himself unable to function sexually, no matter how hard he tried. His family doctor had told him that this was a result of age and nothing could be done for him. She required the sexual show of love in order to overcome a feeling of rejection which had dogged her most of her lifetime.

Her husband readily accepted the use of the artificial phallus and again began to make sexual overtures to his wife. He had discontinued this activity when his inability to get an erection would only cause his wife to burst into tears. Knowing that now he could make love to her even without an erect penis, he found himself relaxing in the sex act. To his astonishment, with this lessening of the pressures upon him, his potency returned naturally. His wife told me: "We feel so much better about each other. It makes a big difference. I feel so much better about him now."

Another man, whose wife preferred to awaken him from his sleep during the night for sexual relations, had difficulty at times with a soft penis and premature ejaculation. This would leave his wife in a frustrated, tense state which would carry over to the next day. An artificial phallus served to prolong the act after his ejaculation and saved her day.

This use of the artificial phallus as an aid in premature ejaculation and in impotence will, no doubt, popularize its use and make it of value in marital counseling.

In his booklet, "So You Think You're Impotent!" Dr. G. Lombard Kelly (1957) makes note of letters from satisfied patients using an artificial "Pinus," whose marital problems were resolved by the use of this instrument. To quote one user: "This friend has a wife like mine wanting a party three and four times or more a week and at times he can't get an erection or is not up to it—to please his wife, keep peace and all, he puts the apparatus on and goes to town and she is very satisfied. This friend let me try this today and I must admit it works perfect and I wish I had one."

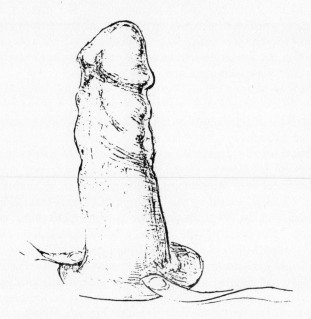

Fig. 1. Artificial Penis

The interested males are those who desire to show their wives love and consideration, who want to please them. A most commendable and marriage-saving attitude.

Concern has been voiced that this device will injure the vagina in some way. The phallus is made of a soft, flexible material and can in no way penetrate or injure the vaginal walls. It may be used with or without lubrication. The one complaint I did hear was from a man who declared that the straps pained him where they circled the scrotum to hold it in place. However, the straps may have been too tight and needed only to be loosened, for other users had no such charge to make. Further, he had an aversion to his wife which was preventing him from having an erection with her. Despite this he needed her and wanted to give her pleasure and to satisfy her sexual longings. In this case he used the phallus manually, with the same pleasant end-results for his marriage. The mail-order houses have now added a harness to hold the device in place more comfortably.

Another question that has arisen relates to its artificiality. A husband insisted that his wife would much rather have "the real thing." Though one wife declared: "The first time I used it, I knew it wasn't real, but afterwards it did feel real and the act was quite nice." Another husband refused to use one for fear it would make him out to be less of a man.

While using the phallus, with the unerect penis inside, a man may secure an erection. There is stimulation through the walls of the device, which is much like a very thick condom. In addition, the consummation of the act, even with a substitute penis, may stimulate a man psychosexually, particularly when he knows that he is acting the male role again with his wife. When this happens, the phallus may be discarded and natural relations continued. If he should again lose his erection, he can resume its use once more.

Other devices, such as penile splints or wimpuses and the Coitus Training Apparatus, work in other ways. They stretch the penis and try to make direct use of it, though the penis may be quite soft. With the artificial phallus this is not done, and it acts only as a substitute penis. In my experience this is an advantage. The majority of men with impotence respond to relaxation with loss of their fear of sexual inadequacy. With the phallus there is no expectation for them to perform and their penises play only a passive role. In contrast, with the former devices, an active attempt is made to force the penis to perform and relaxation is not an integral part of the sexual act.

With the ability to perform the act again, even with a substitute device, the man relaxes, often regains confidence, and gradually experiences a return of his potency. Furthermore, there are not the dangers of the suction type of apparatus, an instrument used to enlarge a limpid penis.

Much has been written of the special artificial phallus used by the Masters-Johnson team. In an interview in *Playboy* magazine, Mrs. Johnson (1968) stated that the instrument had long since been disassembled. She noted that during coition, the research subjects never could achieve orgasm by use of the phallus alone—they all had to employ additional self-stimulation derived from their own personal preferences and previously established patterns. "The point is," she declared, "a female responds sexually to that which is endowed for her with sexual meaning. Over a period of time, all women in our sample probably could have oriented themselves to respond to the exclusive use of a phallic device if they had been so motivated; but to them, the laboratory phallus was nothing in or of itself, and neither the situation nor their own personal interest required that they make it so. Consequently, the only reason for creating and using this device was to provide an opportunity for definition and measurement of the intravaginal environment."

As a prothesis for loss of the penis through disease or accident, it has the advantage of being cheap and useful and continuing a marriage where sex play is important to the wife.

Dr. Kelly (1957) investigated the legal aspects regarding the use of the artificial phallus. He writes: "One of the principal deterrents to the manufacture and supply of artificial phalli to patients who need them is the general belief that such a procedure is illegal. In so far as this writer has been able to determine, this is not true where there are definite medical indications and when the dispensing is done by a licensed physician."

CONSTRICTING DEVICES FOR THE PENIS

Rubber bands placed around the base of the penis have been used to help maintain partial erections. As an improvement upon this possibly dangerous practice, Dr. Pendleton Tompkins (1960) writes of his experiences with a prosthetic device called the Eros. This is a rubber sleeve of the proper size and consistency with an apron in front. When the patient wearing it is in the prone position, the weight of the gonads on the apron elevates the penis and the constricting sleeve produces engorgement. He prescribed it for infertility due to faulty intromission and reported that it helped to achieve stronger erections, vaginal insemination, increased the confidence of husbands and assisted wives to orgasm where it had never before been reached. There were no complaints of discomfort or complications.

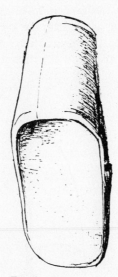

Fig. 2. Eros

THE VIBRATOR IN FRIGIDITY

My first introduction to the use of the vibrator for sexual stimulation in women occurred fifteen years ago. I had a female patient who worked as a masseuse. She related to me that a woman had called to ask if she — my patient — used a vibrator for internal massage. Suspecting some sort of trap she declined the invitation.

I gave no further thought to it until I read about the Masters-Johnson (1963) experimental use of vibration in their studies.

The first patient to whom I advised vibration therapeutically was a 24-year-old nurse, married, complaining of being completely frigid. She had never experienced sexual feelings prior to her marriage, and when this state continued afterward, she was greatly disappointed. Intercourse meant very little to her. She might get a little feeling if her husband awakened her after she had been asleep because, she explained, she was more relaxed then and did not tense up as she generally did.

Sometimes she felt desire and wanted to enjoy the sexual act more than anything else but without success. She loved her man dearly and he was a most cooperative husband. She was a compulsive individual who tended to protect herself against too deep emotional involvement with anyone, and did not like the thought of being beholden to her husband for pleasure. Treatment involved systematic desensitization, relaxation techniques, hypnosis, the use of the Kegel perineometer and the vibrator.

In those days the only vibrator available was the hand device with the fingers extending beyond the instrument. In the past two years they have become more sophisticated: one shaped like a penis, another with a soft finger extension supposed to stimulate the anus but also usable for the clitoris, a regular electric toothbrush with soft bristles.

Mrs. B. used the hand vibrator to good effect. She enjoyed the sensations produced and asked her husband to use it on her. She felt most sensitivity to vibration not on the clitoris but around its base. There was very little feeling if her husband used it on her in contrast to using it herself because, as she said, she knew the places where she was most sensitive. Inserting her fingers into the vagina with vibration did not bring on as much sexual stimulation. However, stimulation of the clitoral area led to the spread of feeling to the vagina: "a sexy feeling."

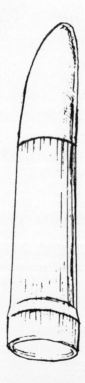

Fig. 3. Vibrator

She applied the instrument five times in the first week. After four to five minutes the stimulation eased off and did not produce as much sensation. She explained: "I think I tensed up then. It reaches a certain point, then just stops. Then there's no feeling at all, like numb. It's the first sex stimulation I've had and it scares me. I get excited to a certain point and then I get scared. I'm afraid of the sexual feeling. But at least I know I'm capable of sex feeling. I'm afraid of getting too used to it, preferring it to my husband. When the sensation dies away, it leaves a pleasant afterglow for a half-hour. I feel relaxed all over."

Six weeks later she reported that she was getting clitoral stimulation without the vibrator. Coincidentally she developed dreams of falling and an increased aliveness in her body.

In contrast, another young married woman described a tremendously rapid build-up and climax with the use of the vibrator applied clitorally, together with increased awareness vaginally without vaginal orgasm. "It makes you reach a climax within a minute, or a couple of minutes at the most. Really fast," she said. However, there was no extension of sexual sensation to the vagina, which she was seeking.

A third, young, married woman who had never experienced a vaginal orgasm spontaneously utilized a soft-bristle electric toothbrush on her clitoral area while her husband was actively involved in intercourse with her. This produced a most pleasureful feeling, with spread of sex sensation from clitoris to vagina for the first time in her life, though not to vaginal orgasm during the periods of its use.

This use of the vibrator opens up a completely new vista for clinical research in frigidity. The concept of clitoral stimulation together with vaginal intercourse is certainly not a new one, but the use of the vibrator as such an adjunct is new. What is required is a flat-tipped soft vibrator which will not interfere with the act of intercourse, is not bulky and cannot get in the way.

Mechanotherapy may lead to desensitization of sexual fears in certain women on a spontaneous basis, particularly if they have a loving and potent husband.

There are many contributions to the etiology of frigidity, and cognizance must be taken of these in therapy, together with other nonsexual complaints which may be present. Mechanotherapy is considered just another tool in our armamentarium.

Patient-acceptance of the vibrator is mixed. Women may object to the non-romantic character of this approach, or even consider it degrading. Men are likely to reject its use because it makes them out to be incapable of producing orgasm in the female on their own; emasculating them, so to speak. However, a couple who are aware of the problem, are mature and want to undo the frigidity may be able to make good use of these therapeutic devices.

Another objection was voiced in an article by Romm (1959), who described a woman who was almost completely frigid sexually. On occasion she could achieve a clitoral orgasm by manipulating her clitoris with the aid of an electric vibrator. She discarded it because it gave her merely a clitoral orgasm. She preferred to have none if she could not attain a vaginal orgasm.

Still another objection came from a married woman suffering from an intense fear of orgastic sensation tied into conflict with her father, an intensely anti-sexual upbringing, and death fears. She was afraid that enjoyment of sex with her husband would cause him much harm. She was not psychotic and knew this could not be true. All the same, it was a thought she could not shake off. She had worked through a great deal of this material in psychotherapy but without much gain in sexual pleasure. She enjoyed the intimate embrace with her husband but had no genuine sensations in the vagina. In using the vibrator she found that it stimulated her to a clitoral climax very quickly but when she attempted to use it vaginally, it had no effect. That was—at first. Then she began to experience mild sensations vaginally which panicked her and which she instantly blocked. She had reached the stage with her husband where the penis in the vagina caused her to panic. "I never had such a violent reaction. All I could think of was get it out of me. I thought that I'd have a clitoral climax and it would go into a vaginal climax." She rejected the use of the vibrator for fear it would lead her toward orgastic expectation.

The vibrator has been used as a preparatory device to bring a female to increased excitation sooner, and to shorten the lag so often present between the male and the female orgasms. The instrument is then discarded with the usual continuation of sex play to completion.

It has also been used as a completion device when the male has reached climax ahead of his partner. Particularly when she is left congested, frustrated, perhaps angry or tearful. In some instances, the compassionate husband has effectively brought his wife to completion.

What of the possible dangers in the use of the vibrator? To date, I know of none. As previously mentioned, one woman feared she might prefer it to her husband. However, it is my experience that as long as a woman has a good relationship with her spouse she will prefer the meaningful satisfaction of intimacy with him to the simple gratification of masturbation. One other stated warning has been that a person may become addicted to its use and that it should be used sparingly in conjunction with professional counseling. In my short experience I have not known this to happen.

THE VIBRATOR IN IMPOTENCE

What of the use of vibrators for potency difficulties in men? A spoon-shaped device, apparently meant to stimulate the penis to erection, appeared for a short time on the mail-order market, but the seller was convicted of mail fraud for allegedly misrepresenting the value of the purported sex device. It sold for $25 and was merely a battery-operated facial massage instrument purchasable at many cosmetic counters for $1.35; so the Post Office said.

Similar devices which use water have been hawked for the same purpose. These are plastic tubes into which the penis is inserted and water forced through in a steady, needlelike spray in order to stimulate the penis to erection. The literature accompanying these devices warn that it may lead to orgasm.

Turning to the scientific literature, wherein electro-stimulation is used to obtain semen for fertility studies and for artificial insemination, Rowan et al. (1962) used a rectal electrode to stimulate to ejaculation the area adjacent to the prostate. Thirty-five patients were studied, four of whom were impotent, and five of whom suffered premature ejaculation; the remaining patients were seen for other than sexual problems. Electrostimulation was accompanied by painful effects. Of the 35 patients, six felt a definite sensation in the urethra, one felt a sensation similar to that occurring with erection, two reported an increase in sexual activity. Psychiatric motivation was possible, it was noted, in these last two.

In 1965, Sobrero, et al., adapted an inexpensive vibrator widely sold for home massage use. A collecting cup was attached to the rubber head with adhesive tape. The cup was then applied with gentle pressure to the glans penis and the current turned on. A reflex ejaculation usually occurred between 15 seconds to 7 minutes later. It was used extensively with more than 100 chronic schizophrenic patients with about 80 percent success in cooperative patients. Among 40 infertile subjects, no full erection was observed, although in some instances a partial, very soft erection was seen at the time of ejaculation; five normal subjects reported similar results. Only five of the 45 reported erotic fantasies during stimulation or orgasmic feelings at ejaculation. It was concluded that the device could stimulate reflex ejaculation but without full erection or orgasm in the great majority of subjects.

Schellen (1968) used an electrovibrator with a cup operated by the subject in the treatment of sterile, married men who had failed to achieve ejaculation. Organicity was ruled out. The cup was placed on the bare glans penis, for which some erection was necessary. Success was achieved in nine of eleven patients, ejaculation with orgastic feeling taking place within 1-6 minutes; in one other, erection improved without ejaculation.

THE KEGEL PERINEOMETER

An article on mechanotherapy of frigidity would be incomplete without mention of the Kegel perineometer (Kegel 1949, 1952). This is a pneumatic cylindrical diaphragm which forms a resistance chamber. It is shaped like a long cylindrical case which inserts

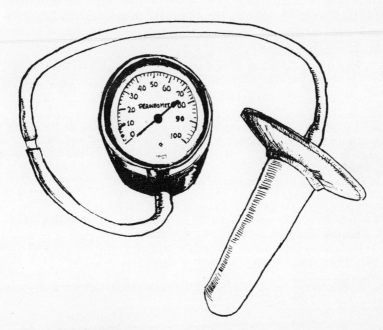

Fig. 4 Kegel's Perineometer

into the vagina and is attached by a long rubber tube to a manometer. Voluntary contractions of the perivaginal muscles cause the pointer to move on the manometer scale, and this can be observed by the user. The stronger the contraction, the higher the scale reading. The apparatus provides a simple means of exercising the muscles against resistance, under visual guidance.

Initially, it was devised to assist women with poor perivaginal muscular tone to overcome urinary stress incontinence. Kegel, however, discovered that it had another, sexual function, leading to sensory perception of the vagina.

He declares that women with a thin, weak pubococcygeus muscle, with a contractile ability measuring zero to three mm. Hg, as measured by the perineometer, frequently show indifference or dissatisfaction regarding sexual activity. In contrast, whenever the perivaginal musculature is well developed, with a contractile strength of 20 mm. Hg or more, sexual complaints are few or transient. He notes, too, that dyspareunia and vaginismus have been successfully treated through muscle education and resistive exercise using the instrument.

CONCLUSION

Mechanotherapy has a place in the treatment of premature ejaculation, impotence and frigidity. The inventiveness of man surpasses itself in the pursuit of sexual pleasure and one may expect more novel and ingenious devices with proper research and controls in order to make good use of the best of them.

The usual cries of dehumanization and deromantization of the sexual act may be raised by those with more sensitive natures. But again, the use of these devices is an aid to increase satisfaction with the sexual act for those who are not securing it. These are not used only as therapeutic instruments. With them, the troubled husband can show that he loves his wife and considers her needs. What could be more important to a marriage than that one would want to pleasure the other?

REFERENCES

Kegel, A.H. The physiologic treatment of poor tone and function of the genital muscles and of urinary stress incontinence. *Western J. Surg. Obstet. Gyn.* 1949, **57**: 527.
Kegel, A.H. Sexual functions of the pubococcygeus muscle. *Western J. Surg. Obstet. Gyn.* 1952, **60**: 521.
Kelly, G.L. So you think you're impotent! *Southern Medical Supply Co.* 1957.
Johnson, V. *Playboy.* 1968.
Masters, W.H. & Johnson, V. *Medical tribune.* Dec. 27, 1963.
Romm, M.E. Influences determining types of regression. *Psy. Q.* 1959, **XXVII**: 170.
Rowan, R. Electro-ejaculation. *J. Urol.* 1962, **87**: 726.
Schellen, T. Induction of ejaculation by electrovibration. *Fert. Steril.* 1968, **19**: 566.
Sobrero, A.J. Technique for the induction of ejaculation in humans. *Fert. Steril* 1965, **16**: 765.
Tompkins, P. Infertility due to faulty intromission successfully treated by prosthetic device. *J.A.M.A.* 1960, **172**: 53.

Part 2

Procedures Focused on Undesired
Sexual Object Choices

All of the articles in Part 1 dealt with common sexual problems experienced (usually) in a heterosexual couple relationship, often the marital relationship. In addition to the commonality of problems, there was also some degree of commonality in the techniques described. But obviously, not all sexual problems are experienced in heterosexual couple relationships, nor are the behavioral techniques available for use with sexual problems limited to those already described. A whole range of sexual problems involving undesired sexual object choices—i.e., those the client may wish to alter—may be brought to the attention of the clinician, and, in fact, Volume II of this book is organized on the basis of these problems. Similarly, a wide range of procedures are available to the clinician to deal with these sexual problems; indeed, many of these techniques are useful in dealing with more than one type of problem (including in some cases problems that involve heterosexual couple relationships). Thus, Part 2 of this volume is focused on these techniques and their evaluation, with most of the case illustrations of their use being presented in Volume II.

Since many sexual problems involve undesired approach behavior, the need for procedures to decrease that behavior, usually well entrenched and reinforced by the sexual gratification and relief it brings, seems obvious. In part because of the generally refractory nature of this problem behavior, and in part because of the very poor record of effectiveness of traditional approaches in this area, one of the commonest sets of procedures for decreasing undesired sexual-approach behaviors has been the use of aversion therapy (*see also* Additional Selected Readings for Volume I). Such therapy involves the use of either the respondent or operant learning paradigm and the application generally of either chemical or more recently, because of its many advantages over chemicals, electrical aversive stimuli to reduce the approach response. The results of such therapy have been encouraging, though not always conclusive, and several examples of the use of aversion therapy in relation to specific sexual problems are available in Volume II. In this Part, however, the focus in the next two articles is on the techniques, per se, of aversion therapy, and their use with one or more types of sexual problems.

In the first article by Abel, Levis and Clancy, "Aversion Therapy Applied to Taped Sequences of Deviant Behavior in Exhibitionism and Other Sexual Deviations," audio-tape recordings were made involving descriptions of each of six clients' problematic sexual behavior with each tape divided into three sequential segments. Five of the six clients were placed on a schedule on which, at first, the final segment of the tape was followed by contingent electric shock, at later sessions the second segment and, ultimately, the first segment. At each session, the shocked-tape runs were followed by runs in which the client avoided shock by verbalizing "nondeviant" sexual behavior in the place of the shocked segment. The sixth client was given shocks out of relation to taped material (noncontingent shock) as a control case. The treatment was evaluated by measuring penile responses to sexually "deviant" and "nondeviant" tapes and by clinical reports. In the five experimental clients, in some contrast to the control client, there was reduction of erectile responses to "deviant" tapes and sustained erectile responses to "non-deviant" tapes. These five clients also reported weaker "deviant responses," less-frequent "deviant" behavior and fewer signs of undesirable behavior in general.

In the next article, Feingold describes "An Automated Technique for Aversive Conditioning in Sexual Deviations." On the grounds that aversive conditioning is a viable technique for decreasing undesired sexual behavior, but a technique that is time consuming, expensive and perhaps boring (for the therapist), Feingold has developed an automated procedure for aversive conditioning. In this procedure, the client imagines those situations associated with the deviant behavior as presented by a tape recorder. He then receives electric shocks, which also are programmed on the tape, to the leg. Feingold presents positive results on six cases involving undesired sexual-object choices, arguing that, to the extent that aversive conditioning is of any value, this automated procedure (perhaps in combination with other therapeutic procedures occurring simultaneously in these cases) is simply an economical way of doing this conditioning.

In the next paper, Moss, Rada and Appel describe the use of "Positive Control as an Alternative to Aversion Therapy." Actually, this report juxtaposes two approaches to cross-dressing behavior. In the first, "traditional" aversion therapy was used effectively. In the second, on the grounds that clinical application of aversive control is not always appropriate, the authors used what they term "positive control" with apparently successful outcome. In positive behavioral control, emphasis is placed upon the development of adaptive behavioral patterns supported by positive reinforcement in the client's own environment. While, for many clinicians, such an approach has built-in ethical advantages, its applicability, like any other procedure, must be based on the availability of empirical evidence and a careful, individualized assessment. For example, in the case reported in this article, there appeared to be ample client and environmental resources on which to build such a program, a situation that obviously is not available in all cases.

An interesting development in the treatment of undesired sexual-object choices is the procedure of orgasmic reconditioning. This technique is described by Marquis in his article, "Orgasmic Reconditioning: Changing Sexual Object Choice through Controlling Masturbation Fantasies." Marquis reviews the history and theoretical considerations of a model for explaining the acquisition and modification of undesired sexual-object choices. The model essentially involves attacking sexual responses to formerly neutral stimuli by pairing them with masturbation. Marquis' elaboration of this model has resulted in a procedure to eliminate undesired sexual-object choices through careful programming of masturbation fantasies. The procedure is described in detail in this article along with 14 case summaries dealing with a variety of sexual problems.

The following article, by Annon, "The Therapeutic Use of Masturbation in the Treatment of Sexual Disorders," contains a careful overview of theory and research on the therapeutic use of masturbation. Annon places this procedure within Staats' A-R-D (Attitude-Reinforcers-Discriminative stimulus) framework, thereby enhancing, at least theoretically, its potential utilization. Annon systematically describes the masturbatory procedure, and illustrates its use with several case examples. Annon concludes with some important cautions in using this procedure, among them, the notion that while successful results may be obtained from its application, this does not automatically mean the treatment is complete. Thus, a broadly-based assessment can be seen as crucial to careful and comprehensive treatment planning.

Marshall, in his article, "The Modification of Sexual Fantasies," describes an approach that combines aversive conditioning and orgasmic reconditioning to reduce problematic sexual behavior. For his work, Marshall suggests that the direct modification of fantasies will provide an effective method for decreasing undesired sexual behaviors. By the end of treatment, the program had eliminated "deviant" behavior in 11 out of 12 clients, a success rate which was maintained at follow-up in at least 75 percent of them.

The next brief article by Serber describes "Shame Aversion Therapy," a procedure developed for treating such sexual problems as cross-dressing behavior, voyeuristic behavior and exhibitionistic behavior. Shame aversion therapy involves having the client who is embarrassed or self-conscious about the act he performs engage in the act on demand in front of a number of observers. The undesired behavior is continued for 15 to 35 minutes and its style kept as close to the actual situation as possible. The client is told to observe himself and be aware of being observed. Serber reports that five of eight individuals so treated have remained free of their dysfunctional sexual behavior during a six-month follow-up.

A very important development in the behavior therapy literature, and another alternative to the use of actual aversive conditioning, is the procedure of covert sensitization. The next article, by Cautela and Wisocki, examines the use of "Covert Sensitization for the Treatment of Sexual Deviations." Covert sensitization is a procedure for decreasing maladaptive approach behavior through pairing an *imagined* aversive stimulus with *imagined* performance of the maladaptive behavior. Hence, covert sensitization, pending further empirical validation, may be useable as a substitute for aversive therapy which relies on such stimuli as electric shock or chemicals. Cautela and Wisocki first describe the advantages of covert sensitization over the use of real aversive stimuli, then provide a detailed discussion of how the procedure is used. They then give examples of the application of covert sensitization to specific sexual behaviors such as exhibitionistic behavior, fetishistic behavior, pedophiliac behavior, homosexual behavior and masochistic and sadistic behavior. The article also reviews evidence of effectiveness of covert sensitization. For those clinicians unwilling or unable to apply actual aversive stimuli, covert sensitization, applied in conjunction with procedures to build an alternate desired behavior where necessary, may prove the procedure of choice for decreasing undesired sexual behaviors.

Maletzky, in the next article, " 'Assisted' Covert Sensitization," reports on a simple but interesting modification to the technique of covert sensitization. He describes the addition of a malodorous substance, valeric acid, at critical points during scene presentations. Maletzky suggests that this addition is safe, inexpensive, readily available, and may considerably strengthen the technique of covert sensitization in selected cases.

The following article (Chapter 19) reports on an important study comparing the effectiveness of covert sensitization with contingent shock in which an electric shock was applied following erection to slides depicting sexual "deviant" material. "Aversion Therapy for Sexual Deviation: Contingent Shock and Covert Sensitization" by Callahan and Leitenberg compared these two treatment methods through relicated, counter-balanced within-subject presentations of each technique in six cases (including two individuals with exhibitionistic behavior, one with cross-dressing behavior, two with homosexual behavior and one with pedophiliac-homosexual behavior). The effects of the two treatments on these clients were monitored by measurement of penile circumference changes during slides presented prior to treatment sessions and by daily subjective recording of sexual urges and fantasies as well as masturbation and sexual acts. On the penile-circumference measure, no difference between the two treatments was found. However, covert sensitization appeared more effective than contingent shock on subjective measures of sexual arousal. Follow-up indicated that both treatments combined led to a favorable outcome.

In the next article, "Increasing Heterosexual Responsiveness in the Treatment of Sexual Deviation: A Review of the Clinical and Experimental Evidence," Barlow points out that there is wide agreement that avoidance of heterosexuality may be a major component in the genesis and maintenance of "sexual deviation" (i.e., undesired or undesirable sexual-object choices). However, despite this, the development of therapeutic procedures to increase heterosexual responsiveness has been largely neglected in favor of aversion therapy to suppress "deviant" responses. This important article critically reviews several techniques used for increasing heterosexual responsiveness (as opposed to decreasing undesired responses), including claims for effectiveness of each technique. The techniques are: aversion-relief procedures in which relief from an aversive stimulus is paired with heterosexual stimuli; systematic desensitization wherein heterosexual avoidance is desensitized either in imagination or in the actual situation; "social retraining" where heterosexual skills are taught; and pairing techniques in which sexual arousal is elicited and associated with heterosexual stimuli. Barlow evaluates the clinical and experimental evidence on these techniques, and concludes with a brief discussion of the relationship between these and aversive procedures. Although the current state of the evidence on the procedures for increasing heterosexual responsiveness does not allow definitive conclusions, the possibility does appear rather strong that future research will demonstrate that, in some instances, such procedures could replace aversive therapy completely or, at least, be consistently used in *conjunction* with aversive procedures.

The next three articles represent a slight departure from most of the other chapters in Volume I. These three articles essentially are case studies (as are most of the articles in Volume II), although each does employ single subject experimental designs. However, the procedures described in these three chapters are not covered extensively in previous chapters in this volume, and are representative of technique innovations, as described in the previous article, for increasing heterosexual arousal. Hence, their inclusion here.

All three of these chapters deal with homosexual behavior, the first two, with attempting to decrease homosexual behavior by increasing heterosexual arousal, and the last one (Chapter 23) with a problem involving erectile failure of a homo- and heterosexual nature. It should be pointed out that the subject of "conversion"—helping the client change from a homosexual "orientation" to a heterosexual one—has been covered extensively in the literature almost to the exclusion of "adjustment"—helping the client become more accepting of and comfortable with his or her homosexual orientation. While this is probably in large part a result of the types of requests for change therapists receive from their clients, this apparent overemphasis on "conversion" at the expense of "adjustment" may be a topic that is deserving of more thorough examination in the literature and in practice.

The first of the three experimental case studies is McCrady's article, "A Forward-Fading Technique for Increasing Heterosexual Responsiveness in Male Homosexuals." This technique involves the incremental fading of a nude female slide into a nude male slide. This "forward-fading" approach, as McCrady notes, is the opposite of other attempts to use fading which fade the male into the female slide. McCrady suggests that his procedure, which was successfully used to condition penile erection to a previously neutral female stimulus, has a major advantage over other fading procedures in that its application is not precluded by the client's initial failure to reach an erection of a given magnitude, and its more ready adaptation for out-patient settings due to the fact that expensive and sophisticated measurement equipment is not necessary.

The following chapter, by Herman, Barlow and Agras describes "An Experimental Analysis of Exposure to 'Explicit' Heterosexual Stimuli As An Effective Variable In Changing Arousal Patterns of Homosexuals." Each of four clients was sequentially exposed to films of female or male sexual content under positive therapeutic instructions. Penile response to female slides in separate measurement sessions was found to increase during exposure to the female film. This increase in objectively measured penile response was accompanied in many instances by changes in masturbatory fantasy and reports of heterosexual arousal and behavior outside of the clinic. However, this increase in heterosexual arousal appeared to have little effect on homosexual responsiveness, thus suggesting that additional procedures to decrease homosexual behavior—if that is desired by the client—may be necessary.

The next article in this volume is "An Experimental Analysis of Feedback to Increase Sexual Arousal In A Case of Homo- and Heterosexual Impotence," by Herman and Prewett. With reports on biofeedback increasing in the literature, this is one of the few instances of its successful use in the treatment of actual sexual problems (i.e., as opposed to analogue studies). In this case, again using a single subject experimental design, penile response to slides of nude males and nude females was significantly increased during treatment phases where sessions consisted of contingent informational feedback. Importantly, this increase in objectively measured penile response was accompanied by achievement of ejaculation during masturbation (which the client previously had been unable to accomplish), changes in masturbatory fantasy, and reports of homo- and heterosexual arousal away from the therapist's office. The article concludes by describing some of the potential advantages of feedback over other methods designed to increase sexual arousal.

As these last few articles illustrate, but as can be seen also from other articles in this book, a variety of paraphernalia and rather esoteric equipment, such as devices to measure penile responding, often have been used in developing procedures to effectively treat sexual dysfunction (see also the articles in Additional Selected Readings for Volume I for discussions of this equipment). But in most cases, these are exploratory studies, attempts to devise procedures that not only will be effective, but practical and readily available to most practitioners. Thus, this use of elaborate equipment and instruments may be viewed as an important but preliminary stage in the development of the behavioral armamentarium for dealing with sexual problems. While the use of such equipment likely will never be eliminated completely, it is hoped that the near future will see available to the practitioner a range of procedures for dealing with similar problems—as has been illustrated by the articles in this volume—so that the individual clinician will be able to make a rational decision about which procedure to use with which problem depending on the procedure's simplicity, clarity, efficiency, ethical suitability, and, of course, its demonstrated effectiveness in bringing about positive change for clients.

The final article in this volume is "Basic and Applied Research in Human Sexuality: Current Limitations and Future Directions in Sex Therapy" by Higginbotham and Farkas. This important review article, prepared specifically for this book, is a summary and critique of much of the behavior therapy literature dealing with sex-related problems. This paper can serve as a model for careful evaluation of the literature with the guiding principle being not to accept and use a given procedure simply because its origin is from a theoretical orientation with which one is "comfortable." Indeed, Higginbotham and Farkas point to several areas of therapeutic practice with sex-related problems that currently are, if not unvalidated, certainly "under-validated." Thus, the task for the future seems to be to continue and expand the experimental evaluation of therapeutic approaches to sex problems so that the clinician will be able to have available a flexible package that can not only be adjusted to specific client needs, but will be demonstrably effective as well.

10

Aversion Therapy Applied to Taped Sequences of Deviant Behavior in Exhibitionism and other Sexual Deviations: A Preliminary Report

GENE G. ABEL, DONALD J. LEVIS AND JOHN CLANCY

Although current opinions favors the use of psychotherapeutic and correctional programs in the treatment of deviant sexual behaviors, Freund (1960) and Smith (1968) indicate that conventional approaches such as psychoanalysis and group therapy have not produced impressive results. By contrast, Feldman (1966) describes encouraging initial findings with behavior therapy.

Rachman (1966), using conditioning techniques, has developed fetishistic responses in nondeviant subjects. Feldman and MacCulloch (1965), Marks, Rachman and Gelder (1965), Rachman (1963), Raymond (1956) and Thorpe et al. (1964), have treated deviants by developing avoidance of deviant sexual expression or by increasing the reward value of desired sexual behaviors. Following Freund's (1960) and Davison's (1968) suggestions, both these principles were utilized in this study.

In designing our treatment procedure, we gave consideration to the following facts: 1) A deviant act is often followed and strengthened by primary reinforcement, that is, orgasm; 2) Deviant sexual acts usually involve a sequence of discrete behaviors. The fact that orgasm often follows deviant behavior is a unique feature of these disorders and may be a major reason for their persistence. To extinguish the deviant behavior, it was important to prevent the terminal reward in the form of orgasm. In addition, pairing pain with the terminal deviant act (or fantasy), e.g., exposure of the genitals, was expected to inhibit its occurrence.

The second factor, the sequence of behaviors preceding the deviant act, has been frequently overlooked as a potential relevant variable. It is not a single condition which precipitates the deviant act, but rather a chain or sequence of behaviors. This sequence is evident in the following description of a typical exhibitionist's experience.

The sequence begins with sexually stimulating memories of previous exposures. This ideational material is followed by driving to a place where he has previously exposed himself. The urge for a new experience now appears. After locating a young girl, the patient circles the area, rehearsing mentally. He then stops the car and calls the girl. As she approaches, he anticipates with pleasurable excitement her reaction to the sight of his genitals. Finally, he exposes himself and terminates the sequence by masturbating.

Every exhibitionist patient reports such a sequence with only minor variations before each deviant act. As the sequence progresses, sexual arousal increases, and so does the difficulty of self-control. These reports suggest the desirability of extinguishing as many phases of the sequence as possible. Additional advantages of separating and conditioning distinctive phases have been emphasized by Levis (1966) and Stampfl (1966). By presenting rats with stimuli ordered serially, they produced an avoidance conditioning with extreme resistance to extinction following minimal shock presentation.

In addition to the above measures designed to combat the deviant behavior, nondeviant sexual behavior was reinforced. This is especially relevant when a negative reinforcer such as pain is used. The danger exists that the pairing of deviant sexual material with an aversive stimulus may result in the generalization of aversiveness to nondeviant sexual material. In order to counteract this possibility, the patients were able to avoid punishment at some trials by substituting "normal" for deviant sexual material.

METHOD

Subject Selection

To facilitate follow-up, patients were solicited only from psychiatrists and legal authorities within a 75-mile radius, including three state psychiatric hospitals. These were advised of "a new treatment program for male sexual deviants" and were asked for referrals. Excluded were patients classified by history or clinical interview as psychotic, retarded, organic or homosexual. Of ten consecutive referrals, three were excluded on these criteria. A fourth was excluded because frequent progress reports to the court were legally required, and it was feared that this might influence follow-up findings.

The remaining six subjects were three exhibitionsts with histories of voyeurism, two transvestites and one masochist. They were 21-31 years old—four married, two single. Four had recent histories of arrest following deviant acts, but only one faced criminal charges. Four had had no previous psychotherapy; the remaining two had had five and seven years of intermittent psychotherapy, with 3 and 4 psychiatric hospitalizations respectively. Five subjects had had frequent heterosexual petting and intercourse; the sixth had petted occasionally but had never attempted intercourse.

Procedure

There were 4 stages.

Stage 1. Each patient's pre-treatment pathology was estimated on the basis of a clinical interview, two rating scales, and the Minnesota Multiphasic Personality Inventory (MMPI). The interview served two purposes: 1) to provide a detailed account of the patient's specific deviant behavior, and 2) to afford a general impression of personality, sexual behavior, occupational ability, and social competence. The first of the two rating scales consisted of ten phrases. Five described those deviant behaviors judged to be most sexually arousing to the patient. The other five described nondeviant behavior judged sexually arousing to most men. These latter items were of course the same for all patients.

The subjects rated the 10 items from least to most exciting. The second rating scale, the Weekly (Clancy & Abel, 1967), consisted of 21 items in three categories: a) specific deviant behavior practiced by the patient; b) deviant behavior not practiced by him; and c) nondeviant sexual behavior. Each of these categories was subdivided into fantasized and overt behaviors. The patients reported the frequency of each listed behavior during the week past. At the end of Stage 1, they were each given a supply of Weekly scales and asked to fill out and mail one every Sunday for the duration of the experiment.

Stage 2. A modification of the penile transducer described by Bancroft, Jones and Pullan (1966) was applied to the patient's penis. This apparatus records changes in penile diameter, and is used to measure the degree of his activities—deviant sexual, normal sexual and general (nonsexual) daily routine—was recorded on audio tape while the penile responses were recorded. The subject described in detail the behavior sequences and thoughts involved in three actual deviant sexual experiences. In addition, he discussed normal sexual experiences and other nonsexual activities.

The experimenter then selected sections from the audio recordings of the six patients to produce for each of them six experimental tapes, each 120 seconds in length. The first 30 seconds of each tape consisted of a description of nonsexual behavior. The last 90 seconds of three of the tapes contained deviant sexual material, and the other three contained normal sexual material. The selected passages were in all cases those associated with the greatest penile responses. Two patients did not exhibit much in the way of penile responses. For them the experimenter facilitated arousal by recounting the recorded sexual experiences, expanding on those parts of the original description which had previously produced even a minimal penile response. By this means, tapes were finally obtained that elicited marked arousal.

When the 120 seconds of experimental tapes were completed a 5 second silent period was inserted after each 30-second segment. Each 30-second period of the last 90 second then comprised an ideational link in a behavioral sequence preceding either a deviant or a normal sexual act. Of an individual's three deviant tapes the one producing the greatest penile response was selected for use in Stage 3—the conditioning phase (*see* Fig. 1).

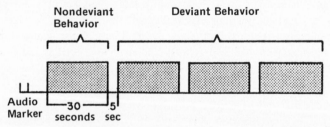

Fig. 1. Tape-recorded Sequence of a Sexual Deviant Experience

Stage 3. Five patients were randomly assigned to a contingent shock schedule,* and one patient to a noncontingent shock schedule. Throughout this stage the patient wore the penile transducer, as well as two silver electrodes on the left forearm through which a painful shock could be given. The patient's selected deviant tape was then played, and he was asked to imagine the material being described. The last three 30-second segments of the tape contained the deviant material, as described above. The tape was run 10 times at

*Delivery of shock was contingent on i.e., followed exclusively, the presentation of a particular tape segment containing deviant material, as indicated in Fig. 2.

a session. In the first three runs the 4th segment was immediately followed by shock. With regard to the remaining seven runs the subject was told that he could avoid shock if at the 4th segment of the tape he would verbalize and fantasize alternative nondeviant sexual behavior. In the implementation of this the tape was stopped as soon as the patient spoke. He usually spoke for 2 or 3 minutes. If the patient failed to verbalize nondeviant sexual material, the 4th segment was played through and followed by shock as in the first three runs.

During sessions 5 to 7, only the first three segments of the tape were presented; and for sessions 8 to 10, only the first two. Thus, in sessions 5 to 7, it was the third segment that was followed by shock in the first 3 runs, and replaced by the patient's verbalizations of non-deviant sexual material in the subsequent 7 runs; and in sessions 8 to 10 it was the second segment to which this schedule applied (*see* Fig. 2).

Each tape run was followed by an intertrial interval of 4 minutes: 1 minute of silence, 2 minutes in which the patient did simple mathematical computation and another minute of silence. The mathematical computations were designed to inhibit thinking of sexual material so as to allow the penile response to return to a baseline level. Each session was conducted on a separate day. At the end of the ten training sessions, each subject had received a total of 30 shock conditioning trials and 70 avoidance trials.

The noncontingent shock subject underwent the same procedure as the shock

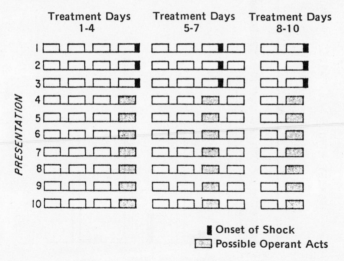

Fig. 2. Conditioning Schedule for the Contingent Shock Group during the 10 Days of Treatment.

contingent group except that the shock was never avoidable and was administered at random and only during the mathematical computation period of the intertrial interval. This subject, furthermore, was matched with one of the patients in the shock contingent group for number and sequence of shocks.

Stage 4. The effectiveness of treatment was evaluated at 1, 8 and 18 weeks following conditioning. The subjects were clinically interviewed (the interviewer being unaware of the subject's treatment condition) and were given the 10 item scale and the MMPI. In addition, the six tapes constructed in Stage 2 were played back to the subject while his penile responses were recorded. The first tape presented was the one used during conditioning. The remaining five tapes (two containing deviant and three non-deviant material) were randomly presented.

The degree of sexual arousal elicited by the tapes was estimated by subtracting the highest transducer reading during the initial, neutral 30 second period, from the highest reading during the presentation of sexual material.

RESULTS

The penile response to the deviant tape that figured in the aversive conditioning was found to be suppressed up to 18 weeks following shock-contingent conditioning (Fig. 3). Marked suppression of response was also observed with the deviant tapes that had not been used in the treatment, indicating good generalization. Arousal to nondeviant sexual material continued, indicating that discrimination had been achieved.

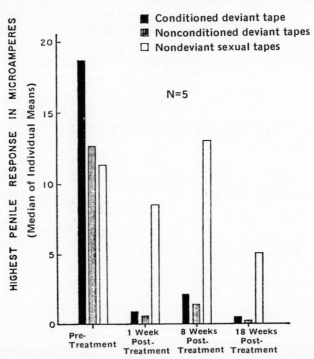

Fig. 3. Transducer Responses of the Shock Contingent Group Before and After Conditioning.

Figure 4 shows the penile responses of a shock contingent patient to the three deviant and the three nondeviant tape sequences 1 week before treatment and 1 week after treatment. The post-treatment penile response to deviant material is manifestly inhibited, while the response to normal sexual material is enhanced.

The general clinical assessment of the shock contingent group appears in Fig. 5, expressed as the median percentage of normality on a scale ranging from zero to 100 percent. A rank of 100 means that a clinical judgment was made that the patient was free

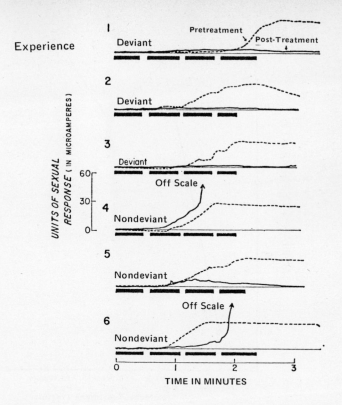

Fig. 4. Polygraph Recording of a Shock-Contingent Patient's Penile Responses 1 Week Before and 1 Week After Aversive Conditioning. Only experience 3 was used during conditioning (marked with asterisk).

from pathology. The group's clinical status can be seen to have improved by about 35 percent after treatment.

The shock contingent group's 10-item ranking scales (Fig. 6) were determined by adding the deviant preferences and subtracing 15. If the five highest rankings all consisted of deviant items, a maximal score of 25 would be obtained $(10 + 9 + 8 + 7 + 6 - 15)$. A considerably decreased preference for deviant items followed treatment. The group's total clinical MMPI scales (T scores) greater than 70 also declined after treatment (Fig. 6).

In the shock contingent group only one overt incident of deviant behavior was reported during the 18 weeks following treatment. The patient, while intoxicated, had acted out one of the deviant taped experiences not used in his treatment 15 weeks after termination of the treatment. In the Weekly reports, no new patterns of overt sexual behavior were recorded. Deviant sexual fantasies were less frequent after treatment, and nondeviant fantasies more frequent. Normal sexual behavior either increased or was the same as before the treatment.

Analysis of the data obtained from the noncontingent shock subject indicated that 1 week after his treatment there was a marked reduction in his penile response to the deviant material conditioned. However, there was only minimal reduction in his response to the other deviant tapes. Moderate suppression of the penile response to nondeviant sexual material was also observed. In interesting contrast to the shock contingent

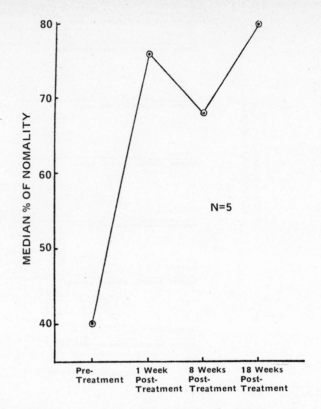

Fig. 5. Clinical Assessment of the Whole Shock Contingent Group. 100 Means Free from Psychopathology.

subjects, the penile response was reduced to both deviant and nondeviant tapes 8 weeks after treatment. The global clinical assessment rating and MMPI remained the same after treatment. No new patterns of sexual behavior developed. However, preference for deviant material on the 10-item scale dropped considerably after pseudoconditioning. Unfortunately, the 18-week follow-up data could not be obtained from this patient.

DISCUSSION

The object of the treatment was to extinguish the deviant sexual behavior and encourage socially acceptable, normal sexual outlets. Etiology and individual differences were not considered in the deployment of the technique. The results achieved suggest that the treatment was successful in suppressing deviant sexual behavior for at least 18 weeks. Continued follow-up may yield evidence of sustained benefit.

It is clear that in the laboratory environment deviant sexual responses were inhibited in all patients. The Weekly reports also indicate that this suppression was generalized in the shock contingent group to the life situation.

Although the noncontingent shock subject showed suppression of his sexual response to the deviant material that was used during his treatment, this suppression did not generalize to other deviant material. There was also the undesirable result of a reduction in his sexual responses to normal stimuli. On the other hand, it appears that he benefited from his experience, as shown by the absence of any overt deviant sexual behavior and a reduction in his 10-item scale score.

On the basis of the clinical assessment ratings, all patients were only 80 percent "normal" 18 weeks following treatment, indicating residual pathology. This could be due to nonsexual problems. Further investigation might have revealed the details of the remaining unadaptive behavior so that appropriate treatment might have been instituted.

Additional studies involving greater numbers of both experimental and control subjects with long term follow-ups are clearly necessary.

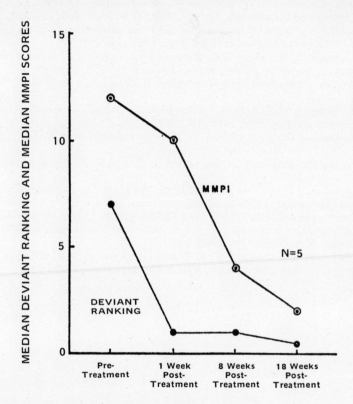

Fig. 6. Deviant Item-Ranking Scale and MMPI Scores of the Shock Contingent group. Lower scores indicate less preference for deviant items and less reporting of pathologic symptoms respectively.

REFERENCES

Bancroft, J.H.J., Jones, H.G. & Pullan, B.P. A Simple transducer for measuring penile erection, with comments on its use in the treatment of sexual disorders. *Behav. Res. Therapy,* 1966, **4**, 239-241.

Clancy, J. & Abel, G.G. Unpublished material available on request, 1967.

Davison, G.C. Elimination of a sadistic fantasy by a client-controlled counterconditioning technique. *J. Abnorm. Psychol.* 1968, **73**, 84-90.

Feldman, M.P. Aversive therapy of sexual deviations; A critical review. *Psychol. Bull.* 1966, **65**, 65-79.

Feldman, M.P. & MacCulloch, M.J. The application of anticipatory avoidance learning to the treatment of homosexuality. I. Theory, technique and preliminary results. *Behav. Res. Therapy.* 1965, **2**, 165-183.

Freund, K. Some problems in the treatment of homosexuality. In (Ed. H.J. Eysenck) *Behavior therapy and the neuroses.* Oxford: Pergamon Press, 1960, 331-326.

Levis, D.J. The effects of serial CS presentation and other characteristics of the CS on the conditioned avoidance response. *Psychol. Rep.,* 1966, **18**, 755-766.

Marks, J.M., Rachman, S. & Gelder, M.G. Methods for assessment of aversion treatment in fetishism with masochism. *Behav. Res. & Therapy.* 1965, **3**, 253-258.

Rachman, S. Aversion therapy: Chemical or electrial? *Behav. Res. & Therapy.* 1963, **2**, 289-299.

Rachman, S. & Hodgson, R.J. Experimentally-induced "sexual fetishism": Replication and development. *Psychol. Rec.* 1968, **18**, 25-27.

Raymond, M.J. Case of fetishism treated by aversion therapy. *Brit. Med. J.,* 1956, **2**, 854-857.

Smith, C.E. Correction treatment of the sexual deviate. *Am. J. Psychiat.* 1968, **125**, 615-621.

Stampfl, T.C. Avoidance conditioning reconsidered: An extension of Mowrerian theory. Unpublished manuscript, 1960. Data review in Levis, D.J. Implosive therapy, Part II: The subhuman analogue, the strategy, and the technique. In (Ed. by S.G. Armitage) *Behavior modification techniques in the treatment of emotional disorders.* Battle Creek, Michigan: V.A. Publication, 1960, 22-37.

Thorpe, J.G., Schmidt, E., Broun, P.T. & Castill, D. Aversion-relief therapy: A new method for general application. *Behav. Res. & Therapy.* 1964, **1**, 293-296.

11
An Automated Technique for Aversive Conditioning in Sexual Deviations

LEONARD FEINGOLD

The treatment of sexual deviations has been incorporating aversive conditioning procedures (Thorpe, Schmidt, Brown, & Castell, 1964; Feldman & MacCulloch, 1965; Bond & Evans, 1967). The techniques involve at least two elements and sometimes a third one.

1. Looking at or imagining the symbolic or real stimuli that are associated with the act. Touching the actual stimuli was used by Blakemore (Blakemore, Thorpe, Barker, Conway, & Lavin, 1963) in the case of transvestism.
2. The presentation of an aversive stimulus, usually electric shock, immediately following the looking at or imagining of the stimuli associated with the deviant act.
3. A third element that is more frequently included is differential conditioning (Solyom & Miller, 1965) in which a symbolic heterosexual stimulus is presented without shock or with the offset of shock. The purpose of this procedure is to condition approach behavior toward normal sexual behavior.

From a practicing therapist's point of reference, the aversive treatments are time-consuming and probably boring. Any movement toward automation of aversive techniques may lead to far greater applicability of these techniques. The technique developed here relies on the patient's imagination. The presentation of the stimuli for imagination and the aversive shock are all automatically programmed.

APPARATUS AND PROCEDURE

The procedure for the automated treatment involves the patient imagining those situations associated with the deviant act as presented by a tape recorder and then receiving electric shocks to the leg. The shocks are programmed on the tape itself. In addition, the patient imagines heterosexual situations without electric shock.

Apparatus

The Uher Universal 5000 (about $300) lends itself to automation very easily. (A cheaper tape recorder—the Wollensak T-1600—can also be used.) The tape recorder was used in a fashion similar to the one in which Migler and Wolpe (1967) used it for automated self-desensitization. Two features to the recorder lend themselves to automated usage. It has a pause switch which makes it possible to stop the tape at any time. This pause switch is wired out to a remote control microswitch which the patient holds in his hand. The patient, by a simple depression of the microswitch, can easily stop the tape. The second feature allows for rewinding the tape to a preset place on the tape. This is necessary in order to repeat a scene. The recorder has two metal sensing guides on each side of the recording heads. When a metal foil on the tape makes contact with the sensing guides on the left, the tape recorder goes from playback to rewind. These two guides were bypassed by the tape and a push button was wired in parallel with the two guides, so that a momentary depression of the push button would rewind the tape. The second pair of sensing guides to the right of the recording heads functions to stop the rewinding and return to playback when the metal foil makes contact with the sensing guides. These guides were left alone.

On the tape each scene was preceded by a 1-inch metal foil. After each scene, the patient could either repeat the scene by pressing the rewind button or he could go on to the next scene by releasing the pause switch.

Shock is programed by putting a signal on tape with a Uher accessory called UHER DIA-PILOT. The tape bypasses the pick-up reel and goes around the heads of the DIA-PILOT. With this device, one can put an inaudible signal on the bottom one-quarter of the tape which, when played back through the device, triggers a built-in relay which is connected to the shock apparatus. Shock was delivered through an auto-transformer plugged into 120-V ac.

Procedural Steps

1. The patient is asked to prepare a hierarchy of sexually deviant stimuli and rank the items from most stimulating to least stimulating.

2. The deviant scenes are put on tape in hierarchal order with the least exciting scene first and the most exciting scene last; 1-minute relaxation instructions precede each scene in order to have the subject relaxed to enhance imagination. After every three or four deviant scenes, a heterosexual scene appears in which there are verbal descriptions of arousing heterosexual situations recorded by a seductive female voice. Each scene is preceded by 1-inch metal foil.

3. Shocks are programmed on the tape following each deviant scene. The heterosexual scenes are not shocked and are only repeated once every three or four scenes.

4. The subject holds two remote control switches in his hand. The pause switch enables him to stop and start the recorder at any time. The rewind switch allows him to rewind the tape in order to repeat a scene if he feels any arousal on the scene.

5. The patient is instructed via the tape to imagine the deviant scene and stop the recorder until the scene is clear. He starts the recorder again as soon as he pictures the scene clearly and then automatically receives anywhere from one to three brief shocks.

He is then asked if he felt any sexual arousal on the scene. If he felt any arousal, he is asked to press the rewind button which automatically rewinds the tape to the beginning of the scene, and the scene is repeated. He continues to repeat the scene until there is no arousal. If there is no arousal, he does not press the rewind button, and the tape proceeds to the next scene in the hierarchy. The patient goes as far as he can on the tape. The session runs anywhere from 45 minutes to 1-1/2 hours. If he completes the tape in less than 45 minutes, he repeats the entire tape again.

6. The patients have usually been treated every day for the first week and then treatment has been thinned out. As a result of inquiries to the patient, new scenes may replace ones that no longer arouse him. Even though he may report no arousal, scenes are still repeated until arousal is not reported for more than five sessions.

7. There is no hard and fast rule for how long to treat a patient. It depends on his report of behavior outside the office. Generally, patients have been run 20 hours and booster treatments given after, if possible.

RESULTS

Case 1

The first patient was a 17-year-old youth who was an in-patient in the hospital because of difficulties in adjusting at home and in school. He had been a promiscuous homosexual both before and during hospitalization, although this was not the reason for hospitalization. He reported impotence with girls, and at the time of the aversive conditioning, was seeing a girl at the hospital but was impotent. After three sessions on the tape, he reported a successful heterosexual experience with this girl, which she corroborated. After ten sessions with the tape, the patient stated that he did not want to give up his homosexuality but wanted to be bisexual. On a year follow-up, he reported bisexual activity.

Case 2

A 23-year-old exhibitionist was admitted to the hospital in lieu of going to jail. He had been arrested eleven times for exhibitionism and reported that he had been exhibiting two to three times a week for the last eight years. He received twenty treatments over four weeks while in the hospital, concurrently reporting a decrease in impulses. After leaving the hospital, he was seen weekly for ten weeks, biweekly for five weeks, and monthly for three months. He reported no acting-out for this period. Six months after the last treatment, he called up and reported an incident and asked for treatment. He was seen twice in a two-week period, receiving two treatments. On an eight-month follow-up, he reported no exhibitionism and increased adult heterosexual activity.

Case 3

A 17-year-old American youth came from West Germany for treatment. He had a history of homosexual activity from age 13 to 15 in various boarding schools. For the last two years there had been no acting-out, but he reported frequent and strong impulses to do so that were making him extremely anxious. He had little activity with females and in one case was impotent. He was seen for two months and received 25 treatments. He reported an immediate lessening of obsessive homosexual thoughts and later, during treatment, that female sexual stimuli were becoming arousing. One month after treatment, he reported a successful intercourse. One year after treatment, he reports that he still has homosexual thoughts which are considerably weaker and less frequent than previously. He continues to be aroused by females and has sexual contact with them.

Case 4

An 18-year-old youth was committed to the hospital because he had been caught in a pedophiliac incident with a 12-year-old boy. The patient reported that he had many pedophiliac impulses toward boys per day (10 to 12 per day). He had a diary which, from age 14, showed erotic interest in young boys. According to his diary he had 25 pedophiliac incidents in four years and no heterosexual ones. He received 23 treatments while in the hospital for ten weeks. He reported diminution of pedophiliac impulses to zero and no acting-out. He was seen for six additional times during the next months, receiving a treatment each time. He reported that he had few deviant impulses and had begun dating girls. Contact was lost with this patient, preventing further follow-up.

Case 5

A 35-year-old married man came in for treatment of a pedophiliac problem with his six-year-old daughter. Two to three times a week he would fondle her and have an orgasm. Heterosexual contact with his wife was low in frequency and not rewarding. He reported pedophiliac tendencies toward little girls ever since he reached puberty. Previous to coming for treatment, he had seen a psychiatrist for five sessions with no diminution in the pedophiliac acts. He was extremely depressed and was having suicidal thoughts because he could not get over the problem. For the first three weeks, he received nine treatments. He reported no acts during this period and added that this was the longest interval in the last three years in which he did not have sexual contact with his daughter. After the third week, he had one pedophiliac incident. He felt extremely hopeless at this point. Because he lived a very long distance from the hospital, he was only able to come in once a week. The shock treatment was discontinued and we switched to covert sensitization for the next two sessions. On a year follow-up, he reports minimal pedophiliac impulses and no acts. When he does have the impulses, he uses covert sensitization. Heterosexual relations with his wife have considerably improved.

Case 6

A 35-year-old homosexual social worker came for private treatment. His sexual experience since puberty had been homosexual. At the time of treatment, he was seeing a girl and having successful intercourse with her. This was the first such experience in his life. He had not had homosexual experiences for the last year. However, he reported strong impulses in the homosexual direction and lack of satisfaction in the heterosexual relationship; the heterosexual aspect did not bring the same satisfaction as the homosexual one. He received 42 treatments over a three-month period. There was no change. He still reported strong homosexual impulses and lack of strong satisfaction in the heterosexual situation.

DISCUSSION

The technique appears to be as successful as those reported in the literature. It has the advantage of minimal therapist time and long sessions to allow for overlearning. No special stimuli are needed. The only investment in time is the preparation of the tape and splicing in of the metal foils. Once the tapes have been spliced, they can easily be used with other patients by just erasing the old deviant scenes and putting new ones on. The author could never have given as many treatments as he did, nor ones as long as he did, without this automated device. The machine makes it possible to have one patient running through the tape while another patient is being seen.

A word of caution is necessary in evaluating the technique. Other therapeutic maneuvers were going on more or less simultaneously with these patients in addition to the aversive conditioning. Such techniques as systematic desensitization, assertive training and environmental manipulation were used with some of the above patients. Therefore, no claim is being put forward for the efficacy of aversive conditioning by itself. To the extent that the research literature indicates that aversive conditioning is of value, then the present technique may have value as an economical way of doing this conditioning.

REFERENCES

Blakemore, C.B., Thorpe, J.G., Barker, J.C., Conway, C.G. & Lavin, N.I. The application of faradic aversion conditioning in a case of transvestism. *Behaviour research and therapy,* 1963, **1**, 29-34.

Bond, I.K. & Evans, D.R. Avoidance therapy: Its use in two cases of underwear fetishism. *Canadian Medical Association Journal.* 1967, **96**, 1160-1162.

Feldman, M.P. & MacCulloch, M.J. The application of anticipatory avoidance learning to the treatment of homosexuality. I. Theory, technique and preliminary results. *Behaviour research and therapy.* 1965, **2**, 165-183.

Migler, B. & Wolpe, J. Automated self-desensitization: A case report. *Behaviour research and therapy.* 1967, **5**, 133-135.

Solyom, L. & Miller, S. A differential conditioning procedure as the initial phase of the behaviour therapy of homosexuality. *Behaviour research and therapy.* 1965, **3**, 147-160.

Thorpe, J.G., Schmidt, E., Brown, P.T. & Castell, D. Aversion-relief therapy; a new method for general application. *Behaviour research and therapy,* 1964, **2**, 71-82.

12
Positive Control as an Alternative to Aversion Therapy*

GENE R. MOSS, RICHARD T. RADA and JAMES B. APPEL

Aversion therapy is a behaviorally oriented treatment that uses an aversive or noxious stimulus, such as electric shock or apomorphine, to rid the patient of some undesirable behavior, such as a sexual deviation or alcoholism (Moss, 1969). The aversive response can be paired either with a stimulus secondarily associated with the undesirable behavior, or with the behavior itself. When paired with a second stimulus, the paradigm is generally a respondent (Pavlovian) one; when paired with the undesirable behavior, the paradigm is generally an operant (Skinnerian) one.

Whatever the paradigm invoked, aversion therapy has assumed the status of a laboratory-based therapy derived from the experimental analysis of behavior. The literature has been devoted to matters of technique and outcome with relatively little attention to the issue of the desirability of instituting aversive control in the clinical context. Nevertheless, aversive control of human behavior may carry with it significant drawbacks in addition to the obvious one of intentionally inflicting discomfort upon the patient.

The recent development of techniques utilizing aversive imagery, i.e., verbal representations of noxious exteroceptive or interoceptive stimuli, may reflect a response to the drawbacks of instituting aversive control in the clinical situation (Cautela, 1967). Although a step removed from the use of noxious physical stimuli, it is likely that aversive imagery techniques will be found to suffer some of the same basic drawbacks common to all forms of aversive control.

The popularity of aversive control reflects its ease of application and the immediacy of response. However, sustained behavioral change through aversive control usually requires the continuing threat of presentation of the aversive stimulus in a situation that denies escape. In addition to offending humanitarian values, this may lead to undesired consequences such as aggressive retaliation, depression or physiological disturbances culminating in illness or even death (Appel, 1964).

*The opinion or assertions contained herein are the private views of the authors and are not to be construed as official or as reflecting the views of the Department of the Army or the Department of Defense.

The extrapolation of behavioral technology from the animal laboratory to the psychiatric clinic requires caution. Procedures demonstrated to be effective with animal subjects may not be appropriate to human patients. Even though aversive procedures can achieve behavioral control, it would seem far more desirable clinically to generate behavioral change through positive reinforcement rather than aversive control.

Two similar cases of transvestism illustrate some theoretical and practical differences between aversive and positive control. Both cases fell into the category of transvestite and not "transsexual" on the criteria of Kubie and Mackie (1968). Neither patient engaged in exhibitionistic or homosexual activities, and neither reported viewing his gender as female. With treatment, the frequency of cross-dressing in both cases decreased to zero.

Case 1

Mr. H., a man in his middle twenties who had been married without children for 3 years, sought treatment for transvestism that had begun in childhood. For the past several years he had cross-dressed 3 to 4 times a week on the average. He was of above-average intellect, a college graduate. He manifested no signs of psychosis. He had had psychoanalytically oriented psychotherapy weekly for 7 months without improvement. Because of the persistence of the problem plus a limited time for treatment, aversion therapy was considered.

Aversion therapy was conducted for a total of 25 sessions over an 8-week period, each session lasting from 30 to 50 minutes. The session began with a brief discussion of events since the previous meeting. The patient then disrobed to his underclothes, and shock electrodes were attached to the skin overlying the deltoid muscle mass. After electrode placement, the patient commenced cross-dressing. Electric shock delivered by a shock generator through a resistance in series with the patient was presented randomly during the cross-dressing. Each shock lasted 100 milliseconds and occurred at 1 second intervals until the patient began to remove the female clothing. Thus shock acted as both a punishment for cross-dressing and as a discriminative stimulus for undressing, i.e., escape. During the early sessions, shock was presented every trial. Although the initial shock level was reported by the patient as mildly painful, as treatment progressed habituation occurred, and the level was raised. Concomitantly, the frequency of shock presentation was decreased on a variable ratio schedule averaging every fourth trial. This schedule was designed to increase the patient's resistance to extinction of the effects of shock (Estes, 1944).

In addition to the aversion therapy, two joint interview sessions were held with the patient and his wife. It was suggested to the wife that she refuse to support her husband's perversion by insisting that he not engage in it in her presence. If necessary, she was to leave home until he had finished. In order to minimize the probability that Mr. H. would resort to auto-erotic behavior, the suggestion was offered that the couple explore patterns of mutually satisfying sexual behavior.

Favorable effects were immediate. After the first aversion therapy session and prior to the first joint interview, his rate of cross-dressing decreased to zero and remained at zero as reported by both husband and wife. At the second and final interview, the couple reported a definite improvement in their relationship. They had explored alternative patterns of sexual behavior that they both found rewarding. The husband also reported improvement in his general level of adaptation and his sense of well-being. At a follow-up meeting 1 month after termination, he reported complete abstinence from cross-dressing but also a slight but significant deterioration both in his marriage and in his general level of adaptation. He subsequently failed to return for further follow-up visits.

Case 2

Mr. R., a man in his middle twenties who had been married for 2 years without children, sought treatment for transvestism dating back to early adolescence. He was of above-average intellect, a college graduate and without signs of psychosis. He had gained some insight into the psychodynamics of his problem through extensive reading of the psychiatric literature; but his transvestism had continued unabated.

An extensive account was obtained from both husband and wife of the frequency and magnitude of the problem behavior and of the environmental variables associated with it. In contrast to the previous case, aversion therapy was never instituted.

The therapeutic program instituted consisted of definitive suggestions given to both husband and wife to achieve mutually satisfactory sexual relations without transvestism. Fortunately, the patient already possessed an appreciable sexual repertoire in relation to his wife. It was suggested to the wife that she refuse to support her husband's perversion by insisting that he not engage in it in her presence, and that she encourage alternate sexual behaviors already current to some extent in her husband's repertoire.

To the husband it was suggested that he bring his transvestite behavior under more explicit stimulus control. Stimulus control refers to the procedure of limiting the occurrence of a behavior to a specific set of stimulus conditions. In this case, it was suggested that the husband cross-dress as often as he must but limit the activity to a storage area in the rear of the home. In addition, he was asked to keep a daily cumulative record of the number of days he dressed only as a man, i.e., abstained from cross-dressing, as well as a record of the frequency and duration of the occasions he did cross-dress. These records were designed to serve both as information for the therapist and as an incentive for the patient to dress appropriately. The therapy sessions, involving primarily the husband but occasionally the wife, were used to assess the effects of the therapeutic program and to alter the program accordingly.

Formal therapy lasted 125 days and consisted of 22 therapy sessions. Prior to therapy, the patient used to cross-dress episodically. He would refrain for as long as 2 to 3 weeks, then cross-dress daily for days for weeks at a time. The results of treatment were somewhat less immediate than in Case 1. After 6 weeks, the rate of cross-dressing decreased to zero and remained at zero throughout the rest of the treatment and through a follow-up period of 8 months. In addition, the patient reported a significant improvement in his general level of adaptation and in his sense of well-being. No subsequent deterioration occurred in the patient's sexual behavior, in his general level of adaptation or in his sense of well-being. In fact, he reported continuous improvement in all these areas with time.

DISCUSSION

The program of aversion therapy instituted in Case 1 was based upon a punishment paradigm. Punishment refers to the presentation of an aversive stimulus contingent upon the occurrence of a behavioral event, the effect of which is to decrease the probability of that event occurring again. However, even with animal subjects, behavioral control through punishment presents technical problems. It has been demonstrated with animal subjects and with humans that the suppression of behavior by punishment may last only so long as the punishment contingency remains in effect (Powell & Azrin, 1968). Furthermore, animal studies by Hunt and Brady (1955) have indicated that punishment-induced suppression generalizes little outside the punishment situation. In addition, Moss and Appel (1968) have demonstrated on animals that once the punishment contingency has been removed, stimuli associated with a high rate of behavior facilitate recovery from the suppressive effects of punishment. Control through punishment often may be insufficient to obtain lasting behavioral change.

In Case 1, the aversion program was effective in achieving an immediate and complete suppression of the problem behavior.

In Case 2, therapeutic emphasis was upon the development of adaptive behavioral patterns supported by positive reinforcement from the patient's own environment. Previous case reports of aversion therapy indicate that relatively little emphasis has been given to the environmental variables associated with the problem behavior. Successful psychiatric treatment, whatever its theoretical orientation, would seem to demand the establishment of stable, adaptive behavioral patterns leading to positive reinforcement. Fortunately, the desired behaviors and the appropriate reinforcers were already current in Case 2 and required mainly strengthening and direction. Goldiamond has suggested that it is a good clinical strategy to utilize reinforcers already current in the patient's environment to strengthen desirable though weak behaviors already current in the patient's repertoire. The foundation of treatment was the instruction offered to the patient and his wife to institute programs of positive behavioral control through differential positive reinforcement and stimulus control. Although some attention was given to the patient's environment in Case 1, neither the diagnostic exploration nor the therapeutic intervention into the environment were at all comparable.

The successful therapeutic response in Case 2 does not validate the methodology employed, but it does serve to illustrate that a behaviorally oriented alternative to aversion therapy does exist and can be effective in cases as resistant to treatment as sexual deviations.

REFERENCES

Appel, J.B. Analysis of aversively motivated behavior. *Arch. gen. psychiat.* 1964, **10**, 71-83.

Cautela, J. Covert sensitization. *Psychol. rep.,* 1967, **20**, 459-468.

Estes, W.K. An experimental study of punishment. *Psychol. mon.,* 1944, **57**, No. 3.

Goldiamond, I. Personal communication.

Hunt, H.F. & Brady, J.W. Some effects of punishment and intercurrent "anxiety" on a simple operant. *J. comp. physiol. psychol.* 1955, **48**, 305-310.

Kubie, L.S. & Mackie, J.B. Critical issues raised by operations for gender transmutation. *J. nerv. ment. dis.,* 1968, **147**, 431-443.

Moss, G.R. An outline of behavior therapy. *Int. J. Psychiat.* 1969, 8, 883-895.

Moss, G.R. & Appel, J.B. Facilitated recovery from punishment-induced suppression. *Psychol. rep.,* 1968, **23**, 815-822.

Powell, J. & Azrin, N. The effects of shock as a punisher for cigarette smoking. *J. appl. behav. anal.,* 1968, **1**, 63-71.

13
Orgasmic Reconditioning: Changing Sexual Object Choice through Controlling Masturbation Fantasies

JOHN N. MARQUIS

The idea that stimuli can become capable of eliciting sexual arousal and overt sexual behavior by being paired with the release of sexual tension is not a new one. A bibliophile could surely find the idea set forth in some moldering manuscript written centuries before the advent of drive-reduction learning theory. Certainly Miller and Dollard (1950) had gathered together all of the facts necessary to suggest that directed masturbation fantasies could be used to alter a person's choice of sexual objects:

> General observations on man and also on animals (Beach, 1947) show that sexual excitement can readily be learned as a response to previously neutral cues and result in a considerable increase in drive. Similarly such observations indicate that previously neutral cues can acquire learned reinforcement value by association with sexual reinforcement. (p. 85.)

The only thing missing is fantasy. However, this element is mentioned in a footnote on the same page. Miller and Dollard followed Hull (1943) in believing that only the rapid reduction of a drive state would increase the habit strength of a preceding response. Therefore, they were troubled by the possibility that the acquisition of secondary reinforcement value by sexual stimuli might constitute a genuine exception to Hull's position that only drive reduction is reinforcing. They go on to say, however:

> ... sexual subgoals that are reinforcing in spite of an apparent increase in excitation tend to lose their reinforcing value and to be avoided rather than sought if they consistently fail to be associated with *eventual* drive reduction, either directly *or through the mediation of phantasies associated with masturbation or nocturnal emission.* (author's italic.)

In a later discussion of ways of getting rid of symptoms, Miller and Dollard point out that masturbation may be valuable in generalizing to other sexual behavior and extinguishing fears about sexual behavior. However, they caution:

Finally, the patient may be having undesirable phantasies during masturbation. Associating the strong sexual reward of the orgasm with the cues involved in these phantasies may increase his appetite for childish, perverse, or extramarital sex outlets. (p. 387).

They go on to suggest that the therapist "try to exert some control over the phantasies and direct them toward the heterosexual marital goal." (p. 387). Unfortunately Miller and Dollard do not give any case material or any more systematic or specific suggestions for applying their excellent advice.

In historical perspective their adumbrating of this technique is ironic. In 1950 scientific psychology and psychotherapy were worlds apart. The attempt of Miller and Dollard to reconcile psychoanalysis and learning theory generally confused the issues, led psychoanalysis in through the back door to a few more years of respectability, and probably led many emerging seekers of scientific methods of behavior change to follow the torch of learning theory to continue wandering in the wilderness of psychoanalysis for a few more years.

Yet their formula for directed masturbation fantasies foreshadows the bridge between the animal lab and clinic which enabled Wolpe (1958) to found his branch of behavior therapy as a method of individual treatment to deal with almost all problems in such a way as to satisfy therapists who are both thoroughly scientific and thoroughly clinical. Indeed the formulation contained three crucial elements of systematic desensitization:

1. The patient is recognized as a human being with the ability to conjure up images which can be used as stimulus material in modifying his approach or avoidance tendencies.
2. A powerful physiological response is used which is incompatible with anxiety and compatible with desirable behavior (relaxation in systematic desensitization, and sexual arousal and reduction in Miller and Dollard).
3. Emphasis is placed on shifting of stimuli in the desired direction.

The mere mention of mental content, although it undeniably exists as a private event, was the conditioned stimulus for derision and bad language on the part of behavioristic scholars in the 1940's and early 1950's. Obviously, this position has changed by 1970. The last chapter of each of several new books of great respectability is devoted primarily to the conditioning of private events (Bandura, 1969; Franks, 1969; Mischel, 1968).

Indeed many students of perception feel that most perceptions of external events are on the basis of matching of memory images and external sensory data. This position holds that all that sensory inputs do, except under circumstances of unusual novelty, is to call up a stored image. The efficacy of changing behavior by conditioning private stimulus material is supported by the dramatic results achieved by techniques such as systematic desensitization and covert sensitization (Cautela, 1967, Anant, 1969). In the latter technique use is made of private stimuli, both as unconditioned stimuli and conditioned stimuli.

In 1964, Thorpe, Schmidt, Brown and Castel reported one case in which directed masturbation was used to modify sexual preference. The client, a homosexual, was simply told to masturbate as frequently as possible, looking at pictures of attractive women which they provided, and using the pictures as a starting point for purely heterosexual fantasies. He reported some difficulty at first. The heterosexual fantasies he was able to conjure up were brief and it took him an unusually long time to reach orgasm. He stated that he felt no personal attraction to the girl in the picture at first. However, by the seventh session he was able to achieve sustained heterosexual fantasies and ejaculate in a usual amount of time. He had considerable feelings of attraction and affection for the girl in the picture. This interest generalized to real women and when treatment was terminated he was dating a woman to whom he felt a strong attraction.

This case serves to illustrate the fact that a powerful method of changing behavior is often effective even if used in a rather crude or unsystematic manner. However, a note of caution is indicated. The most crucial aspect of Wolpe's systematic desensitization (Wolpe, 1958; Marquis & Morgan, 1968) is that it is systematic, and many of the principles of modern operant techniques were well known for centuries before Skinner (1938) systematized the technology of operant conditioning. The improvement in results has come from applying sound learning principles to the fine texture of the process of behavior modification and carefully dealing with such variables as anxiety level and level of item difficulty. A prime bad example of pre-scientific attempts to modify behavior is the standard Victorian practice of sending boys to the local house of prostitution in order to desensitize their sexual anxieties. As Masters and Johnson (1970) have pointed out, conditions at the brothel can often provide for the conditioning of premature ejaculation and impotence.

McGuire, Carlisle and Young (1965) present a cogent and comprehensive case for the position that most sexual deviations are conditioned primarily through masturbation fantasies. Conditioned aversions to normal sexual objects, and modeling certainly contribute to this process, but choice of sexual object is probably crystalized by masturbation and overt sexual behavior leading to orgasm, or at least high levels of sexual arousal in the presence of real or imagined stimuli. McGuire, Carlisle and Young (1965) are primarily interested in explaining the etiology of sexual deviations, but they do propose implications for treatment. They make the general statement that they have had successful results with sexual deviates by ". . . instructing them whatever the initial stimulus to masturbation, the fantasy in the 5 seconds just before orgasm must be of normal sexual intercourse" (McGuire, Carlisle & Young, 1965).

Here are two refinements over the technique of Thorpe et al. (1964). First, recognition is made of the importance of temporal proximity of the stimulus to the orgasm. Second, the habitual masturbation fantasy is made available for use in achieving a higher level of sexual arousal and thus preventing the attenuation of sexual response evidenced by the long latency of orgasm reported in the previous work.

It is not clear where the figure of 5 seconds comes from. Actually Masters and Johnson (1966) state that the onset of orgasm can be anticipated by 2 to 4 seconds. In the case of the female there is an initial isolated contraction of the orgasmic platform 2 to 4 seconds before the onset of the rhythmic contractions of orgasm. In the case of the male the secondary organs of reproduction (the prostate and possibly the seminal vesicles contract once approximately 4 seconds before ejaculation. These phenomena correspond exactly to the subject's report of feeling the inevitability of orgasm. At this point in time the orgasm cannot be aborted and will run off no matter if sexual stimulation stops. Thus, the client can safely shift to picturing the desired sexual object.

Davison (1968) devised a more sophisticated programming of masturbation stimuli. This involved the substitution of gradually less salient heterosexual stimuli for the client's original sadistic fantasies progressing from pictorial to imaginal females and from naked women to clothed women. At each step in the progression, loss of sexual arousal was made the occasion for switching back to the previous step in the program—the back-up fantasy. The case he reported is of particular interest because the client, armed with an understanding of how the technique operates, went through the process of reconditioning himself to respond to his original sadistic fantasies and then eliminated them again in favor of the normal heterosexual stimuli.

As Miller and Dollard (1950) speculated, arousal without orgasm has proved capable of serving as the unconditioned response for conditioning sexual arousal to a formerly neutral stimulus. Rachman (1966) established sexual responses (Penile volume increase as measured by a penis plethysmograph) in response to a slide depicting a pair of boots by immediately following it with slides of attractive naked women. Three subjects were conditioned in 24 to 65 trials and extinction and spontaneous recovery of the response were demonstrated. In a replication to eliminate a methodological criticism, Rachman and Hodgson (1968) used five subjects who were conditioned in 21 to 38 presentations (contrast with Thorpe et al.'s 7 masturbations). McConaghy achieved faster conditioning in a design using colored geometric designs as CS and moving pictures of nudes (male for homosexual subjects) as UCS. The intensity of the CR was highly correlated with the intensity of the UCR.

Because arousal short of orgasm can be conditioned to neutral stimuli, the deviant stimulus must be faded for extinction to take place, the sooner the better. The problem with this is that it interferes with the most rapid and enjoyable performance of masturbation, as both Thorpe et al. (1964) and Davidson (1965) report. This could be disastrous for a client-controlled technique which should be made as easy and reinforcing to the client as possible. Therefore, as with most behavior modification techniques, maximum effectiveness comes from the carefully balanced programming of ease and progress.

The main effect of orgasmic reconditioning follows the classical conditioning paradigm. Before conditioning takes place a stimulus is determined to evoke the unconditional response or UR, whether innately or by previous conditioning. This stimulus is called the unconditioned stimulus or US. In the present case the US would include both the physical stimulation of masturbation and the pre-existing, perverse masturbation fantasy. The UR would include sexual arousal and orgasm. Conditioning takes place by presenting the UCS and CS (appropriate fantasy) contiguously or serially, but preceding the UR. Through repetition the CS takes on the power to evoke some elements of the UR which then constitute the CR. This process of stimulus substitution is called SS contiguity learning and it can take place in the absence of reward. The CS will share its ability to arouse the CR (sexual arousal) with similar stimuli (appropriate sexual cues) through a process of stimulus generalization.

METHOD

The procedure used is generally as follows: First, a careful diagnosis of the problem is made, including exploration of the specific stimuli which elicit sexual arousal and those which do not, or even arouse anxiety. The matrix of sexual behavior is studied to determine if other procedures are indicated and if so all of them are instituted as soon as possible. Assertive training may be indicated to break a pattern of parental domination or a fear of being dominated by persons of the opposite sex. Shyness or sensitivity to criticism may need to be desensitized and social or sexual skills taught in order to make it possible to approach persons of the opposite sex effectively. Often covert sensitization or aversive conditioning to the perverse stimuli are indicated, but are not usually instituted until the client feels attracted by appropriate objects. Some clients need a great deal of information about sex.

Once diagnosis and preliminary planning are completed, the client is given an explanation of the process of conditioning in general, and specifically told how the process of orgasmic reconditioning will change his responses to sexual stimuli. Questions are carefully sought to make sure that the process is thoroughly understood. If the client is generally tense he is instructed to relax before masturbating, because sexual arousal and anxiety are incompatible (Wolpe, 1969). If he reports feeling guilty after masturbating he is instructed to relax after masturbating as well. It may be suggested that he increase the frequency of masturbation in order to speed the process of reorientation or to decrease the frequency in order to increase drive level if he masturbates more than once a day. It is often helpful to suggest the use of a lubricant to enhance physical stimulation.

US, or appropriate fantasies, are usually carefully specified. It seems desirable to specify variations in the appropriate fantasy if the client is unattached and to insure that they are appropriate to his situation. Thus, a 14-year-old might picture dancing or kissing rather than intercourse. A *Playboy* magazine centerfold is probably inappropriate for most men and can lead to the client's becoming a "beauty freak" who sits at home alone or trades more undesirable characteristics for more beauty in the sex object, depending on his own assets.

The client is instructed to masturbate to the point where he feels the inevitability of orgasm using whatever fantasy is most arousing. Then he is to switch to the appropriate fantasy. He is warned that he may experience some difficulty at first, but that he will not lose his sexual arousal at that point. After he has successfully shifted to the appropriate stimulus four or five times (this is arbitrary but seems to work), he is instructed to start moving the introduction of the appropriate fantasy backward in time toward the beginning of masturbation. An attempt is made at the outset to get a commitment from the client never to continue picturing the inappropriate fantasy through the occurrence of an orgasm, whether in masturbation or overt sexual behavior. Any decrease in sexual arousal upon switching is seen as evidence that the client has exchanged fantasies too soon and he is instructed to drop back to the original fantasy and switch at a higher level of sexual arousal.

The procedure is seen as accomplishing five things: 1) Interpreting the client's perversion in terms of conditioning as the result of a simple, mechanical, and often accidental or capricious process can be very reassuring to someone who has thought of himself as having an unspeakable taint or character flaw. 2) The technique is particularly reinforcing because it adds guilt-free (because it is doctor's orders) sexual pleasure to the usual reinforcement that comes from expecting and seeing improvement in a distressing problem. 3) It attaches sexual arousal and rehearses sexual behavior in response to socially acceptable stimuli. 4) It desensitizes anxieties which the client originally felt in response to the appropriate stimulus through pairing it with powerful sexual responses which block the occurrence of the anxiety response. 5) It extinguishes sexual responses to the deviant stimulus by preventing them from being paired with orgasm and eventually decreasing to zero the amount of arousal with which they are paired.

The writer has been using orgasmic reconditioning since 1965. All of the cases described below were seen because they were suffering human beings seeking help, and not as experimental subjects. Most were treated for other related or unrelated difficulties, as well as for their sexual problems. As a result, contamination of results by treating other problems and using other techniques is added to the uncertainty resulting from variations in the evolving use of orgasmic reconditioning.

CASE SUMMARIES

Two cases will be presented in greater detail than the others to illustrate the use of orgasmic reorientation along with other techniques.

Case 1

26-year-old clerk seen for 44 hours. He was referred by a colleague who had despaired of trying to save his marriage of 8 months' duration because of the extreme hostility between the partners who were now separated. He came in such a state of fury and despair that for several weeks the therapist lived in fear that he would act on his threats to kill himself or his estranged wife. Although he had been sexually active for 10 years he had never become sexually involved with any girl whom he really liked or respected and who was gentle and nice to him. This had forced him into marriage with a woman who was extremely vituperative and destructive.

The client's father was a busy executive who had found most of his reinforcements outside the home. His mother was domineering. He was very dependent on the mother but very much embarrassed and bitterly defensive about this fact. His feelings of inadequacy and resulting bitterness were increased by the awareness that he had hypospadias and by his having dropped out of high school once and college three times with poor grades despite very superior intelligence. He remained insanely jealous of his wife even after they were separated, in spite of the fact that he hated her. He felt that everyone was out to get him and was in constant, severe pain from stomach tension except when he was drunk, which was frequently.

During the early weeks of therapy much of the time was spent in trying to overcome the client's despair and cynicism in order to get him to try to stop raging and work on learning to relax. Within 6 weeks he was able to relax without help, but was still too angry and cynical to try it most of the time. At that time he reported bowling a line and receiving a score of 110. He thought a little about relaxing and his second line was 140. Thus reinforced, he worked hard at relaxing and scored 190. Thereafter he had good weeks, but would still often come in in a state of fury and hopelessness.

Two months after treatment started, orgasmic reconditioning was instituted, as we continued to work with relaxation and desensitization of several hierarchies. He was handsome and heterosexually active and was usually dating one or two "nice girls" as well as one or two whom he categorized as active or potential sexual partners. He was asked to picture having intercourse with a current "nice girl" with the inevitability of orgasm whether he was masturbating or having intercourse with a "bad girl." He was inconsistent at first because of his usual scepticism, but soon found he could switch earlier in the process and that he was finding "nice girls" more arousing. He then was diligent and by the end of 2 months was trying to seduce a "nice girl" of his own religion. They broke up, but he became interested in another nice girl a month or so later and began to relate much better to her as he became more relaxed and was desensitized to criticism and competition. Four months after starting orgasmic reconditioning he was able to enjoy both sex and tenderness in the same relationship. Shortly before termination of therapy he met another girl who was one step closer to home than the preceding one who was from Europe. They were married before the last interview.

Three years later the therapist met the client and his wife at a party. She is an exceedingly nice girl. Both reported an inspiring marriage. The client had continued to grow since the end of therapy into a very remarkable and creative young man of great poise, genuine social concern, and some scholarly accomplishment. He was in the process of choosing between several good graduate schools.

Case 2

This was a 21-year-old female assembler. Her parents had been prevented from marrying and she had been reared by her mother who was an extremely tense, worried and submissive woman. The mother had thoroughly dominated her and taught her to be afraid of everyone. She was very shy and uncomfortable with people, especially those she saw as wiser than herself, and attractive men her own age. She had been actively homosexual for 4 years and involved in the gay world for 3 years.

Shortly before coming for help, she had had her first heterosexual relations with a black man 11 years her senior. She had been orgasmic and generally enjoyed the relationship, but felt she had little in common with the man, who was happy and extroverted. Somehow she associated him with her Lesbian friends and was unable to generalize the erotic response to other men.

She learned to relax rather quickly, worked hard at staying relaxed and was soon able to be comfortable most of the time when alone. She was attending night classes in a local junior college. Because she had difficulty concentrating on her studies, a program was devised of gradually increasing periods of study followed by reinforcing activity. This was successful in solving this problem and helped her general level of anxiety considerably.

However, her greatest fear was of saying something stupid and it soon became apparent that she became tense the moment she started to talk. The response-produced stimuli resulting from opening her mouth were initially enough to break a deep relaxation. Desensitization to a criticism hierarchy having failed to ameliorate this reaction, she was asked to say "Mary" and then relax completely again. After some 10 minutes of this, she proceeded to "Mary had," and then to "Mary had a little lamb." When she could do this comfortably, she was given homework of staying relaxed while she read aloud and talked to herself in the mirror. At this point the criticism hierarchy was repeated having her say her part of the dialogue aloud, with good results.

She was asked to picture talking to attractive men her own age when she masturbated and was able to do so without loss of sexual arousal or resort to back-up fantasies of women or less appropriate men. She quickly progressed to picturing intercourse with appropriate men and found that she could talk to attractive men comfortably. Meanwhile, we rehearsed assertive episodes and her general confidence increased rapidly.

Three weeks after starting orgasmic reconditioning she met an attractive man at a party. She described him in glowing terms, but then said that there was one thing wrong with him—he didn't talk. The therapist was about to be sympathetic and let the matter drop, but she said: "Wait a minute, you're supposed to be able to change peoples' behavior. Isn't there some way we can teach him how to talk?" We conceived a plan for her to reinforce anything he said with her rapt attention. The following week she reported that he was talking at a great rate but that he constantly repeated himself. It was decided that she would continue to reinforce anything that he said for the first time. If he repeated himself she was to act bored, look away from him or look at her watch. If he said anything for the third time she was to find some excuse to arise and leave. The following week she returned to report that he no longer repeated himself, but that the quality of his remarks varied from fascinating to deadly dull. The same three levels of response were instituted depending on the quality of his conversation. At her next hour she reported that he was rapidly becoming a good conversationalist and that his friends at work had commented on the great improvement in his personality.

Therapy was terminated at this 22nd hour. Three months later she reported that she was having comfortable, satisfying relationships with men and that her confidence was steadily increasing.

Case 3

A 30-year-old male unemployed junior executive was seen for 10 hours. As an adolescent he had masturbated with fantasies derived from pornography with themes of sado-masochistic and group sexual activities. These included whips, leather clothing, grovelling, picturing wife's intercourse with another man and a shoe fetish. These fantasies had persisted in marriage and many problems arose when the wife was asked to play roles in these fantasies. The client was instructed to switch from his perverse fantasy to picturing looking into his wife's face when he felt the inevitability of orgasm during masturbation. (He and his wife were temporarily separated during treatment). Covert sensitization (Cautela, 1967) was used to reduce fetish fantasies. Initially, he had great trouble in controlling his fantasies, but after the ninth hour visited his wife and was able to have intercourse several times without other fantasies intruding. This caused a marked increase in his self-esteem and greatly improved his relationship with his wife.

Case 4

A 27-year-old male business executive was seen for 18 hours. Following homosexual relations with his brother at 13, he had used homosexual fantasies for masturbation. He had been a confirmed homosexual, frequenting gay bars for 3 years, but had only once had heterosexual intercourse, when drunk, 4 months before starting treatment. Covert sensitization and hand shock for homosexual situations was combined with orgasmic reorientation. Within a month he was having regular intercourse with a woman. Several times he returned to homosexuality for a night following a heterosexual rejection and heavy drinking, with a subsequent resurgence of homosexual impulses for a week or so. When transferred to a colleague nearer his home he was functioning better sexually with women than he ever had with men and enjoyed the competition of pursuing women.

Case 5

A 27-year-old male law student was seen for 13 hours. He usually pictured men when masturbating, but could use a heterosexual fantasy from the beginning of masturbation, and occasionally did. He was afraid of women and uncomfortable in close contact with men because of homosexual impulses. Previous treatment for 3 years by an analytic therapist had ended with a suicide attempt. He was told never to picture men when masturbating and given assertive training and desensitized criticism and heterosexual situations, along with shock-aversion conditioning to homosexual fantasies. In 6 weeks he had heterosexual relations with some difficulty, but this greatly increased his confidence. A couple of months later he was having satisfying sexual relations in the context of a somewhat platonic relationship and had no more doubts about his adequacy. He had escaped from a pervasive sick role.

Case 6

A 33-year-old carpenter was seen for 150 hours. He had spent most of 4 years in hospital with depression and chronic alcoholism. He had enjoyed manual and oral contact with his baby daughter while she slept. He had also once masturbated after beating a 2-year-old niece. He later used all three things as fantasies while masturbating or having intercourse with his wife. He had severe guilt feelings as a result of this and saw himself as a comtemptible freak. The mere explanation of the impulses resulting from his masturbation fantasies relieved him greatly. After desensitization to *Playboy* pictures he was unable to muster his pedophilic sadistic impulses for aversive conditioning. He is now comfortable around little girls and is a moderate drinker. It should be noted that orgasmic reconditioning was not formally used in Case 6; but the case is included here because it seems that the patient may have ceased to picture his perverse fantasies as a result of my explanation of his impulses.

Case 7

A 21-year-old male student, a confirmed homosexual, had had one isolated heterosexual intercourse several months before starting treatment, without generalization. A week or two after starting orgasmic reconditioning, he was enjoying heterosexual intercourse. He relapsed to homosexuality at times when things were going poorly with his current girl friend and when drinking. Was firmly bisexual when transferred to a colleague closer to his residence.

Case 8

A 27-year-old male technician was seen for 23 hours. He had a fetish for white socks and enjoyed being spat upon and cursed during homosexual relations. His attentions to adolescent boys had thrice landed him in the State Hospital for the criminally insane. He had been married to a female homosexual but had never had sexual relations with her. Orgasmic reconditioning was instituted together with covert sensitization and shock aversion to homosexual situations and socks. Within 10 days he was noticing attractive women in the street. Several times he pictured homosexual relations through orgasm, usually while intoxicated on marijuana, and each time experienced a resurgence of homosexual impulses. He was desensitized to homosexual situations and criticism and given assertive training. When treatment was terminated he had a steady girl friend with whom he had had oral intercourse and was no longer irritable or self-conscious. He had rare homosexual impulses but no interest in socks. He had stopped using heavy drugs and cut down markedly on his consumption of marijuana and alcohol.

Case 9

A 23-year-old male printer had been seen over 200 hours by several behavioral therapists. He was severely schizoid and passive and could never relax with another human being in the same room. Although generally unimproved, he was cured of homosexual behavior by orgasmic reconditioning and explaining to him the unimportance of penis size.

Case 10

A 29-year-old divorced teacher was seen for 40 hours. She had used masochistic fantasies for many years and was self-defeating and sexually uninterested in men who were nice to her. Following orgasmic reconditioning, she became less self-defeating and able to be attracted to men who treated her kindly, although still turned off by a man who did not seem sure of himself.

Case 11

A 45-year-old male mortgage broker was seen for 18 hours. He was extremely shy, having been the victim of severe maternal domination. Although he had been homosexual for many years he had been seduced by aggressive women twice. Orgasmic reconditioning was not effective, nor were other therapeutic measures.

Case 12

A 26-year-old physician who was not sexually aroused by kissing was told to kiss his wife during the late plateau period of sexual arousal and on through orgasm. He now enjoys kissing more, and his wife has more frequent orgasms as a result of prolonged foreplay.

Case 13

A 24-year-old male computer programmer who was very shy had had intercourse rarely but had frequently masturbated to fantasies and pictures of beautiful girls. As a result he was completely unattracted to girls who were not strikingly beautiful. This was a serious problem since he was homely and inarticulate. Orgasmic reconditioning led to considerable improvement, but he remains a little bit too particular.

Case 14

A 22-year-old female student was seen for 18 hours with extremely good results. She had used sado-masochistic masturbation fantasies and as a result thought of herself as being a freak. She was capable of carrying through masturbation with normal hetero-sexual fantasies and rapidly got over her morbid fantasies when told to do so exclusively.

In respect to the sexual problem alone, the results of these fourteen cases can be classified: five cured, four much improved, three improved with treatment continuing, one slightly improved, and one unimproved.

REFERENCES

Anant, S.S. (Ed.) *Readings in behavior therapies.* New York: MSS Educational Publishing Co., 1969.

Bandura, A. *Principles of behavior modification.* New York: Holt, Rinehart and Winston, 1969.

Cautela, J. Covert sensitization. *Psychol. Rep.,* 1967, **30**, 459-468.

Davison, G.C. Elimination of a sadistic fantasy by a client-controlled technique: A case study. *J. abnorm. psychol.,* 1968, **73**, 84-90.

Franks, C.M. *Behavior therapy, appraisal and status.* London: McGraw-Hill, 1969.

Hull, C.L. *Principles of behavior.* New York: Appleton-Century-Crofts, 1943.

Marquis, J.N. & Morgan, W.G. *A guidebook for systematic desensitization.* Palo Alto: Veterans Workshop, 1968.

Masters, W.H. & Johnson, V.E. *Human sexual response.* Boston: Little, Brown, 1966.

Masters, W.H. & Johnson, V.E. *Human sexual inadequacy.* Boston: Little, Brown, 1970.

McConaghy, N. Penile response conditioning and its relationship to aversion therapy in homosexuals. *Behav. therapy,* 1970, **1**, 213-221.

McGuire, R.J., Carlisle, J.M. & Young, B.G. Sexual deviations as conditioned behavior: A hypothesis. *Behav. res. & therapy.* 1965, **2**, 185-190.

Miller, N.E. & Dollard, J. *Personality and psychotherapy.* New York: McGraw-Hill, 1950.

Mischel, W. *Personality and assessment.* New York: Wiley, 1968.

Rachman, S. Sexual fetishism: An experimental analogue. *Psychol. rec.* 1966, **16**, 293-296.

Rachman, S. & Hodgson, R.J. Experimentally induced "sexual fetishism": Replication and development. *Psychol. rec.* 1968, **18**, 25-27.

Skinner, B.F. *The behavior of organisms.* New York: Century, 1938.

Thorpe, J.G., Schmidt, E., Brown, P.T. & Castell, D. Aversion-relief therapy: A new method for general application. *Behav. res. & therapy.* 1964, **2**, 71-82.

Wolpe, J. *Psychotherapy by reciprocal inhibition.* Stanford University Press, Stanford.

Wolpe, J. *The practice of behavior therapy.* New York: Pergamon Press, 1969.

14

The Therapeutic Use of Masturbation in the Treatment of Sexual Disorders

JACK S. ANNON

The importance of masturbatory fantasy in therapy has long been stressed by the psychoanalytic school. In theory, Murphy (1965) sees such fantasies as developing from extremely intense Oedipal longings, while others (Eidelberg, 1945; Hammerman, 1961) use the concept of unconscious masturbatory fantasies. In his review of the psychoanalytic literature in this area, Bonime (1969) points out the stress on the strong association between the unconscious masturbatory fantasy and the pathological character structure. Generally, the fantasy is seen as an emotional metaphor for a wide range of interpersonal practices of which the person using the fantasy is unaware. Clinical use of this material is similar to the use of symbolic dreams. For example, affective association to the fantasy is used to help the patient arrive at insightful experiences.

From a learning point of view, McGuire, Carlisle, and Young (1965) have advanced the hypothesis that continual masturbation to a fantasy may play an important role in the formation and shaping of the sexually deviant behavior itself. Clinically, learning-oriented therapists have attempted to use masturbation primarily as a means of conditioning arousal responses to stimuli that have not previous elicited such a response.

One of the first reports on the attempted use of such conditioning was by Thorpe, Schmidt, and Castell (1963) with a homosexual patient. Initially they had the patient stand in a small dark room where he masturbated to whatever fantasy he wished and at the point of orgasm a picture of a scantily clad female was lighted. However, by the eleventh session there was no change in the patient's homosexual masturbation fantasy, and a series of alternate procedures, including shock aversion therapy, were instituted. On an 8-month follow-up after termination of treatment, the patient reported one attempt at heterosexual intercourse and several homosexual experiences. He also reported a few minor attempts at exhibitionism, but he now showed interest in persons of both sexes rather than just young men and boys. It appears that regardless of the methodological difficulties, the positive masturbatory conditioning was more successful than the aversive conditioning.

The following year Thorpe, Schmidt, Brown, and Castell (1964) reported giving pictures of attractive females to patients and asking them to use them in their masturbatory fantasies. This was also done in conjunction with aversion treatment. Their overall reported results were much more encouraging.

In 1968 Davison reported the elimination of a sadistic fantasy in a client through use of a number of procedures, one of which was client-controlled masturbation sessions. Davison (1968) had suggested that the client use his sadistic fantasy initially, then switch to pictures from *Playboy* magazine as soon as possible. The client reported some success along with several "breakdowns." He was then moved to the use of real-life pictorial stimuli of girls in bathing suits or lingerie, with the *Playboy* pictures as back-up stimuli. Again the client reported only limited success. Davison then instituted a form of covert sensitization to the sadistic fantasies, along with instructions on continuing to masturbate to pictures of girls in bathing suits. By the end of the sixth session, the client reported that the sadistic fantasies had dropped out, and he was using real-life and imaginal appropriate sexual stimuli for his fantasies. A 1-month follow-up indicated that the client was no longer using the sadistic fantasies, though he still had not started dating.

Jackson (1969) described the successful treatment of voyeurism after only eight sessions by asking his client to masturbate to the most exciting pornographic pictures that he could find with particular concentration at the point of orgasm. He instructed his client to do this every time he felt an urge to peep. After 2 weeks he was moved to the use of nude pictures from *Playboy*. From that time progress was rapid and the client reported no urges to peep and two satisfactory heterosexual relations. A 9-month follow-up showed continual gains. It should be noted that in contrast to the Davison (1968) procedures, Jackson first used stimuli that were sexually arousing to the client before moving him to general *Playboy* nudes.

Gray (1970) used a number of different procedures in the treatment of a client with homosexual fantasies and heterosexual anxiety. One suggestion was to request that the client stop using homosexual masturbatory fantasies and switch to heterosexual ones. Apparently, the client was able to achieve this on his own by the fifteenth session. Fortunately, the client was also closely involved with a young woman who was aware of his problem and who apparently contributed immeasurably to the treatment. He initially reported no arousal to the woman and was able to experience arousal only after an extended series of *in vivo* desensitization procedures. It is somewhat puzzling why there was no attempt to have the client use the woman in his masturbatory fantasies and thus increase the probability of his experiencing arousal to her.

Most recently, Marquis (1970) has described a procedure called *orgasmic reconditioning* for eliminating perversions through careful programming of masturbation fantasies. He instructs his clients to masturbate with whatever fantasy is most arousing and then switch to the more appropriate fantasy at the point of orgasm. After the client has been able to do this successfully four or five times he is asked to introduce the appropriate fantasy backward in time toward the beginning of masturbation. If the client reports any decrease in arousal upon switching he is instructed to drop back to the original fantasy and switch to a higher level of sexual arousal. Marquis describes his method as an adjunctive technique for changing sexual object choice, and he illustrates his procedure with 14 case summaries dealing with homosexual, fetishistic, masochistic, and other related problems. His paper offers the first systematic approach to the use of fantasy in this area.

As may be seen by this brief overview, the therapeutic use of masturbation by learning-oriented therapists has been limited and somewhat fragmented, and, with the exception of Marquis (1970), when such a procedure has been used, it has been used in a relatively unsophisticated manner. The purpose of the present paper is to describe a number of therapeutic masturbatory procedures that may be used in the treatment of various sexual problems. The primary emphasis is on the overt behavior itself, the use of fantasy, and the use of pictorial stimuli.

THEORY AND RESEARCH

In their original theoretical paper, McGuire et al. (1965) suggest that the orgasm experienced during masturbation provides the critical reinforcing event for the conditioning of the fantasy preceding or accompanying masturbation. They argue that what particular fantasy is used may be arbitrarily determined by a random experience to which an individual was subjected at some point in his life. One of the many implications of this theory is that it allows for the acquisition of any sexual deviation. In support of their view they cite numerous case histories that illustrate the possibility of such conditioning. Though further case descriptions from a learning-oriented view have supplied additional grounds for this hypothesis (Annon, 1971), it is interesting to note that perhaps the greatest clinical case support for this theory may be found in the psychoanalytic literature. Many of the carefully detailed psychoanalytic histories of masturbatory fantasies provide excellent illustrations of how sexually deviant behavior may have been learned through such a conditioning process. Examples of such histories may be found in Berest's (1970) report on a case of sadism; Friedemann's (1966) description of two cases of male transvestism; McCawley's (1965) paper on cases of exhibitionism. Shenken's (1964) account of bestiality cases; Yalom's (1960) study of cases of voyeurism; and Gorman's (1964) report on fetishism in identical twins.

Of course, direct experimental testing of the theory is not possible ethically, though several experimental studies have indirectly tested the hypothesis. Evans (1968) attempted to decondition exhibitionistic behavior by using emotive imagery and aversive conditioning with two groups of exhibitionists, one with normal masturbatory fantasies and the other with deviant fantasies. As was predicted, the deviant behavior of acting out (and the urge to do so) was deconditioned significantly more rapidly in the normal fantasy group (median of 4 weeks) than in the deviant fantasy group (median of 24 weeks).

Rachman (1966), and Rachman and Hodgson (1968) demonstrated that it is possible to experimentally condition arousal in males to previously neutral stimuli (slides of black boots) by pairing their presentation with sexually arousing stimuli (colored slides of nude women). Similarly, McConaghy (1970) reported conditioned penile volume changes to the presentation of slides with red circles or green triangles after such presentations were repeatedly followed by pictures of nudes (female nudes for heterosexual subjects and male nudes for homosexual subjects). Barlow and Agras (1971) further demonstrated that it was experimentally possible to directly alter sexual arousal to heterosexual stimuli in a subject with a homosexual problem. They used a fading technique whereby they gradually and systematically increased the brightness of a slide of a female nude (which had elicited no arousal response) while simultaneously decreasing the brightness of a superimposed slide of a male nude (which had elicited a high arousal response as measured by penile volume change). They used a design where the fading was introduced, reversed, and reintroduced again while associated changes in sexual arousal were measured. Not only did they demonstrate arousal responses to the female slide used, but the response generalized to other female slides and, during the first fading-in phase, the client reported sexual attraction to females in his daily life.

In their original theoretical paper, McGuire et al. (1965) mentioned a number of implications for treatment, one of which was that positive conditioning to heterosexual stimuli could be carried out along lines similar to the manner that the deviant stimuli were conditioned. The authors briefly mentioned successful results by having their patients use imagery of normal sexual intercourse in the 5 seconds preceding orgasm, regardless of the initial stimuli used. They provide no further details. While it seems reasonable to assume that the orgasm experience would be an extremely effective reinforcing event for any stimuli preceding or accompanying the occasion, Staats (1970) has recently pointed out that each instance of a sexual act constitutes a whole series of classical conditioning trials, since a sexual act extends over a considerable length of time. Probably many subjects with homosexual problems have had no opportunity, or interest in taking advantage of opportunity, to discover specific details of female anatomy, so it would be expected that their attempts at such imagery would be "fuzzy" and difficult to obtain without some further help in addition to being told to "imagine heterosexual intercourse."

Recently, Staats (1968, 1970) has advanced the concept of a human motivational system which he refers to as the Attitude-Reinforcer-Discriminative (A-R-D) system. He suggests that the same stimulus may have multiple functions in relation to both classical and operant conditioning. The A-R-D system stands for the three functions that a stimulus may serve. An Attitudinal stimulus is defined as a stimulus which has come to elicit an emotional response through the principles of classical conditioning. He then points out that this same stimulus will also function as a Reinforcing stimulus, as well as serve as a Discriminative stimulus that may elicit overt behavior. The A-R-D system has many important implications for the treatment of complex sexual disorders. One is in the assumed hierarchical nature of the system, where deprivation or satiation procedures may alter the reinforcing intensity of a given stimulus.

Another implication is that once a stimulus comes to elicit an emotional response, thereby becoming a reinforcer, it will continue to do so unless further conditioning or extinction procedures are encountered. In treating homosexual problems this would suggest that altering a client's response to members of the opposite sex, along with acquisition of appropriate heterosexual behavior, would have little effect on the client's responses to members of the same sex. This, perhaps, suggests why some clients are reported as leaving treatment as "bisexuals," or why the fading procedures of Barlow and Agras (1971) appeared to have no effect on the strong arousal responses of the client to male slides.

The assumed interaction effect of the three A-R-D functions of a given stimulus has further implications for treatment. Changing the value of one function is believed to also affect the other two functions. For example, it would be expected that, with the use of masturbation, changing the attitudinal response of a male to females would not only change the reinforcing value of females for him, but that females would elicit different behaviors from him.

Finally, the assumption that altering the individual's A-R-D system may induce changes in his instrumental behavior repertoire has an important implication for the ordering of interventions. For example, altering the attitudinal response of a male to a female from negative to positive might change her discriminative value to elicit approach behaviors, the frequency of which would increase as a function of her increased reinforcing value. On the other hand, altering a male's A-R-D system in relation to females will not be sufficient if he has obvious deficits in his heterosexual behavior repertoire. However, an important theoretical point is that altering such an attitudinal response may facilitate the acquisition of such behaviors. It would appear that attempts to teach such new behaviors through modeling and operant principles without working within the A-R-D system first would be much more difficult. The therapeutic implication in such cases is clear: work to alter the A-R-D system *prior* to teaching new instrumental behaviors.

The current stress by many behavior therapists on a broad-spectrum approach to treatment has no virtue unless there is some theoretically based plan for ordering their various interventions. Without such a plan, broad-spectrum treatment may be just as much a shotgun approach as is using the same one or two procedures for all problems. The A-R-D system offers one such promising conceptual framework for the ordering of such problems and their treatment.

Space demands do not permit more than this brief background presentation of the A-R-D system, and a more detailed explication of the use of this system in the analysis of complex sexual problems is available elsewhere (Annon, 1971). In summary, the A-R-D system is seen as providing the theoretical framework for the appropriate use of masturbatory conditioning, and such conditioning is seen as a promising procedure for changing attitudinal sexual responses.

DESCRIPTION OF THE PROCEDURE

The general procedure is usually as follows: First, an initial analysis of the client's sexual problem from within the A-R-D framework, followed by a behavioral diagnosis of relevant behavioral repertoires is made. This usually takes from four to ten 1-hour sessions. The use of this approach offers a plan for the simultaneous consideration of the full range of the client's circumstances. Such a scheme also allows for the ordering of priorities for intervention and provides guidance for the timing of multiple interventions. In addition, the use of such a conceptual analysis is not tied to any particular behavioral technique or procedure, but fosters the development of appropriate procedures based upon theoretical analysis.

During this initial assessment period the client is also usually referred to his or her own physician for a medical evaluation to determine if there is any genetic, constitutional, hormonal, or disease factors contributing to his problem. Throughout assessment (and treatment), various opportunities are also taken where appropriate to orient the client to general learning principles and to suggest how such principles might account for some aspect of his problem. In addition, along the lines suggested by Tinling (1970), a new vocabulary of behavioral description is generally suggested. For example, the client may learn the different implications of saying "I had a homosexual experience" rather than "I am a homosexual."

Upon completion of assessment, a tentative rational treatment program based upon a learning-oriented conceptual analysis of the obtained information is made and then thoroughly discussed with the client. Generally, at this point many clients appear greatly relieved to hear that their behavior may be interpreted as resulting from experiences that follow general learning principles, rather than the result of some "disease" or "character flaw" within them. The rationale and purpose of the tentative program is explained and, if agreeable to them, put into effect (as of to date, no client has ever refused to try to plan, though some were initially skeptical that it would "do any good"). If it becomes apparent from the ongoing evaluation that a particular procedure, or the entire program, does not appear to have a functional relationship with the client's behavior, then modifications are made.

If the initial analysis of the assessment information indicates that the use of masturbation is appropriate, then one of the procedures to be described is initiated. Unlike some other therapeutic orientations that may see masturbation as pathological or distorted (see Marmor, 1969), a learning-based approach places no value judgment on the behavior. The activity itself is seen as neither bad nor good except in relation to the goals of the client or the laws of the society of which he is a member. Therefore, suggesting masturbation to a client—provided it is acceptable to him—is just as therapeutically appropriate as any other theoretically grounded, researched based procedure.

Not only is the self-regulated use of masturbation by the client viewed as a means of altering attitudinal responses to appropriate stimuli, but it is also seen as a way of extending perceptions of bodily sexual responses and of learning new sexual behaviors through approximation principles. As described previously, these procedures may involve the behavior itself, the imagery used (fantasy or pictorial), or, more generally, both. For clarity of exposition, procedures involved in each of these areas will be presented separately. After each general presentation, brief case examples will be described to illustrate the application of the procedure. Specific details of treatment are not given; however, a more detailed description of the majority of the cases along with the conceptual assessment and treatment scheme described earlier may be found elsewhere (Annon, 1971).

Masturbatory Behavior

Direct use of overt masturbatory behavior is primarily concerned with female clients with complaints of some form of orgasmic dysfunction or lack of sexual arousal. The goal of the procedure is generally to help the client gradually become more aware of her own sexual responsiveness until she eventually is able to experience orgasm. The usual next step is then successive approximation of heterosexual behaviors with her partner similar to the procedures suggested by Masters and Johnson (1970). The rationale of the approach is first discussed with the client as a means of "self-exploration" that she will eventually teach her partner. (The term *masturbation* is seldom used to avoid eliciting any conditioned negative attitude she may have toward the term.) In addition to discussion, it is generally helpful to provide the client with various articles that explain the methods and advantages of such self-exploration. Wright's (1969) short book has been particularly helpful in introducing female clients to this procedure, and many women have responded positively to reading what another woman has to suggest. The client is asked to refrain from sexual intercourse temporarily so as to avoid any further experiences of a negative value taking place. She is then encouraged to explore at her own pace and to report back her progress. If she appears to reach a plateau, it is often helpful to introduce the suggestion of using a vibrator, along with appropriate reading materials. Again she is encouraged to continue her self-exploration at her own pace with the eventual goal of sharing her new-found responsiveness with her partner. The client is also encouraged to be more aware of her own bodily feelings in her breasts and genitals on other occasions such as when she is taking a shower, bath, or drying herself.

Generally, clients soon report increased arousal feelings until they eventually reach orgasm. However, a word of caution is in order. Some clients may become very frightened and stop when they discover they are about to reach a climax. They usually report a fear of "something happening" like they are going to "fall into pieces" or "explode." It seems generally wise not to push them further and to allow them to proceed at their own pace with the assurance that their feelings are quite normal and to be expected and merely demonstrates their capacity for sensation. Usually the experience of orgasm is a highly positive experience, and most women report that they feel like a sexually normal woman for the first time in their life. Others, using similar procedures, have reported similar results (see Clark, 1968; Dengrove, 1971; Hastings, 1963). Once orgasmic return is achieved, successive approximation of heterosexual intercourse through arms, legs, and body positions, as well as movement from clitoral stimulation to labial and vaginal stimulation, may proceed. Finally, successive approximation to sexual intercourse with a partner may be advisable. The ongoing imagery during their exploration will be more fully discussed later.

Example 1. A 24-year-old woman reported that she had never experienced an orgasm by any means, and all sexual contact of any type left her with a "blank" feeling or only a slight degree of arousal. One aspect of her treatment was to suggest that she start on a program of self-exploration as described above. At the end of the first week she reported experiencing positive sensations that she had never felt before. At this point she was asked to continue her exploration and gradually move from direct clitoral stimulation to the general mons and vulval area. At the same time it was suggested that she begin to share her knowledge of herself by gradually guiding her partner. By the end of the second week she reported going beyond the suggested limits, and she had sexual intercourse with her partner on four different occasions. Her response ranged from "extremely pleasurable and arousing" on the first occasion to experiencing her first orgasm on the fourth.

Example 2. A 27-year-old female married 5 years reported never having experienced an orgasm by any means. She was started with self-exploration but soon reached a plateau beyond which she did not seem able to respond. It was then suggested that she experiment with a vibrator but she felt hesitant about using it herself, so she began using it in joint relations with her husband. She soon went beyond her usual stage of arousal but stopped just short of orgasm, reporting that she was afraid to "just let go." She was not pushed but asked to proceed at her own pace and to continue exploring her own potential. A week later she related experiencing her first orgasm with the vibrator. (Initially she reported that it took her an hour, but this eventually was reduced to 10 or 15 minutes.) After her experience she reported that for the first time in her life she felt like a "sexually normal woman."

Example 3. A 23-year-old female reported never having experienced orgasm through sexual intercourse, though she was multiorgasmic through masturbation. She masturbated through direct clitoral stimulation using a sideways motion, and she related noticing no feeling in her vaginal area. Through small successive steps she was moved to a circular motion of the clitoral shaft, dorsal-ventral motions of the mons area, then downward to the vulval area and eventually into the vaginal rim (each new movement being first attempted at the point of orgasm). Her body positions were also gradually changed from lying with her legs extended and her body rigid, to a position with her knees bent and legs flexed and body movement approximating sexual intercourse. It is interesting to note that once she reported a definite responsiveness in the vagina to the point of climax, she no longer found direct clitoral stimulation as satisfying.

Masturbatory Fantasy

The guided use of fantasy in masturbation appears to offer the most potential for therapeutic use in conditioning arousal to previously neutral stimuli. The research previously cited indicates that a wide range of sexual problems may be helped with this adjunctive technique. However, it is important to note that merely asking a client to change his fantasies is seldom sufficient. It appears that the most fruitful approach is to provide a systematic procedure that follows successive approximation principles. Marquis (1970) has offered an excellent description of the systematic use of masturbatory fantasy in the treatment of a wide range of sexual problems, and further elaboration of his procedure will not be given here. However, his technique of moving the appropriate fantasy from orgasm gradually back to the beginning of masturbation does not appear to take into account all the possible conditioning trials that may take place to the deviant fantasy prior to the final inclusion of the appropriate fantasy. Research is necessary to see if this delays the positive conditioning process. An alternate method of changing a deviant fantasy will be described, as well as a procedure for dealing with homosexual problems where the client has difficulty in fantasizing a female.

Example 1. A 23-year old female with a complaint of orgasmic dysfunction in intercourse reported using masochistic masturbatory fantasies of large groups of men attacking and raping her. Just prior to entering into treatment, these fantasies had begun to lose their arousal value, and she began using fantasies of engaging in sexual relations with horses and dogs. It is theoretically important to note that shortly after switching to these fantasies she reported exposing herself on two different occasions to pet dogs of friends of her, but they failed to respond. At this point the theory of masturbatory conditioning was explained to her (which greatly relieved her feeling that she was becoming "mentally sick"), and she was started on a program of successive changes in her masturbatory fantasy. She was first asked to return to her imagery of large groups of men in a somewhat improbable situation rather than in vicious attack situations. She was next requested to use small groups of men in such situations, to single men in such situations, then to single men in more probable situations, and finally to her current partner in a probable situation. The strength of the conditioning may be judged by her report that once when she was angry with her partner (and her therapist) she purposely reverted to her former masochistic and animal fantasies. She was quite upset when she found that they were no longer very arousing to her, and even more upset when she once more tried the imagery of her partner and found it even more arousing than before. This was discussed with her as an example of how such conditioning may take place, but it was also pointed out to her that this knowledge gave her the ultimate responsibility for her own behavior, as she was free to choose whatever fantasy she wished.

Example 2. A 24-year-old male with an extensive history of homosexual contact (over 200 different males) reported that he could not recall ever having experienced any arousal toward female stimuli of any type. At the beginning of his treatment program he was *not* asked to use imagery of heterosexual intercourse with which he was totally unfamiliar, but to use features of his past imagery in combination with females. In other words, his past behavior and masturbatory fantasy had always involved having a male perform fellatio on him or engaging in anal intercourse, with the other male as receiver. He was merely asked to substitute females performing these same behaviors in his fantasy. This did not require any new knowledge of female anatomy or use of imagery that was beyond him. Even at this, however, he still described his first attempt as seeing the female in a somewhat "fuzzy" situation. He also reported feeling "strange and alienated," which seems to be a common first reaction. In this case continued practice led him to feel "proud" and then finally highly aroused to the imagery. He also reported that for the first time he began noticing females around him and really looking at them, suggesting that changing the attitudinal value of female stimuli may have also changed the discriminative function of females, as the A-R-D theory would predict. Most important, his arousal response appeared to generalize to the actual environment when he discovered himself aroused to the point of erection when looking at a "real woman." This was a completely new experience for him and something that he did not think possible. This all happened within a 1-week period.

Masturbatory Pictorial Stimuli

If the client reports failure in using a suggested fantasy and reversal to previous fantasy, it may be taken as a possible indication that the therapist has suggested stimuli that might be anxiety provoking, or, because of the lack of familiarity, stimuli that are too difficult to imagine without specific training procedures being instituted. Various training procedures in imagery are used with systematic desensitization when the client reports difficulty in imagery, and there is no reason to believe that such procedures would not be effective in masturbatory conditioning. Supplying the client with pictorial materials that are individually selected by the client as eliciting some degree of interest seems to be one promising approach. If questioning reveals some anxiety response to the materials, then perhaps systematic desensitization to the material may be necessary before such positive conditioning procedures are initiated. Again, merely suggesting to the client that he use pictures from *Playboy* is seldom sufficient. A systematic approach that follows successive approximation principles appears to offer the best results.

Example 1. A 23-year-old male with a homosexual problem reported that he had been sexually afraid of women since his first and only contact at age 16 when he found himself impotent. His masturbatory fantasy was limited to males, except for one occasion when he attempted to visualize intercourse with a female, but the imagery had been too "fuzzy" and unsatisfactory. This case was seen prior to the full development of the conceptual scheme of analysis advanced previously, and it further illustrates the pitfalls of inadequate analysis. First, an attempt was made to change the discriminative value of females by concentrating on supplying the client with appropriate information of female sexual anatomy and function by using readings, diagrams, charts, and models. He soon became quite knowledgeable in this area and was proud to find that he was the "authority" with most of his friends. He was then given further materials and information of relevant techniques in heterosexual stimulation and coitus. However, it appeared that even though there was a change in the discriminative function of females (he felt confident of his ability to "at last" perform in such a situation and he thought it would be "interesting" if it happened), there was no corresponding change in his attitudinal response to women. As he put it, "they just don't turn me on. What a waste of all my new knowledge." At this time the use of masturbation to fantasies of females was attempted but resulted in "breakdowns" because the imagery was too "fuzzy." Then the use of controlled pictures in place of fantasy was instituted. He was given a series of pictures to use according to the degree of interest that he showed in them. At each therapy session he was given new pictures to replace those that he had used the previous few days. The eventual graded sequence ran as follows: color close up pictures of female genitalia (he had no idea of what a female looked like "down there"); pictures of breasts and genitalia; pictures of the complete nude female body in a variety of positions; pictures of couples engaging in intercourse and other sexual behavior; and, finally, motion picture films of couples engaging in various forms of sexual behavior. Here too, the client described a series of changing responses starting with a "strange" feeling, eventually a "warm" feeling, and finally a high degree of arousal. Shortly thereafter, he began to experience arousal to females in his natural environment. However, even though he now was eager to have sexual relations with a female, his deficit in social and dating behaviors prevented him from further immediate progress. As he aptly put it, "I want to—and I know what to do when I get them there—but how in the hell do I get them to bed?" At this time behavior rehearsal and successive approximation of social contacts was begun. Initial analysis from within the A-R-D framework would have suggested a possibly more fruitful sequence of working with his attitudinal response first, followed by behavioral training of social skills along with cognitive information pertaining to sexual knowledge and skills.

Example 2. A 32-year-old male with a pedophilic problem reported that he had been sexually attracted to little girls since his early teens, and he had a 10-year history of physical contact with young girls. His masturbatory fantasies had always been devoted to prepuberal females. An initial A-R-D analysis of the clients problem indicated that female sexual stimuli had a high negative value for him. We conjectured that if he were asked to discontinue using young females in his fantasies and to start using stimuli of negative value, masturbation would lose its reinforcing value and thus possibly increase the reinforcing value of actual contact with children (which was much higher on his sexual reinforcing hierarchy than adult female contact). Accordingly, the negative attitudinal response to adult female sexual stimuli was first altered through the use of systematic desensitization procedures. Next an attempt was made to have him masturbate to adult female fantasy, but this was abandoned when he reported an immediate "breakdown" and reversal to previous imagery. He was then supplied with several magazines containing pictures of nude women engaging in a variety of activities. From these magazines pictures were selected by him that elicited some "interest" on his part, mostly of teenagers with small breasts and a light growth of pubic hair. Those pictures that showed younger, preteenage girls were excluded, but he was allowed to take several where breast development had just begun, or where the pubic hair was relatively scanty. We hoped that these would serve as a first step in successive approximation to adult females. In addition, we suggested that he imagine himself engaging in fondling and petting behaviors with the women in the pictures, similar to those behaviors that he had used with children. At the point of orgasm he was to concentrate on imagining intromission with the adult female with all the accompanying sensations he could imagine. He soon reported that he was able to use the pictures exclusively, but they were not particularly "arousing" to him. We explained that they were not expected to be arousing initially, but that the intent of the procedure was eventually to help them become arousing. At each session his pictures were exchanged for those of slightly older women with more breast development and more pubic hair growth. By his fifth session, he was selecting rather large-breasted women with well-developed genitalia of about 20 years of age. He reported one "breakdown" on his twelfth session but was surprised and disappointed to find that his old fantasy was not particularly arousing and satisfying as the more recent ones involving adult females. He also began to report arousal to older girls (age 16-18) in the natural environment. He was then moved to pictures of couples engaging in petting and intercourse, and he soon reported these as being very arousing. At this time social behavior training was begun, and, somewhat later, covert sensitization procedures to behavior with young girls was instituted. In a 5-month period after the withdrawal of all treatment procedures, the client continued to report strong arousal to, and heterosexual behavior with, adult females. He reported no arousal or contact with female children during the same period. His case is still being followed.

DISCUSSION

There are a number of practical considerations that should be considered when these procedures are used. First, in order to help the client experience as much success as possible and to prevent regression to his previous fantasies, the therapist must keep in close contact with the client. This may mean that when such treatment is initiated, daily contacts may be necessary so that any reversals or other difficulties can be examined and alternate procedures immediately suggested. Generally, starting with three contacts a week and then two a week seems to be sufficient.

Since the eventual goal of these treatment procedures is to help the client experience arousal to real-life stimuli, the therapist must suggest any procedures that he feels might be of aid to the particular client in helping him to generalize his response to the natural environment. For example, when working with homosexual problems the therapist may suggest that the client engage in "mentally undressing" different women he encounters; or he may give the client homework assignments of noticing and recording the different shapes and sizes of female breasts; or he may only suggest that he just look for the "female butt of the week." Another technique that might be of help in increasing generalization is *fantasy masturbation*. This technique was developed when a client reported that he experienced no arousal to women in the natural environment, only interest. But later when masturbating to women he had seen, he found them highly arousing. It was suggested that whenever he encountered such women in the natural setting he was to imagine that he was using them in his masturbation at that very moment. Inasmuch as the thought of masturbation appeared to be a discriminative stimulus for arousal and masturbation, it was hoped that by pairing this thought with actual stimuli these stimuli would become conditioned to arousal. At his next session he reported two occasions of high arousal lasting an hour each. He had sat in the park and associated his fantasy masturbation with various women walking by him. He was encouraged in his progress, but it was suggested that he attempt such fantasy more with women he knew and was considering dating. Regardless of the technique, the important point is that the client attempt to associate arousal with real-life stimuli as well as fantasy or pictures.

Finally, it should be pointed out that successful results from the application of these procedures will rarely mean that treatment is complete. The reported success of Jackson

(1969) in his treatment of voyeurism appears to be a rare exception. Generally these procedures are seen as only one of a number of necessary interventions for dealing with complex sexual problems. For example, in working with homosexual problems, sexual arousal to heterosexual stimuli might be seen as a good starting point. (It appears to have a strong reinforcing effect on the client who usually reports a positive feeling of "normality" and generally sees "hope" for the first time.) However, numerous other difficulties remain, such as the possibility of continued arousal to the same sex stimuli, or major deficits in appropriate heterosexual social behaviors. On the other hand, changes in the client's attitudinal response does appear to affect related functions of the stimuli and tend to make other procedures such as social behavior training much more reinforcing for the client.

In closing, it should be pointed out that because of the comprehensive approach used, the results of the procedures described in the case examples are confounded by the use of a number of other interventions for different aspects of the sexual problem. Experimental research is definitely needed to identify the most relevant variables in such procedures, to discover the most effective methods for establishing conditioned arousal (e.g., masturbation, slides, motion pictures, etc.), as well as determining the lasting effects of such conditioning.

REFERENCES

Annon, J.S. *The extension of learning principles to the analysis and treatment of sexual problems.* (Doctoral dissertation, University of Hawaii) Ann Arbor, Mich.: University Microfilms, 1971, No. 72-290.

Barlow, D.H., & Agras, W.S. An experimental analysis of "fading" to increase heterosexual responsiveness in homosexuality. Paper presented at the 17th annual meeting of the Southeastern Psychological Association, Miami Beach, Florida, April 1971.

Berest, J.J. Report on a case of sadism. *Journal of Sex Research,* 1970, 6, 210-219.

Bonime, W. Masturbatory fantasies and personality functioning. In J.H. Masserman (Ed.), *Science and psychoanalysis.* Vol. 15. *Dynamics of deviant sexuality.* New York: Grune & Stratton, 1969. Pp. 32-50.

Clark, L. The range and variety of questions people ask about sex. In C.E. Vincent (Ed.), *Human sexuality in medical education and practice.* Springfield, Ill.: Thomas, 1968. Pp. 552-565.

Davison, G. Elimination of a sadistic fantasy by a client-controlled counterconditioning technique. *Journal of Abnormal Psychology,* 1968, 73, 84-90.

Dengrove, E. The mechanotherapy of sexual disorders. *Journal of Sex Research,* 1971, 7, 1-12.

Eidelberg, L. A contribution to the study of masturbatory phantasy. *International Journal of Psychoanalysis,* 1945, 26, 127-137.

Evans, D.R. Masturbatory fantasy and sexual deviation. *Behaviour Research and Therapy,* 1968, 6, 17-19.

Friedemann, M.W. Reflection on two cases of male transvestism. *American Journal of Psychotherapy,* 1966, 20, 270-283.

Gorman, G.F. Fetishism occurring in identical twins. *British Journal of Psychiatry,* 1964, 110, 255-256.

Gray, J.J. Case conference: behavior therapy in a patient with homosexual fantasies and heterosexual anxiety. *Journal of Behavior Therapy and Experimental Psychiatry,* 1970, 1, 225-232.

Hammerman, S. Masturbation and character. *American Psychoanalytic Association, Journal,* 1961, 9, 287-311.

Hastings, D.W. *Impotence and frigidity.* Boston: Little, Brown, 1963.

Jackson, B.T. A case of voyeurism treated by counterconditioning. *Behaviour Research and Therapy,* 1969, **7**, 133-134.

McCawley, A. Exhibitionism and acting out. *Comprehensive Psychiatry,* 1965, **6**, 396-409.

McConaghy, N. Penile response conditioning and its relationship to aversion therapy in homosexuals. *Behavior Therapy,* 1970, **1**, 213-221.

McGuire, R.J., Carlisle, J.M., & Young, B.G. Sexual deviation as conditioned behaviour: a hypothesis. *Behaviour Research and Therapy,* 1965, **2**, 185-190.

Marmor, J. Discussion of "masturbatory fantasies and personality functioning." In J.H. Masserman (Ed.), *Science and psychoanalysis.* Vol. 15. *Dynamics of deviant sexuality.* New York: Grune & Stratton, 1969. Pp. 47-50.

Marquis, J.N. Orgasmic reconditioning: changing sexual object choice through controlling masturbation fantasies. *Journal of Behavior Therapy and Experimental Psychiatry,* 1970, **1**, 263-271.

Masters, W.H., & Johnson, V.E. *Human sexual inadequacy.* Boston: Little, Brown, 1970.

Murphy, W.F. *The tactics of psychotherapy.* New York: International Universities Press, 1965.

Rachman, S. Sexual fetishism: An experimental analogue. *Psychological Record,* 1966, **16**, 293-296.

Rachman, S., & Hodgson, R.J. Experimentally-induced "sexual fetishism": Replication and development. *Psychological Record,* 1968, **18**, 25-27.

Shenken, L.I. Some clinical and psychopathological aspects of bestiality. *Journal of Nervous and Mental Disease,* 1964, **139**, 137-142.

Staats, A.W. Social behaviorism and human motivation: principles of the Attitude-Reinforcer-Discriminative system. In A.G. Greenwald, T.C. Brock, & T.M. Ostrom (Eds.), *Psychological foundations of attitudes.* New York: Academic Press, 1968. Pp. 33-66.

Staats, A.W. Social behaviorism, human motivation, and the conditioning therapies. In B.A. Maher (Ed.), *Progress in experimental personality research.* Vol. 5. New York: Academic Press, 1970. Pp. 111-168.

Thorpe, J.G., Schmidt, E., & Castell, D. Aversion-relief therapy: A new method for general application. *Behaviour Research and Therapy,* 1964, **2**, 71-82.

Thorpe, J.G., Schmidt, E., & Castell, D. A comparison of positive and negative (aversion) conditioning in the treatment of homosexuality. *Behaviour Research and Therapy,* 1963, **1**, 357-362.

Tinling, D.C. Cognitive and behavioral aspect of aversive therapy. Paper presented at the 4th annual meeting of the Association for the Advancement of Behavior Therapy, Miami Beach, Florida, September 1970.

Wright, H. *More about the sex factor in marriage.* (3rd corrected impression) London: Benn, 1969.

Yalom, I.D. Aggression and forbiddenness in voyeurism. *Archives of General Psychiatry,* 1960, **3**, 305-319.

15

The Modification of Sexual Fantasies: A Combined Treatment Approach to the Reduction of Deviant Sexual Behavior

W. L. MARSHALL

INTRODUCTION

Aversion therapy of one sort or another has been the main, if not the only, component of most successful behavioral treatment methods aimed at reducing the frequency of deviant sexual behaviors. Feldman and MacCulloch (1965) have described a procedure that associates a noxious stimulus (painful electric shock) with pictures representing the deviant object or activity. Recent evidence indicates that this procedure successfully reduces the frequency of homosexual behavior (Feldman & MacCulloch, 1970), exhibitionism (Evans, 1968; MacCulloch et al., 1971), and pedophilia (Marshall, 1971).

In addition to pairing analogues of the deviant stimuli with a noxious event, this procedure permits the patient to avoid the shock by producing a response that terminates exposure to the deviant material. This latter component has been shown to be unnecessary to successful treatment (Feldman & MacCulloch, 1970). A further component of this variant of aversion therapy, involves the presentation of slides depicting appropriate heterosexual material consequent upon termination of the deviant pictures.

In a recent modification of this procedure, Abel et al. (1970) successfully modified deviant behavior by using taped sequences that described the behavioral events involved in the deviant activity. They noted that the sequence of discrete behaviors involved in deviant sexual acts is frequently overlooked in treatment designs, despite evidence indicating that aversive conditioning is enhanced by delivering the noxious stimulus to various responses in the approach sequence (Levis, 1966a; 1966b). Abel et al., chose a single taped sequence for treatment purposes basing their selection on the patient's penile responses to various tapes. They divided the approach sequence into three segments, and delivered a painful electric shock at the end of different segments at different points in the treatment program. By this means Abel et al., were able to move the delivery of punishment backward in the response sequence from the final segment to the first segment as treatment progressed. They also provided the S with the possibility of avoiding the noxious event but, unlike Feldman and MacCulloch, they used the Ss

verbalizations of nondeviant sexual behaviors as the avoidance response.

Abel et al.'s technique differs from that of Fedlman and MacCulloch in one important respect, and on one minor point. Most importantly they prefer taped descriptions of the behavior to Feldman and MacCulloch's method of visual representations. This allows the therapist to deliver shock at different points in the approach sequence leading to the possibility of punishing the behaviors that initiate deviant acts rather than simply associating shock with stimuli that elicit the terminal behavior. The minor point of difference concerns the different kinds of avoidance responses employed. Since there does not appear to be any advantage to be gained from including such a component in treatment, this point of difference is not one for concern.

Since Feldman and MacCulloch specifically request their patients to fantasize to the deviant slides, they presumably consider the production of fantasies to be important to treatment. If this is true then obviously any method that explicitly uses fantasies has an advantage over a method that relies on the subject to produce his own. It has been suggested by others (Evans, 1968; McGuire & Carlisle, 1965; Rachman, 1966; Rachman & Hodgson, 1968) that fantasies may play an important role in the genesis and maintenance of sexually deviant behavior. Davison (1968) and Marquis (1970) have described methods for modifying masturbatory fantasies, and they provide evidence that such procedures can lead to a reduction in deviant behavior.

If fantasies do play an important part in maintaining deviant behavior, then direct methods of modifying them should provide an effective treatment for sexual deviance. Such a treatment method should have advantages over any alternative procedure that exerts little direct control over the production of fantasies. Abel et al.'s aversion therapy procedures obviously describe one quite direct way of modifying fantasies. Davison's masturbatory therapy and Marquis' orgasmic reconditioning likewise represent direct methods for changing fantasy content. Combined treatment programs have been advocated before (Marshall, 1971; Solomon & Marshall, 1973) and perhaps the most sensible approach is to include both an aversion therapy and a masturbatory therapy component in an initial evaluation of a treatment program aimed at reducing deviant behavior by directly modifying the patient's fantasies. The value of each component of a well-defined program can be readily determined in later studies once the over-all efficacy has been demonstrated.

AIM

It is hypothesized that a combined aversion therapy/orgasmic reconditioning treatment program will be effective in: a) reducing the attractiveness of deviant fantasies; and b) increasing the attractiveness of appropriate fantasies. Since it is suggested that the content of fantasies plays an important role in maintaining deviant behavior, such changes in the attractiveness of fantasies should be reflected in changes in behavior. Patients treated in this way should show a reduction in the frequency of their deviant behavior, and a change in their attitudes toward the deviant stimuli or activities.

METHOD

Assessments

a) *Behavior.* In view of the difficulties in establishing baseline rates of the deviant behavior (either reliance on the patient's recall or the imposition of the altered conditions of self monitoring), Ss were asked to report only on the frequency of the undersirable behavior over the final week of treatment and at follow-up.

b) *Attitudes.* Feldman et al. (1966) report the use of the Sexual Orientation Method (SOM) which is essentially a technique for assessing attitudes to categories of sexual material, and may be used to measure changes in these attitudes with treatment. It was originally designed for use with homosexuals, but has recently been used to assess attitude changes with an exhibitionist (MacCulloch et al., 1971). In adapting the SOM to novel problems all that is necessary is to substitute appropriate material for "men" and "women" in the adjective pairs. The results provide scores between 6 and 48 on both stimulus classes (i.e., appropriate and inappropriate sexual material).

c) *Ratings of Sexual Attractiveness.* A method for rating the sexual attractiveness of various fantasies was described to the patients. They were required to assign a number from 1 to 10 to each stimulus so that the number assigned indicated the sexual attractiveness of that stimulus. In this scale 1 represents an absence of attractiveness, and 10 indicates extreme attractiveness. Two sets of fantasies were composed for each patient with one set matching the deviant behavior, and the other set corresponding to more appropriate responses. These fantasies served as the material to be rated.

d) *Penile Responses.* The patient's responses to the fantasies were recorded as penis circumference changes by a mercury strain-gauge providing a write-out on a Beckman Type R Dynograph (*see* Barlow et al., 1970, for a more detailed description). Penile responses were recorded in two ways: 1) amplitude of response was measured as a percentage of full erection where the magnitude of full erection was established before assessment began; and 2) latency of response was recorded as the point at which the pen deflection reached 25 percent of the maximal response to that particular stimulus.

These latter three assessments were administered before treatment; immediately after treatment, and at follow-up appointments occurring at various times after treatment.

Treatment

a) *Aversion therapy.* In view of the findings of Feldman and MacCulloch (1970) that anticipatory therapy offers no advantages over a straight classical conditioning procedure, the avoidance component was not included in the present program.

At least three detailed fantasies were composed for each patient on the basis of discussions with him. The fantasies chosen for inclusion in treatment were those rated as most attractive by the S, and which produced the largest amplitude penile response. Each fantasy was associated with a slide prepared for presentation by a projector onto a screen mounted in front of the S. The patient selected the slides, and matched them with the fantasies, so that they facilitated his imagining the scene.

The chosen fantasies were broken up into six segments that included: 1) thinking about engaging in the deviant behavior; 2) approaching the situation where deviant behavior usually occurred; 3) seeking out the object of the deviant response; 4) approaching the object; 5) commencing the deviant behavior itself; and 6) completion of the deviant behavior and resulting orgasm. The fantasies were taped, and a 3-second pause was allowed between each of the segments.

Each of the segments in the sequence was associated with an unpleasant electric shock. The intensity of the shock was established for each subject prior to treatment by increasing the intensity until the subject described it as painful. The presentation of the shock was slightly preceded by the command "Stop" in the hope that this command would thereby become a conditioned punisher.

Initially shocks were delivered every time the segment to be punished occurred in order to facilitate the suppression of the deviant response. After six shocked trials the delivery of shock was moved to a 75 percent variable schedule of reinforcement for another six trials, and finally a 50 percent variable schedule for the last six trials. The nonshocked trials were terminated by the therapist's command "Stop." Thus the nonshocked trials differed from the shocked trials only in terms of the withdrawal of the faradic stimulus.

Each segment, therefore, was associated with punishment (either shock or the conditioned punisher) on 18 occasions. Since there were six segments in each fantasy and at least three fantasies per S, each patient received at least 324 pairings of the deviant fantasy material with punishment. Twelve pairings occurred at each treatment session for at least 27 sessions. Treatment had to be adjusted for each individual patient, but all Ss were seen for at least 4 weeks and none for more than 8 weeks.

Lovibond (1968) has illustrated the generally aversive nature of uncertainty, and he has argued that aversive conditioning will be enhanced if the S is unable to predict particular components of the treatment especially the onset of the noxious stimulus. For this reason the point (or segment) in the total sequence of a fantasy at which punishment was delivered was randomized. However, the modal point for punishment, in any one session, varied across sessions such that in the first session segment 6 was the modal point, and by the last session the modal point for the delivery of punishment had shifted to segment 1.

Immediately at the command "Stop" both the taped deviant fantasy and the slide depicting inappropriate material were switched off, and the shock followed if it was required by the program. The next step was to immediately present the patient with a slide depicting more appropriate sexual material. For most patients it seemed to be artificial to use fantasies to match this material, since before treatment these fantasies were not judged to be particularly attractive. Consequently the patient was simply urged to create his own fantasies if possible.

During this part of the treatment the S was seated in a darkened room separated from the therapist, although they could communicate quite readily.

b) *Orgasmic Reconditioning.* Each patient was given material for his private use that illustrated appropriate heterosexual material, and he was asked to derive from it appropriate fantasies. Ss were then told of the important role that fantasies play in maintaining deviant behavior, and how it was essential to change those fantasies that occurred during masturbation. It was explained to the patient that the fantasies that occurred during the course of masturbation could be divided into three parts: 1) the thoughts that were used to stimulate him to masturbation; 2) the thoughts that occurred during masturbatory activity; and 3) the stimuli imagined immediately before, during, and after ejaculation. The patient was told that section 3) was the most important since it was associated with the very reinforcing properties of orgasm. He was told to use his deviant fantasies to initiate masturbation, and to continue to imagine them until immediately before ejaculation at which time he was to switch to the appropriate fantasy. The patient carried on this practice until he was able to control his fantasy content at ejaculation. At this time the therapist advised the patient to begin to extend the appropriate fantasy further back in the sequence until it would finally serve as the initiating stimulus.

Treatment components a) and b) were conducted concurrently, and it was suggested to the patient that he utilize the appropriate fantasies of the orgasmic reconditioning component when viewing the heterosexual material during aversion therapy.

Subjects

A total of 12 patients have so far been treated by the methods outlined above. Their mean age was 26.4 yr (range = 19-38), and their deviant behavior included homosexuality (three patients), fetishism (two patients), rape (two patients), and pedophilia (2 homosexual pedophiles, two heterosexual pedophiles, and one mixed pedophile). Five of the patients (including both rapists) were referred for treatment by the local helping agencies or private practitioners.

RESULTS

Table 1 shows the group scores on all objective assessments, while Table 2 shows the results of statistical analyses of the differences in the scores at the different occasions.

Table 1. Group Scores on the Objective Measures

Method of Assessment		Deviant Fantasies			Appropriate Fantasies		
		Pre-treatment	Post-treatment	Follow-up	Pre-treatment	Post-treatment	Follow-up
SOM	X	39.2	17.8	12.3	37.8	44.5	45.0
	Md.	39.0	19.0	9.0	44.0	47.0	46.0
	S.D.	7.16	10.56	10.33	14.15	4.98	3.85
Ratings of Attractiveness	X	6.7	4.1	4.4	6.5	8.6	8.4
	Md.	6.9	3.9	4.3	6.5	7.6	8.0
	S.D.	1.64	1.23	1.97	2.46	1.35	1.03
Penometer Latencies	X	40.8	54.8	72.9	68.6	52.1	47.2
	Md.	38.6	54.8	76.6	52.8	51.3	50.6
	S.D.	12.18	20.44	29.77	31.11	10.76	5.95
Penometer Amplitudes	X	77.5	48.5	45.0	67.1	85.6	94.1
	Md.	79.5	46.9	35.6	60.4	85.8	93.1
	S.D.	14.5	12.48	20.64	23.12	11.52	2.01

All the Pre- versus Post-data are based on $N = 12$. The Post- versus Follow-up-data for the SOM are based on $N = 8$, and the corresponding data for the remaining assessments are based on $N = 5$.

In addition to these data, all patients reported a complete absence of any deviant behavior over the final week of treatment.

The single set of follow-up assessments were completed at varying times after treatment as a result of varying degrees of success in securing the patient's cooperation in returning for assessment. One of the major problems in this regard was the fact that a number of patients were living at a distance of some hundreds of miles from the hospital. The minimum period between completion of treatment and follow-up was 3 months, and the maximum was 16 months.

Table 2. t-Values of the Differences between Means*

Method of Assessment	Deviant Fantasies		Appropriate Fantasies	
	Pre- vs. Post-Assessment Means	Post vs. Follow-up Assessment Means	Pre- vs. Post-Assessment Means	Post vs. Follow-up Assessment Means
SOM	$t = 10.95$ $p < 0.01$	$t = 1.40$ NS	$t = 2.44$ $p < 0.05$	$t = 1.18$ NS
Ratings of Attractiveness	$t = 7.98$ $p < 0.01$	$t = 0.04$ NS	$t = 4.82$ $p < 0.01$	$t = 1.21$ NS
Penometer Latencies	$t = 4.55$ $p < 0.01$	$t = 2.05$ NS	$t = 2.54$ $p < 0.05$	$t = 0.78$ NS
Penometer Amplitudes	$t = 5.46$ $p < 0.01$	$t = 0.25$ NS	$t = 3.26$ $p < 0.01$	$t = 1.06$ NS

*The analyses are based on Edwards (1962) model for correlated data.

Seven patients did not return for assessment, and of these two refused to complete the SOM, and two did not respond at all. Of those eight Ss who completed the SOM and replied to the question about relapse, two were homosexuals, one had a fetish, two were rapists, two were homosexual pedophiles, and the remaining patient was the mixed pedophile. Of these one of the homosexuals, the mixed pedophile, and one of the homosexual pedophiles did not return for the laboratory assessments. The two Ss who did not respond at all to the request for follow-up were one of the patients with a fetish and one of the heterosexual pedophiles.

Of those ten Ss who replied to the question about relapse at follow-up, all but two reported a complete absence of any deviant behavior or indeed of any difficulties related to their former problems. One of the heterosexual pedophiles reported a single incident over a 16-month period, and one homosexual declared that he had completely returned to his former behavior.

An important point to note is that in this latter case the objective assessments obtained immediately after treatment indicated that the procedures had been successful. On the other hand, the only patient whose immediate post-treatment evaluations suggested a failure to respond, nevertheless reported a complete absence from difficulties despite the fact that follow-up assessments confirmed the post-treatment measures.

DISCUSSION

The results indicate that for 11 out of the 12 patients there was a reduction in the rated attractiveness of deviant fantasies, and a corresponding increase in the rated attractiveness of the appropriate fantasies at the end of treatment. These rating changes were matched by changes in penile responses to the material. For those subjects who were available for further assessments these changes were maintained at varying follow-up periods. All 11 *Ss* who altered their evaluation of the fantasies, also reported a disappearance of their deviant behaviors and showed changes in their attitudes toward such behaviors immediately after treatment. One of these cases subsequently relapsed, and another reported a single instance of the deviant behavior. In the single case where the attractiveness of the fantasies remained unaltered, behavioral changes nevertheless were positive. Attitude changes, however, were not apparent in this patient.

The treatment program, then, appeared to be immediately successful in eliminating deviant behavior in all cases (100%). If we accept the reports of patients as valid, and allocate those two patients who did not respond to follow-up requests to the failure category, then the procedures produce 75 percent maintained success at follow-up. Describing the two patients who failed to respond to requests as failures is the safest course, but not necessarily accurate. A patient who has been freed from a previously unacceptable, and possibly embarrassing, behavior may not wish to be reminded of his earlier failings.

The apparent success rate is indeed quite high and appears to be at least as good, if not better than, most other reported treatment programs. Further investigations employing factorial designs and including untreated controls seem justified, and are essential before any firm conclusions can be reached. There does, however, appear to be something wrong with the general argument that altering fantasies will have a direct effect on behavior in all *Ss*. It was observed that in one case positive changes in ratings and corresponding changes in penile responsivity, although predictive of immediate modifications in attitudes and behavior, did fail to indicate later relapse. In another case the absence of positive changes in ratings and penile responsivity was associated with immediate and maintained changes in both attitudes and behavior. Again the need for further research is indicated.

REFERENCES

Abel, G.G., Levis, D.J. & Clancy, J. Aversion therapy applied to taped sequences of deviant behavior in exhibitionism and other sexual deviations: A preliminary report. *J. Behav.ther. & exp. psychiat.* 1970, **1**, 59-66.

Barlow, D.H., Becker, R., Leitenberg, H. & Agras, W.S. A mechanical strain gauge for recording penile circumference change. *J. appl. behav. anal.* 1972, **3**, 73-76.

Davison, G.C. Elimination of a sadistic fantasy by a client-controlled counterconditioning technique. *J. abnorm. psychol.* 1968, **73**, 84-90.

Edwards, A.L. *Statistical methods for the behavioral sciences.* New York: Holt, Rinehart & Winston, 1962.

Evans, D.R. Masturbatory fantasy and sexual deviation. *Behav. res. & therapy.* 1968, **6**, 17-19.

Feldman, M.P. & MacCulloch, M.J. The application of anticipatory avoidance learning to the treatment of homosexuality. I. Theory, technique and preliminary results. *Behav. res. & therapy.* 1965, **2**, 165-183.

Feldman, M.P. & MacCulloch, M.J. *Homosexual behaviour: Therapy and assessment.* Oxford: Pergamon Press, 1970.

Feldman, M.P., MacCulloch, M.J., Mellor, V. & Pinschoff, J.M. The application of anticipatory avoidance learning to the treatment of homosexuality. III. The sexual orientation method. *Behav. res. & therapy.* 1966, 4, 289-299.

Levis, D.J. The effects of serial CS presentation and other characteristics of the CS on the conditioned avoidance response. *Psychol. rep.,* 1966a, 18, 755-766.

Levis, D.J. Implosive therapy, Part II: The subhuman analogue, the strategy, and the technique. In *Behavior modification techniques in the treatment of emotional disorders* (Ed. S.G. Armitage). Battle Creek, Michigan: V.A. Publication, 1966b, 22-37.

Lovibond, S.H. The aversiveness of uncertainty: an analysis in terms of activation and information theory. *Aust. J. psychol.* 1968, 20, 85-91.

MacCulloch, M.J., Williams, C. & Birtles, C.J. The successful application of aversion therapy to an adolescent exhibitionist. *J. Behav. ther. & exp. psychiat.* 1971, 2, 61-66.

Marquis, J.N. Orgasmic reconditioning: Changing sexual object choice through controlling masturbation fantasies. *J. Behav. ther. & exp. psychiat.* 1970, 1, 263-264.

Marshall, W.L. A combined treatment method for certain sexual deviations. *Behav. res. & therapy,* 1971, 9, 293-294.

McGuire, R.J. Carlisle, J.M. & Young, B.G. Sexual deviations as conditioned behavior: A hypothesis. *Behav. res. & therapy.* 1965, 2, 185-190.

Rachman, S. Secual fetishism: An experimental analogue. *Psychol. rec.* 1966, 16, 293-296.

Rachman, S. & Hodgson, R.J. Experimentally-induced "sexual fetishism": Replication and development. *Psychol. rec.,* 1968, 18, 25-27.

Solomon, E. & Marshall, W.L. A comprehensive model for the acquisition, maintenance, and treatment of drug-taking behavior. *Brit. J. addict.* (in press), 1973.

16
Shame Aversion Therapy

MICHAEL SERBER

Shame aversion therapy is a technique that developed as an incidental result of photographing a transvestite patient cross-dressing. The patient, a 23-year-old law student, had been cross-dressing for over 10 years in private, using his mother's undergarments. He would terminate the cross-dressing by masturbating. He had cross-dressed 2 to 3 times a week in either his bedroom or the bathroom. He was referred to me by a private psychiatrist who, after 2 years of treatment, had been unable to alter the transvestite behavior in any way. I had planned to use classical aversion therapy—to project photographed scenes of the patient cross-dressing and then administer painful electrical shocks to one of his extremities (Blakemore et al., 1963, Feldman & McCulloch, 1965). I had explained the procedure to the patient and supplied him with women's lingerie so that I could begin photographing him. He appeared reluctant to begin. He said he was too embarrassed and ashamed to be observed while cross-dressing. I urged him on while taking still photographs at different stages of his cross-dressing. He became markedly anxious. He flushed, felt weak, had to sit down several times. He was unable to get sexually excited in the least. He reported that the photographic session had completely "turned him off" and had changed his entire feeling about cross-dressing. The session had lasted 25 minutes.

The patient was asked to repeat his cross-dressing on two subsequent occasions in front of me and two other mental health workers. He was instructed to observe himself in a large dressing-mirror and also to observe his observers. No judgmental remarks were made before, during, or after the cross-dressing sessions, and the patient was only encouraged to go on, closely observing himself and his observers. At times he hesitated, cried and asked to stop. He was unable to achieve an erection during either session. The patient reported having nightmares and intermittent anxiety between shame aversion sessions but had no desire to cross-dress when he was alone. After the last session he was shown slides of himself cross-dressing in front of observers and was instructed to look at them in case he felt the desire to cross-dress again. After a 1-year follow-up, the patient has not cross-dressed and denies any urge to do so.

Eight patients have now been treated by shame aversion therapy. They include cases of transvestism, voyeurism, exhibitionism, pedophilia and frotteurism, all of at least 10 years' duration. Most of the patients had psychotherapy, and had not in any way been altered by this.

Modified techniques had to be devised for voyeurs, frotteurs and pedophiles. Voyeurs were placed on the observer side of a one-way mirror to look at someone undressing behind the mirror. The observers stood in the observation room away from the mirror, observing the patient observing. Each situation was set up in such a way as most carefully to replicate the *in vivo* conditions of the act. In the case of the frotteur* an attractive girl was asked to participate, and the frotteur was requested to rub against her just as he would rub against strangers in buses and subways. The pedophile was placed in a room with a consenting young secretary, who had agreed to stand in for his usual sexual objects, a neighbor's child or his own niece.

PATIENT SELECTION

In general there are two prerequisites for successful shame aversion therapy:

1. The patient must be ashamed of the act and desire not to be observed in its execution. Even the exhibitionist who desires to shock people with his genital exposure really does not wish to be observed by people who are not the object of his exhibitionism. The patient who, in shame aversion therapy, performs the act without any feeling of self-consciousness or anxiety, will not improve.
2. The patient must be in contact with what he is doing. He must be aware he is performing the asocial act. (I have observed schizophrenic sexual deviates who cannot tell one after they have performed an asocial act, what they have done.)

Table 1. A List of Patients Treated by Shame Aversion Therapy

Age	Sex	Behavior Observed	Years of Practice	Act-Frequency per Month	S.A. Sessions	Follow-up
23	M	transvestism	11	8-11	3	1 year - no repetition of behavior
31	M	transvestism	18	5-6	3	6 months - no repetition of behavior
24	M	transvestism	12	10-15	3	1 year - no repetition of behavior
52	M	pedophilia	30	1-2	2	6 months - no repetition of behavior
32	M	exhibitionism	21	1	3	6 months - no repetition of behavior
34	M	voyeur-exhibitionism	15	1-2	3	6 months - 1 episode of voyeurism
33	M	frotteurism	18	3-4	2	no change
34	M	transvestism	20	4-10	2	no change

*A frotteur rubs himself against someone, usually in a crowd, receiving sexual excitation and frequently coming to orgasm.

One patient, a 34-year-old voyeur-exhibitionist, had a history of psychotic behavior and had to be placed on phenothiazines for a few weeks following shame aversion therapy. He showed dissociated thought-content during the shame aversion therapy and was unable to tolerate the high level of anxiety evoked during the session. Patients with a psychotic history have to be treated very cautiously, if at all. Previous psychotherapy appears not to correlate with success or failure in shame aversion therapy.

DISCUSSION

A question of importance is, how many shame aversion therapy sessions are optimal. Certainly, in two or three sessions the aversive elements predominate, and habituation to the therapy has not yet occurred. Theoretically, as the number of shame aversion therapy sessions increases, there could be habituation of the shame reaction. This premise has yet to be tested.

Shame aversion may also be applicable to a number of deviant behaviors such as petty thieving and various secretive behaviors.

It is possible that, as in most aversive therapies, "booster" treatments at some later date may be required (Rachman, 1961). The patients so far treated will be observed for exacerbation of symptoms.

Shame aversion therapy would be most likely to succeed and produce enduring effects when coupled with the establishment of appropriate alternative behavior (Cautela & Wisocki, 1968, and Serber & Wolpe, 1970). For example, if a transvestite had no other sexual outlet besides his cross-dressing behavior, his "cure" would be less likely to be stable than if alternative sexual behavior were to be established. Fortunately, all the patients treated to date have had a history of normal heterosexual experience along with their deviant behavior.

REFERENCES

Blakemore, C.B., Thorpe, J.C., Barker, J.C., Conway, C.G. & Lavin, N.I. The application of faradic aversion conditioning in a case of transvestism. *Behav. res. & therapy.* 1963, 1, 29-34.

Feldman, M.P. & MacCulloch, M.J.A., The application of anticipatory avoidance learning to the treatment of homosexuality. I. Theory, technique and preliminary results. *Behav. res. & therapy.* 1965, 2, 165-183.

Rachman, S. Sexual disorders and behavior therapy, *Am. J. psychiat.* 1961, 118, 235-240.

Cautela, J.R. & Wisocki, P.A. The use of male and female therapists in the treatment of homosexual behavior. *Advances in behavior therapy.* (Ed. by Rubin R. & Franks C.) New York: Academic Press, 1968, 165-173.

Serber, M. & Wolpe, J. The behavior therapy treatment of the sexual offender. *The treatment of the sexual offender.* (Ed. by Resnik, H.L.P. & Wolfgang, M.E.). (In press) Boston: Little, Brown & Co., 1970.

17
Covert Sensitization for the Treatment of Sexual Deviations

JOSEPH R. CAUTELA AND PATRICIA A. WISOCKI

The problem of sexual deviations has long been regarded as one of faulty learning (Binet, 1888; Max, 1935; Curran & Parr, 1957; Ullmann & Krasner, 1965). Rachman recently demonstrated this point in an experimental analogue study in which he successfully conditioned (and later extinguished) sexual fetishistic behavior in human *Ss* (1966; 1968) by pairing a neutral stimulus (a picture of black boots) with a sexually arousing stimulus (picture of a nude woman).

Treatment of sexual deviations is frequently centered about the elimination of the result of such contiguous pairings. That is, the deviant sexual behavior is paired with noxious stimuli until *S* develops an avoidance response to the sexual object. Treatment studies employing chemical and electrical aversion techniques as the noxious stimuli have reported successful results with transvestites (Lavin, et al., 1961; Thorpe, et al., 1964; Barker, 1965; Morgenstein, Pearce & Rees, 1965), exhibitionists (Bond & Hutchinson, 1960; Evans, 1968), fetishists (Raymond, 1956; Oswald, 1962; Clark, 1963), homosexuals (Feldman & MacCulloch, 1965; Robertson 1968), and persons engaging in sadistic fantasy (Mees, 1966). Some investigators (Max, 1935; Cooper, 1963; McGuire & Vallance, 1964; Feingold, 1968) have found the combination of external aversion techniques with imagery successful in the treatment of maladaptive sexual behaviors. In these studies *Ss* were shocked while they imagined or fantasized imagery of their sexual deviations.

Despite the generally high success rate with faradic and chemo aversion techniques, there are many disadvantages in the use of these procedures. Drug use is time-consuming, requires hospital admittance and a team of personnel available at all times; drugs may cause dangerous physical disturbance, and their administration cannot always be properly controlled (Barker, 1965). The use of electric shock is time-consuming, expensive, and often results in a high drop-out rate from treatment (Morgenstein, Pearce, & Rees, 1965), an overgeneralization of treatment effects (Sanderson, Campbell & Laverty, 1963) and a build-up of tolerance to shock (Barker, 1965). Furthermore, neither method is readily employable as a self-control device and is not practical for use in private practice.

The imagerial technique of covert sensitization (Cautela, 1966; 1967), on the other hand, has none of these disadvantages and has also been quite successful in the treatment of maladaptive approach behaviors (Anant, 1967; Stuart, 1967; Barlow, Leitenberg & Agras, 1968; Davison, 1968; Ashem & Donner, 1968; Mullen, 1968; Viernstein, 1968; Barlow, Agras & Leitenberg, 1969; Cautela, 1969).

The advantages of a technique in which both the aversive stimulus and the maladaptive behavior are presented in imagination are many: a) it is not necessary to employ actual stimuli; b) there is a greater range of applicability to a variety of aspects in the stimulus situation; c) patients are less likely to leave therapy through fear; d) its use is more likely to receive acceptance in settings in which physical methods are impractical (e.g., in clinical practice and in some institutions); e) it can be used as a self-control measure by the patient whenever needed. Furthermore, based on evidence of some investigators (McGuire, Carlisle & Young, 1965; Evans, 1968) that the habits of sexual behaviors are strengthened by the experience of sexual fantasies related to those behaviors, one may suggest that an imagerial procedure may be more effective in weakening the sexual habit than physical methods.

Because the covert sensitization procedure appears to be a valuable tool for the clinician in the treatment of maladaptive approach behaviors in general and because some evidence has accumulated regarding its efficacy with sexual problems, it is the primary purpose of this paper to provide clinicians with a detailed procedural description of the technique applied to a variety of sexual deviations. Empirical support for covert sensitization in this area is also provided for the generation of novel and researchable hypotheses.

PROCEDURE

When a patient desires treatment for maladaptive sexual behaviors, those behaviors are analyzed in terms of the stimuli that evoke sexual arousal, the amount of arousal evoked, and the frequency of its occurrence in specific situations for each stimulus. For this purpose special questionnaires have been developed for use with homosexuals (Cautela, 1968b) and patients reporting other sexual behaviors (Cautela, 1970b). Patients are also asked to complete a Life History Questionnaire (Wolpe & Lazarus, 1966), a Fear Survey Schedule (Wolpe & Lang, 1964) and a Reinforcement Survey Schedule (Cautela & Kastenbaum, 1967), each of which have been found valuable in the over-all treatment program (Cautela, 1968a). The Fear Survey Schedule provides not only an idea of the number, type and intensity of specific fearful items, but functions as an immediate checklist of aversive or noxious stimuli (as bats, spiders, etc.) for use in the application of covert sensitization. The Reinforcement Survey Schedule supplies a list of reinforcers available for inclusion in anxiety-reduction scenes and for the application of various behavior therapy techniques (Catutela & Wisocki, 1969b).

After the behavioral analysis, the rationale for treatment is explained to the patient by means of the following points: a) through a process of conditioning he has learned to respond inappropriately (with sexual arousal) to particular stimuli; b) if a noxious stimulus can be presented when the stimulus occurs, he will no longer respond with pleasure, but with displeasure or lack of arousal; c) the entire covert sensitization procedure is carried out in imagination.

Covert sensitization is described to the patient as an aversive conditioning technique in which he, in imagination, pairs the pleasurable object (e.g., a sexually attractive male, a fur glove, a child, etc.) within a noxious setting (e.g., a cesspool, a dungeon) with the image of himself vomiting on himself, the sexual object, and every aspect of the stimulus situation.

"Scenes" are constructed from material presented by each patient concerning his desirable sexual objects and the contact situations available to him for sexual stimulation. The material is arranged in hierarchical form, and a scene is constructed for each item. The most desirable item is generally treated first.

Some examples of scenes used in therapy are these:

The Dungeon Scene. You are in a dungeon. It is dark, smelly and altogether loathsome. As your eyes get accustomed to the light, you can just barely see an attractive male nude in a corner of the dungeon. He is gesturing for you to come nearer to him. As you begin to approach him, you think to yourself: "Boy, this is going to be good." As you think that, you begin to get a funny, queasy feeling in the pit of your stomach. Some chunks of food come into your mouth and taste bitter. You swallow them down. Your throat feels raw. But you continue to approach the guy. The closer you go, the sicker you get. Your eyes are watery. Snots and mucous from your nose are running down into your mouth. Your stomach is churning. Just as you're about to touch him, you start to vomit. You vomit all over him, all over yourself, all over the floor. You can see him all covered with yellow and brown bits of slimy vomit. His entire body is covered with it, especially his penis. You continue to retch your insides out. Your clothes are full of vomit. You get sick over and over again and vomit all over everything again. You turn away from _____(name of contact) and start to run out of the dungeon. He grabs for you and you trip and fall face down into a huge pile of vomit. The odor overcomes you and you vomit again, but nothing comes up . . . you have the dry heaves. Somehow you pick yourself up, push him away and run from him. As you run out the door you start to feel better and better. When you get out into the clean fresh air, you feel wonderful. You go home and clean yourself up.

Rape Scene. You are walking downtown on a warm day. You see a girl in a miniskirt. She has beautiful legs. You say to yourself "I've got to have some of that" and you start approaching her. As soon as you have that thought, you start to feel sick to your stomach. But you keep on going. As you get closer, bitter spit comes into your mouth. You feel really sick now. You are very close to her now—just about to grab her leg, and food comes into your mouth. Just as you touch her you feel so sick that you vomit all over her leg, all over yourself. Snots come out of your nose. Your clothes are full of vomit. The girl screams and people gather around to stare at you. You start to run away from her and immediately feel better.

Cesspool Scene. Imagine that you are in a hotel room, completely naked. There's a real sexy looking fellow about three feet away from you—also naked. You say "Oh boy" and start to go toward him. He giggles and says, "You'll have to catch me." He opens the door of the room and runs out. You follow him. He runs down a long corridor. At the end of the corridor is a door. He opens it and shuts it behind him. You hear a splash just as you reach the door. You open it and go in. You can't believe your eyes. There he is, floating on his back in a cesspool. There's an awful stench—from fecal matter and urine. It's smeared all over him. He laughs and suggests that you come in and join him. You immediately start to feel sick to your stomach. You feel extremely nauseous. Your spit is bitter. Food comes into your mouth. You see him swimming around in all that disgusting crap. Then you puke. It goes all over you and some of it goes into the cesspool. He swims toward you and says again "Come on in" and reaches out for you. Now you're really disgusted. You turn away and start running toward the door. He gets out of the pool and starts chasing you. He's right behind you. As you get to the door, his hand, full of garbage, is just about to touch your shoulder. You open the door and bolt it behind you. You feel relieved. You go back to the room and take a shower, get dressed and go home. You feel wonderful—rejecting sex with another guy.

A scene such as one of these is described to the patient while he is relaxed. He is told to imagine it as vividly as he can—trying to actually experience the nausea at each of the various steps in his approach to the sexual object. After one scene description by the therapist, the patient is asked to visualize the same scene by himself. Approximately ten of these scene pairs are presented in a therapy session. Ten additional trials are described in which the patient confronts the sexual object or has the intention of doing so, but turns away from it and immediately feels relieved (this is an application of the escape conditioning paradigm).

The following is a typical relief scene:

You are walking near _____(favorite meeting place for homosexual contact) and you say to yourself, "I think I'll go and see if _____(usual partner) is available." As soon as you say that, you get a pain and feel sick to your stomach. Then you say to yourself: "The hell with it; I'm not going near him." As soon as you think that, you feel better and walk away from the place. You feel proud of yourself because you were able to resist the temptation.

After the scenes have been presented in the office, the patient is instructed to practice them at home (or on the ward) twice a day. (Although most patients report practicing fewer times than prescribed for each day, most usually report practicing about twenty scenes a week.) The patient is also told to imagine himself vomiting on the desirable sexual object whenever he sees it or intends to approach it. The use of the procedure in this way gives the patient a self-control response for future use, as well as providing for "in vivo" sensitization.

Problems in Imagery

Some patients report difficulty in obtaining clear imagery when asked to imagine scenes. Several things can be done in cases of this sort: a) the therapist may describe the scene in more detail; b) the therapist may describe scenes employing more than one sensory modality; c) the patient may be asked to make more careful observations of the environment in which the sexual behavior occurs; d) pictures of appropriate scenes may be employed; e) a tape recorder may be used for those patients who claim they are unable to achieve imagery outside the office.

Only one patient reported serious difficulty in imagining the scenes after all these methods were attempted. Usually after several trials most patients were capable of visualizing the presentations clearly.

Examples of Applications to Specific Sexual Behaviors

Covert sensitization has been applied clinically with cases of exhibitionism, fetishism, pedophilia, masochism, sadism, rape, homosexuality and sadistic fantasies. In each type of case the patient is instructed to imagine himself in one of these situations: a) intending to approach the sexual object (i.e., thinking about it in a positive way); b) about to approach the sexual object; c) actually reaching for it (but never getting it, in imagination). After each approach response the patient imagines himself either vomiting or confronted with an aversive item, as maggots crawling on the sexual objects, bats flying into his hair, etc.

In cases of masochism, however, while it may appear inappropriate to use aversive conditioning methods on behavior that is presumably already unpleasant, studies by Lovaas (1967) with electric shock and Cautela and Baron (1969) with covert sensitization indicate that self-destructive behavior can be eliminated by aversive conditioning methods. Marks, Rachman and Gelder (1965) demonstrated successful treatment by faradic aversion of a patient who hit his genitals with his boots and demanded that his wife kick and stand on him to provoke sexual arousal.

In order to apply covert sensitization in such cases, it is first necessary to determine which stimuli are sufficiently aversive to the patient. If feelings of nausea and vomiting are ineffective, other stimuli as spiders, dirt, worms, decaying matter, etc. may be used. Ideas for these stimuli may be acquired from the patient's responses to the Fear Survey Schedule. During treatment the patient is instructed to imagine scenes in which the aversive stimuli are presented immediately prior to inflicting pain on himself and on attempts to achieve sexual pleasure through self-destructive activities.

Kolvin (1967) used images of falling out of bed while dreaming and looking from a great height to condition an aversive reaction to the behavior of a "fetishistic" boy who reported he was compelled to put his hand up the skirts of women on the street. After 8 months of aversive imagery, treatment was terminated successfully. An 11-month follow-up indicated no further occurrence of the maladaptive behavior.

In the cases described briefly above, the imagery technique of covert sensitization was employed to reduce the frequency of overt sexual behaviors. Covert sensitization has also been used to eliminate other imagery behavior. That this is theoretically possible has been suggested by Franks (1967, p. 218) and Bandura (1969, p. 506) and demonstrated by Davison (1968).

Davison reports a case in which a sadistic fantasy of 10-years duration was eliminated in five sessions over a 10-week period. While Davison used a counter-conditioning technique for the patient's sexual responses (from masturbating while imagining the sadistic fantasy to masturbating while focusing on a picture of a sexy, nude woman), he credits the application of covert sensitization during the third through fifth sessions as instrumental in changing the content of the fantasies. For a covert sensitization scene, Davison depicted to the patient a large bowl of "soup," composed of steaming urine with reeking fecal bolli bobbing around on top. Five minutes were spent portraying the client drinking from the bowl and feeling nauseous while watching a sadistic situation typical for him.

In describing each of these applications of covert sensitization, we have emphasized the treatment of the specific sexual deviation to the exclusion of the patient's other behavioral problems. In actual therapy, of course, many aspects relating to the individual's maladaptive behavior are examined and treated. For example, in the treatment of homosexual behavior, a program was designed utilizing a male and female therapist (Cautela & Wisocki, 1969a). The patient's anxiety responses to females and heterosexual social situations are treated by the female therapist using covert reinforcement (Cautela, 1970a), relaxation (Jacobsen, 1938), desensitization (Wolpe, 1958), thought-stopping (Cautela, 1969). The patient's maladaptive sexual attraction to males and his inability to behave assertively are treated by the male therapist who employs covert sensitization and provides assertive training (Salter, 1949). This program appears to provide well for discrimination learning—the patient learns to associate the female (who treats only anxiety-related behaviors) with anxiety reduction, and the male is the recipient of any aggression resulting from the application of aversive conditioning (Gantt, 1944).

After two years, three of the eight homosexuals seen in this therapy program have reported that they are happily married and engaging exclusively in heterosexual behavior with no sexual urges to males. Two patients are in various stages of learning appropriate heterosexual behavior and report infrequent urges to males. The other three decided to remain homosexual after a few initial sessions. Of the five patients who remained in therapy, only one had had previous sexual experience with females and none had ever experienced heterosexual fantasies before entering therapy.

In the course of this program we have found it relatively easy to eliminate the sexual attraction to males but more difficult to reduce heterosexual anxieties and instill proper approach behavior.

Failures in Therapy

The failures we have experienced in therapy have been usually attributed to premature termination (within 3 months) by the patient. Patients who remain in treatment and follow the instructions of the therapist generally modify their sexual behavior in a desirable direction. Reasons for premature termination are these:

1. Some homosexuals become fearful of losing their entire social structure as soon as they realize the treatment may be effective (i.e., as they begin to decrease the frequency of sexual urges for persons of the same sex). The *Es* tried to insure against this occurrence by proceeding slowly with covert sensitization at the beginning of therapy, while first establishing new social behaviors toward the opposite sex.

2. Some patients neglect their "homework" assignments and feel that they

are not cooperating fully and that, therefore, the treatment will be ineffective. Since this observation, the authors have stressed the importance of homework for a more rapid remission of their sexual problems, but emphasize that it is not crucial to success. For patients who do not practice assigned scenes, for a greater number of conditioning trials, the *Es* try to spend more time in the office describing scenes.

3. Some patients feel the procedure is too "superficial" and simple: that its use neglects the "real cause" of their problems. To guard against this attitude, great pains are taken to explain the rationale for the approach in the first several sessions.

The authors are not aware of any experimental study which indicates that the covert sensitization procedure is ineffective in modifying sexual deviations. In fact, when the technique has been put to rigid experimental test within an operant paradigm (Barlow, Leitenberg & Agras, 1968), it was demonstrably effective in eliminating the deviant behavior of a homosexual and a pedophile.

Barlow, Leitenberg and Agras (1968) first obtained baseline measures of sexual arousal for patients with long histories of homosexual and pedophiliac experiences. These measures were acquired while the *Ss* were imagining sexually arousing scenes. In each treatment session *Ss* were given relaxation instructions and presented with scenes in which they imagined themselves approaching the desirable sexual object, feeling nauseous, and vomiting. Alternate scenes in which *Ss* imagined themselves about to approach the object, began to feel sick and turned away, feeling relieved and relaxed were also presented. The *Es* found that all measures of sexual arousal (GSR and self report) decreased during this phase of treatment. After six acquisition sessions, extinction was introduced. The extinction procedure consisted of presentations of the sexually arousing scene without the aversive imagery. During this phase, all measures of arousal increased. The final phase of reacquisition was then initiated and all measures dropped to zero.

One could assert, however, that the results of treatment were due to the expectancies established in *S* by the covert sensitization procedure itself. Indeed, Murray and Jacobson (1969) claim that the treatment outcome in all behavior modification procedures employing imagery, such as desensitization (Wolpe, 1969), implosive therapy (Stampfl, 1967) and emotive imagery (Lazarus & Abramovitz, 1962), is more parsimoniously explained in terms of the expectancies of the *S* who is convinced the procedure will be effective.

To test this assumption Barlow, Agras and Leitenberg (1969) employed an operant paradigm to manipulate the instructions in the application of covert sensitization with two male homosexuals. After establishing a baseline of arousal, with measures of penile volume while viewing sexual scenes, ratings of those scenes and self-report, *Ss* were told that their arousal would decrease if they relaxed and viewed slides of male nudes. During this phase arousal increased, contrary to the expectations of the *Ss*. Then *Ss* were told that their sexual urges would increase a bit if they paired sexually arousing scenes with images of vomiting (covert sensitization), because the investigators felt it necessary to "heighten the tension." During this period their measures of arousal decreased. A 6-month follow-up indicated no relapse. Therefore, it appears that *Ss'* expectancies had no significant effect on treatment outcome.

DISCUSSION

The anecdotal evidence presented in this paper and the experiments cited lead us to believe that covert sensitization can be a powerful technique in the modification of sexual behavior. While emphasizing the direct treatment of the sexual deviation by aversive conditioning, it is also occasionally necessary to eliminate the drive component of the behavior. In these cases relaxation, desensitization and assertive training are effective procedures. Stevenson and Wolpe (1960) and Bond and Hutchinson (1960) report successful results with these procedures alone. It is our impression from clinical experience, however, that in treating long-term cases the use of aversive conditioning increases the probability of successful treatment outcome.

In treating sexual deviations it is also important to provide alternate modes of behavior. Ulmann and Krasner (1969, p. 488) state that "a sexual outlet should probably not be changed by a technique such as aversive conditioning unless 1) a better outlet is available; 2) one can teach and reinforce such an alternative outlet, and 3) failing the above, the present outlet is so socially reprehensible that its pursuit leads to increasingly negative social consequences."

Some clinicians (private communications) have expressed concern that the aversion will overgeneralize, for example, to the sight of any male, all shoes, etc. In practice, we have found that overgeneralization will not occur if the aversive imagery is paired with the *intent* to perform the maladaptive behavior, rather than the performance of the behavior itself.

Another point of inquiry concerns the probability of the patients actually vomiting. We have not had a case in which one actually vomited, but Wolff* reports the successful treatment of a homosexual who, while testing the efficacy of covert sensitization procedure after treatment, vomited fifty yards away from a homosexual bar he was attempting to enter. There are probably some patients, however, who are extremely sensitive to instructions of nausea and vomiting. Perhaps in these cases other aversive items may be paired with the intent to obtain the sexual object.

*Wolff, R., Personal communication, May 20, 1969.

REFERENCES

Anant, S.S. A note on the treatment of alcoholics by the verbal aversion technique. *Canadian Psychologist.* 1967, 1, 19-22.

Ashem, B. & Donner, L. Covert sensitization with alcoholics: A controlled replication. *Behavior Research and Therapy.* 1968, 6, 7-12.

Bandura, A. *Principles of behavior modification.* New York: Holt, Rinehart, & Winston, 1969.

Barker, J.A. Behavior therapy for transvestism: A comparison of pharmacological and electrical aversion techniques. *British Medical Journal.* 1965, 111, 268-276.

Barlow, D.H., Agras, W.S. & Leitenberg, H. The effect of instruction on the use of Covert Sensitization. Unpublished study, Univ. of Vermont, Burlington, 1969.

Barlow, D.H. Leitenberg, H. & Agras, S.W. Preliminary report of the experimental control of sexual deviation by manipulating of the US in Covert Sensitizaton. paper presented at the Eastern Psychological Association meeting, Washington, D.C. In press, *Journal of Abnormal Psychology.*1968.

Binet, A. *Le fetishisms dans l'amour.* Paris, 1888.

Bond, I. & Hutchinson, H. Application of reciprocal inhibition therapy to exhibitionism. *Canadian Medical Association Journal.* 1960, 83, 23-25.

Cautela, J.R. Treatment of compulsive behavior by covert sensitization. *Psychological Record.* 1966, **16**, 33-41.

Cautela, J.R. Covert Sensitization. *Psychological Reports.* 1967, **20**, 459-468.

Cautela, J.R. Behavior therapy and the need for behavioral assessment. *Psychotherapy: Theory, Research and Practice.* 1968a, **5**, 175-179.

Cautela, J.R. Homosexual questionnaire. Unpublished data. Boston College, Chestnut Hill, Mass., 1968b.

Cautela, J.R. Behavior therapy and self-control: Techniques and implications. In C. Franks (Ed.) *Behavior therapy: Assessment and status.* New York: McGraw-Hill, 1969.

Cautela, J.R. Covert reinforcement. *Behavior Therapy.* 1970a, **1**, 33-50.

Cautela, J.R. Sexual behavior questionnaire. Unpublished data. Boston College, Chestnut Hill, Mass., 1970b.

Cautela, J.R. The use of covert sensitization in the treatment of alcoholism. *Psychotherapy: Theory, Research and Practice.* 1970c, **7**, 86-90.

Cautela, J.R. & Baron, M.G. The behavior therapy treatment of self-destructive behavior. Unpublished study. Boston College, Chestnut Hill, Mass., 1969.

Cautela, J.R. & Kastenbaum, R. A Reinforcement Survey Schedule for use in therapy, training and research. *Psychological Reports.* 1967, **20**, 1115-1130.

Cautela, J.R. & Wisocki, P.A. The use of male and female therapists in the treatment of homosexual behavior. I.R. Rubin & C. Franks (Eds.), *Advances in behavior therapy.* 1968. New York: Academic Press, 1969a.

Cautela, J.R. & Wisocki, P.A. The use of the Reinforcement Survey Schedule in behavior modification. Paper presented to the Association for the Advancement of Behavior Therapy, Washington, D.C., September, 1969b.

Clark, D.F. Fetishism treated by negative conditioning. *British Journal of Psychiatry.* 1963, **109**, 695-696.

Cooper, J.E. A study of behavior therapy in thirty psychiatric patients. *Lancet.* 1963, **1**, 411-415.

Curran, D. & Parr, D. Homosexuality: An analysis of 100 male cases in private practice. *British Medical Journal.* **1**, 797-801.

Davison, G. Elimination of a sadistic fantasy by a client-centered counterconditioning technique: A case study. *Journal of Abnormal Psychology.* 1968, **73**, 84-89.

Evans, D.R. Masturbatory fantasy and sexual deviation. *Behavior Research and Therapy.* 1968, **6**, 17-20.

Feingold, L. An automated technique for aversive conditioning in sexual deviation. Paper presented at the Association for the Advancement of Behavior Therapy, San Francisco, August, 1968.

Feldman, M., & MacCulloch, M. 1965. The application of anticipatory avoidance learning to the treatment of homosexuality: 1. Theory, technique, and preliminary results. *Behavior Research and Therapy.* 1965, **2**, 165-183.

Franks, C. 1967. Reflections upon treatment of sexual disorders by the behavioral clinicians: An historical comparison with the treatment of the alcoholic. *The Journal of Sex Research.* 1967, **3**, 212-222.

Gantt, W.H. *Experimental basis for neurotic behaviors.* New York: Hoeber, 1944.

Jacobsen, E. *Progressive relaxation.* Chicago: Univ. of Chicago Press, 1938.

Kolvin, L. "Aversive imagery" treatment in adolescents. *Behavior Research and Therapy.* 1967, **5**, 245-249.

Lavin, N., Thorpe, J., Barker, J., Blackemore, C., & Conway, C. Behavior therapy in a case of transvestism. *Journal of Nervous and Mental Disorders.* 1961, **133**, 346-353.

Lazarus, A.A. & Abramovitz, A. The use of "emotive imagery" in the treatment of children's phobias. *Journal of Mental Science.* 1962, **108**, 191-196.

Lovaas, I.O. Behavior therapy approach to the treatment of childhood schizophrenia. Minnesota symposium on child development. Minneapolis: Univ. Minn. Press, 1967.

Marks, I., Rachman, S. & Gelder, M. Methods of assessment of aversion treatment in fetishism with masochism. *Behavior Research and Therapy.* 1965, **3**, 253-258.

McGuire, R., Carlisle, J. & Young, B. Sexual deviation as conditioned behavior. *Behavior Research and Therapy,* 1965, **2**, 185-190.

McGuire, R.J. & Valance, M. Aversion therapy by electric shock: A simple technique. *British Medical Journal,* 1964, **1**, 151-153.

Mees, H.L. Sadistic fantasies modified by aversive conditioning and substitution: A case report. *Behavior Research and Therapy,* 1966. **4**, 317-320.

Morgenstein, F.S., Pearce, J.F. & Rees, W. Predicting the outcome of behavior therapy by psychological tests. *Behavior Research and Therapy,* 1965, **2**, 191-200.

Mullen, F.G. The effect of covert sensitization on smoking behavior. Unpublished study, Queens College, Charlottesville, N.C., 1968.

Murray, E.J. & Jacobson, T.L. The nature of learning in traditional psychotherapy. In A.E. Bergin & S.L. Garfield (Eds.), *Handbook of psychotherapy and behavior change.* New York: Wiley, 1969.

Oswald, L. Induction of illusory and hallucinatory voices with considerations of behavior therapy. *Journal of Mental Science.* 1962, **108**, 196-212.

Rachman, S. Sexual fetishism: An experimental analogue. *Psychological Record.* 1966, **16**, 293-296.

Rachman, S. & Hodgson, R.J. Experimentally-induced "sexual fetishism": Replication and development. *Psychological Record.* 1968, **18**, 25-27.

Raymond, M.J. Case of fetishism treated by aversion therapy. *British Medical Journal.* 1956, **2**, 854-857.

Robertson, M. The use of stimulus hierarchy combined with avoidance learning in the treatment of homosexuality. Paper presented to the Association for the Advancement of Behavior Therapy, San Francisco, September, 1968.

Salter, A. *Conditioned reflex.* New York: Farrar, Strauss, 1949.

Sanderson, R.E., Campbell, D. & Laverty, S.G. An investigation of a new aversive conditioning treatment of alcoholism. *Quarterly Journal of Studies of Alcoholism.* 1963, **24**, 261-275.

Stampfl, T.G. Implosive therapy, Part I: The theory. In S.G. Armitage, (Ed.), *Behavior modification techniques and the treatment of emotional disorders.* Battle Creek, Mich.: U.S. Publications, 1967.

Stevenson, I. & Wolpe, J. Recovery from sexual deviations through overcoming non-sexual neurotic responses. *American Journal of Psychiatry.* 1960, 116, 737-742.

Stuart, R.B. Behavioral control of overeating. *Behavior Research and Therapy.* 1967, 357-365.

Thorpe, J., Schmidt, E., Brown, P. & Castell, D. Aversion-relief therapy: A new method for general application. *Behavior Research and Therapy.* 1964, **2**, 71-82.

Ullmann, L. & Krasner, L. (Eds.) *Case studies in behavior modification.* New York: Holt, Rinehart & Winston, 1965.

Ullmann, L. & Krasner, L. *A psychological approach to abnormal behavior.* Englewood Cliffs: Prentice-Hall, 1969.

Viernstein, L. Evaluation of therapeutic techniques of Covert Sensitization. Unpublished data, Queens College, Charlottesville, N.C., 1968.

Wolpe, J. *Psychotherapy by reciprocal inhibition.* Stanford: Stanford Univ. Press, 1958.

Wolpe, J. *The practice of behavior therapy.* New York: Pergamon Press, 1969.

Wolpe, J. & Lang, P. A fear survey schedule for use in behavior therapy. *Behavior Research and Therapy.* 1964, **2**, 27-30.

Wolpe, J. & Lazarus, A.A. *Behavior therapy techniques: A guide to the treatment of neurosis.* New York: Pergamon Press, 1966.

18
"Assisted" Covert Sensitization: A Preliminary Report

Despite early acclaim, several critical reports of covert sensitization demonstrating only marginal effect have now been published (Ashem & Donner, 1968; Sachs, Bean, & Morrow, 1970). This has also been our experience. To bolster the strength of conditioning in such cases, an odiferous substance, valeric acid,[1] was introduced at points during scene presentations coincident with verbal suggestions of nausea and vomiting. The following examples demonstrate the use of this technique:

CASE REPORT 1

A 52-year-old house painter complained of a long-standing compulsion to commit fellatio five to seven times monthly. For the past 35 years he had "given in" and solicited men in public toilets for this purpose. He came to our clinic because, as he grew older, religion became important to him and, in addition, he feared apprehension. He denied other forms of homosexual behavior, and he and his wife described adequate heterosexual adjustment.

Failing to diminish soliciting thoughts or behaviors to any significant degree with routine covert sensitization, the following modification was attempted: when the therapist introduced verbal suggestions of nausea and vomiting coincident with the act of fellatio, he also introduced an offensive odor by uncapping a bottle of valeric acid and holding it under the patient's nose. He also practiced with tape recordings of scenes and by smelling this acid in the rest rooms he used to frequent. This technique induced rapid sensitization with brief but extreme feelings of nausea and several episodes of actual vomiting.

After 15 sessions of sensitization using valeric acid, neither acts of fellatio nor

---

[1] I am indebted to Dr. Donald Molde for first experimenting with the use of valeric acid in conditioning therapies. Valeric acid is an inexpensive, relatively noncorrosive substance easily purchased from many chemical supply firms. Its odor is powerful, yet it can be used repeatedly without loss of potency.

bothersome urges to perform the act were reported. Verification was obtained from his wife and associates. "Booster" sessions were held at 3-month intervals for 1 year. A 12-month follow-up indicated sensitization had been sustained.

Eight additional homosexual patients have now been sensitized using this "assisted" technique and a 12-month follow-up indicates a total absence of homosexual urges, dreams, and overt behavior. A tenth patient has achieved only a partial remission. The technique has been applied to other types of maladaptive approach behaviors as well.

CASE REPORT 2

A 27-year-old married woman was progressing slowly in a weight-control group. She had difficulty not eating anything made of chocolate. After relaxation training she was presented with scenes of chocolate goodies she had just tasted infested with lice and maggots. At the appropriate moment, the smell of valeric acid was introduced, inducing nausea and gagging. After 10 such sessions, she has refrained from eating chocolate on most occasions and a 7-month follow-up revealed a continued weight loss.

There is ample precedent for the use of foul-smelling substances to sensitize behavior (e.g., Kennedy & Foreyt, 1968; Wolpe, 1969). Valeric acid seemed remarkably suitable in these cases, however, as the protocols called for imagining fecal and putrid odors and tastes in various scenes. This substance not only assaults the olfactory senses with an odor benignly termed foul, but adds a certain human decaying quality as well, which seemed appropriate in helping these subjects more vividly experience a noxious visceral response. Moreover, as Bandura (1969) has recently reported, stimuli producing nauseous reactions may yield "more natural and symbolically reproducible aversions" than the more commonly used electroshock techniques.

The purist may well assert that the procedure employed with these subjects is hardly covert sensitization inasmuch as a physical stimulus was utilized. This is indisputably correct; nonetheless, the procedure originally derived from covert sensitization which, when proving too tenuous for these particular patients, was modified accordingly.

REFERENCES

Ashem, B., & Donner, L. Covert sensitization with alcoholics: A controlled replication. *Behaviour Research and Therapy,* 1968, **6**, 7-12.

Bandura, A. *Principles of behavior modification.* New York: Holt, Rinehart and Winston, Inc., 1969, pp. 507-508.

Kennedy, W.A., & Foreyt, J. Control of eating behavior in an obese patient by avoidance and conditioning. *Psychological Reports,* 1968, **23**, 571-573.

Sachs, L.B., Bean, H., & Morrow, J.E. Comparison of smoking treatments. *Behavior Therapy,* 1970, **1**, 465-472.

Wolpe, J. *The practice of behavior therapy.* New York: Pergamon Press, 1969.

19
Aversion Therapy for Sexual Deviation: Contingent Shock and Covert Sensitization

EDWARD J. CALLAHAN AND HAROLD LEITENBERG

Control of societally defined deviant behavior has traditionally been a difficult area of therapeutic intervention. This has proven especially true in sexual deviation (Curran & Parr, 1957; Eysenck & Rachman, 1965), possibly because of the immediate pleasure inherent in orgasm regardless of its method of occurrence. Recent attempts to alter patterns of sexual arousal using learning techniques have met with some success, however, so that the behavior therapist is now faced with a selection of techniques from which he may choose (Rachman & Teasdale, 1969).

Basically, aversion therapies pair an unpleasant event with some form of undesirable behavior. The aversive events have ranged from nausea-inducing drugs to electric shock to unpleasant scenes presented in imagination. Emetic drugs have been found unacceptable because of their unpredictable onset in time and their unpleasantness for those administering treatment (Rachman & Teasdale, 1969). Further, their success has not been outstanding (Freund, 1969), although McConaghy (1969, 1970) presented recent evidence that this technique might be effective with homosexuality. Electric shock and imagined aversive events currently seem to be preferred by therapists for their ease of administration and control. To date, however, no direct comparisons of the relative effectiveness of these two techniques have been made, although a number of studies have investigated each technique separately.

Electric shock as an aversive technique for treatment of sexual deviation has been reported to be effective in numerous case reports and in various larger studies (e.g., Fookes, 1969; MacCulloch & Feldman, 1967; Marks, Gelder, & Bancroft, 1970; McConaghy, 1970; and *see* the review by Rachman & Teasdale, 1969). Shock intensity and duration are easily quantified, and shock can be administered in a number of different paradigms, including avoidance (MacCulloch & Feldman, 1967) and punishment (Marks & Gelder, 1967). It has been shown that the actual administration of shock to the patient is necessary for the suppression of homosexuality in an avoidance conditioning

*This paper is based on a portion of a dissertation submitted to the Department of Psychology, University of Vermont, in partial fulfillment of the requirements for the Ph.D. degree.

treatment paradigm (Birk, Huddleston, Miller & Cohler, 1971). Further, there are indications that shock punishment is most effective if it is applied during the actual deviant act or a close representation of that act (*see* Fookes, 1969; Marks & Gelder, 1967). Since penile erection is a necessary prerequisite to most male sexual activity, the applicaton of electric shock might be made optimally effective if it were made contingent upon evidence of penile erection. This is a conclusion also reached by Bancroft (1969) and Rachman and Teasdale (1969). Contingent shock was one therapeutic technique used in the present study; it provides a marked contrast to the second technique—covert sensitization.

Verbal description of nauseous and repulsive scenes in conjunction with imagined sexual behavior has been reported successful in controlling deviant sexual behavior in various single case reports (e.g., Cautela, 1966; Gold & Neufeld, 1965; Miller, 1963). In controlled within-subjects studies, such description also has been isolated as the effective therapeutic ingredient in covert sensitization (Barlow, Leitenberg & Agras, 1969; Barlow, Leitenberg, Agras, Callahan & Moore, in press).

It was the purpose of this study to compare within individual subjects these two forms of aversion therapy since they offer contrasting, yet reportedly effective, approaches to the treatment of sexual deviation. On the one hand, covert sensitization provides an imagined aversive event following imagined sexual behavior, while contingent shock provides a physical aversive event contingent upon a physical response, erection. These two therapies were administered in counterbalanced order to each of a series of six sexually deviant patients, while ongoing penile circumference changes to erotic slides were objectively monitored and a daily subjective report of sexual feelings and activities was recorded. Detailed procedure and results for two of these subjects are provided, and the results for the remaining four subjects are briefly summarized.

METHOD

Subjects

Six subjects were selected from a group of 23 referrals during a 2-year period. Selection was made on the grounds of desire to undergo aversion therapy and the consistent occurrence of measurable erection during presentation of slides depicting their deviant form of arousal. Seven referrals decided against treatment (two of these were court referred), two subjects dropped out during the first phase of treatment, and eight subjects were not included because they did not show consistent erections to slides during the base-line assessment period. Two of the six patients reported were under court supervision for their sexual acting out (exposure). These six patients all showed penile circumference changes while watching slides depicting stimuli appropriate to their own sexual deviation. Stable penile response was necessary for research assessment of the two therapies, and for application of contingent shock punishment.

The subjects included two exhibitionists (one of whom was also pedophilic and homosexual), one transvestite-transsexual, two homosexuals, and one pedophilic homosexual. Their problems were diverse and their patterns of sexual arousal highly individualized. For reasons such as these, as well as the limited number of subjects available for study, within-subject analysis of treatment effects was thought preferable to a group design study (*see* Chassan, 1967; Sidman, 1960). Each subject received both treatments, while the order of treatments was counterbalanced across subjects.

Instructions

Each referral was offered free treatment as part of a research program evaluating aversion therapies for sexual problems. He was instructed that two equally powerful therapies were to be used. These therapies were said to be complementary because of their different modes of operation; together they were said to provide a more thorough eradication of the problem under attack. Every effort was made to lead each subject to expect equal improvement under both treatments. An attempt was made to provide a friendly supportive atmosphere throughout, but extensive discussions of nonsexual difficulties were discouraged. It was made clear that the two aversion therapies were *the* therapies.

Treatment Procedures

Contingent shock. Moderately painful shock levels were first determined by psychophysical intensity scaling for levels of subjective perception, report of pain, and absolute peak tolerance level. Shock levels varying from "pain" to "tolerance" were then randomly selected for administration as part of a punishment procedure which made shock contingent upon erection. These shock levels ordinarily ranged from .5 milliampere to 4.5 milliampere, and shock duration was varied randomly from .1 second to .5 second. Erection was monitored by a penile strain gauge (*see* Barlow, Becker, Leitenberg & Agras, 1970). Five slides of deviant material and two heterosexually oriented slides were presented for 125 seconds apiece in each session while the subject was instructed to imagine whatever was sexually arousing with the person on the slide. An attempt was made to obtain slides appropriate to each person's idiosyncratic sexual arousal. If during the "deviant" material slide, the penile circumference increase exceeded a level of 15 percent of full erection, shock was administered through electrodes on the first and third fingers on the subject's right hand. This level was sufficient to allow subjects to report awareness of penile engorgement prior to shock in most instances.

This procedure was quite similar to that reported by Bancroft (1969). However, in Bancroft's study, shock could be delivered only at five fixed times (15 seconds apart) across the 75 seconds the slide was left on following onset of erection. In the present study, shock could be delivered at the onset of erection and any time thereafter that the degree of erection increased. In both procedures, the absence of erection avoids shock. In Bancroft's procedure, five shocks were possible over the 75 seconds subsequent to the occurrence of erection; in the present study, as many as 15 shocks were delivered over the course of the slide presentation.

Covert Sensitization. As reported by Cautela (1966), this technique involves the presentation of verbal descriptions of "deviant" acts and the description of aversive consequences, such as nausea, vomiting, discovery by family, etc. Scenes were presented to each subject after he was relaxed using Jacobson's technique (Wolpe, 1958); relaxation training was conducted for 1-3 sessions. Individual hierarchies of sexually arousing "deviant acts" were constructed, and each subject was interviewed to determine the most subjectively aversive events he could imagine. Each session contained six scenes describing deviant arousal. Four of these were described as leading to unpleasant consequences. For example, a man might be asked to imagine going to the apartment of a homosexual contact, approaching the man's bedroom, initiating sexual activity, feeling increasingly nauseous, and finally vomiting on the contact, on the sheets, and all over himself. A variation of this scene might involve the patient finding the homosexual contact rotting with syphilitic sores, or finding that the contact has diarrhea during the sexual encounter. A socially aversive scene might have an exhibitionist discovered by a girlfriend, or a father caught in the middle of some sexual act by one of his children, his wife or a respected co-worker. In the other two scenes, the "deviant" act was described as beginning, leading to discomfort or nausea, then being escaped from by leaving the scene and approaching an arousing girl in an appropriate heterosexual manner. As therapy continued, aversive events were introduced progressively earlier in the imagined sequence, that is, when the subject's hand reached for his belt instead of as he exposed himself. The subjects were repeatedly questioned about fantasies and urges in order to directly mold the ongoing therapy to the subject's current arousal patterns. They were not instructed to practice covert sensitization at home.

Measures

Penile Plethysmograph. Changes in penile circumference were recorded on the Grass Model-7 polygraph by means of a penile transducer (*see* Barlow et al., 1970). Each subject was instructed before each session to imagine that he was alone with the person(s) presented by a slide projector on the screen, engaging in whatever act was most sexually arousing. During base line, measures of sexual arousal were taken during presentation of three slides of deviant and three slides of heterosexual stimuli. During treatment phases, these measurements were taken for two slides of each type before the therapy was administered; thus, in a sense, the sessions measured the effects of the previous treatment, which usually had occurred 2 days before. Erectile responses were averaged over two session blocks during treatment. It is important to note that assessment during the contingent shock administration took place before shock electrodes were attached for treatment.

Of 16 potential subjects evaluated extensively on this measure, 8 showed great enough and stable enough erection for inclusion in the research program. Two of these dropped out during treatment. The plethysmograph was calibrated daily by mechanically spreading the wings of the gauge 1-15 millimeters. In this way, daily recording variations were accounted for. Deflections of the pen could then be compared to the standard of a response designated by the patient as a full erection, thus producing "percentage erection."

Subjective Clinical Report. Each subject was given a notebook to record daily sexual urges (a quick striking sexual arousal), sexual fantasies (prolonged imagination of sexual scenes), masturbation and its accompanying fantasies, as well as any overt sexual acts with other people. The therapist never discussed the actual recorded data with the patient, but instead made broad verbal inquiries about this information in order to keep the therapy situation as natural as possible. The therapist did not analyze these data until all phases of treatment were complete.

Subjective reports were averaged over the day of treatment and the following 3 days. One average was then taken for each 2 successive treatment days. In addition, an over-all average of each type of report was determined for each phase. In most cases, only "urges" were reported frequently enough after treatment began to allow a meaningful comparison between treatments.

Outside Report. This method of evaluation of treatment was only possible in the cases of the two exhibitionists who were both on parole. One of these was under close surveillance by a state institutional school, and the other had periodic visits with a court-appointed psychiatrist. Neither outside report revealed information relevant to the comparative evaluation of the two therapies. Of the other four cases, two were married men whose wives were unaware of their sexual problems and two were single living away from home.

Experimental Design

Single case research methodology was employed in this study. An attempt was made to compare each treatment within the subject rather than between groups. The small number of subjects available for study and the idiosyncratic nature of each subject's sexual problems required such within-subject research strategy. Before either treatment was introduced, 3-9 sessions were devoted to obtaining relevant baseline measures. Following the baseline, one of the treatment procedures was introduced. Three subjects received covert sensitization first, and three received contingent shock first. For four of the six subjects, Treatment A was maintained for 10 sessions before switching to Treatment B. For one subject, treatments were switched after six sessions, and for the remaining subject after eight sessions. Attempts were made to replicate each treatment condition twice for each subject, although this turned out to be impossible in some of the cases.

RESULTS

Since the nature of the sexual problem was different for each subject, since length of phases and number of times a given treatment was provided to each subject also varied somewhat across subjects, and since the response of each subject to each treatment was by no means identical, no attempt was made to combine the data into a single figure. Ideally, individual figures for each subject should be presented. Unfortunately, this demands too much journal space. As a compromise, detailed results for two of the subjects are described, and the results for each of the remaining subjects are briefly summarized.

Subject 2

The patient was a 38-year-old depressed married man with a 13-year history of active homosexuality and depression. The patient sought behavioral treatment after 4 years of psychiatric counseling which had not alleviated either problem. He continued psychiatric counseling for the depression, with the stipulation that no sexual matters be discussed.

His homosexual activity consisted of seeking contacts 2-3 times a week, usually without success. Sexual relations with one regular contact occurred once every other week. Sexual relations with his wife occurred once every other week also; however, these were always accompanied by a fantasy of watching another male having intercourse with her. Kissing and petting had become aversive to him, although these activities had been enjoyable early in the marriage. He sought treatment to reduce homosexual urges since he felt they led to frustration, depression and an inability to concentrate on work.

Baseline. Baseline measures were taken five times over a 5-week period. Penile circumference changes during slides of males resulted in between 85 percent and 100 percent erection, while slides of females never resulted in more than 15 percent erection (*see* Fig. 1). Homosexual urges averaged 3.7 per day (*see* Fig. 1), while fantasies about men occurred about three times per day. Masturbation accompanied male fantasy twice, while homosexual imagery was involved in all of the four instances of intercourse during this period. Homosexual "cruising" or loitering to find male partners occurred seven times during this phase.

Phase 1. Covert sensitization was administered for 10 sessions, at a frequency of three sessions per week. Sexual arousal as measured by penile circumference changes during slides of males showed a reduction in average erection to about 70 percent, while erection during slides of female increased very little to an average of about 15 percent.

Homosexual urges were reduced to an average of .75 per day, with no urges on 23 of the last 27 days of this treatment period. Homosexual fantasies were reduced to an average of .6 per day, and beyond this point in treatment homosexual fantasies never again led to masturbation. Intercourse was accompanied by homosexual fantasy twice early in this phase, but such fantasy was never again reported with intercourse. Intercourse remained stable in frequency (five times over 34 days), but the patient said he began to initiate intercourse himself. Cruising was first reduced in frequency, then stopped and was never again reported after the halfway point of this phase.

Phase 2. Contingent shock was administered for 10 sessions. Penile circumference changes during slides of men showed a marked increase back to the pre-treatment level of almost 100 percent erection. Penile circumference changes during slides of females also became greater, approaching an average of almost 100 percent erection. Thus, all penile responding was facilitated during this phase. Reported homosexual urges increased in frequency to an average of 1.3 per day, while homosexual fantasies continued to decrease, averaging .3 per day. Intercourse remained stable in frequency.

Phase 3. Covert sensitization was reintroduced for 10 sessions. This treatment phase resulted in a decrease in penile circumference changes during slides of men, although never below an average of 50 percent erection during the slides. Penile circumference changes during slides of females remained at close to 100 percent erection. Reported homosexual urges decreased in frequency to less than one per day (.6), while homosexual fantasies did not occur. Intercourse continued at about the same rate, while fantasies of sexual relations with females first occurred during this time.

The subject's only homosexual contact during treatment occurred during a 2-week break in treatment in this phase. The patient reported an inability to reach climax during this contact. During a later talk to a former contact, the patient felt the symptoms of impending vomiting and left the situation. He later connected this feeling with experiences felt during treatment.

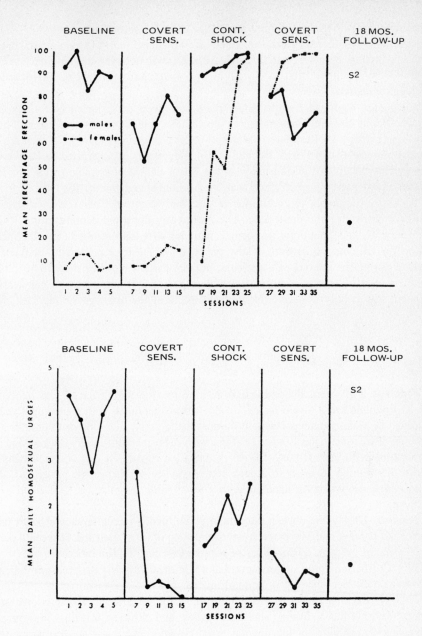

Fig. 1. Subject 2: Mean Percentage of Erection to Slides and Mean Daily Homosexual Urges.

Summary. Covert sensitization was clearly more effective than contingent shock in suppressing homosexual arousal for this patient. In fact, contingent shock reversed prior improvement on the objective measure of penile circumference and on the subjective measure of homosexual urges. It did not reverse the previous suppression of homosexual fantasy and masturbation with homosexual fantasy. The second administration of covert sensitization again decreased erection to slides of men and reported homosexual urges. A surprising finding, however, was the substantial increase in penile circumference response to heterosexual stimuli that occurred in the first contingent shock phase and was sustained thereafter.

Follow-up. Eighteen months later, there had been no recurrence of homosexual contacts. Penile circumference measures showed less responsiveness to all stimuli at this follow-up (*see* Fig. 1). Response to slides of males was again greater (27%) than response to slides of females which had declined (17%). Depression was reported to be alleviated somewhat by treatment; it recurred with the threat of loss of employment at one point, however. Systematic desensitization was then administered briefly for fears of job loss and fears of criticism for job performance and family support. Elavil was later prescribed by a psychiatrist for the depression. This transiently improved depression but lessened sexual arousal, and temporary impotence with his wife also resulted. This lessened his satisfaction with sexual aspects of the marriage. Urges for homosexual contacts had occurred during the periods of depression, but the patient reported these to be mild and infrequent. Sexual aspects of his marriage are reported still improved over pre-treatment status but not as fully as before. Nonsexual aspects of the marriage are reported greatly inproved.

Subject 4

This was a 19-year-old homosexual with no prior sexual or dating experience with girls. The patient had a 6-year history of overt sexual contacts with males and 3 years of "cruising" or seeking male partners in homosexually active areas. Sexual contacts at the beginning of treatment consisted of relations with older men once every 2 weeks and daily masturbation with male fantasy. Sexual contacts led to guilt feelings and vacillation over whether he wanted to learn to accept homosexuality or change his pattern of sexual arousal. After discussing his dilemma with a few friends and relatives, he decided to seek treatment.

Baseline. During the 3-week assessment phase, penile circumference changes ranged between 70 percent and 100 percent erection during slides of men and between 3 percent and 52 percent erection during slides of women (*see* Fig. 2). Homosexual urges (*see* Fig. 2) and masturbation about men occurred at a rate of slightly less than one per day, while homosexual fantasies occurred at a rate of one per day.

Phase 1. Contingent shock was administered for 10 sessions. Penile circumference changes were reduced during slides of males and females initially; however, this suppression during slides of females was only transient. There was an increase in average daily homosexual urges to slightly more than two per day and a slight increase in frequency of daily homosexual masturbation, while homosexual fantasies were slightly decreased. The patient was somewhat disturbed by the experience of shock but was willing to undergo it in order to change his sexual arousal pattern. He had one homosexual contact late in this phase.

Phase 2. Covert sensitization was administered for seven sessions. Penile circumference changes to slides of men reduced greatly, and penile circumference changes to slides of women continued to increase. Rapid progress was reported by the subject in this phase. Homosexual urges were quickly reduced to zero as were homosexual fantasies. Following four sessions, masturbation with male fantasies reduced to zero frequency as well. The subject reported his first heterosexual urges, fantasies and masturbation in this phase. After seven sessions, the subject reported he was progressing more quickly than he could stand "psychically." He felt his progress was strong enough to drop treatment and continue to make adjustment alone. After 3 months, however, he returned to treatment

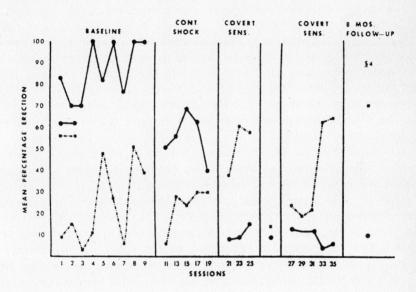

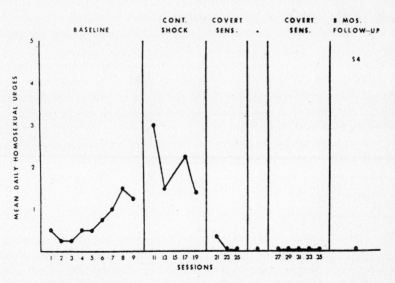

Fig. 2. Subject 4: Mean Percentage of Erection to Slides and Mean Daily Homosexual Urges.

because of an "unwanted" homosexual contact which unnerved him about the stability of his progress.

Covert sensitization was introduced again in order to complete the interrupted phase and was continued for four sessions. Penile circumference changes during slides of women decreased following the no-treatment phase. With reintroduction of covert sensitization, these responses increased again. Homosexual urges, masturbation, and fantasies were reported to have been returning infrequently but were reduced to zero again with reintroduction of treatment. Heterosexual masturbation and fantasy increased, but no heterosexual urges were ever reported.

An attempt was then made to return the subject to contingent shock treatment. The subject became very upset by this and misapplied the electrodes during the first scheduled shock session in order to reduce the shock. At the next session, he explained that he felt shock had not helped him and that he did not want to go through the painful experience since he felt it had no therapeutic effect. At this stage, he said he would have to quit treatment rather than go through contingent shock again. A decision was then made to return to covert sensitization.

Six further covert sensitization sessions showed a continued absence of homosexual arousal in urges, fantasies and masturbation. Heterosexual fantasy and masturbation increased and the subject began dating more frequently.

Summary. Covert sensitization effectively suppressed erection to slides depicting homosexual content; however, contingent shock had previously reduced erection to these slides, although not as completely. Since the subject refused to undergo contingent shock a second time, there was no chance to test whether shock would have continued or reversed the suppression occurring during covert sensitization. At the same time that erection was partially suppressed during the administration of contingent shock, reported homosexual urges increased in frequency. This indicates a lack of correspondence between objective measures (penile erection) and subjective measures (reported occurrences of sexual arousal) of sexual deviation. Covert sensitization reduced subjective reports of deviant sexual arousal after they had increased during contingent shock therapy.

Follow-up. After 8 months, penile circumference changes during viewing of slides of males remained low (10%), while erection during slides of females remained great (86%; *see* Fig. 2). The subject reported continued arousal to females and no homosexual urges (*see* Fig. 2). He engaged in one homosexual contact early in this period but claimed not to find excitement in it. His heterosexual dating had led to increased petting and sexual arousal but had not yet led to intercourse. He reported homosexual thoughts were bland to him and that he thoroughly enjoyed dating and petting with girls.

Subject 1

The patient was a 15-year-old boy with a 4-year history of exposure. He had previously been committed for this for 18 months and had been released to the custody of his parents as the exposures seemed to have abated. However, the subject reported that he continued to expose himself during the next year home. He was then returned to a state institution after repeated police complaints about his exposure. Just prior to this referral, he had been expelled from public high school for exposure. Previous treatment had included weekly psychiatric conferences and meetings with a social worker, which had not been successful.

Following baseline, four phases of covert sensitization and three phases of contingent shock were provided; each phase consisted of six treatment sessions. Perhaps because of the brevity of each alternating treatment condition, it was difficult to ascertain any substantial difference in the relative effectiveness of each treatment. However, by the end of treatment and at an 18-month follow-up, there was considerable improvement on all measures taken. On follow-up, the subject's erectile response to slides of nude females under instructions to think of intercourse was 83 percent of maximum, while only 14 percent erection occurred during the same slides under instructions to think of exposure. Mean daily urges to expose declined from four to five per day during baseline to less than one per day at follow-up. Incidents of reported exposure decreased from once every other day to zero. He also reported dating one girl steadily for 8 months during the period from the end of treatment to follow-up measurement.

Subject 3

The patient was a 30-year-old man who had been arrested for exposure to young boys. He was given a suspended jail sentence on condition that he seek treatment.

He had a long history of sexual activity with teenage boys dating from his own adolescence. He had intercourse for the first time with a prostitute while in the service. At the same time, he became more aware of his sexual interest in children and began to expose to them. Exposure continued even during his one short-term sexual relationship with a woman. His one attempt to establish homosexual relations during this period of time also failed, so that exposure to and fondling of children were his only sexual activities for a period of 5 years before treatment. Masturbation was most frequently accompanied by fantasies of these acts. Following baseline, eight sessions of covert sensitization, eight sessions of contingent shock, and then again eight sessions of covert sensitization were provided in sequential phases.

During baseline, erections to slides of boys, girls and women were about equivalent. As treatment progressed, there were some separation in these curves with the erectile response to slides of women increasing to about 65 percent and the response to young boys and girls declining to about 20 percent. No clear differences between treatments on this measure were observed. The most sensitive subjective measure seemed to be the subject's sexual fantasies during masturbation. Thinking about children while masturbating averaged about twice per day during baseline, declined to once per day during the first covert sensitization phase, rose again to twice per day during contingent shock, and declined once more to once per day during the final covert sensitization phase. An inverse effect was noted for fantasies of sexual intercourse with women.

Regular follow-up interviews with no booster sessions indicated a gradual deterioration of progress over the subsequent 4 months. This deterioration was not evidenced by measurements of penile circumference changes during slides; it was evident only from verbal reports of fantasy and sexual urges.

Subject 5

The patient was a 29-year-old married man referred after being apprehended by police while walking along a main street in women's clothing. This was his first police contact in 17 years of cross-dressing, and no charges were pressed. His treatment was voluntary; his reported reason for wanting therapy was the desire to feel sexually "normal." Although married, the patient reported intercourse occurred only twice a year. According to the patient's description, 2-week periods of frequent masturbation and cross-dressing were interspersed between month-long sex-free periods.

The patient reported spontaneous transsexual fantasies, urges, and masturbation too infrequently to allow any comparison of these measures for treatment effects. Research measurement relied exclusively on changes in penile circumference during fantasies of a) being a woman and b) being a man making love to a woman. The same slides of nude women were used for both fantasies, differing only in the verbal instruction preceding slide presentation. While instructed to imagine being a woman, 35 percent—72 percent erection occurred; while instructed to imagine intercourse with a woman, only 2 percent—15 percent erection occurred. All measurements of penile circumference change during slide presentation were taken while the patient was dressed in woman's clothing. This served to heighten transsexual arousal but did not seem to affect heterosexual response. There was no evidence of greater heterosexual response when dressed as a man.

Treatment consisted of one phase of contingent shock and one phase of covert sensitization. There was rapid and substantial suppression of erection to transsexual fantasies during the first phase. (Note that measurement was taken without the shock electrodes attached.) Intercourse was reported to increase to once a week, although independent confirmation with his wife was impossible since the patient claimed that his wife was unaware of his tranvestism, and he did not wish us to contact her. Improvement continued during the subsequent covert sensitization, and thus no differential effect of treatments could be observed. The patient reported feeling that shock suppressed his transsexual desires but that he did not trust the permanence of the suppression. He first reported that covert sensitization could not work for him, but later claimed it brought about a "permanent" suppression of transsexual and transvestitic arousal.

Final evaluation is difficult because of the sporadic history of the problem. At an eight-month follow-up, penile circumference changes remained slight during fantasy of being a woman and fantasy of intercourse with a woman (4 percent and 10 percent erection, respectively). He reported that he had maintained improvement but had turned down the therapist's suggestion of further marriage counseling as unneccessary. Intercourse was reported to occur three times per week at this stage. This case showed the best evidence of effectiveness of contingent shock. It is also the only case in which the punishment took place while the deviant act was occurring, that is, while the subject was dressed in woman's clothing and imagining being a woman.

Subject 6

The patient was a 22-year-old male medical student with homosexual and pedophiliac desires but no overt experience. No aversion to females was expressed, but the patient had not dated because of a fear that a girl would demand sexual performance; he felt that he could not perform sexually with women because of small genitals. Recent kareotyping had ruled out Klinefelter's syndrome, but this did not diminish his heterosexual fears. His sexual arousal centered around fantasies of stroking the chest and arms of young muscle builders and very young boys, requiring such fantasy for erection. He sought treatment because he wanted marriage and a family and because he felt homosexual and pedophiliac activity would not be appropriate in his planned medical career.

In the baseline period, measurable penile circumference changes during slides of boys ranged between 55 percent and 80 percent erection, while slides of women consistently resulted in about 10 percent erection. Homosexual urges occurred at a rate of about 1.5 per day, while both homosexual fantasy and masturbation occurred once every 3 days. No dating or heterosexual arousal was reported in this phase.

Ten sessions of contingent shock were administered in the first treatment phase. No significant decrease in the frequency of homosexual urges, fantasies or masturbation was noted; all of these measures remained essentially at the pre-treatment frequency level. Despite this lack of clinical indices of progress, penile circumference changes during slides of boys were significantly reduced by treatment by the fifth and sixth sessions. Penile circumference changes during slides of females, however, did not increase. The subject reported some upset at the lack of generalization of treatment effects at the end of this period.

Ten sessions of covert sensitization were administered in Phase 2. Penile response during slides of males remained suppressed through this treatment, while penile response during slides of females increased and surpassed the pedophilic penile responses. However, penile circumference changes during slides of females never surpassed 30 percent, so no strong heterosexual interest was evidenced in this measure. Dating began sporadically at this time, but medical rotations served to keep the frequency quite low. Homosexual urges were significantly reduced to an average level of .4 per day, compared to 1.5 per day during baseline and 1.3 per day during contingent shock. This measure is slightly confounded because the patient reported that he began to record nonarousing glances at boys as "urges" after sexual urges became less frequent in this phase. Homosexual fantasy stopped altogether halfway through this period as did masturbation with homosexual imagery. Heterosexual urges and fantasies began and masturbation was accompanied exclusively by heterosexual imagery after the halfway point of this phase.

Unfortunately, treatment was terminated at this point because the patient felt that his time commitments were too heavy to justify further treatment which he felt was no longer needed. This prevented a return to contingent shock treatment.

In summary, contingent shock was successful in suppressing penile response during slides of young boys, while covert sensitization successfully continued that suppression. Thus, no difference is apparent between the treatments on this measure. However, while shock suppressed erection, it did not change the frequency of reported pedophiliac urges. Covert sensitization did produce such a suppression and therefore was apparently more effective than contingent shock in control of the subject's subjectively recorded indices of arousal. However, there might have been continued suppression if shock had been reintroduced.

Seven months after the end of treatment, the subject reported no further attraction to young boys. Penile circumference changes remained greater during slides of women than during slides of boys. Masturbation was still accompanied exclusively by heterosexual imagery, and the subject reported heterosexual urges with nurses in the hospital.

His dating had increased, but he still wondered how well he would be able to perform sexually when intercourse is finally available to him.

Summary

In several of these cases, the desired number of two replications of each treatment was impossible. In addition, even when such frequent alterations in treatment were possible, clear-cut differences in treatment effects were not always apparent. In general, however, the covert sensitization appeared somewhat more effective. Consider first the results with the penile circumference measure. Covert sensitization was used during 12 treatment phases. It reduced deviant arousal on this measure in nine of those applications below the level established in the preceding phase, although this was not often a substantial reduction. In the other three phases, erection had previously been reduced and covert sensitization continued that suppression. Contingent shock was used during eight treatment phases, and it produced a suppression of erection from the level established in the preceding phase in three of these applications. It continued previously produced suppression in three other phases and produced suppression in three other phases and produced an increase in erection to deviant stimuli in two phases.

Only five of the six subjects provided subjective measures, so there were 11 covert sensitization phases and seven contingent shock phases providing data on this measure. In 8 of 11 covert sensitization phases, recorded subjective measures of deviant arousal were suppressed below the level established in the preceding phase. In the other three phases, subjective measures remained at a previously suppressed rate. During the seven phases in which contingent shock was administered, no change in subjective measures was observed in five instances, while an increase in subjective measures of deviant arousal was observed twice. In four patients (Subjects 2, 3, 4 and 6) covert sensitization clearly showed greater suppression of these subjective measures. In one patient (Subject 5), subjective measures of deviant arousal were too infrequent to allow comparison, while in the other patient (Subject 1) phases were too short to allow a clear comparison of treatment effects. These differences were seen most clearly in frequency of reported "urges," while the less frequently reported categories (fantasies, masturbation, sexual acts) usually were not frequent enough to allow clear comparison of treatment effects. In the one instance in which fantasies were reported more frequently than urges (Subject 3), fantasies showed greater suppression during covert sensitization, while urges showed a general decline. On none of these subjective measures was contingent shock more suppressive than covert sensitization. It should be noted that these differences were apparent even though we were unable to reverse treatment procedures more than once in the last three subjects.

Because of the low frequency of actual deviant behavior during treatments, the two techniques cannot be compared meaningfully on these grounds. Two patients (Subject 5 and Subject 6) never engaged in any deviant sexual acts during treatment. Two patients (Subject 2 and Subject 3) reported a homosexual contact and an exposure, respectively, during covert sensitization, while one patient (Subject 3) reported a homosexual contact during contingent shock therapy. The sixth patient (Subject 1) reported exposure during both treatments. It is also impossible to determine whether sexual behavior in follow-up is attributable to one treatment or the other since each patient received both treatments.

In summary, then, no substantial difference between contingent shock therapy and covert sensitization could be found on degree of suppression of penile erection to deviant stimuli or on the frequency of deviant sexual behavior. Greater suppression of subjective report of sexual arousal (especially urges) was found during covert sensitization than during contingent shock therapy, however. Also, follow-up in general indicated that both treatments combined led to a favorable outcome.

DISCUSSION

Prior research has already questioned the validity of erection to visual stimuli as a measurement of sexual arousal. In these studies, it has been shown that subjects can inhibit their erections during presentation of visually erotic material (Laws & Rubin, 1969), even when effort is made to assure attention to the erotic material (Henson & Rubin, 1971). However, these studies involved instructions requesting that subjects inhibit erection. In the present study, patients were asked to produce as much erection as possible during all slides. Under such conditions, erection has been validated as a measure of sexual preference (Bancroft, 1971; Bancroft & Mathews, 1967; Freund, 1963, 1965, 1967; McConaghy, 1967, 1969, 1970; see reviews by Zuckerman, 1971a, 1971b). However, in the present study only 50 percent of referrals produced erection consistently and reliably enough to allow them to serve as research patients receiving contingent shock therapy. Bancroft (1971) also found only 50 percent of his patients showing substantial erection. Erection to slides may be a fairly valid indicant of sexual preference, but erection is not a reflexive response which allows the therapist an automatic laboratory analogue of a person's sexual behavior in his natural environment. This partially undermines the idea that shock contingent upon erection in the laboratory can be used to punish deviant sexual behavior fairly directly.

In the present study, the contingent shock therapy was designed to reduce erection to deviant sexual stimuli on the premise that erection is a necessary prerequisite to sexual behavior. This is a faulty assumption. For example, Lazarus (1965) reported on a case in which a man learned to masturbate without an erection because of punishment received for erection as a teenager. In this case, masturbation did not require erection; nor does any passive sexual activity, including exposure, require erection. At the same time, erection to pictures of women does not guarantee that sexual activity will occur with women whom the patient encounters. A whole series of preliminary social behaviors are necessary prior to this.

The second question that must be examined in the use of erectile response changes as an index of ongoing sexual arousal patterns is whether changes in this response during and following treatment correlate with other indices of change in sexual arousal. Previous indications have been that improvement on clinical criteria correlates with decreases in deviant erection (Barlow et al., in press; Marks & Gelder, 1967; McConaghy, 1969). However, Bancroft (1970) recently compared systematic desensitization and contingent shock therapy between groups of homosexuals. When he compared subjects who had improved and subjects who showed no change, he found no difference between them in degree of suppression of deviant erection. In the present study, contingent shock produced suppression of erection in one case with a concurrent increase in subjective measures of deviant arousal (Subject 4), while in another case suppression of erection occurred without any change in frequency of these subjective measures (Subject 6).

Suppression of erection, then, does not necessarily mean clinical improvement. Penile erection is one measure of sexual arousal; it need not correlate with all other measures. As Lang (1968) has previously emphasized in the context of fear, there are physiological, verbal and behavioral aspects of abnormal behavior. Therapy will not produce equivalent measures of change in each indicator of the abnormal behavior.

This does not imply that the subjective reports are unquestionably accurate in gauging treatment effects. These reports are determined by each patient's recording in a tally book. The measures reported here are pencil marks, not objectively observable sexual acts. It seems unlikely that every patient defined these measures in exactly the same way. However, since each patient served as his own control by receiving both treatments, differences across subjects in response definition should not confuse the within-subjects comparisons.

Two other questions about reports of sexual behavior need to be considered. First, are these reports related to actual sexual arousal so that they can be used as an accurate pre-treatment assessment? With cooperative patients, this seems likely. In each of these six patients, pre-treatment subjective reports of sexual arousal and activity indicated a preference for the sexual deviation over heterosexuality. This group included two patients under court jurisdiction who might have wanted to fake improvement; both of these patients reported a predominance of deviant sexual urges and acts during the pre-treatment assessment. This is not to say that all referrals will report honestly. For example, one referral who refused treatment reported that he never thought of or engaged in exposure. His arrest for an exposure which occurred during baseline contradicted his verbal report. Thus, the recording of subjective measures of sexual arousal can be a relatively accurate pre-treatment assessment, but only if the patient is cooperative.

A second question is that of the accuracy of changes in this measure during treatment. The therapist never analyzed these data or talked with the patient about data during treatment in this study in order to avoid reinforcing changes in the frequency of various tallies. Despite this precaution, patients might still be motivated to fake changes. Subject 1 and Subject 3, for example, were under court jurisdiction. It might have been expected that both would report rapid and sustained improvement to end treatment quickly. This did not occur. Both patients reported early improvement with treatment but later reported some degree of relapse during and subsequent to treatment.

Despite the fact that their absolute reliability cannot be determined by concurrence of outside observation (see Nelson & McReynolds, 1971; Simkins, 1971a, 1971b), subjective measures did yield some suggestive information on the differential effectiveness of the two treatments. Although the results are not crystal clear because of the major difficulties in conducting controlled within-subject experimental comparisons on this patient population, it seemed that in five of the six subjects subjective measures of sexual deviation were more substantially and consistently reduced by covert sensitization than by contingent shock. Prior studies have indicated covert sensitization to be effective in controlling reported sexual thoughts, urges and behavior (Barlow et al., 1969; Cautela, 1966; Gold & Neufeld, 1965; Miller, 1963); Bancroft has previously shown contingent shock to be fairly ineffective in controlling sexual deviation (Bancroft, 1969) and that it is no more effective than systematic desensitization on outcome in treatment of homosexuality (Bancroft, 1970). This was true despite the fact that it was more effective in reducing penile response to homosexual stimuli. The results of this study tend to support these prior findings.

REFERENCES

Bancroft, J.H.J. Aversion therapy of homosexuality. *British Journal of Psychiatry.* 1969, **115**, 1417-1431.

Bancroft, J.H.J. A comparative study of aversion and desensitization in the treatment of homosexuality. In L.E. Burns & J.L. Worsley (Eds), *Behaviour therapy in the 1970's.* Bristol: Wright and Sons, 1970.

Bancroft, J.H.J. The application of psychophysiological measures to the assessment and treatment of sexual behaviors. *Behaviour Research and Therapy.* 1971, **9**, 119-130.

Bancroft, J.H.J. & Matthews, A.M. Penis plethysmography: Its physiological base and clinical application. Proceedings of the 7th European Conference on Psychosomatic Medicine. *Acta Medica Psychosomatica.* 1967, **7**, 475-480.

Barlow, D.H., Becker, R., Leitenberg, H. & Argas, W.S. A mechanical strain gauge for recording penile circumference change. *Journal of Applied Behavior Analysis.* 1970, **3**, 72.

Barlow, D.H., Leitenberg, H. & Agras, W.S. The experimental control of sexual deviation through manipulation of the noxious scene in covert sensitization. *Journal of Abnormal Psychology.* 1969, **74**, 596-601.

Barlow, D.H., Leitenberg, H., Agras, W.S., Callahan, E.J. & Moore, R.C. The contribution of therapeutic instructions to covert sensitization. *Behaviour Research and Therapy,* in press.

Birk, L., Huddleston, W., Miller, E. & Cohler, B. Avoidance conditioning for homosexuality. *Archives of General Psychiatry.* 1971, **25**, 314-323.

Cautela, J.R. Treatment of compulsive behavior by covert sensitization. *The Psychological Record.* 1966, **16**, 33-42.

Chassan, J.B. *Research design in clinical psychology and psychiatry.* New York: Appleton-Century-Crofts, 1967.

Curran, D. & Parr, D. Homosexuality: An analysis of 100 male cases seen in private practice. *British Medical Journal.* 1967, **1**, 797-801.

Eysenck, H. & Rachman, S. *The causes and cures of neurosis.* London: Routledge and Kegan Paul, 1965.

Fookes, B.H. Some experiences in the use of aversion therapy in male homosexuality, exhibitionism and fetishism. *British Journal of Psychiatry.* 1969, **115**, 339-341.

Freund, K. *Homosexuality in the male.* Cited in S. Rachman & J. Teasdale (Eds.), *Aversion therapy and behavior disorders: An analysis.* Coral Gables, Fla.: University of Miami Press, 1969.

Freund, K. A laboratory method for diagnosing predominance of homo- and hetero-erotic interest in the male. *Behaviour Research and Therapy.* 1963, **1**, 85-93.

Freund, K. Diagnosing heterosexual pedophilia by means of a test of sexual interest. *Behaviour Research and Therapy.* 1965, **3**, 229-234.

Freund, K. Erotic preference in pedophilia. *Behaviour Research and Therapy.* 1967, **5**, 339-348.

Gold, S. & Neufeld, I. A learning theory approach to the treatment of homosexuality. *Behaviour Research and Therapy.* 1965, **2**, 201-204.

Henson, D.E. & Rubin, H.B. Voluntary control of eroticism. *Journal of Applied Behavior Analysis.* 1971, **4**, 37-44.

Lang, P.J. Fear reduction and fear behavior: Problems in treating a construct. In J.M. Schlein (Ed.) *Research in psychotherapy. Vol. 3.* Washington, D.C.: American Psychological Association, 1968.

Laws, D.R. & Rubin, H.B. Instructional control of an autonomic sexual response. *Journal of Applied Behavior Analysis.* 1969, **2**, 93-99.

Lazarus, A.A. The treatment of a sexually inadequate man. In L. Ullmann & L. Krasner (Eds.) *Case studies in behavior modification.* New York: Holt, Rinehart & Winston, 1965.

MacCulloch, M.J. & Feldman, M.P. Aversion therapy in the management of 43 homosexuals. *British Medical Journal.* 1967, **113**, 711-729.

Marks, I. & Gelder, A.M. Transvestism and fetishism: Clinical and psychological changes during faradic aversion. *British Journal of Psychiatry.* 1967, **113**, 711-729.

Marks, I., Gelder, A.M. & Bancroft, J.H.J. Sexual deviants two years after electric aversion. *British Journal of Psychiatry.* 1970, **117**, 173-185.

McConaghy, N. Penile volume change in moving pictures of male and female nudes in heterosexual and homosexual males. *Behaviour Research and Therapy.* 1967, **5**, 43-48.

McConaghy, N. Subjective and penile plethysmograph responses following aversion-relief and apomorphine aversion therapy for homosexual impulses. *British Journal of Psychiatry.* 1969, **115**, 723-730.

McConaghy, N. Subjective and penile plethysmograph responses to aversion therapy for homosexuality: A follow-up study. *British Journal of Psychiatry.* 1970, **117**, 555-560.

Miller, M.M. Hypnotic-aversion treatment of homosexuality. *Journal of the National Medical Association.* 1963, **55**, 411-414.

Nelson, C.M. & McReynolds, W.T. Self-recording and control of behavior: A reply to Simkins. *Behavior Therapy.* 1971, **2**, 594-597.

Rachman, S. & Teasdale, J. *Aversion therapy and behavior disorders: An analysis.* Coral Gables, Fla.: University of Miami Press, 1969.

Sidman, M. *Tactics of scientific research.* New York: Basic Books, 1960.

Simkins, L. The reliability of self-recorded behaviors. *Behavior Therapy.* 1971a, **2**, 83-87.

Simkins, L. A rejoinder to Nelson and McReynolds on the self-recording of behavior. *Behavior Therapy.* 1971b, **2**, 598-601.

Wolfe, J. *Psychotherapy by reciprocal inhibition.* Stanford, Calif: Stanford University Press, 1958.

Zuckerman, M. Does the penis lie? Paper presented at the annual meeting of the 79th American Psychological Association, Washington, D.C., September 1971a.

Zuckerman, M. Psychological measures of sexual arousal in the human. *Psychological Bulletin.* 1971b, **75**, 347-356.

20
Increasing Heterosexual Responsiveness in the Treatment of Sexual Deviation: A Review of the Clinical and Experimental Evidence*†

DAVID H. BARLOW

Despite wide agreement that avoidance of heterosexuality is a major component in the genesis and maintenance of sexual deviation, the development of therapeutic procedures to increase heterosexual responsiveness has been largely neglected in favor of aversion therapy to suppress deviant responsiveness. Therapeutic procedures that have been employed to increase heterosexual responsiveness include: aversion relief techniques in which relief from an aversive stimulus is paired with heterosexual stimuli; "Systematic Desensitization procedures" in which heterosexual avoidance is desensitized either in imagination or in the real situation; social retraining where heterosexual skills are directly encouraged and taught; or pairing techniques in which sexual arousal is elicited and associated with heterosexual stimuli. Clinical and experimental evidence for the effectiveness of these procedures, as well as some newly developed techniques which cannot be classified in the above categories, is evaluated and the relationship of these procedures to aversion therapy in the treatment of sexual deviation is discussed.

A strikingly similar viewpoint on homosexual behavior and to some extent deviant sexual behavior in general is held by psychoanalytic and behavioral theorists. This view emphasizes the importance of fear of or avoidance of heterosexuality in the genesis and maintenance of such behavior. Analysts such as Rado (1949), Ovesey, Gaylin and Hendin (1963), and Bieber et al., (1963), and behaviorists such as Wolpe (1969), Ramsey and Van Velzen (1968), and Feldman and MacCulloch (1971) view heterosexual fear and avoidance as major determinants of homosexuality. In addition, both Ovesey et al. (1963) and Stevenson and Wolpe (1960) speak of the necessity of increasing more appropriate and assertive heterosocial behaviors in the treatment of sexual deviation.

Despite these views, aversion therapy aimed at eliminating sexual deviation is increasingly advocated as the treatment of choice (Barlow, 1972), due in part to the

*Preparation of this manuscript was supported by National Institute of Mental Health Grant MH-20258.

†The assistance of Stewart Agras and Ed Blanchard, who read an earlier version of this manuscript, is gratefully acknowledged.

growing application of the experimental behavioral sciences to the clinic and in part to the relative success of this technique (MacCulloch & Feldman, 1967; Feldman & MacCulloch, 1971) compared to psychoanalytic psychotherapy (Bieber et al., 1963). In a period of 10 years, seven series of cases containing at least ten patients (Freund, 1960; Feldman & MacCulloch, 1965; MacCulloch & Feldman, 1967; Bancroft, 1969; Gelder & Marks, 1969; Evans, 1968; Morganstern, Pierce & Rees, 1965; Fookes, 1968) and four controlled outcome studies (McConaghy, 1969; Bancroft, 1970; Birk, Huddleston, Miller & Cohler, 1971; MacCulloch & Feldman, 1971) have reported on the effectiveness of aversion therapy for sexual deviation.

The emphasis on aversion therapy suggests that most clinicians are ignoring a second treatment goal in sexual deviation, that of increasing heterosexual responsiveness. This attitude is exemplified by Bond and Evans (1967) who state: "It is probable that if they can abstain from their deviant behavior for a sufficient period of time, normal outlets for the control of sexual arousal will develop" (p. 1162). The potential dangers of this are obvious. As West (1968) points out: "Aversion therapy may cause some patients to undertake heterosexual experiments who otherwise might not have done so, but it will leave others impotent and frustrated and in a worse state than they were before" (p. 260).

Findings from two recent studies support earlier theories on the importance of heterosexual responsiveness in the treatment of sexual deviation. Feldman and Mac-Culloch (1971), in a large, controlled study comparing aversion therapy and psycho-therapy, report that the most important predictor of success in treatment is prior heterosexual experience. Of those patients with prior heterosexual experience, fully 80 percent improved while only 20 percent with no prior heterosexual experience improved. These results are similar to those of Bieber et al. (1963), who reported that 50 percent of those homosexuals who were bisexual at the time of treatment became exclusively heterosexual, while only 18 percent of those who were exclusively homosexual at the time of treatment (but may have had heterosexual experiences earlier) became hetero-sexual.

In this same vein, an important finding was recently reported by Bancroft (1970) who divided homosexuals who had received either aversion therapy directed at homo-sexual responsiveness or systematic desensitization to heterosexual themes into clinically improved and unimproved at a follow-up. Those patients who improved had demon-strated significantly greater increases in heterosexual arousal as measured by penile circumference changes and positive heterosexual attitudes during treatment irrespective of mode of treatment. Decreases in homosexual arousal and attitude during treatment occurred equally in both improved and unimproved groups, and were not related to clinical outcome. Although the over-all percentage of success was not high, the implication is that when success is achieved, increasing heterosexual responsiveness, by whatever technique, is a more important factor in treatment than decreasing homosexual responsiveness. To the extent that clinical judgments of improvement are valid, these correlational findings suggest the necessity of discovering effective techniques to increase heterosexual responsiveness.

Although clinicians employing aversion therapy emphasize the suppression of deviant arousal, many of these therapies include procedures intended to increase heterosexual arousal. Since these procedures are most often embedded in aversive therapy, it is difficult to determine if they are clinically effective. Furthermore, most case studies and series of cases systematically measure and report only changes in deviant behavior.

On the other hand, a few recent case studies (Kraft, 1967; Huff, 1970) report successful treatment of sexual deviation through the exclusive use of techniques designed to increase heterosexual responsiveness resulting in these single cases in declines in reports of homosexual responsiveness as well as increases in heterosexual responsiveness. These observations, as well as those of Bancroft (1970), raise the possibility that when these techniques are tacked onto aversion therapy they may contribute more to a successful outcome than reports emphasizing aversion therapy would indicate.

This paper critically examines the evidence for the effectiveness of such techniques. These procedures will be classified into four categories, based on similarities in practice or common theoretical underpinnings: aversion relief; systematic desensitization procedures; social retraining and pairing. Other techniques which do not fit into these four categories, comprise a fifth category.

AVERSION RELIEF

Aversion relief treatment involves pairing a heterosexual stimulus with relief from a noxious stimulus. This technique has been widely utilized to increase heterosexual responsiveness, probably because it is very convenient to apply in conjunction with aversion therapy. The use of an aversive stimulus insures that a period of relief following the termination of that stimulus will occur. It is, therefore, easy to pair a heterosexual stimulus with the relief. Because of this, aversion relief has always been used in conjunction with aversion therapy.

Aversion relief was first used in treating sexual deviation by Thorpe, Schmidt, Brown and Castell (1964) who treated three homosexuals, one transvestite and one fetishist. The aversion therapy procedure consisted of projecting, on a screen, a number of words (up to 23) connotating deviant experiences. Shock accompanied each presentation. The last word in the series, however, described "normal" activities, such as "heterosexual" and signified the end of the shock session. Thorpe et al. reported that "tremendous relief" was experienced at this time and, presumably, this word became associated with that relief. Following treatment, all patients reported some increased heterosexual interest although no measure of this was taken and no follow-up reported. Thorpe et al. speculated that this procedure worked either by inhibiting heterosexual anxiety, or positively reinforcing heterosexual approach behavior.

In the numerous case studies and series of cases since this report, the heterosexual "relief" stimulus has taken two forms, verbal, usually words or phrases depicting heterosexual interest such as "intercourse" (Gaupp, Stern & Ratliff, 1971) or pictorial such as slides of nude females (Larson, 1970). Most case studies anecdotally report increases in heterosexual responsiveness.

The aversion therapy and aversion relief procedure devised by Feldman and MacCulloch (1965) is perhaps the best known and has been applied to the largest number of cases; a total of 78 through 1971. The authors state that the goal of the aversion relief procedure is to reduce "heterosexual anxiety."

In a controlled study comparing two groups of homosexuals, each receiving a form of aversion therapy with an aversion relief component, with a third group receiving psychotherapy (Feldman & MacCulloch, 1971), heterosexual interest, as measured by an attitude scale, increased initially in all three groups with no difference among groups. Because the purpose of the experiment was to compare the effects of these therapies on homosexual interest rather than heterosexual interest, experimental design considerations made further comparison of heterosexual interest among the three groups at follow-ups impossible.

McConaghy (1969) compared electrical aversion therapy containing an aversion relief paradigm with chemical aversion therapy which contained no element designed to increase heterosexual behavior in two groups of homosexuals. Subjective reports of heterosexual desire and relations two weeks after treatment revealed no significant difference between the group receiving aversion therapy with aversion relief and the group receiving aversion therapy in which no attempt was made to increase heterosexual interest.

Solyom and Miller (1965) applied aversion relief to six homosexuals while continually monitoring a physiological response, in this case finger plethysmograph, to heterosexual stimuli. Although they noted a "trend" to greater plethysmograph response to female pictures, when the individual data are examined only two patients showed increased responding to female pictures over treatment, while three showed decreased responding. This result is further confused by the fact that the two patients who showed increased responding to females did not report any increased heterosexual interest or behavior.

In the only series to assess heterosexual interest continually by means of a valid objective measure, penile circumference change, Abel, Levis and Clancy (1970) administered aversion therapy to five nonhomosexual deviates by shocking verbalization of the deviant acts at different points in the chain of behavior. After the initial series of shocks, verbalizing a sequence of heterosexual behavior was associated with relief from shock. The results one week after treatment indicate that heterosexual arousal dropped somewhat, although at an 8-week follow-up heterosexual arousal was higher than baseline levels. Thus, aversion relief had no immediate effect.

In view of the well-documented observation that heterosexual responsiveness increases during aversion therapy in the absence of any attempt to accomplish this goal (Bancroft, 1969; Gelder & Marks, 1969; Barlow, Leitenberg & Agras, 1969), all clinical reports that aversion relief is effective are suspect since aversion relief has never been used in the absence of aversion therapy to isolate treatment effects.

Currently, then, there is no evidence that aversion relief increases heterosexual responsiveness. Furthermore, the stated goals of aversion relief differ from therapist to therapist; but, if the specific goal of aversion relief is to reduce heterosexual anxiety (Feldman & MacCulloch, 1971) there is no experimental evidence anywhere in the literature that aversion relief does, in fact, reduce anxiety, heterosexual or otherwise, in humans.

It is revealing that in the empirical field of behavior modification, the use of a therapeutic technique has now been reported in the literature on approximately 150 cases and continues to be employed clinically without any evidence that it is effective.

SYSTEMATIC DESENSITIZATION TECHNIQUES

Although the mechanism of action is not clear, (Agras et al., 1971) systematic desensitization, either in imagination or *in vivo* aims at eliminating fear of anxiety associated with heterosexual behavior. This approach is most consistent with the various theories on the genesis and maintenance of homosexual behavior mentioned above, and is further buttressed by two surveys.

Bieber et al. (1963) noted that 70 of the 106 patients in his survey reported fear or aversion to female genitalia. Ramsay and Van Velzen (1968) collected questionnaires from 25 homosexuals, 24 heterosexuals and 17 bisexuals. The answers to a series of questions indicated that homosexuals are not merely indifferent to heterosexual situations, but have strong negative emotional feelings concerning them, much as many heterosexuals find homosexual practices aversive.

Recently Freund et al. (1973) documented that homosexuals and heterosexuals both react negatively to nude slides of the nonpreferred sex on attitudinal and penile response measures.

The use of desensitization, or a close variant, has been reported in conjunction with aversion therapy in four instances. In a large series containing 15 homosexuals, 7 exhibitionists, and 5 fetishistic transvestites, Fookes (1968) paired relaxing music with heterosexual slides after a course of electrical aversion. Fookes reported that this variant of desensitization produced increases in heterosexual behavior in some patients. Levin et al. (1968) also reported success in desensitizing a homosexual using the standard desensitization in imagination procedure in conjunction with aversion therapy. Using systematic desensitization in the real situation, Cooper (1963) successfully treated a fetish by chemical aversion and by instructing the patient to lie in bed naked with his wife until he felt comfortable and to attempt small steps progressively leading to sexual intercourse only when he felt no anxiety when engaging in the previous step. Gray (1970) used a similar procedure in conjunction with covert sensitization for treatment of a homosexual.

Unlike aversion relief, desensitization has been used in the absence of aversion therapy. Kraft, in several reports (1967a,b; 1969a,b), suggests that decreasing heterosexual anxiety alone may be sufficient not only to increase heterosexual behavior, but to eliminate homosexual behavior, and reports that in several cases of homosexuality (1967a,b) desensitization in imagination apparently accomplished this goal. Huff (1970) and LoPiccolo (1971) also reported increases in heterosexual responsiveness after desensitizing homosexuals in imagination although LoPiccolo's patient began engaging in the target behavior before he was desensitized!

Successful desensitization in the real situation, in the absence of aversion therapy, has been reported by DiScipio (1968) with a homosexual, and Wickramasekera (1968) with an exhibitionist, although DiScipio's patient later relapsed.

Whatever the therapeutic mechanism of action, systematic desensitization in the real situation offers the naive patient the advantage of learning the intricacies of sexual approach behavior first hand from a cooperative partner.

The only attempt to evaluate the efficacy of systematic desensitization in treating sexual deviation was reported by Bancroft (1970) who treated two groups of 15 homosexuals each. One group received systematic desensitization in imagination to heterosexual themes, the second group was treated by electrical aversion therapy. No difference was noted between groups either after treatment or a 6-month follow-up on reports of homosexual or heterosexual behavior or sexual arousal as measured by penile circumference change. However, when changes from beginning of treatment to the follow-up are examined within groups, both treatments increased heterosexual arousal, as measured by penile circumference change, immediately after treatment, with aversion (surprisingly) increasing heterosexual arousal slightly but not significantly more than the systematic desensitization. Only aversion, however, significantly reduced homosexual arousal immediately after treatment.

Bancroft then dichotomized the groups into improved and unimproved, based on the *reports of behavior* at a 6-month follow-up and found that *during treatment*, reduction of homosexual arousal occurred in both the improved and unimproved groups, but that significant increases in heterosexual arousal occurred only in the improved group. This suggests that development of heterosexual responsiveness, whether through systematic desensitization or through aversion, is the prerequisite for clinical improvement and that aversion therapy may work not because it decreases homosexual responsiveness but, paradoxically, because it increases heterosexual responsiveness. However, all conclusions are tentative since the study did not include a placebo control or a no-treatment control. Thus, the relatively modest therapeutic results (only 5 out of the original 15 were rated as much improved or improved after treatment in the systematic desensitization group) could be due to placebo factors or the passage of time.

Thus, there is no experimental evidence that desensitization procedures increase heterosexual responsiveness. However, the clinical reports of success in the absence of aversion therapy would justify further investigation of these techniques.

SOCIAL RETRAINING

Another approach is assertive training, or a variant, behavior rehearsal. Essentially, these procedures teach new social skills to those patients who, because of avoidance or behavioral deficiencies, are unable to function effectively in heterosocial situations. In one of the first reports, using this approach exclusively, Stevenson and Wolpe (1960) taught three sexual deviates to be more assertive. This resulted not only in the establishment of strengthening of social and sexual aspects of heterosexual behavior based on the patients' report, but also eliminated most deviant behavior. Edwards (1972) reported that a similar procedure was successful with a pedophilic.

As part of a comprehensive treatment program including aversion therapy, Cautela and Wisocki (1969) provided behavior rehearsals with a female to teach correct social and assertive behavior to six homosexuals who then reported increases in heterosexual responsiveness.

The establishment of adequate social behavior would seem to be a necessary precursor to sexual behavior. This approach is similar to techniques that Salter (1949) and Ellis (1956, 1959) use, in which homosexual activity is largely ignored and the patient is taught in the first instance to be more assertive, and second, is given instructions and encouragement on appropriate heterosocial and heterosexual behavior. Ellis (1956) reports 75 percent of a series of 40 homosexuals were improved. Improvement is not defined, however, and there is reason to believe that homosexual behavior had not diminished in the series. No follow-up is reported.

Although exact procedures are seldom reported, other clinicians practicing individual psychotherapy (Ovesey et al., 1963) or group psychotherapy (Birk, Miller & Cohler, 1970) describe the teaching of assertiveness and more effective heterosexual approach behavior during the course of therapy. It is possible that this aspect of therapy accounts for reports of success using this approach. In view of the seeming importance of teaching appropriate heterosocial behavior, it is surprising that no research at all has been reported in this area.

PAIRING

Another grouping of techniques shares a common basic procedure in which elicited sexual arousal is paired with heterosexual stimuli for the purpose of increasing heterosexual arousal. When close attention is paid to timing relationships, the procedure is sometimes called classical conditioning. In other reports it is called counterconditioning, or pairing. When masturbation is used to produce sexual arousal the procedure has been called masturbatory conditioning or orgasmic reconditioning.

Although the notion that sexual arousal patterns are learned through association is not new (Binet, 1888; Dollard & Miller, 1950), several analog studies have recently verified this hypothesis. Both Lovibond (1963) and Wood and Obrist (1968) conditioned autonomic responses to neutral stimuli that were repeatedly paired with sexual arousal. McConaghy (1970) paired erotic slides with geometrical configurations and produced penile circumference changes to the configurations in 10 heterosexual and 15 homosexual subjects.

In a somewhat closer approach to the clinical situation, Rachman (1966) paired a slide picturing a pair of women's boots with slides of nude females and obtained increases in penile circumference to the boots in three volunteer, normal subjects, and later replicated these findings with five additional subjects (Rachman & Hodgson, 1968). These procedures were termed classical conditioning.

Early attempts at applying the principles of classical conditioning or pairing to clinical populations were made using hormonal injections to elicit sexual arousal (Freund, 1960; James, 1962). Freund (1960) was the first to attempt this in his pioneering report of the treatment of a series of male homosexuals. After a course of aversion therapy, 10 mg. of testosterone propinate were injected and approximately 7 hours later pictures of nude or semi-nude women were shown to the patient. Results are reported for 47 patients. Forty and four-tenths percent made a "heterosexual adjustment" immediately following treatment. This percentage dropped to 25.5 percent after 3 years. Unfortunately, it is not clear whether the "adjustment" was due to a drop in homosexual behavior, a rise in heterosexual behavior or both, and there is no evidence that the hormone treatment increased heterosexual responsiveness.

In another physiological approach, Moan and Heath (1972) reported increased heterosexual responding in a homosexual after pairing heterosexual stimuli and behavior with septal stimulation.

In a procedure close to that employed by Rachman (1966), Beech, Watts and Poole (1971) increased heterosexual arousal to mature females in a heterosexual pedophilic by pairing sexual arousal elicited by pictures of young females with slides of increasingly older females. Interest in young girls spontaneously declined although no aversion was used.

Several case studies have reported pairing sexual arousal produced by masturbation with heterosexual stimuli in the treatment of homosexuality (Thorpe, Schmidt & Castell, 1963; Marquis, 1970; Annon, 1971), sado-masochism (Davison, 1968; Mees, 1966;

Marquis, 1970), voyeurism (Jackson, 1969), and heterosexual pedophilia (Annon, 1971). In most cases, subjects are instructed to masturbate to a series of pictures or fantasies which progressively approximates the desired heterosexual activity.

Evidence for the efficacy of masturbatory conditioning does not go beyond the case study level. In only one case (Jackson, 1969) has this procedure been the sole therapeutic technique. However, it is interesting to note that pairing masturbatory arousal with various fantasies has been hypothesized to play an important role in the etiology of specific deviant sexual preferences. McGuire, Carlisle and Young (1965) suggested that deviates have some critical first sexual experience with a person or object which need not be sexually arousing at the time, but later provides a fantasy for masturbation. Historical evidence for the process is presented in a series of 45 deviates by McGuire et al. (1965) and in a second series reported by Evans (1968). Thus, altering masturbatory fantasy may be the most direct and efficient method of changing sexual preferences and deserves further investigation.

In one series of single case experiments the pairing procedure has been experimentally analyzed (Herman, Barlow & Agras, in press). In this experiment the principles of classical conditioning were closely followed. Three exclusive male homosexuals chose slides or movies of males as unconditioned stimuli (UCS) and a female slide as the conditioned stimulus (CS). The experimental design consisted of backward pairing, classical conditioning, backward pairing and classical conditioning once more. During backward pairing none of the three subjects showed any increase in heterosexual responsiveness as measured by penile changes to female slides and scores on attitude scales. During classical conditioning two subjects showed sharp increases in heterosexual arousal although one subject first required alteration of the temporal relationship of the CS and UCS. This arousal dropped somewhat after a return to the control phase and returned during the last classical conditioning phase. Homosexual responsiveness decreased to near zero for one subject but remained high for the second subject. The third subject demonstrated no clinically useful change during classical conditioning despite the presence of an adequate response to the UCS.

These studies suggest that classical conditioning is capable of increasing heterosexual arousal in homosexual patients. However, in all cases occasional procedural difficulties in temporal relationships between the CS and UCS and the maintenance of an adequate response to the UCS were noted. Furthermore, clinical follow-ups revealed that the two subjects who improved had difficulty in implementing their new-found heterosexual arousal, due to deficits in social skills.

This experimental evidence, along with evidence from analog studies, suggests that the various pairing procedures are therapeutically useful. Future research should determine the extent of their usefulness and the advantages and disadvantages of different methods of eliciting sexual arousal.

OTHER PROCEDURES

Several techniques have recently been reported which do not easily fit in the previous categories. Two of these procedures are based on operant methodology, a third employs intensive exposure to heterosexual stimuli.

Shaping. In case reports by Quinn, Harbison and McAllister (1970) and Harbison,

Quinn and McAllister (1970) attempts were made to increase penile response to heterosexual stimuli through selective positive reinforcement, a technique better known as shaping, in two cases of homosexuality. After a course of aversion therapy the patients were fluid deprived and then reinforced with a drink of lime juice for longer heterosexual fantasies and/or progressively greater increases in penile circumference to slides of nude female. Penile responses increased over the course of treatment as did the heterosexual score on an attitude scale. The homosexual score on the attitude scale also declined over pre-treatment values. No report of behavior was given.

Fading. A second "operant" approach concentrates on introducing or "fading in" heterosexual stimuli during periods of sexual arousal in an effort to change stimulus control of sexual responsiveness. This technique has been investigated in a series of three controlled, single case experiments with homosexuals (Barlow & Agras, in press). In this procedure, one male and one female slide were superimposed on one another. Through the use of an adjustable transformer, an increase in the brightness of the female slide resulted in a simultaneous decrease in the brightness of the male slide. During treatment the female stimuli was faded in contingent on the subject maintaining 75 percent of a full erection as measured by a strain gauge device through a series of 20 steps ranging from 100 percent male brightness to 100 percent female brightness. The experimental design consisted of fading, a control procedure where fading was reversed or stopped, followed by a return to fading.

The first homosexual completed the fading procedure in that he became sexually aroused to the female slide alone in six sessions. This arousal generalized to female slides in separate measurement sessions and to reports of behavior. In a control phase, when fading was reversed, heterosexual arousal and reports of behavior dropped considerably. When the female slide was faded in once more, heterosexual arousal increased. Homosexual responsiveness remained high throughout the experiment.

In the second experiment heterosexual arousal rose during the initial fading, continued rising, but then dropped sharply during a control phase in which fading was stopped at the halfway point and the slides shown separately, and rose once again when fading was reintroduced. Again, homosexual arousal remained high but had dropped sharply after termination, *without* therapeutic attempts to accomplish this goal, at follow-ups of 1 and 3 months. This experimental procedure and result was replicated on a third homosexual.

Although these experiments suggest that a fading procedure is effective in instigating new patterns of sexual arousal, clinical assessments following treatment indicated that the first two subjects needed training in heterosocial skills to implement their newly acquired arousal.

Exposure. One final technique to increase heterosexual responsiveness (Herman, Barlow & Agras, 1971; Herman, 1971) involved exposing homosexuals to high intensity movies of a nude, seductive female. This technique was experimentally analyzed in three single cases with two homosexuals and a pedophiliac.

The procedure was straightforward. An 8-mm movie of a nude, seductive female was shown daily for 10 minutes. During the control phase, a movie of a nude, seductive male was shown accompanied by a therapeutic rationale. The third phase consisted of a return to the female exposure condition.

In all subjects, exposure to the female film increased heterosexual arousal. During the homosexual film, heterosexual arousal dropped for all subjects and rose once again when the heterosexual film was reintroduced. All subjects reported generalization to fantasies and behavior outside of treatment. Homosexual arousal had earlier been decreased in one subject through aversion therapy. In other subjects homosexual arousal did not decrease during treatment. Follow-ups of from 3 months to 1 year revealed that two subjects had difficulty in heterosexual relations, despite continued arousal, due to deficient social skills.

Although the experimental analysis isolates exposure as responsible for changes in patterns of sexual arousal, the mechanism of action is not clear. The authors consider that this process may be similar to the "flooding" or "implosion" treatment of fear (Stampfl & Lewis, 1967) which is consistent with the notion that heterophobia is a major component of sexual deviation. Another possibility is that it provides the subjects with new fantasy material which is then associated with sexual arousal outside treatment.

CONCLUDING COMMENTS

In view of the long-standing agreement among therapists on the importance of instigating heterosexual behavior, it is surprising how little research has been done. Thus the plethora of techniques described in this paper are more often based on assumption and hypothesis rather than evidence of effectiveness, although several different approaches do show promise.

Furthermore, these techniques often have different goals. For instance, systematic desensitization in the first instance is directed at reducing heterosexual "anxiety." Pairing procedures or fading techniques, on the other hand, are designed to instigate heterosexual arousal while social retraining aims to teach adequate heterosocial skills. Many clinicians have concentrated on one of the above goals implicitly assuming that other appropriate behavior will follow. There is clinical evidence from our lab (Herman, 1971) and others (Annon, 1971) that an increase in heterosexual arousal is not always followed by acquisition of the necessary social skills to implement the arousal. On the other hand, many clinical anecdotes note that decreasing heterosexual anxiety or increasing hetero-social skills does not result in increased arousal. This suggests that heterosexual responsiveness is not a unitary concept, but actually consists of several distinct behavioral components. If this is the case, some combination of the above techniques such as a pairing procedure or fading techniques to instigate heterosexual arousal and social training to build heterosocial skills may constitute the most effective approach to the problem. Some patients may require intervention in only one area. There is an immediate need for a precise delineation of the various behavioral components constituting heterosexual responsiveness, and for the development of reliable and valid measurement devices to assess the extent of deficiencies in each component so that the appropriate technique or combination of techniques can be administered.

Finally, the relationship of aversion therapy and procedures to increase heterosexual responsiveness in the treatment of sexual deviation is not clear. Some evidence now exists suggesting that aversion therapy may not be necessary. In several cases where heterosexual responsiveness was increased without therapeutic attempts to suppress deviant responsiveness, deviant responses declined anyway, either during treatment (Kraft, 1967; Herman, 1971) or immediately after treatment (Barlow & Agras, in press). Since the ready use of aversive techniques has precluded this type of observation in most cases to date, more information is needed on the generality of this phenomenon and the patient variables which may predict its occurrence. Similarly, the observation noted independently by several investigators that aversive techniques alone set the occasion for rises in heterosexual responsiveness (Bancroft, 1971; Barlow, Leitenberg & Agras, 1969; Gelder & Marks, 1969) is a paradoxical and puzzling phenomenon worthy of further investigation. This finding is reminiscent of side effects noted when aversive techniques are applied to disruptive behavior in children and psychotic adults. In these cases, socially appropriate behavior appears concurrent with deceleration of disruptive behavior and in the absence of any positive contingencies (Sajwaj & Risley, in press; Wahler et al., 1970). If this phenomenon is verified by future clinical research, then variables responsible for this effect should be isolated and arranged to maximize therapeutic benefit.

REFERENCES

Abel, G., Levis, D. & Clancy, J. Aversion therapy applied to taped sequences of deviate behavior in exhibitionism and other sexual deviation: A preliminary report. *Journal of Behavior Therapy and Experimental Psychiatry.* 1970, **1**, 59-60.

Agras, W.S., Leitenberg, H., Barlow, D.H., Curtis, N.A., Edwards, J. & Wright, D. The role of relaxation in systematic desensitization. *Archives of General Psychiatry.* 1970, **25**, 511-514.

Annon, J.S. The extension of learning principles to the analysis and treatment of sexual problems. *Dissertation Abstracts International.* 1971, **32**(6-B), 3627.

Bancroft, J. Aversion therapy of homosexuality: A pilot study of 10 cases. *British Journal of Psychiatry.* 1969, **115**, 1417-1431.

Bancroft, J. A comparative study of aversion and desensitization in the treatment of homosexuality. In L.E. Burns and J.L. Worsley (Eds.), *Behavior therapy in the 1970's.* Bristol: Wright, 1970. Pp. 12-33

Bancroft, J. The application of psychophysiological measures to the assessment and modification of sexual behavior. *Behaviour Research and Therapy.* 1971, **9**, 119-130.

Barlow, D.H. Aversive procedures. In W.S. Agras (Ed.). *Behavior modification: Principles and clinical applications.* Boston: Little, Brown, and Co., 1972, 87-125.

Barlow, D.H. & Agras, W.S. Fading to increase heterosexual responsiveness in homosexuals. *Journal of Applied Behavior Analysis* (in press).

Beech, H.R., Watts, F. & Poole, A.D. Classical conditioning of sexual deviation: A preliminary note. *Behavior Therapy.* 1971, **2**, 400-402.

Bieber, B., Bieber, I., Dain, H.J., Dince, P.R., Drellich, M.G., Grundlach, H.G., Grundlach, R.H., Kremer, Malvina W., Wilber, Cornelia B. & Bieber, T.D. *Homosexuality.* New York: Basic Books, 1963.

Binet, A. *Etudes de psychologie experimentale.* Paris, 1888.

Birk, L., Miller, E. & Cohler, B. Group psychotherapy for homosexual men by male—female cotherapists. *Acta Psychiatrica Scandinavica.* Supplementum **218**, 1970, 9-36.

Birk, L., Huddleston, W., Miller, E. & Cohler, B. Avoidance conditioning for homosexuality. *Archives of General Psychiatry.* 1971, **25**, 314-323.

Bond, I. & Evans, D. Avoidance therapy: Its use in two cases of underwear fetishism. *Canadian Medical Association Journal.* 1967, **96**, 1160-1162.

Cautela, J.R., & Wisocki, P.A. The use of male and female therapists in the treatment of homosexual behavior. In R. Rubin and C. Franks (Eds.), *Advances in behavior therapy.* 1968. New York: Academic Press, 1969. 165-174.

Cooper, A.A. A case of fetishism and impotence treated by behavior therapy. *British Journal of Psychiatry.* 1963, **109**, 649-652.

Davison, G.C. Elimination of a sadistic fantasy by a client-controlled counterconditioning technique: A case study. *Journal of Abnormal Psychology.* 1968, **73**, 84-90.

DiScipio, W. Modified progressive desensitization and homosexuality. *British Journal of Medical Psychology.* 1968, **41**, 267-272.

Dollard, J. & Miller, N.E. *Personality and psychotherapy.* New York: McGraw-Hill, 1950.

Edwards, N.B. Case conference: Assertive training in a case of homosexual pedophilia. *Journal of Behavior Therapy and Experimental Psychiatry.* 1972, **3**, 55-63.

Ellis, A. The effectiveness of psychotherapy with individuals who have severe homosexual problems. *Journal of Consulting Psychology.* 1956, **20**, 58-60.

Ellis, A. A homosexual treated with rational psychotherapy. *Journal of Clinical Psychology.* 1959, **15**, 338-343.

Evans, D.R. Masturbatory fantasy and sexual deviation. *Behaviour Research and Therapy.* 1968, **6**, 17-19.

Feldman, M.P. & MacCulloch, M.J. The application of anticipatory avoidance learning to the treatment of homosexuality. I. Theory, technique, and preliminary results. *Behaviour Research and Therapy.* 1965, **2**, 165.

Feldman, M.P. & MacCulloch, M.J. *Homosexual behaviour: Theory and assessment.* Oxford: Pergamon Press, Ltd., 1971.

Fookes, B.H. Some experiences in the use of aversion therapy in male homosexuality, exhibitionism, and fetishism-transvestism. *British Journal of Psychiatry.* 1968, **115**, 339-341.

Freund, K. Some problems in the treatment of homosexuality. In Eysenck, H.J. (Ed.), *Behavior therapy and the neuroses.* London: Pergamon Press, 1960, 312-326.

Freund, K., Langevin, R., Cibiri, S. & Zajac, Y. Heterosexual aversion in homosexual males. *British Journal of Psychiatry.* 1973, **122**, 163.

Gaupp, L.A., Stern, R.M. & Ratliff, R.G. The use of aversion-relief procedures in the treatment of a case of voyeurism. *Behavior Therapy.* 1971, **2**, 585-588.

Gelder, M.G. & Marks, I.M. Aversion treatment in transvestism and transsexualism. In R. Green (Ed.), *Transsexualism and sex reassignment.* Baltimore; Johns Hopkins Press, 1969, 383-413.

Gray, J.J. Case conference: Behavior therapy in a patient with homosexual fantasies and heterosexual anxiety. *Journal of Behavior Therapy and Experimental Psychiatry.* 1970, **1**, 225-232.

Harbison, J., Quinn, J. & McAllister, H. The positive conditioning of heterosexual behavior. Paper presented to Conference on Behavior Modification, Dublin, 1970.

Herman, S.H. An experimental analysis of two methods of increasing heterosexual arousal in homosexuals. Unpublished Doctoral dissertation, University of Mississippi, 1971.

Herman, S.H., Barlow, D.H. & Agras, W.S. Exposure to heterosexual stimuli: An effective variable in treating homosexuality? *Proceedings of the American Psychological Association 79th Annual Convention.* Washington, D.C.: American Psychological Association, 1971, 699-700.

Herman, S.H., Barlow, D.H. & Agras, W.S. An experimental analysis of classical conditioning as a method of increasing heterosexual arousal in homosexuals. *Behavior Therapy* (in press).

Huff, F. The desensitization of a homosexual. *Behaviour Research and Therapy.* 1970, **8**, 99-102.

Jackson, B. A case of voyeurism treated by counter-conditioning. *Behaviour Research and Therapy.* 1969, **7**, 133-134.

James, B. Case of homosexuality treated by aversion therapy. *British Medical Journal.* 1962, **1**, 768-770.

Kraft, T. A case of homosexuality treated by systematic desensitization. *American Journal of Psychotherapy.* 1967a, **21**, 815-821.

Kraft, T. Behavior therapy and the treatment of sexual perversions. *Psychotherapy and Psychosomatics.* 1967b, **15**, 351-357.

Kraft, T. Desensitization and the treatment of sexual disorders. *The Journal of Sex Research.* 1969a, **5**, 130-134.

Kraft, T. Treatment for sexual perversions. *Behaviour Research and Therapy.* 1969b, **7**, 215.

Larson, D. An adaptation of the Feldman and MacCulloch approach to treatment of homosexuality by the application of anticipatory avoidance learning. *Behaviour Research and Therapy.* 1970, 8, 209-210.

Levin, S., Hirsch, I., Shugar, G. & Kapche, R. Treatment of homosexuality and heterosexual anxiety with avoidance conditioning and systematic desensitization: Data and case report. *Psychotherapy: Theory, Research and Practice.* 1968, **5**, 160-168.

Lo Piccolo, J. Case study: Systematic desensitization of homosexuality. *Behavior Therapy.* 1971, 2, 394-399.

Lovibond, S.H. Conceptual thinking, personality, and conditioning. *British Journal of Social Clinical Psychology.* 1963, 2, 100-111.

MacCulloch, M.J. & Feldman, M.P. Aversion therapy in the management of 43 homosexuals. *British Medical Journal.* 1967, 2, 594-597.

Marquis, J.N. Orgasmic reconditioning: Changing sexual object choice through controlling masturbation fantasies. *Journal of Behavior Therapy and Experimental Psychiatry.* 1970, **1**, 263-271.

McConaghy, N. Subjective and penile plethysmograph responses following aversion relief and apomorphine aversion therapy for homosexual impulses. *British Journal of Psychiatry.* 1969, **115**, 723-730.

McConaghy, N. Penile response conditioning and its relationship to aversion therapy in homosexuals. *Behavior Therapy.* 1970, **1**, 213-221.

McGuire, R.J., Carlisle, J.M. & Young, B. G. Sexual deviations as conditioned behavior. *Behaviour Research and Therapy.* 1965, 2, 185-190.

Mees, H.L. Sadistic fantasies modified by aversive conditioning and substitution: A case study. *Behaviour Research and and Therapy.* 1966, 4, 317-320.

Moan, C.E. & Heath, R.G. Septal stimulation for the initiation of heterosexual behavior in a homosexual male. *Journal of Behavior Therapy and Experimental Psychiatry.* 1972, 3, 23-30.

Morgenstern, F.S., Pearce, J.P. & Rees, L. Predicting the outcome of behavior therapy by psychological tests. *Behaviour Research and Therapy.* 1965, 2, 191-200.

Ovesey, L., Gaylin, W. & Hendin, H. Psychotherapy of male homosexuality. *Archives of General Psychiatry.* 1963, 9, 19-31.

Quinn, J., Harbison, J. & McAllister, H. An attempt to shape human penile responses. *Behaviour Research and Therapy.* 1970, 8, 213-216.

Rachman, S. Sexual fetishism: An experimental analogue. *The Psychological Record.* 1966, **16**, 293-296.

Rachman, S. & Hodgson, R.J. Experimentally induced "sexual fetishism": Replication and development. *The Psychological Record.* 1968, 18, 25-27.

Rado, S. An adaptational view of sexual behavior. In P. Hoch and J. Zubin (Eds.), *Psychosexual development in health and disease.* New York: Grune and Stratton, 1949.

Ramsey, R.W. & Van Velzen, V. Behaviour therapy for sexual perversions. *Behaviour Research and Therapy.* 1968, 6, 17-19.

Sajwaj, T.E. & Risley, T.R. Punishment techniques in behavior modification. *Journal of Applied Behavior Analysis* (in press).

Salter, A. *Conditioned reflex therapy.* New York: Farrar, Strauss, 1949. Republished: New York: Capricorn Books, 1961.

Solyom, l. & Miller, S. A differential conditioning procedure as the initial phase of behavior therapy of homosexuality. *Behaviour Research and Therapy.* 1965, 3, 147-160.

Stampfl, T.G. & Levis, D.J. Essentials of implosive therapy: A learning theory based psychodynamic behavioral therapy. *Journal of Abnormal Psychology.* 1967, **72**, 496-503.

Stevenson, I. & Wolpe, J. Recovery from sexual deviation through overcoming nonsexual neurotic responses. *American Journal of Psychiatry.* 1960, **116**, 789.

Thorpe, J., Schmidt, E., Brown, P. & Castell, D. Aversion-relief therapy: A new method for general application. *Behaviour Research and Therapy.* 1964, **2**, 71-82.

Thorpe, J., Schmidt, E. & Castell, D. A comparison of positive and negative (aversive) conditioning in the treatment of homosexuality. *Behaviour Research and Therapy.* 1963, **1**, 357-362.

Wahler, R.G., Sperling, K.A. Thomas, M.R., Teeter, N.C. & Luper, H.L. Modification of childhood stuttering: Some response-response relationships. *Journal of Experimental Child Psychology.* 1970, **9**, 411-428.

West, D.J. *Homosexuality.* 3rd Edition. London: Penguin Books, 1968.

Wickramasekera, I. The application of learning theory to the treatment of a case of sexual exhibitionism. *Psychotherapy: Theory, Research, and Practice,* 1968, **5**, 108-112.

Wood, D. & Obrist, P. Minimal and maximal sensory intake and exercises as unconditioned stimuli in human heart-rate conditioning. *Journal of Experimental Psychology.* 1968, **76**, 254-262.

Wolpe, J. *The practice of behavior therapy.* New York: Pergamon Press, 1969.

21
A Forward-Fading Technique for Increasing Heterosexual Responsiveness in Male Homosexuals

RICHARD E. McCRADY

The client was a 27-year-old male college student who had become aware of his homosexual desires at approximately 14. He had had his first overt homosexual experience at age 16 and had numerous irregularly occurring homosexual experiences subsequently. For both moral and practical reasons, when he entered therapy he was highly motivated to increase his heterosexual behavior (and to decrease his homosexual behaviors).

METHOD

The client was seen weekly (except between treatment sessions 10 and 11 when 2 weeks elapsed) in an out-patient psychophysiological laboratory setting, for a total of 13 sessions. Two 35mm slide projectors and a polygraph were operated by the therapist in a separate room adjacent to the treatment room. The slides were projected on to a rear-projection screen which was installed in the wall separating the two rooms. All communication between therapist and client was conducted through an intercom system.

Measures of sexual arousal to slides of nude males and females were obtained by means of a Sexual Preference Rating Scale (SPRS) consisting of nine categories of sexual arousal extending from −4 through 0 to +4 (0=neutral, 1=little, 2=fair amount, 3=much, 4=very much). Three ratings (slides presented in 3 different orders) were averaged to indicate the degree of arousal of 10 female and 10 male slides, in both the pre- and posttreatment evaluations.

The client was also required to keep a daily record of each discrete incident of covert (urges and fantasies) and overt homo- and heterosexual activity.

During sessions 2-12 the client was exposed to a procedure in which a female image was gradually faded into a male image while penile circumference changes were being monitored. The images were of a highly arousing male (Slide 7) as reflected by the SPRS rating, and a female figure (Slide 10) chosen primarily for its superimposability on the male figure. Each fade process consisted of 21 female:male light intensity combinations

199

(100 percent female:0 percent male, 95 percent female:5 percent male, ... 5 percent female:95 percent male, 0 percent female:100 percent male). Zero percent represented the light intensity of the projector lamp corresponding to the minimum reading on a graduated rheostatic control at which a projected slide was just perceptible to the therapist. One hundred percent represented the intensity corresponding to the rheostatic setting at which the slide image was maximally perceived by the therapist. The points of minimum (lower) and maximum (upper) intensity were determined separately for the male and female slides by the method of limits. Intermediate settings for each slide were obtained by dividing the difference between the upper and lower rheostatic settings by 20. For example, a 95 percent female:5 percent male light intensity combination corresponded to rheostatic settings of one increment below the highest setting on the rheostat controlling intensity of the female slide and one increment above the lowest setting on the rheostat controlling the intensity of the male slide. These incremental changes in light intensity were made mechanically by the therapist by a simultaneous adjustment of the rheostats every 15 seconds for a total of 21 settings. A notation of each setting was made on the polygraph chart by mechanical activation of an event marker immediately following adjustment of the rheostats. This 5¼-minute fading sequence, resulting in a smooth and gradual transition from a total female image through female-male combinations to a total male image, was repeated four times per session. Each sequence was followed by a 2-minute exposure to a blank illuminated screen.

Penile circumference changes occurring throughout the fading sessions (and during the posttreatment exposure of the client to three female slides) were monitored by a Barlow et al. (1970) type of penile circumference transducer and a Grass Model 7 polygraph. The measure obtained during each fading sequence was the time (in seconds) from the start of the sequence (100 percent female:0 percent male) to the point at which maximum erection was initially achieved. This time lapse was expressed in terms of the number of 15-second fade increments, to the nearest whole number necessary for maximum erection to be achieved. For example, if the initial point of maximum deflection of the polygraph pen for monitoring penile circumference were to occur at a point more than halfway into fade increment No. 9 as indicated by the event marker on the polygraph time channel, the fade increment of initial point of maximum erection would be recorded as No. 10, and would represent about a 135-second time lapse from the beginning of the fading sequence to the initial point of maximum erection.

At the beginning of each treatment session the client was instructed as follows: "Now we shall go through the fading procedure. Each fading will take approximately 5 minutes. The procedure will be carried out a total of four times during this session. There will be a brief rest period at the end of each fading sequence. During this period, blot out thoughts of the figures which you have just viewed." Immediately before each fading sequence the client was told: "Now I would like you to imagine yourself in a sexually arousing situation with the person shown in the slides to follow."

In the posttreatment session, Session 13, in addition to completing the Sexual Preference Rating Scale, the client viewed three nude female slides (Nos. 10, 2 and 25) for 2 minutes each while penile circumference changes were monitored. This was done to test the client's ability to achieve erection to the nude female image (Slide 10) in the absence of a male image, and to determine whether the effect could be produced by presenting other female images.

RESULTS

Figure 1 shows the mean fade increment points at which initial peak erection occurred during weekly treatment sessions. The means represent an average of only those fade values at which the client reported at least 75 percent erection. Also shown are initial points of peak erection for the four separate fade processes during each treatment session. The figure reveals that in treatment sessions 1-4 peak erection was not achieved until near the end of the fades when the male figure was nearly 100 percent illuminated, indicating the male image as the primary if not the only arousing stimulus. A sharp break occurred at Session 5, when the average initial point of peak erection occurred at the eleventh fade increment or 2½ minutes into the fade. By session 9 the initial point of peak erection occurred at increment 6, where it remained through Session 10. This was approximately 1¼ minutes from the setting of 100 percent female:0 percent male. (Increment 6 was where the male figure first came into view each time, as reported by the client at the end of treatment on each of three stimulus threshold tests. For this test the client was exposed to the fade sequence in the same way as during treatment and was asked to report when the male image first began to be visible.) In Session 11, 2 weeks after Session 10, the initial point of peak erection was displaced toward the male end of the fade but was still within the range of values for sessions 5-10.

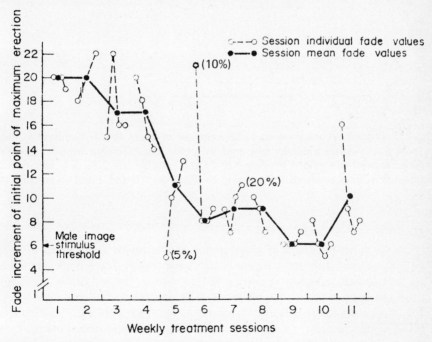

Fig. 1. Number of 15-second fade increments to the initial point of maximum erection for weekly treatment sessions and for individual fades per session. Percentage values in parentheses correspond to reports of less than 75 percent erection and are not included in mean fade values. In session 1 the first fade value was missed because of equipment failure; in session 2, two values were missed due to polygraph pen deflecting off chart; and in session 8 only three fades were conducted.

Figure 2, a polygraph record, shows the penile circumference changes associated with the three 2-minute exposures of female slide Nos. 10, 2, and 25, presented in that order, in the posttreatment session. Full erection was reported by the client to slides 10 and 2, as confirmed by the polygraph record, and no erection to Slide 25.

Throughout the treatment sessions, with few exceptions the client reported full or nearly full erection during each fade. Where the reported maximum erection was less than 75 percent the percentage is shown in parentheses in Fig. 1.

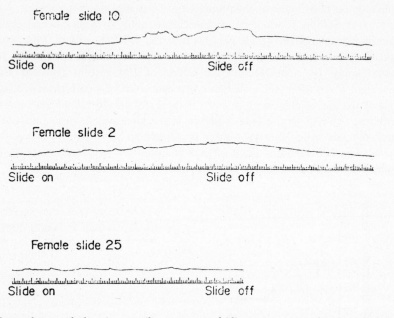

Fig. 2. Polygraph record showing penile response of client to a two-minute exposure to each of three female slides as measured by penile circumference transducer, indicating stimulus control was gained by slide No. 10 and by slide No. 2 (a slide not used during treatment). (Client reported full erection to slide Nos. 10 and 2 and no erection to slide No. 25.)

Table 1 shows the degree of sexual arousal, as determined by the SPRS, to 10 female and 10 male slides before and after the 11 treatment sessions. It is notable that the female slides were neutral to slightly negative (−0.4) in arousal "power" before treatment, and did not change as a result of treatment (−0.3); and that overall the male slides were slightly more arousing after treatment than before (+2.8 versus +2.1).

The weekly records of covert and overt homo- and heterosexual behavior revealed that the client engaged in no overt heterosexual activity and that he had two overt homosexual experiences during the three months of treatment. One of these experiences occurred between treatment sessions 3 and 4 and the other between treatment sessions 7 and 8. Covert homosexual activity was reported on only 10 occasions throughout the 3-month period, but the client admitted that this was misleading because frequently the activity reported as a single occurrence was more or less continuous over several hours.

More important, the client reported 14 occasions of heterosexual fantasy between Sessions 3 and 13 (none during the pretreatment week or between treatment Sessions 1 and 2), 10 of these occasions being associated with masturbation. In addition, he reported having a "heterosexual" dream between treatment sessions 6 and 7.

There was an attitudinal change accompanying treatment session 5, in which he found his penis could become erect to a female figure. After this "breakthrough," in group therapy sessions co-led by the experimenter, he frequently used or implied the phrase, "When I used to be homosexual." Experiencing sexual arousal to a female image seemed to convey to him that he was sexually normal and that he could realistically hope for a heterosexual future.

Table 1. Degree of sexual arousal elicited by male and female slides as indicated by mean of three SPRS ratings

	Female			Male	
Slide No.	Before treatment	After treatment	Slide No.	Before treatment	After treatment
1	0·0	0·0	1	+2·3	+3·7
2	0·0	0·0	3	+1·7	+2·7
5	-1·0	0·0	4	+1·0	+1·7
6	-0·3	0·0	6	+2·7	+2·0
*10	+0·3	+0·3	*7	+3·0	+2·3
11	-3·0	-3·0	8	+1·3	+3·0
18	0·0	0·0	11	+1·7	+2·0
21	0·0	0·0	13	+2·7	+3·0
22	0·0	-0·7	14	+3·0	+4·0
25	0·0	0·0	15	+1·3	+3·7
Mean	-0·4	-0·3		+2·1	+2·8

*Slides used in the fading treatment.

DISCUSSION

The results show that a procedure which was reverse of the Barlow-Agras fading procedure—that is, a forward conditioning technique with a female figure faded into a male figure—brought penile erection under the control of a stimulus which had not previously set the occasion for sexual arousal. Furthermore, stimulus control was shown to generalize to one of two female slides not used in the treatment procedure.

Comparison of the results obtained by the three different measuring procedures employed in this experiment revealed that while penile circumference measures and verbal reports of the client as to the number of heterosexual fantasies and urges reflected concomitant increases in heterosexual arousal, there was no appreciable change in heterosexual arousal as indicated by pre- and posttreatment SPRS ratings. Similar measurement discrepancies were reported by Barlow and Agras (1971) and by Herman et al. (1971).

If further testing of the present conditioning procedure proves its effectiveness in conditioning arousal to female stimuli with other homosexual cases, it will have certain advantages over the Barlow-Agras procedure. The procedure should be (a) more generally usable since its use is not precluded by the client's having to achieve an erection, and (b) more easily adaptable to an out-patient setting since there is no need for precise penile volume measures (needed in the Barlow-Agras technique to establish the subject's 75 percent full erection criterion), permitting the use of considerably less expensive equipment and less sophisticated operators.

REFERENCES

Barlow, D.H. & Agras, W.S. (1971) *An experimental analysis of "fading" to increase heterosexual responsiveness in homosexuality.* Paper presented at the 17th Ann. Mtg. Southeastern Psychol. Assoc., Miami Beach, Florida, April, 1971.

Barlow, D.H., Becker, R., Leitenberg, H. & Agras, W.S. (1970) A mechanical strain gauge for recording penile circumference change. *J. Appl. Behav. Anal.* **3**, 73-76.

Herman, S.H., Barlow, D.H. & Agras, W.S. (1971) Exposure to heterosexual stimuli: An effective variable in treating homosexuality, *Proceedings of the Ann. Conv. of the Amer. Psychol. Assoc.* **6** (Pt. 2), 699-700.

22

An Experimental Analysis of Exposure to "Explicit" Heterosexual Stimuli as an Effective Variable in Changing Arousal Patterns of Homosexuals

STEVEN H. HERMAN, DAVID H BARLOW and W. STEWART AGRAS

Both psychoanalytic and behavior theorists view the genesis and maintenance of homosexual behavior as due to fear and avoidance of, or deficits in, heterosexuality (e.g. Rado, 1949; Ovesey et al., 1963; Wolpe, 1969; Feldman & MacCulloch, 1971). This view is supported by data from Bieber et al. (1963), who noted that 70 of 106 homosexuals surveyed reported fear or aversion to female genitalia. Similarly, Ramsey and Van Velzen (1968) found that homosexuals are not merely indifferent to heterosexual situations, but have strong negative feelings about them, much as many heterosexuals view homosexual practices.

Despite the desirability of modifying sexual disorders by increasing heterosexual responsiveness, most attempts to date have stressed the use of aversion therapy to decrease the deviant sexual arousal (Barlow, 1972), due in part to the relative success of this technique compared to other approaches (e.g. Feldman & MacCulloch, 1971).

However, recent fine analysis of patients undergoing psychoanalysis (Bieber et al., 1963) and aversion therapy (Feldman & MacCulloch, 1971) have again suggested the importance of instigating heterosexual responsiveness during the treatment of sexual deviation, since both studies report minimal success in those homosexuals with little or no prior heterosexual experience. In addition, there is some recent evidence to indicate that when aversion therapy does work on sexual disorders, it succeeds *not* because it decreases deviant arousal, but, paradoxically, because heterosexual responsiveness increases (Bancroft, 1970).

In spite of the disadvantages and potentially dangerous side effects of aversion therapy (Azrin & Holz, 1966; West, 1968), only a few techniques designed primarily to increase heterosexual responsiveness have been employed clinically and fewer still have been experimentally evaluated (*see* Barlow, 1973, for a review). The overall research strategy in our laboratory was to use a series of single case experimental designs to extend these uncontrolled single case observations and to tease out the relevant variables suggested by anecdotal case studies. At a later date, the most promising of these variables could be combined to form a treatment paradigm, which could then be tested by group outcome procedures. This research approach constitutes a major recommendation emanating from the massive review of the status of psychotherapy research undertaken by Bergin and Strupp (1970).

In the process of evaluating one technique hypothesized to increase heterosexual arousal, masturbatory conditioning, where heterosexual stimuli are paired with masturbatory activity (e.g. Marquis, 1970; Annon, 1971), an unexpected finding ensued. During an initial control phase, heterosexual arousal in a homosexual subject increased sharply in a condition where he viewed a film explicitly depicting a nude, young, attractive female assuming various sexual poses. Subsequent to this serendipitous finding, the effect of 'explicit exposure' to nude female stimuli on heterosexual arousal was experimentally analyzed in four homosexuals in a series of single case experimental designs. The purpose of the experiment was to determine if viewing explicit heterosexual films was functionally related to increases in heterosexual arousal in homosexuals. Since heterosexual arousal is a necessary condition for heterosexual behavior, techniques to increase heterosexual arousal may play an important role in the treatment of sexual deviation.

METHOD

Subjects

The subjects for the present study were four males; three homosexuals and one homosexual pedophiliac. Each had voluntarily presented himself for treatment and each expressed a strong desire to change his behavior.

The first subject was a 24-year-old male who had recently attempted suicide. Homosexuality began at age 13. For the last year the frequency of homosexual encounters was one to three per day and usually occurred in public toilets. During this period, he was arrested twice and mugged once. He had two heterosexual contacts in college, but these were initiated by the females and he was not able to maintain an erection or ejaculate. This patient was seen daily as an inpatient on the hospital's Clinical Research Unit.

The second subject was a 27-year-old homosexual pedophiliac who reported a ten year history of sexual behavior with young boys. He reported minimal attraction toward females. After a series of covert sensitization treatments, he was able to control his deviant urges and his arousal to young boys was minimal. However, there was no change in his low level of heterosexual arousal and therefore, he was accepted for the present study. He was seen daily as an inpatient on the Clinical Research Unit.

The third subject was a 38-year-old male with a sporadic history of homosexual relationships beginning in Junior High School. As he approached his thirties, heterosexual behavior, which had been limited to isolated instances of petting with some arousal, had disappeared and homosexual behavior became more frequent. However, he then decided to get married and have a family. After his marriage, homosexual contacts continued. He had intercourse with his wife about twice a week, but it was quite aversive to him as he had to use a homosexual fantasy to maintain an erection. He never ejaculated during intercourse, but was able to ejaculate while masturbating to homosexual fantasies. He was followed as an outpatient approximately three times a week.

The fourth subject was an 18-year-old male who reported two homosexual experiences at age 10. Although he had not engaged in overt homosexual behavior since that time, he had frequent homosexual urges and fantasies. Masturbation fantasies were mostly homosexual. He had dated girls on two occasions with no arousal or sexual behavior. The subject was quite depressed as treatment began. He was seen daily as an inpatient on the Clinical Research Unit.

Measurement

Penile circumference changes in response to colored slides of nude males (young boys, for subject 2) and females were recorded by a mechanical strain gauge (Barlow et al., 1970), using a Grass polygraph, model 7. Each subject chose slides that were arousing (in the case of the male slides) or least unattractive (in the case of the female slides) from a larger collection; subject 1 chose 22 male and 19 female slides; subject 2, 12 adolescent male and 20 female; subject 3, 14 male and 13 female; and subject 4, 20 male and 21 female. In addition, each subject was asked to select an 8-mm film of a nude, seductive female that was the least unattractive to him to be used during treament.

During each measurement session, four male and four female slides were presented to subject 1, and three male and three female slides, to subjects 2, 3 and 4. One of the female slides was a still of the female pictured in the film. Each slide was presented for two-minute periods during which each subject was instructed to "imagine yourself in a sexually arousing situation with the person in the slide." The order of slides was random and the interval between slides was 30 seconds of baseline recording, or a return to baseline, whichever was longer.

In addition to the objective penile measure, subjective reports of hetero- and homosexual behavior and arousal were collected (Herman et al., 1971; Herman et al., 1974).

Procedure

Each subject was told, "We are using a new treatment for homosexuality which contains several different phases. Although this treatment has been effective with other cases like yours, every treatment, no matter how successful, has its ups and downs, so don't get discouraged." This last sentence was designed to allay any fear of ultimate failure which might have arisen when control procedures were introduced.

Baseline. During the baseline phase, penile measurements as well as subjective reports of arousal and behavior were recorded, but no treatment was administered. Baseline continued for 9 sessions for subject 1 and 6 sessions for subjects 2, 3 and 4.

Phase 1. Exposure to females. The subject was seated in a comfortable chair and instructed to imagine engaging in heterosexual behavior with the female in the film. An 8-mm film of a nude, seductive female assuming various sexual poses was shown for 10 minutes. Penile circumference change to slides of nude males and females as well as the subjective measures continued to be recorded in separate measurement sessions. Typically, treatment sessions took place during the afternoon and measurement sessions occurred the next morning. The exposure to explicit female stimuli phase continued for 18 sessions for subject 1, 8 sessions for subject 2, 16 sessions for subject 3 and 6 sessions for subject 4.

Phase 2. Exposure to males. Subjects were told, "For the next few sessions we are going to change the procedure. We have noticed from your responses that it is time to begin the second phase of treatment. Your heterosexual responses are now strong enough that you can begin testing your homosexual tendencies by confronting them in the controlled laboratory atmosphere. You will learn to control your homosexual arousal and your heterosexual arousal will continue to increase." Although subject 2 had not had a pedophiliac experience since the beginning of the present study, the rationale for male exposure came from the fact that he would eventually leave the hospital and be confronted with situations which formerly elicited pedophiliac behavior.

The subject was seated in a chair and a 10-minute film depicting homosexual activities (a Boy Scout Jamboree, for subject 2) was shown. Responses to male and female slides as well as the subjective measures continued to be recorded for each subject in separate measurement sessions as in the previous phase. The male exposure control phase lasted for 9, 4, 8 and 6 sessions for subjects 1, 2, 3 and 4, respectively.

Phase 3. Female exposure. The female film was reintroduced as previously described and continued for 9, 28, 5 and 9 sessions for subjects 1, 2, 3 and 4, respectively.

In most instances, each phase continued until clear trends in the data emerged. However, additional criteria for changing phases for individual cases are noted in the results. In addition, specific reasons for discrepancies in the number of sessions per phase among subjects are also detailed in the results section.

RESULTS

Figure 1 shows penile circumference change, expressed as a percentage of full erection, to nude male and female slides in the separate measurement sessions for the first subject. The responses to females was averaged over blocks of three sessions while responses to males are averaged over each phase.

During baseline, penile response to female slides stabilized between 26 and 36 percent of full erection. Penile response to male slides was slightly higher and averaged 37 percent for the entire phase. Behaviorally, the subject reported that he had at least four homosexual encounters, but added that he cruised almost continually. All masturbatory fantasy was reported as homosexual.

Due to the unexpected increase during female exposure, which was originally intended as a control phase, the phase was extended to 18 sessions to insure that the increase was stable. During this phase, penile response to females in measurement sessions increased to 56 percent of full erection. The increase in female responding was not specific to the slide of the female in the film, but generalized to the other female slides. The greatest response, however, was to the slide of the female in the film. Male responding also increased and averaged 47 percent for the phase. The reported frequency of the subject's homosexual behavior declined during this period. Masturbatory fantasies became increasingly heterosexual. The subject began to date women and reported being aroused by females in the environment.

In the male exposure phase, penile responses to females dropped from 57 to 24 percent of full erection. Male responding also declined and averaged 36 percent for the phase, which was equivalent to male responding during baseline. Heterosexual behavior, such as dating, continued in the early part of the phase; however, male responding began to increase and he stopped dating in the latter part of the phase. He began to cruise more actively and had two homosexual encounters. Masturbatory fantasies became exclusively homosexual once more.

When exposure to the female film phase was reinstated, penile responding to female slides increased to 60 percent during the separate measurement sessions. Male responding varied around baseline levels and averaged 36 percent for the phase. Masturbatory fantasy became heterosexual once more, the subject reported being aroused by females in the environment and he soon began dating again. However, although he verbalized much dislike for homosexual acts, he did occasionally cruise and habitually frequented male restrooms.

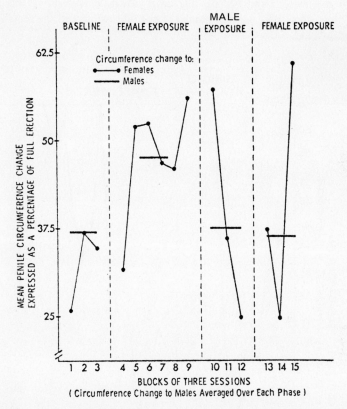

Fig. 1. S1: Mean penile circumference change expressed as a percentage of full erection, to nude female (averaged over blocks of three-sessions) and nude male (averaged over each phase) slides.

Figure 2 shows penile circumference change, expressed as a percentage of full erection, to nude male and female slides in measurement sessions for the second subject. The response to females was averaged over blocks of two sessions, while response to males was averaged over each phase.

During baseline, penile response to female slides decreased steadily from 41 to 29 percent of full erection, with responses to the slide of the female in the film somewhat greater than responses to generalization slides. Penile responses to male slides remained at low levels and averaged between 9 and 14 percent throughout the entire experiment.

During the first female exposure phase, penile response to female stimuli (both test and generalization slides) increased substantially from 9 to 64 percent of full erection. The subject also reported an increase in heterosexual urges outside the hospital and he began to date.

When the male exposure phase was introduced, responses to female slides decreased markedly from the previous phase and stabilized below baseline levels at 21 percent of full erection. Interestingly, the only pedophiliac urges reported throughout the study were reported during this phase. Behaviorally, the subject became quite agitated and depressed. For this reason, and because the drop in female responding was sharp and remained very low, this phase was terminated after four sessions and the female exposure phase was reintroduced.

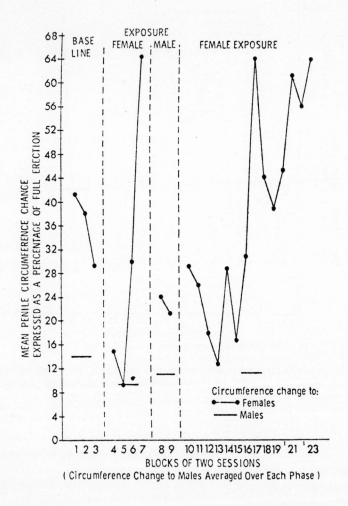

Fig. 2. S2: Mean penile circumference change expressed as a percentage of full erection, to nude female (averaged over blocks of two sessions) and nude male (averaged over each phase) slides.

During the early part of the second female exposure phase, penile responses to females was variable, showing occasional signs of recovery. When recovery finally occurred, responses increased sharply to an average of 64 percent of full erection. Since the recovery was slow, this phase was extended 12 more sessions to check the stability of this heterosexual arousal. By the end of the phase, female responding had again increased to 64 percent of full erection. In addition, the subject reported that he felt less depressed and was attempting to begin dating again.

Figure 3 shows penile circumference change, expressed as a percentage of full erection, to nude male and female slides in measurement sessions for the third subject. The response to females was averaged over blocks of two sessions, while response to males was averaged over each phase.

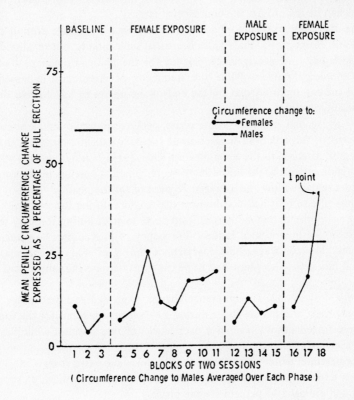

Fig. 3. S3: Mean penile circumference change expressed as a percentage of full erection, to nude female (averaged over blocks of two sessions) and nude male (averaged over each phase) slides.

During baseline, penile response to female stimuli stabilized below 11 percent of full erection. There did not appear to be any difference between responses to the slide of the female in the film and the generalization slides. Penile response to male stimuli was variable but averaged 59 percent for the entire phase. The subject reported that he had three homosexual contacts during this phase and attempts at heterosexual intercourse with his wife (which averaged once every 2 weeks) required the use of homosexual fantasy.

During the female exposure phase, response to female stimuli increased to 25 percent, then dropped below 12 percent but increased again and stabilized at 20 percent of full erection. Inspection of the data indicates that the initial increase was equivalent for both test and generalization slides. However, after the decrease, the responses to generalization slides remained low. The major increase in female responding was to the test slide, and in fact, at one point, reached a high of 55 percent of full erection. Male responding, while variable, increased over baseline levels and averaged 75 percent for the phase. There were six homosexual contacts reported during this phase, which took 10 weeks to complete, since the subject took a vacation after the eighth session. Intercourse became somewhat more frequent (once per week) and the subject reported that there were occasions when he did not use the homosexual fantasy.

During the male exposure phase, penile response to female stimuli decreased to baseline levels. Responses to male slides decreased substantially, but remained higher than female responding and averaged 28 percent for the phase. Homosexual contacts continued at sporadic intervals. While the frequency of intercourse increased (twice per week), the subject reported that by the end of the phase, he had to rely on the homosexual fantasy once again.

During the second female exposure phase, penile response to female stimuli increased to 41 percent of full erection. Inspection of the data indicates however, that the major increase was in response to the generalization slides (as high as 57 percent) while response to the test slide, after a slight initial increase, remained at baseline levels. Penile response to male slides remained low and averaged 28 percent for the phase.

Although the subject had one homosexual contact during the two week duration of the phase, he reported that he was able to become erect during foreplay with his wife without the use of homosexual fantasy. Frequency of intercourse, however, declined to once a week. He still was unable to ejaculate during intercourse and masturbated to homosexual fantasies. This phase had to be cut short because the subject had to return to school.

Figure 4 shows penile circumference change, expressed as a percentage of full erection, to nude male and female slides during measurement sessions for the fourth subject. The response to females was averaged over blocks of two sessions, while the response to males was averaged over each phase.

During baseline, penile response to female slides decreased from 22 to 11 percent of full erection with no difference between test and generalization slides. Response to males was higher and averaged 43 percent for the phase.

During the female exposure phase, penile response to female slides increased and reached a high of 88 percent of full erection. Male responding also increased and averaged 53 percent for the phase. Although the subject reported more arousal to females, he seldom left the hospital.

During the male exposure phase, penile response to female slides decreased from 51 to 34 percent of full erection. Male responding, however, continued to increase and averaged 62 percent of full erection for the phase. Reports of homosexual arousal in the environment increased sharply toward the end of this phase and the subject reported strong desires to go cruising although he had not engaged in this behavior previously. In this subject, who had not engaged in homosexual behavior as an adult, homosexual films produced strong homosexual arousal.

When the female exposure phase was reinstated, response to female stimuli increased gradually to 82 percent of full erection. Male responding decreased to below baseline levels and averaged 33 percent for the phase. Reports of homosexual arousal in the environment decreased steadily but remained slightly more frequent than heterosexual urges and fantasies.

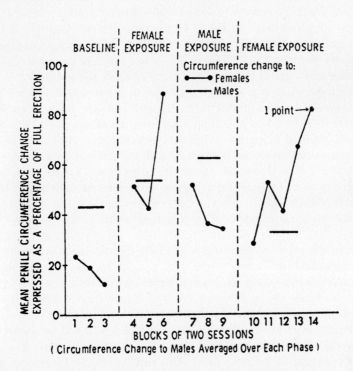

Fig. 4. S4: Mean penile circumference change expressed as a percentage of full erection, to nude female (averaged over blocks of two sessions) and nude male (averaged over each phase) slides.

DISCUSSION

The findings of the present series indicate that exposure to explicit heterosexual stimuli modifies the sexual arousal of homosexuals. Responding to female stimuli in the separate sessions increased during the female exposure phase, decreased during the male exposure phase, and increased once again when the female exposure phase was reinstated. In addition, the effects of exposure were separated from the usual psychotherapeutic variables such as therapist attention, rapport, and expectancy of improvement since these variables were still present during the male exposure control phase and yet heterosexual arousal decreased.

Although all subjects were 'exposed' to slides of females during initial preliminary assessment sessions and during the baseline phase, there was no increase in heterosexual arousal during this time. Increased responsiveness only followed exposure to the female film, a more 'intense' or explicit stimulus. It seems then, that the effectiveness of exposure may be dependent on the 'intensity' of the heterosexual stimulus used.

The pattern of responsiveness during the testing sessions was not specific to the female pictured in the film. During exposure to this film, responsiveness increased to a slide of the female pictured in the film and also to slides of other females. In addition, the increase in penile response to female stimuli was paralleled by changes in masturbatory fantasy (subjects 1 and 2), reports of arousal (all subjects) and heterosexual behavior outside the laboratory (subjects 1, 2 and 3). In case three, the increased arousal to female stimuli during treatment appeared to have generalized to reports concerning sexual intercourse. During the female exposure phase, the patient reported greater enjoyment and less use of homosexual fantasies than during baseline or male exposure phases.

The third subject showed major inconsistencies in the increased responding to test and generalization slides and appeared to do less well than the other cases. This case, however, differed in at least two important ways from the other cases: (1) since he was married, he was required to engage in behavior (sexual intercourse) that was aversive *before* any heterosexual interest had been established, and this may have slowed considerably the development of heterosexual interest during treatment. (2) He came to sessions less often than the other subjects (three times a week, when he came regularly; once a week for several sessions; and frequent periods of nonattendance for upwards of three weeks) and had less concentrated trials, therefore, possibly retarding any ongoing learning.

Nevertheless, this exposure technique is generally effective and appears to overcome many of the procedural difficulties noted with other techniques designed to increase heterosexual responsiveness, such as classical conditioning (Herman et al., 1974) and fading (Barlow & Agras, 1971). Exposure to explicit heterosexual stimuli is a simple, straightforward technique; all that was needed was to show a film.

It is interesting to note that homosexual arousal also increased somewhat the first time they saw the heterosexual stimuli in those three subjects who were homosexually aroused at the beginning of the experiment. Although the reasons for this are not clear, we have observed this phenomenon in other subjects in our laboratory. Subjects later report that during this first phase, they are generally more aroused, suggesting that the initial effect of this procedure is an increase in sex drive which is undifferentiated. In this experiment, however, homosexual arousal in these three subjects returned to either baseline levels or below, suggesting that it is a transitory phenomenon. In any case, it deserves further investigation.

Although exposure to high intensity heterosexual stimuli appears to be effective in modifying heterosexual arousal patterns, in cases one and four, when heterosexual arousal increased, there was no concomitant decrease in homosexual arousal. In case three, when homosexual arousal did decrease somewhat, reports of homosexual behavior did not seem to change. These results appear to confirm findings from previous research (e.g. Herman et al., 1974), that increasing heterosexual arousal may not be sufficient in the treatment of homosexuality and techniques to decrease homosexual arousal and behavior, such as aversion therapy, may still have to be used. In addition, although all subjects did attempt to implement new social-sexual behaviors in the environment after heterosexual arousal had increased, all had considerable difficulties. It therefore seems important to teach the patient sufficient hetero-social skills to implement his new arousal. These observations suggest that a more comprehensive approach than heretofore employed is necessary for the treatment of sexual deviation (Barlow, 1974).

It should be emphasized that we are not proposing the exposure procedure as a treatment for homosexuality, since obviously many more factors such as hetero-social skills must be considered. Nor is it the purpose of this experiment to compare the efficacy of this therapeutic procedure with other procedures designed to increase hetero-sexual arousal. This type of comparison is best carried out in a group design. What this experiment does indicate, however, is that exposure to explicit heterosexual films is functionally related to increases in heterosexual arousal outside the treatment session.

Based on the initial serendipitous (but now replicated) finding that exposure to heterosexual stimuli produced increases in heterosexual arousal, it is possible to interpret previous anecdotal case studies in this light. These include systematic desensitization to progressively more intimate heterosexual themes (e.g. Huff, 1969); shaping successive increases in penile response to heterosexual stimuli by positive reinforcement (Harbison, Quinn & McAllister, 1970); associating strong sexual arousal, such as masturbatory (Davison, 1968) or drug induced (Freund, 1960) arousal with heterosexual stimuli; and classical conditioning, using the deviant stimuli as the UCS to condition a response to a more appropriate sexual stimulus (Beech et al., 1971). Common to these procedures is exposure to heterosexual stimuli, both in treatment and in real life, often avoided by homosexual subjects.

It is possible that the effectiveness of exposure is due to extinction of avoidance behavior. In the present series, subjects were confronted with representations of hetero-sexual stimuli in such a way that neither the avoidance response nor the aversive conse-quences (especially in case three) could occur. Interestingly, toward the end of the experiment, one subject (case one) remarked that seeing the girl in the film was like being with an old friend, in front of whom he could not be embarrassed. Another possibility is that exposure provided the subjects with new fantasy material which is then associated with sexual arousal outside treatment, thus strengthening heterosexual arousal.

Finally, mention should be made concerning the strength and appropriateness of the single case experimental design, which allowed us to change strategies and test the effect of exposure immediately, rather than confound it with the masturbation variable (see Barlow & Hersen, 1973). Without this flexibility, it would have been quite difficult to 'tease out' the relevant therapeutic variable.

REFERENCES

Annon, J.S. The extension of learning principles to the analysis and treatment of sexual problems. *Diss. Abst. Int.* 1971, **32**, (6-B), 3627

Azrin, N.H. & Holz, W.C. Punishment. In *Operant Behavior: Areas of Research and Application* (Ed. W.K. Honig), New York: Appleton-Century-Crofts, 1966.

Bancroft, J. A comparative study of aversion and desensitization in the treatment of homosexuality. In *Behavior Therapy in the 1970's* (Eds. L.E. Burns and J.L. Wosley), Bristol: Wrights, 1970.

Barlow, D.H. Aversive procedures. In *Behavior Modification: Principles and Clinical Applications* (Ed. W.S. Agras), Boston: Little, Brown, 1972.

Barlow, D.H. Increasing heterosexual responsiveness in the treatment of sexual deviation: A review of the clinical and experimental evidence. *Behav. Therapy,* 1973, **4**, 655-671.

Barlow, D.H. The treatment of sexual deviation: Towards a comprehensive behavioral approach. In *Innovative Treatment Methods in Psychopathology* (Eds. K.S. Calhoun, H.E. Adams and K.M. Mitchell), New York: Wiley, 1974.

Barlow, D.H. & Agras, W.S. An experimental analysis of 'fading' to increase heterosexual responsiveness in homosexuality. Paper presented at *Southeastern Psychological Association Meeting,* Miami Beach, Florida, 1971.

Barlow, D.H., Becker, R., Leitenberg, H. & Agras, W.S. A mechanical strain gauge for recording penile circumference change. *J. Appl. Behav. Anal.,* 1970, **3**, 73-76.

Barlow, D.H. & Hersen, M. Single case experimental designs: Uses in applied clinical research. *Archs gen. Psychiat.* 1973, **29**, 400-402.

Bergin, A.E. & Strupp, H.H. New directions in psychotherapy research. *J. abnorm. Psychol.,* 1970, **76**, 13-26.

Bieber, B. et al. *Homosexuality.* New York: Basic Books, 1963.

Davison, G.C. Elimination of a sadistic fantasy by a client-controlled counterconditioning technique: A case study. *J. abnorm. Psychol.,* 1968, **73**, 84-90.

Feldman, M.P. & MacCulloch, M.J. *Homosexual Behavior: Theory and Assessment.* Oxford: Pergamon Press, 1960.

Freund, K. Some problems in the treatment of homosexuality. In *Behavior Therapy and the Neuroses* (Ed. H.J. Eysenck), Oxford: Pergamon Press, 1960.

Harbison, J., Quinn, J., & McAllister, H. The positive conditioning of heterosexual behavior. Paper presented to *Conference of Behavior Modification,* Dublin, 1970.

Herman, S.H., Barlow, D.H., & Agras, W.S. Exposure to heterosexual stimuli: An effective variable in treating homosexuality? *Proceedings of the American Psychological Association 79th Annual Convention,* pp. 699-700. Washington, D.C.: American Psychological Association, 1971.

Herman, S.H., Barlow, D.H., & Agras, W.S. An experimental analysis of classical conditioning as a method of increasing heterosexual arousal in homosexuals. *Behav. Therapy,* 1974, **5**, 33-47.

Huff, F. The desensitization of a homosexual. *Behav. Res. & Therapy,* 1970, **8**, 99-102.

Marquis, J.N. Orgasmic reconditioning: Changing sexual object choice through controlling masturbation fantasies. *J. Behav. Therapy & Exp. Psychiat.* 1970, **1**, 263-271.

Ovesey, L., Gaylin, W., & Hendin, H. Psychotherapy and male homosexuality. *Archs Gen. Psychiat.,* 1963, **9**, 19-31.

Rado, S. An adaptational view of sexual behavior. In *Psychosexual Development in Health and Disease* (Eds. P. Hoch and J. Zubin). New York: Grune & Stratton, 1949.

Ramsey, R.W., & Van Velzen, V. Behavior therapy for sexual perversions. *Behav. Res. & Therapy,* 1968, **6**, 233.

West, D.J. *Homosexuality.* 3rd edn. London: Penguin Books, 1968.

Wolpe, J. *The Practice of Behavior Therapy.* New York: Pergamon Press, 1969.

23

An Experimental Analysis of Feedback to Increase Sexual Arousal in a Case of Homo- and Heterosexual Impotence: A Preliminary Report

STEVEN H. HERMAN and MICHAEL PREWETT

Although informational feedback paradigms have been successfully used to modify such behaviors as phobias (Leitenberg et al., 1968), posture (O'Brien & Azrin, 1970), muscle tension and tension headaches (Budzynski, Stoyva & Adler, 1970), heart rate (Brener & Hothersall, 1966) torticollis (Bernhardt, Hersen & Barlow, 1972) and EEG-alpha (Stoyva & Kamiya, 1968), there has been no systematic application of feedback procedures to the treatment of sexual disorders. Biofeedback paradigms have enabled subjects to detect and control previously indiscriminable physiological reactions. Modification of sexual arousal patterns might be accomplished by providing the patient with information concerning ordinarily undetectable changes in penile response, thus making it possible for the patient to gain fine discriminative control over this response system. The purpose of the present investigation was to determine, using a single case experimental design, whether informational feedback can be used effectively to increase sexual arousal in a case of impotence.

METHOD

Subject

The subject was a 51-year-old male who reported a homosexual history dating from age 13. Homosexual activity was greatest during his mid-twenties, but he had never been able to maintain an erection for more than a few minutes and had ejaculated during only one encounter. He also reported a brief heterosexual history beginning with sporadic dating in high school. He attempted unsuccessfully on several occasions to have intercourse, but was unable to achieve or maintain an erection. There was a 1-year marriage but it was never consummated. His sexual difficulties exacerbated to the extent that he was unable to maintain an erection during masturbation, nor was he able to ejaculate. In addition, he seldom attempted any sexual activity and would go weeks without sexual urges towards males or females.

PROCEDURE

Baseline measurement

Penile circumference changes in response to viewing slides of nude males and females were recorded by a mechanical strain gauge (Barlow et al., 1970), using a Grass polygraph, model 7. From a pool of 10 male and 23 female slides, initially selected by the subject as being the most attractive, three slides of each gender were shown during each measurement session. Slides were presented for 2-minute periods and the subject was to imagine himself in a sexually arousing scene with the person in the slide. The order of slides was random and the interval between slides was 30 seconds of baseline recording, or a return to baseline, whichever was longer.

During the six sessions of the baseline phase, the objective penile measure, as well as subjective reports of hetero- and homosexual arousal and behavior (Herman, Barlow & Agras, 1971) were recorded, but no treatment was administered.

Phase 1: Contingent feedback

The subject was seated in a comfortable chair in front of a bank of 10 lights which were operated by an add-subtract counter and his penile responses were monitored. He was told, "We are ready to begin treatment. When I tell you to begin, you may use any means you wish, outside of manipulation, to achieve an erection. The lights in front of you will tell you how you are doing. As your arousal increases, more lights will come on; if your arousal decreases, lights will go off. If all the lights are on and your arousal is still increasing, the lights will quickly flash and start again from the first light. Continue to try to turn on as many lights as possible until I tell you to stop." No pictorial sexual stimuli were presented during these treatment sessions.

The polygraph was monitored by the therapist who also operated the add-subtract counter. Beginning from a baseline level of responding, for each mm increase in pen deflection, one light was turned on. If, after the response had begun to increase, the response began to subside, one light was turned off for each mm decrease in pen deflection. In the present case, the sensitivity settings of the polygraph were such that 1 mm readout of pen deflection turned out to be 4 percent of the deflection caused by a full erection. (This, of course, was determined in a later phase of the study. Barlow et al., 1970, point out that although reliably recorded, the patient is often unaware of changes in penile response in the vicinity of 3 percent of full erection.) Four feedback trials of 3 minutes each were given during each treatment session. After each trial, the lights were reset; the interval between trials was 60 seconds of baseline recording, or a return to baseline, whichever was longer.

After each treatment session, the patient was given a one-half hour rest period and then his penile responses to male and female slides were assessed in a separate measurement session, identical to that of baseline, where no lights or feedback were included. Subjective measures were also recorded. The contingent feedback phase continued for 10 sessions.

Phase 2: Non-contingent feedback

During this phase, penile response was monitored as before, but changes in the light display were no longer contingent upon the response of the subject. The patient was told, "We are going to change the procedure a bit. We have found that this is the best course of action at this time. Keep trying to achieve an erection. However, now the lights may or may not come on." While penile response was being recorded, lights were turned on and off in a manner approximating the pattern that was observed during contingent feedback. Four 3-minute trials were given at each session. Penile responses to male and female slides as well as the subjective measures continued to be recorded in separate sessions as before. The non-contingent feedback phase continued for six sessions.

Phase 3: Contingent feedback

The contingent feedback condition, as described in phase 1, was reinstated for 10 sessions.

RESULTS

Figure 1 represents penile circumference changes, expressed as a percentage of full erection, to male and female slides during the separate measurement sessions, averaged over blocks of two sessions.

During baseline, responses to male and female stimuli stabilized at minimal levels. Penile response to female slides decreased from 18 to 12.6 percent of full erection, while responses to male slides ranged from 17.4 to 13.6 percent. Although the patient reported several attachments to male ward members with some urges toward one young male doctor, there were no masturbation attempts, nor were there any instances of overt sexual behavior.

During the separate measurement sessions of the contingent feedback phase, penile responses to both male and female slides increased sharply. Responses to females increased from 17.6 to 48 percent while responses to males increased from 20 to 46 percent of full erection. In addition to the increases in penile response, the subject reported that he was able to masturbate to ejaculation on three occasions. He began to date a woman during this phase and masturbation fantasies primarily concerned her. Homosexual urges toward young doctors in the hospital continued to be reported.

Penile response to both male and female stimuli decreased during the non-contingent feedback phase. Penile responses to female slides stabilized at 27 percent of full erection, while penile responses to males averaged 28 percent for the entire phase. Although the subject reported that he was attracted to females in the environment and felt that he was making progress in treatment, he indicated that he had again become unable to masturbate successfully. Heterosexual behavior, limited to light petting with arousal at the beginning of the phase, had become unsuccessful by the end of the phase.

When the contingent feedback phase was reinstated, penile response to female slides increased steadily to 68 percent of full erection. Responding to male stimuli was variable; after an initial increase, responding decreased to 30 percent, but then increased sharply to

56 percent of full erection by the end of the phase. Concurrent with the increase in penile responding, the subject again reported success in masturbation, with accompanying heterosexual fantasies. He began dating again, but the woman rejected him after a short time. He then reported increasing attraction to males in the environment and had two successful homosexual encounters.

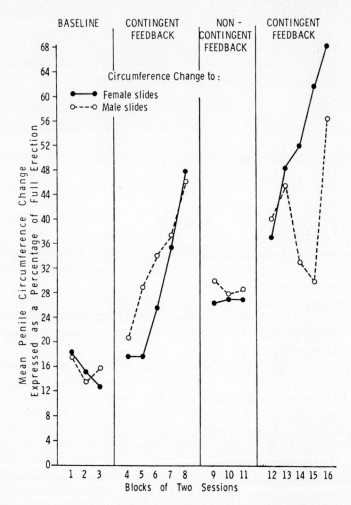

Fig. 1. Mean penile circumference change, expressed as a percentage of full erection, to nude male and female slides, averaged over blocks of two measurement sessions.

DISCUSSION

The results of the present study indicate that informational feedback can be used to systematically modify penile responding. An impotent subject's penile response to male and female stimuli were significantly increased during a contingent feedback phase, decreased when feedback was administered non-contingently, and increased, once again when contingent feedback was reinstated.

The increase in penile responding was paralleled by the achievement of ejaculation during masturbation, changes in masturbatory fantasy, and reports of homo- and heterosexual behavior outside the laboratory. However, approximately 7 months after discharge, the subject was readmitted to the hospital for medical complications following excessive drinking. He indicated that he had been "jilted" in a homosexual affair, attempted reconciliation, failed and began to drink excessively. He then noted a decrease in sexual urges and fantasies and overt sexual behavior ceased. A measurement session revealed that penile response had decreased to within baseline levels. It appears that even when sexual arousal had been increased, this subject's low level of social skills made achievement of long-term social-sexual behavior improbable. This strengthens the observation that teaching the patient sufficient social skills to implement his new arousal is crucial for therapeutic success (Herman et al., 1974).

Nevertheless, the feedback technique is an effective method of modifying penile responsiveness. In addition, it appears to overcome many of the procedural difficulties noted with techniques designed to increase heterosexual arousal, such as classical conditioning (Herman et al., 1974) or fading (Barlow & Agras, 1973), especially since these techniques require a large initial response amplitude in order to initiate treatment. Furthermore, feedback can be used when desensitization hierarchies or exposure (Herman et al., 1971) stimulus dimensions are not readily apparent, especially in the case of sexual disorders (primarily, erectile difficulties) that are related to medical-surgical complications, such as in renal dialysis or spinal cord injury patients. In this latter case, the feedback technique may prove as important in the areas of assessment, evaluation and prognosis as it is for treatment.

An important factor for the successful outcome of this procedure appears to be the capacity for the objective measurement of very low level responses (below 3 percent of full erection). Such response definition permits the contingent feedback and/or reinforcement of these target responses, enabling the patient to gain fine discriminative control over his responding.

REFERENCES

Barlow, D.H. & Agras, W.S. Fading to increase heterosexual responsiveness in homosexuals, *J. Appl. Behav. Anal.* 1973, 6, 355-366.

Barlow, D.H., Becker R., Leitenberg H. & Agras, W.S. A mechanical strain gauge for recording penile circumference change, *J. Appl. Behav. Anal.* 1970, 3, 73-76.

Bernhardt, A. & Hersen, M. Measurement and modification of spasmodic torticollis: An experimental analysis, *Behav. Therapy,* 1972, 3, 294-297.

Brenner, J. & Hothersall, D. Heart rate control under conditions of augmented sensory feedback, *Psychophysiology,* 1966, 3, 23-28.

Budzynski, T., Stoyva, J. & Adler C. Feedback-induced muscle relaxation: Application to tension headache, *J. Behav. Ther. & Exp. Psychiat.,* 1970, 1, 205-211.

Herman, S.H., Barlow, D.H. & Agras, W.S. Exposure to heterosexual stimul: An effective variable in treating homosexuality? *Proceedings of the American Psychological Association 79th Annual Convention,* 1971. Pp. 699-700. Washington, D.C.: American Psychological Association.

Herman, S.H., Barlow, D.H. & Agras, W.S. An experimental analysis of classical conditioning as a method of increasing heterosexual arousal in homosexuals, *Behav. Therapy,* 1974, 5, 33-47.

Leitenberg, H., Agras, W.S., Thompson, L. & Wright, D. Feedback in behavior modification: An experimental analysis of two phobic cases, *J. Appl. Behav. Anal.*, 1968, **1**, 131-137.

O'Brien, F. & Azrin, N. Behavioral engineering: Control of posture by informational feedback, *J. Appl. Behav. Anal.*, 1970, **3**, 235-240.

Stoyva, J. & Kamiya, J. Electrophysiological studies of dreaming as the prototype of a new strategy in the study of consciousness, *Psychol. Rev.*, 1968, **75**, 192-205.

24
Basic and Applied Research in Human Sexuality: Current Limitations and Future Directions in Sex Therapy

HOWARD N. HIGGINBOTHAM and GARY M. FARKAS

In this paper, sex therapy and research are placed in a social perspective, with the influence of basic research on both social mores and applied behavioral science outlined. It is then suggested that effective clinical intervention requires a broad knowledge of the genetic, biological, physiological, and sociopsychological aspects of sexuality. Issues of classification and subsequent treatment are examined next, with three levels of intervention identified. Finally, a critical review of the major innovations in sex therapy is presented, with suggestions for an integrated behavioral approach to the treatment of sexual problems.

THE INTERFACE OF SEX RESEARCH AND TREATMENT
WITH CHANGING SOCIAL ATTITUDES AND MORES

Perhaps the best example of a research or applied endeavor that illustrates the intricate link between the scientific enterprise and the prevailing social mood is sex research and therapy. As Holden noted in a recent *Science* article (Holden, 1974), sex therapy is making it as both a science and an industry. The societal factors responsible for this phenomena have been commented upon by a number of writers (Gagnon, 1975; Franks & Wilson, 1974; Jacobs & Whiteley, 1975; Obler, 1975). Most notably, the American sexual revolution has legitimized frank and open discussion of hitherto secretive sexual attitudes, practices and preferences. Similarly, social influence movements such as women's rights and gay liberation have dramatically sensitized society to its discriminatory practices, paving the way for acceptance of alternative life styles for women and homosexuals, while liberalizing abortion and sexual preference statutes.

Following these changes in traditional mores has been the social expectation, or even demand, for sexual sophistication and expertise. Many Americans consider sexual performance (i.e., bringing oneself and one's partner to orgasm on every trial) the major criterion for determining sexual adequacy, and suffer resignation when not living up to the newly created cultural expectations (Obler, 1975).

In fact, Masters and Johnson (1970) estimate that 50% of all couples suffer sexual problems of significant magnitude that their relationship is severely affected. Because of this demand, the psychological service industry has been profoundly changed. Not content with imperfect sexual functioning, clients have pressed therapists to provide them with *valid* and *reliable* sexual treatment strategies (Obler, 1975). Of course, one consequence of a high investment in sex therapies is heightened pre-therapy expectancy and placebo effects attached to being treated at a special center (usually a medical school) designed to "cure" couples presenting similar complaints.

Unfortunately, the push for sexual treatment has carried with it the spawning of thousands of sex clinics, self-appointed experts, "New Therapies," misinformation and misapplication of behavioral techniques (Holden, 1974). Masters and Johnson, in large part responsible for the sex therapy movement, estimate that perhaps 50 out of the 3500-5000 newly opened clinics and treatment centers are administered by sufficiently qualified professionals (*Medical World News,* 1974). Under these conditions, pressure is felt by ethically responsible professionals to delineate guidelines for legitimate sex therapy and empirically validate the host of new techniques currently offered by licensed clinicians (Koch & Koch, 1976; Meyer, 1976).

The historical antecedents of current trends in sex research and treatment offer additional examples of the interface between social context and applied behavioral science. Without question, Freud's impact on the development of 20th century sexual ideology has been omnipotent. One damaging aspect was his distinction between the vaginal and clitoral orgasm, the former being sole evidence of psychosexual maturity for women, and the latter evidence of fixations, unresolved Oedipal conflicts, penis envy, and other conditions causing guilt in women. It is interesting to note that the citoral orgasm was a major issue with many of the sexologists following Freud. Such notables as Havelock Ellis, Kelly, Kinsey, and even Albert Ellis strongly advocated the position that masturbation and petting enable women to have better orgasms than through intercourse, and that such information should be known and used. This paramount topic of sexological concern culminated in Masters and Johnson's (1966) direct measurements of the orgasmic process, where they empirically demonstrated that masturbation resulted in more intense orgasms than those elicited via coition.

From its onset, the pattern of sex research begun by one of the first modern authorities, Ellis (1935, 1936), has resulted in dispelling myths, changing parochial attitudes, and lending the weight of scientific legitimacy to variation in sexual repertoires. The impact on the American public can be unobtrusively measured by the rapidity with which research surveys and experimental outcomes have become both popular books in their own right (e.g., Hunt, 1974; Kinsey, Pomeroy, & Martin, 1948; Kinsey, Pomeroy, Martin, & Gebhard, 1953; Masters & Johnson, 1966, 1970), as well as non-technical summaries for the layman (e.g., Robbins & Robbins, 1970). The marriage manual era of the 50's and 60's has turned into the sexological book explosion of the 70's. Writers such as Albert Ellis (e.g., *Sex without Guilt,* 1958) are attacking sexual misinformation and creating a new role for people in bed—that of the personal sex-scientist. In this context, Kinsey's survey research of human sexuality, charting rates and varieties of behavior, went the furthest toward influencing social attitudes, public policy, and research interests in the 50's and 60's (Gagnon, 1975). The publication of these surveys was a national event with broad implications. For example, Kinsey's data showing higher than expected rates of homosexual activities among men, fostered a personal sense of normality among gays, kindling the liberation movement, and combating the traditional disease perspective. Moreover, this forced researchers to consider novel classification schemas: for example, it would never again be sufficient to designate someone as being "homosexual." Kinsey's studies emphasized that individuals' sexual behavior would most appropriately be classified as lying on a continuum between exclusive homo- and heterosexuality.

The climate for research created by Kinsey also led to the physio-anatomical studies of Masters and Johnson (1966). Again, it was an established professional who conducted this pioneering work; Masters (like Kinsey) was over 40 years of age and had first established a reputation in a non-sex area. Both operated with the support of a major institution, Kinsey based at Indiana University, Masters located at Washington University Medical School.

BASIC FOUNDATIONS FOR CLINICAL COMPETENCY

Before a therapist can devise an effective intervention for sexual dysfunction, or before clinical research in this domain can be designed, what fundamental information does one require concerning the bio-physiological and anatomical nature of normal sexual arousal? Stated differently, does the underlying physiological nature of sexual response become a consideration in the treatment process of dysfunctional states? Following this, what valid and reliable assessment devices can be used to record sexual behavior, and what variables typically effect these measurements? The following section elaborates on these questions.

Genetic and Bio-Neurological Determinants of Dysfunction and "Deviancy"

Although the vast majority of sexual problems treated clinically are sociopsychological in origin, genetic, neurological, chemical and other non-psychological factors have been shown to play a causal role in certain instances (cf. Kinsey et al., 1948). I. Evans (in press) reviewing the evidence relating genes, hormones, and sexual preference, states that "genetic endowment and normal hormonal development are a necessary but by no means sufficient condition for determining either sexual desire or sexual preference; what little evidence there is for a direct hormonal influence on a sexual behavior is related to hormonal conditions during fetal development." Kaplan (1974) reports that diagnosed organic pathology, the biogenetic determinants of sex dysfunction, accounts for three to 20 percent of the cases seen, and details the possible effects of a variety of medical illnesses on male and female sexuality. Summarizing Kaplan and other sources (Belt, 1973; Farkas & Rosen, 1976; McDowell, 1968; Runcimen, 1975; Weiss, 1972) reveals: male impotency can be caused by (1) endocrine dysfunctions, (2) drug ingestion, (3) cardiovascular anomalies, (4) spinal cord injury, and (5) diabetes mellitus. Other major factors that may contribute to impotency in males include respiratory and genital diseases, and nutritional deficiencies. For females, the primary biological determinants of sexual inactivity are reported to be vulval and vaginal pathology, conditions producing pain or displeasure during intercourse.

A vast medical literature documents sexual dysfunction as arising from organic states (cf. Belt, 1973; Weiss, 1972). However, the present practice within medicine of informed consent, where practitioners convey the *expectation* of dysfunction following certain medical interventions (hypotensive chemotherapy, spinal cord transection, etc.) may in fact promote such side-effects. This follows a model for iatrogenic effects of treatment, where environmental influences such as suggestion and fear of fear prevail (I. Evans, 1972; Schachter & Singer, 1962). While further research is needed to shed light on the difference between organic-dysfunctional patients who do and do not experience sexual anomaly, it is important to note that when attributing dysfunctions to biologic determinants, the more relevant psychologic variables accounting for a larger portion of the variance in human sexuality may be ignored (Kinsey et al., 1948).

Physiological Processes Mediating the Arousal Cycle

At face validity, as well as on the authority of Kaplan (1974), Masters and Johnson (1970), McDowell (1968), and I. Evans (in press), the physiological network mediating the arousal cycle represents an important consideration for clinical attention. Briefly, the sexual arousal cycle moves through four phases that are generally termed: excitement, plateau, orgasm, and resolution (Masters & Johnson, 1966).

Of utmost clinical importance is the distinction in males between the desire for sex (possibly a learned response to a range of specific stimuli) and the neural separation of the sexual arousal mechanism (SAM) and the intromissive and ejaculatory mechanism (IEM) (Beach, 1956). The SAM can be elicited by visual, olfactory, tactile or cognitive stimuli which converge at the limbic and hypothalamic systems. The IEM operates different impulses which activate the lumbar spinal cord center to promote clonic contractions of the compressor urethra, bulbocavernosus, and ischiocavernosus muscles, resulting in expulsion of seminal fluid from the penis (McDowell, 1968). The division between SAM and IEM is noted in the possibility of ejaculation without erection (Beach, Westbrook, & Clemens, 1966). However, what concerns us most in this process is the reciprocal action of sympathetic (SNS) and parasympathetic (PNS) nervous system activities. For both sexes, PNS activity is critical for developing excitement and plateau phases leading to orgasm. At this juncture, sympathetic nervous system dominance arises, inhibiting SAM but initiating ejaculation for males. The fact that SNS is also dominant during anxiety reactions is a cogent physiological basis which accounts for why anxious males may experience impotency, premature ejaculation, or an inability to maintain an erection while anxious females may suffer anorgasmia. As detailed later, the overuse of systematic desensitization for treatment of these conditions has been a consequence of this rationale.

Problems Assessing Sexual Responses: Issues of Veridical Physiology

Due to the need for initial and ongoing assessment in a sexual therapy, the development of methodologies for measuring change in sexual response is crucial. Only recently has progress been made in this endeavor, because paralleling Lang's (1969) findings, sexual arousal is like fear and anxiety: it has physiological, behavioral, and cognitive components, and more often than not they are uncorrelated. In a real sense, sexual arousal *is* fear and anxiety, that is, early studies of psychophysiological correlates of sexual arousal were unable to distinguish it from anxiety or surprise (Bancroft & Mathews, 1971) which frustrated initial attempts at developing reliable assessment criteria. As Zuckerman (1971) reports in his authoritative, *Psychological Bulletin* review, frequently used physiological measures cannot determine the direction of affect attached to the aroused state. Fear and sex do overlap physiologically in terms of pulse rate, blood pressure, adrenalin output and respiration; although, on measures of surface skin color and temperature, tumescence, genital secretions, and mytonia, sex appears to stand alone. Zuckerman further reviews 10 physiological parameters of sexual arousal in humans (e.g., electrodermal, cardiovascular, respiratory, vaginal blood flow, pupillary response) delineating the reliability and limitations of each. Of these, penile erection measurement has received the highest reliability endorsement and has stimulated several lines of research and instrumentation development (Bancroft, 1971; Bancroft, Jones, & Pullan, 1966; Freund, 1963; Freund, Sedlacek, & Knob, 1965; Henson & Rubin, 1971; Laws & Rubin, 1969; Rosen, 1973; Rosen, Shapiro, & Schwartz, 1975). However, in a recent study of the parameters of female sexual response, Hoon, Wincze and Hoon (1976) found that in addition to vaginal vascongestion, blood pressure and forehead temperature reliably discriminated between sexual and dysphoric stimuli. Clearly, with refinements in instrumentation and methodology, more precise experiments will enable the delicate physiological interactions to become known.

Despite its increasing popularity among sex researchers and therapists, penile tumescence and vaginal vascongestion are not simple or "pure" measures of arousal; rather, they are mitigated by a number of factors. In terms of instrumentation, Freund's phallometric device allows recording of total penile volume, but is cumbersome and complicated to attach. Other investigators, e.g., Bancroft, Jones and Pullan (1966), Barlow, Becker, Leitenberg and Agras (1970), and Fisher, Gross and Zuch (1965), have developed alternative types of strain gauges, which although efficient, sacrifice volume for diameter measurement. However, McConaghy's (1974) research suggests that most empirical questions can probably be answered with the more elegant strain gauge device.

Recently, photoplethysmograph devices for assessing vaginal blood flow have made female sexual arousal amenable to objective inquiry (Cohen & Shapiro, 1971; Sintchack & Geer, 1975). The ability of these devices to discriminate between sexual and non-sexual stimuli has been widely reported (Geer, Morokoff & Greenwood, 1974; Heiman, 1974, 1975; Hoon, Wincze & Hoon, 1976).

Farkas (1976) has developed a working model which seeks to incorporate those parameters which have been experimentally demonstrated to influence sexual arousal (see Fig. 1). This model delineates five necessary conditions governing the physiological arousal process, and serves as a focus for future basic and applied investigation.

As illustrated in Fig. 1, the presentation of internal or external stimuli evokes a process of generalized autonomic activation. This activation, if of sufficient intensity, serves as a CS which enhances arousal. Upon cognitive assessment of internal states, the individual is prepared to further attend to the stimuli. This internal assessment is dependent on levels of psychogenic stimuli, ability to maintain attention, and competing proprioceptive cues. For example, if the individual is engaged in deep thought about business demands or has a troubling low back pain, arousal is unlikely to occur. An additional influence on the arousal process is the individual's assessment of the social appropriateness of arousal. Clearly, most humans have sets of discriminative cues which deter-

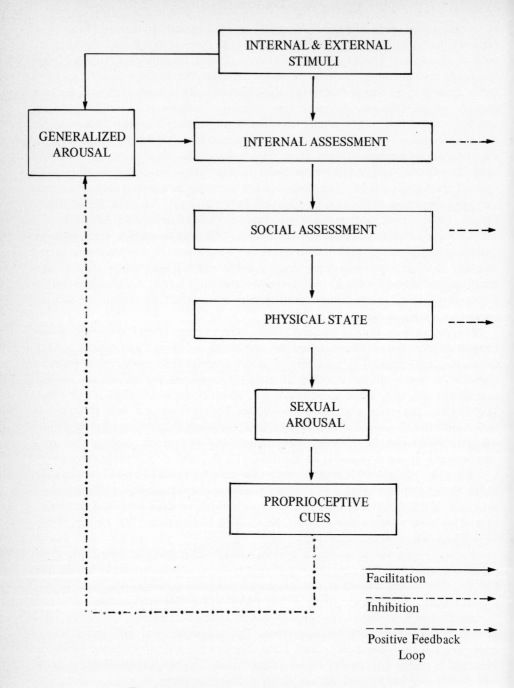

Fig. 1. Cognitive-Physiological Model of Sexual Arousal

mine, the occasion for response; whereas tumescence, for instance, may be elicited while watching a beautiful film star at a movie theater, it is less likely to occur while walking along a crowded beach. A final necessary condition for arousal to occur is the physical capability to respond: denervation and autonomic neuropathy due to organic pathologies or drug states are crucial factors in the ability of the organism to become aroused. However, once aroused, proprioceptive cues become stimuli which continue to sustain arousal.

In sum, we support Masters and Johnson's (1970) dictum that the practicing sex therapist should be fully versed in the literature on sexual arousal. A clearer conceptualization of the technical utility of present treatment techniques, as well as future innovations will thus be fostered. Moreover, without a broad knowledge of the determinants, mediating factors, and the range of sexual behavior, therapists could not begin to allay the fears and misconceptions of their clients. With this broad range of knowledge, information and specific suggestions can be readily given, even in time-limited situations (cf. Annon, 1974).

ISSUES OF ASSESSMENT CREDIBILITY: FACTORS AFFECTING PRETREATMENT DECISIONS

Beyond the descriptive domain of what constitutes sexual dysfunction, how it should be classified, measured, and examined psychophysiologically, comes the more heated and subjective concern of under what conditions is treatment indicated and the sociopsychological rationales for making these decisions (Ullmann & Krasner, 1975). The literature dealing with these concerns appears to fall into three areas. The first deals with the socio-ethical debate of who to treat and when to treat, an issue that arose dramatically when agents of the broader social milieu—gay liberation activists—demanded that behavior therapists cease "treating" homosexuals. The second presents the variety of targets for intervention (what to treat) derived from an equally diverse set of bio-psycho-sociological formulations of etiology. The third returns to the area of "deviancy," and an issue of inappropriate classification and undifferentiated treatment schemas. Also, examples of effective differential treatment in systematic desensitization are mentioned for "non-deviant" disorders. However, prior to any discussion of who, when or what to treat, a brief review of various nosological systems and their utility will be presented.

Classification of Sexual Dysfunction

The three major proponents of sex therapy each have their own idiosyncratic classification systems for sexual dysfunctions (Annon, 1974, 1975; Kaplan, 1974: Masters & Johnson, 1970). For the most part, these typologies are based on a descriptive appraisal of the individual's sexual repertoire in terms of deficits and surfeits. Etiological formulations from the full spectrum of theoretical rationales are available for each diagnostic category in Kaplan's system, while Masters and Johnson remain satisfied in reporting composite histories for each dysfunction. Classification is given a significant role in determining subsequent treatment procedures in all systems. A variety of standard techniques for specific dysfunctions have been developed; for example, Seman's (1956) procedure for premature ejaculation and Kegel's (1952) exercises for increasing the strength and

		MALE	FEMALE
PNS:	vascongestion (erection, vaginal swelling and lubrication, mytonia)	erectile dysfunction (impotence)	general sexual dysfunction (frigidity)
SNS:	orgasmic component (involuntary spasmodic clonic discharge of certain genital muscles)	premature ejaculation retarded ejaculation	orgasmic dysfunction
			vaginismus
			sexual anesthesia or conversion

Fig. 2. Kaplan's Classification System

flexibility of vaginal (pubococcygeal) muscles. However, as later elaborated, Masters and Johnson, Kaplan, Ellis, Lazarus, and others, employ broad spectrum therapy packages, giving the same treatment to all patients (with the exception of deleting or adding specific-problem techniques as required). Others, however, focus on well defined areas, employing only those measures which are problem mandated (Annon, 1974).

More specifically, the three nosologies do show variation in structure. Kaplan interestingly divides her schema long the lines of biphasic sexual functioning (sympathetic and parasympathetic innervation) in both sexes. This is readily shown with a 2 X 2 contingency table with two cells appended on the female variable (see Fig. 2).

Masters and Johnson, on the other hand, classify disorders into ejaculation problems and problems of primary and secondary impotence. For women, they construct four categories: primary orgasmic dysfunction, situational anorgasmia, vaginismus, and dyspareunia. Annon (1974, 1975) dispenses with the descriptive nosology outlined by Masters and Johnson, preferring to follow within the behavioral assessment framework proposed by Kanfer and Saslow (1969), terming sexual problems as either behavioral deficits or surfeits. In addition he expands his treatment perspective to include the full range of sexual deviancy (fetishistic, transvestic, pedophiliac, etc. behaviors). Moreover, unlike the previous mentioned authors, Annon strives to maintain the highest congruity possible between assessment outcome and level of treatment administered.

Who to Treat, and When is Treatment Indicated?

The unquestioned extension of behavior therapy to the treatment of sexual orientation has been recently challenged by a number of behavioral psychologists (Davison, 1974, 1976; Davison & Wilson, 1973; Franks & Wilson, 1974; Money, 1972; O'Leary & Wilson, 1975; Wilson & Davison, 1974). Behavior therapy is touted as an unbiased and neutral set of procedures and principles for *how* to change rather than a system of ethics or social values. In their survey of American and British behavior therapists, Davison and Wilson (1973) report minimal sensitivity to the orientation issue among respondents, but, except for Freund's (1960) aversion therapy enterprise, most programs avoid directly imposing society's values on homosexuals.

However, Davison (1974, 1976) later issued a stronger challenge, supported by Money (1972), that the simple availability of change-of-orientation programs strengthens social prejudices against homosexuals, while increasing their self-hate and desire to change. Clearly, therapeutic intervention *per se* is *not* a neutral event; the availability of behavior change methods encourages their use. Many clinicians surveyed do not attend to factors of why this client population seeks to change; others report that homosexuality *ipso facto* is changeworthy (see Bieber, 1976). Therefore, Davison suggests that we stop engaging in voluntary therapy programs aimed at altering choices of adult partners to whom the client is attracted. The focus instead should be on desensitizing individuals to socially elicited guilt and shame while providing them with skills to ensure adjustment in their chosen sexual orientation. Fensterheim (1972), Lazarus (1971), Kohlenberg (1974) and Halleck (1976) are examples of therapists reporting efforts to help adjust homosexuals to a more satisfactory and permanent homosexual identity.

Several standard-bearers of behavior therapy (Bandura, 1969; Ullmann & Krasner, 1975) have long maintained that the goals of therapy are founded upon the client's personal goals; a laudable position in theory but without applied utility in many instances (e.g., court-ordered interventions). Addressing this issue, I. Evans (in press) has suggested 6 criteria to guide clinicians in determining the harmfulness of a client's deviancy: (1) degree of anxiety, guilt or distress associated with it; (2) conflict with the law; (3) degree to which activity is limited to deviancy; (4) pain, discomfort or distress caused to others; (5) reduction of opportunities to establish close interpersonal relationships with others; and (6) interference with important aspects of life or occupation of an overly important position in life.

What to Treat?

Therapists choose their entree for intervention from among three levels of client functioning: the physiological, the cognitive and the psychosocial. Many practitioners, including Masters and Johnson (1970), Hartman and Fithian (1973), and LoPiccolo (Lobitz & LoPiccolo, 1972; LoPiccolo & Miller, 1975) structure their interventions to deal with all three, using so called "broad spectrum" therapies. However, other therapists legitimately separate their targets of intervention and it is useful to discuss them from the triparte perspective.

Physiological targets

Treating the symptom *per se* is not only possible, but efficacious, as demonstrated by the success of both Kegel's (1952) exercises for promoting a more sexually responsive vagina, and Haslam's (1965) graded dilators for the treatment of vaginismus along the lines of successive approximation (Annon, 1974). In a study reported by Deutch (1968), Kegel exercises alone produced improvement in 65 percent of the non-orgasmic females. Some erectile and orgasmic dysfunctional problems are easily handled through instructions of how and when to masturbate, which provide simple discrimination learning of what constitutes ejaculatory inevitability for males and the orgasmic phase for females.

The "squeeze" technique, genital "teasing" and "caressing" procedures, and mutual examinations to determine sexually responsive zones among partners represent additional procedures employed by Masters and Johnson and Hartman and Fithian with direct consequences for this level of sexual functioning.

Cognitive Targets

Cognitive variables are systematically attacked during the early phases of intervention in most therapies. Misinformation and irrational fears may account for a large percentage of the variance in client problems (Pion, 1975). Sayner and Durrell (1975) go so far as to assert that, "Most impotent men require no formal treatment once accepting that penile-vaginal intercourse is but one way of satisfying a woman." Runciman (1975) purports that 97% of non-orgasmic females are victims of traditional anti-sexual values, unreal concepts of marriage, lack of information about the subject, low body image, preoccupation with other priorities, fatigue, and/or early trauma associated with sex. Carol Lassen (1976) adds that there are positive aspects of self-concept in non-orgasmic women which offer resistance to sexual responsiveness. Notions that sexual license is selfish and unfeminine, it is more important to be respected than be sexual, and the satisfaction of one's partner is paramount are instances of adaptive behaviors and attitudes in certain life situations.

The most commonly mentioned psychological formulation of sexual dysfunction and deviancy for both sexes is founded on the conditioning of fear model (Husted, 1975; Kraft and Al-Issa, 1967; Lazarus, 1963). When sexual situations come to evoke fear of failure, fear of pain, fear of fear (see I. Evans, 1972), heterophobia, and so forth, the concomitant anxiety and innervation of the sympathetic nervous system, as mentioned earlier, effectively interrupts the sexual arousal mechanism — vascongestion, lubrication, tumescence, formation of orgasmic platform—inhibiting performance. The ease with which performance demands for males can be linked with fear of failure, and subsequently conditioned avoidance, is illustrated by Masters and Johnson (1970, p. 164-168) in a discussion concerning secondary impotence attributed to alcohol ingestion.[1]

As a cognitive variable influencing sexual responsivity, fantasy has received little research attention. However, Laws and Rubin (1969) have demonstrated that erection may be achieved with voluntary control, possibly mediated via fantasy. From a theoretical stance, McGuire, Carlisle, and Young (1965) posit that repeated masturbation to deviant fantasies endow these fantasies with exaggerated erotic value, which then function as powerful directors of deviant sexual behavior. On an applied plane, Wish (1975) suggests fantasizing and the use of imagery-based counseling techniques to enhance arousal and overcome inhibitory cognitions. Along similar lines, Runciman (1975) believes that an absence of erotic fantasy life for some non-orgasmic women plays a causal role.

Psychosocial Targets

Masters and Johnson and their followers are dogmatic in their basic premise that the "patient" in sex therapy is the marital relationship. In conjoint marital unit therapy, an

---

[1] A recent study by Farkas and Rosen (1976) examined the *acute* effect of alcohol on penile tumescence in the human male. Their data suggest that high dosages of alcohol cause acute depression of erectile responses.

uninvolved partner is not treated. Sex problems are presumed to be a function of the inadequate information, negative sex attitudes, unrealistic expectations, etc., mentioned before but, more importantly, result from a breakdown of interpersonal communicaton concerning sexual needs and desires. Masters and Johnson state that communication failures in the bedroom will ultimately extend to every phase of married life. Lazarus (1971), however, believes that

> Defensive, guarded, or competitive relationships make gaps in communication of which sexual incompetence is often the most obvious *consequence.* A therapeutic program which focuses *primarily* on establishing or reestablishing open verbal and nonverbal communication between partners and *secondarily* upon the mechanics of sexual performance (e.g., Masters and Johnson, 1970) is more likely to succeed and endure than treatments which emphasize mechanics over and above the context of overt and covert communication. (p. 350) [Editor's italics]

Therefore, when sexual patterns are intricately interwoven with marital patterns, then, as Runciman prosaically put it, "As the husband goes, so goes his penis." Bandura (1969) concurs, arguing that proper assessment requires identifying the critical controlling stimuli and determining the functional value of sexual dysfunction. When orgasmic inadequacy is the result of generalized attitudes of hostility toward men rather than a conditioned avoidance response maintained by sex-specific anxiety, then modification of hostile behavior is the proper target for therapy.

Differential Diagnosis and Treatment

"Deviants"

Wilson (1973) sounds a disquieting note in his appraisal of current practices in assessment: "Matching of different techniques to particular problems in behavior therapy is a matter of guesswork plus trial and error." Nowhere does this ring more true than in the research and treatment carried out on individuals with "deviant" sexual preferences. With regard to homosexuals in particular, behavior therapy stands in judgement of perpetuating the patient uniformity myth (Kiesler, 1966), when it should be tailoring procedures to the individual (Wilson & Davison, 1974). Researchers have concentrated their attention on devising research strategies to suppress deviant responses (see Marks, 1976 for a recent review) and have constructed assessment devices to record the suppression effects. Freund (1963, 1965, 1967) and McConaghy (1967) assert the validity for diagnosing sexual pathology using sensitive penile instrumentation, while the more socially relevant topography of behavior engaged in by homosexuals, the heterosexual aspects of their lives, and even the differences between male and female homosexuals remains uncharted. Responding to this, Money (1972) suggests that behavior therapists design strategies permitting homosexuals to fall in love heterosexually. Money believes that it is not sex (coition) *per se* that should be the target behavior, rather the desire and the ability to fall in love are the most important areas in need of intervention.

However, the treatment of choice among clinicians has been aversion therapy techniques aimed at suppressing erotic attraction to inappropriate stimuli (e.g., Feldman & MacCulloch, 1965). What is emerging, though, is a recognition that homosexuals with little prior heterosexual interest seldom respond favorably to aversion techniques (Feldman & MacCulloch, 1971). The accepted hypothesis that alternative "normal" patterns of attraction would emerge when deviant arousal is eliminated (the hydraulic principle) has not been borne out.

Clearly, as Kinsey (and earlier, Freud, 1962) stated, homosexuals are not alike! Those with a history of pleasurable heterosexual behavior have a favorable prognosis for changing their orientation using aversion procedures or possibly through training in hetero-social skills and desensitization to heterophobic stimuli (Barlow, 1972). This type of individual is termed a "secondary homosexual." Primary homosexuality, on the other hand is refractory to behavior change programs and, according to Feldman and MacCulloch, is probably constitutionally determined (also see, R. Evans, 1972). If the distinction between primary and secondary homosexuality is a valid one, then treatment strategies for primary homosexuality should deal with enabling the person to make a satisfactory homosexual adjustment rather than attempting to reverse his preference. Critics of the Feldman and MacCulloch analysis point out that the logic of their research paradigm using anticipated avoidance precluded behavioral analysis of the presenting problem, while their primary/secondary distinction is a hazardous one based on outcome of a therapy regime (Wilson & Davison, 1974).

"Normals"

For certain "non-deviant" sexual dysfunctions, matching problems with techniques is becoming refined as outcome studies provide more adequate guidelines. This is most apparent in the literature dealing with the selective use of systematic desensitization (Husted, 1975; Kraft & Al-Issa, 1967; Lazarus, 1963). Simply stated, systematic desensitization is applicable when anxiety, fear, and/or repulsion at contact with sex partners are the main inhibiting factors preventing normal sexual responses (Kraft & Al-Issa, 1967). In the graded *in vivo* sensate focus exercises, anxiety decreases through non-demand contact with sexual arousal emerging as a result, thereby inhibiting any residual anxiety.

Systematic desensitization has been used extensively in cases of vaginismus, when there are aversive and anxiety reactions to sexual situations, or even when the reaction is neutral, and possibly hidden. It is contra-indicated in cases where the woman enjoys foreplay and coitus and experiences arousal without orgasm, but reaches orgasm via non-coital stimulation (Husted, 1975). Failures in Lazarus' (1963) desensitization program for anorgasmic women were those who held extremely negative attitudes, could not produce sexual images, were unmotivated, had homosexual preferences and used their sexual disinclinations as leverage in their marital relationship. Of more importance are observations by McGovern, Stewart, and LoPiccolo(1975) and Husted (1975) concerning differences between primary and secondary orgasmic women. McGovern, et al. found that anxiety reduction and skill training cured primary but not secondary anorgasmics. Rather, the latter group of women, who chose to reach orgasm through rigid and con-strained methods of masturbating, required primarily marital interventions. Husted, however, suggests reduction of anxiety significantly increases the rate of performance for women with orgasmic histories, but for those without prior experience, a lack of anxiety does not insure completion of the sexual response cycle. Still, training can thus be suggested, following LoPiccolo's approach (Lobitz & LoPiccolo, 1972).

Brady (1966, 1969) offers a modification of systematic desensitization based on the induction of high levels of relaxation through Brevital. In 16 of 24 frigidity cases treated, Brevital produced "greatly improved" responding. Kraft (1967, 1969) reports Brevital's successful application to premature ejaculation and impotence. Brady adds that Brevital-aided desensitization plus insight oriented psychotherapy is indicated for cases where sexual dysfunctions are presented with other clinical conditions. Finally, Kockott, Dittmar, and Nusselt (1975), in a controlled study, found that desensitization alone did change impotent males' attitudes towards sexual situations but had no effect on their sexual behavior.

TECHNIQUES OF SEX THERAPY: ISSUES OF TECHNICAL ECLECTICISM AND COMPONENT RESEARCH

The literature explicating the therapeutic packages available for treating sexual problems is a rich source for delineating issues pertinent to behavior therapy. Of these, the most crucial is the failure of practitioners to distinguish between the simple application of behavioral techniques (often as an adjunct to other procedures), and the broader theoretical and assessment rationales from which they were derived. In short, this represents the issue of behavior therapies versus behavior therapy; an issue elegantly stated by Wilson and Evans (1967).

The purpose of this section is to demonstrate how techniques of behavioral sex therapy have made a digression from their original use by hard-core behavioral clinicians to become adjuncts to conventional psychotherapy or unindentifiable elements within broader sexual treatment packages. A brief description of the popular "broad spectrum" sex therapies is presented first, followed by cursory mention of the few outcome studies appraising the Masters and Johnson procedures. Finally, a detailed presentation is given of the numerous behavior change programs derived from behavior therapy. For perspective, it can be mentioned that the purpose of this section is to foster a basis for contrast with the final portion of this paper, dealing with integrated behavioral sex therapy.

The Sex Therapy Packages

Masters and Johnson

Although Masters and Johnson are not behavior therapists, their two-week intensive program is decidely behavioral. A social learning analysis of their treatment (O'Leary & Wilson, 1975) reveals that they take a strong pedagogical role; incorporating procedures of extinction, modeling, reciprocal reinforcement, and communication training. While only couples are treated, unmarried singles are seen with a partner. Moreover, a male/female co-therapist team is stipulated as necessary to provide appropriate sex models and sources of identification. The dual therapist team is also assumed to (1) insure sensitivity to the male:female aspects of the problem, (2) serve as a check against biased information and (3) provide spokespersons for the same sex client.

The preliminary sessions are devoted to exhaustive history-taking and a medical exam. These are followed by "round-table" sessions where therapists provide feedback to the couple on how they function sexually and how they affect each other in their marital interactions. Based on the formulation that sexual difficulties are a function of performance-related fear, couples are first prohibited from any sexual activity not specifically sanctioned by the therapists. Then, all couples embark on a program of "sensate focus," where

> Clients are taught to think and feel sensuously by giving and getting bodily pleasure, first by non-genital contact and then by specific genital stimulation. . . . The fundamental significance of the sensate focus exercises is in increasing verbal and non-verbal communication between partners and in teaching them that sexual gratification does not depend on coitus. As sexual arousal spontaneously occurs in these "homework" assignments, the treatment is oriented towards the specific form of sexual inadequacy in question (O'Leary & Wilson, 1975, pp. 292-293).

For each dysfunction a set of tasks is prescribed which offers *in vivo* desensitization and erotic reconditioning. For example, premature ejaculation is dealt with using a modified Seman's technique; a gradual shaping procedure beginning with manual caressing and culminating in mutual thrusting with the female partner squeezing the penis beneath the coronal ridge just prior to ejaculatory inevitability. For impotency, a series of "non-demand" steps are initiated with sensate focus exercises until erection occurs spontaneously, then follows a "teasing technique" of repeated erection and relaxation to extinguish the fear of losing an erection and the inability to re-elicit it. Finally non-demand intromission is begun with the woman controlling the insertion and progressively more vigorous thrusting until orgasm occurs involuntarily. As was mentioned earlier, vaginismus and dyspareunia are dealt with by the male partner inserting a set of graded dilators. To increase orgasmic responses, the woman is first encouraged to show her partner what she finds stimulating, especially with respect to genital stimulation; then the couple proceeds to nondemanding penile insertion with the woman in the superior coital position controlling the pace at all times so as to ensure full expression of her own needs.

Hartman and Fithian

Hartman and Fithian (1973) have extended Masters and Johnson's format with a broader range of therapeutic interventions. Some of the additions they make to the procedures outlined above include the administration of psychological tests such as Draw-A-Person, MMPI, and Luscher Color Test (which appears to be unrelated to later therapy) as well as body imagery exercises where the person stands in front of a mirror to make an objective appraisal of their totally nude body so that fears of flaws are dispelled. Clients are also told to explore body feelings by systematically touching themselves from head to toe. Next they engage in a fantasy excursion through the inner regions of their body reporting on the nature of their "inner environment."

Other innovations from Hartman and Fithian include: the use of hypnosis for relaxing anxious clients and suggesting future arousal, and a formal sexological examination of each client in the presence of their partner for educational purposes. Moreover, there is extensive use of films and videotapes to teach and desensitize. Also included in the 13 day therapeutic program are hair combing and bath assignments, one and a half hours of foot and face caressing, and the therapeutic expression of a non-verbal goodbye at termination (see Hartman & Fithian, 1973, p. 203).

Ellis

Ellis (1975) maintains categorically that his rational-emotive approach encompasses those procedures used by the aforementioned therapy teams. The system postulated by Ellis is founded on the belief that all problems stem from the escalation of irrational beliefs. His broad-spectrum tactics in sex treatment attack inappropriate cognitions, emotions and behaviors. At the cognitive level, therapist testimony, films and other modalities are used to remove irrational ideas regarding sex; imagery methods are used to improve the client's ability to fantasize intensely and face sexually disappointing situations without negative thoughts; "anti awfulizing" and "anti-absolutizing" cognitive practice is also carried out to change irrational thoughts about sexual performance. Sex related emotions are changed therapeutically after the therapist has demonstrated his acceptance of the client and then proceeds to launch a "shame attack" followed by risk-taking exercises and emotive verbalizations of sexual feelings. Finally, Ellis acknowledges the behavior therapists' standard repertoire and the special techniques associated with Masters and Johnson as integral parts of the rational-emotive method.

LoPiccolo

In a sex therapy program at the University of Oregon, LoPiccolo has directed the treatment of approximately 25 couples per year since 1969. Following a social learning framework, a number of techniques have been innovated or adapted from existing procedures to construct a highly successful package for the treatment of sexual dysfunction. Lobitz and LoPiccolo (1972) summarize the clinic's operations and present details of the new methods employed. Essentially there are five classes of innovations: (1) daily record forms detail for the therapists data on pleasure and arousal gains of the couples, and refundable penalty deposits insure that the recordings and other homework are not forgotten; (2) masturbation procedures (Annon, 1973; Davison, 1968; Marquis, 1970) for conditioning clients' arousal to each other are used with fantasy stimuli as well as *in vivo* cues; for non-orgasmic women, LoPiccolo's nine-step masturbation program is implemented first; (3) interpersonal sexual skills are taught through modeling and role playing, focusing on appropriate behaviors for the initiation of sexual contact, refusal, and emotional assertion; (4) disinhibition of sexuality for women is also brought about through role playing and therapist self-disclosure; in role-play the woman is instructed to act out a gross exaggeration of orgasm with violent convulsions and inarticulate screaming, this presumably extinguishes fears concerning loss of control and the demonstration of intense arousal; (5) to maintain therapeutic gains, the final meetings in the 15-session program are planned by the clients themselves, thus insuring their preparation for dealing with problems which may arise after therapy has terminated.

In passing, it is of interest to note that more recently LoPiccolo (LoPiccolo & Miller, 1975) has sought to bond these innovative behavioral techniques with "sensitivity" exercises in a weekend encounter program for enhancing sexual relations of non-dysfunctional couples. Assessing the effects of the group experiences pre-post and against a control group, the Sexual Interaction Inventory (LoPiccolo & Steger, 1973) reflected significant gains that were maintained at a three-month follow-up.

Outcome Studies: Testing the Package and Its Components

By all accounts, Masters and Johnson have an effective treatment program. Of the initial 790 individuals treated, only 18.9 percent were failures at the end of the two-week therapy. The overall success rate five years after the end of therapy showed only a slight drop to 74.5 percent. Divorce statistics also showed an interesting trend at the five year follow-up. Of the 155 couples sampled, eight out of the nine who had either filed for legal separation or who had been divorced during therapy described reconstituted marriages. Only four couples had filed for separation or were divorced during this period.

However, as Franks and Wilson (1974) eloquently question: Are the innovative embellishments added to the traditional behavioral methods in the New Sex Therapies really necessary and do they increase therapeutic efficacy? Clearly, what is required is an analysis of the necessary and sufficient conditions for treating the various forms of sexual inadequacy.

To date, few studies have attempted to isolate the effective elements found in Masters and Johnson's package. However, at least one claim appears to be unsubstantiated. Brady (1969), Lazarus (1963), Madsen and Ullmann (1967), and Wolpe (1969) have all successfully treated sexually dysfunctional women *without* a female co-therapist, while Franks and Wilson (1974) report that many other behavior therapists have stated that a co-therapist of the opposite sex is rarely essential.

Husted (1975) and Obler (1975) add empirical weight to the single-therapist postulate and question the necessity for other components as well. Husted attempted to compare imaginal and *in vivo* (sensate focus) desensitization for orgasmic dysfunctional women with and without partners in therapy. She purposefully excluded sex re-education and attitude change procedures, masturbation instructions, and Kegel exercises. From the outcome, Husted concluded that imaginal systematic desensitization by itself is a fast and efficient method for reducing anxiety and inhibitions regarding sexual behavior, and reliably produces behavioral generalization. Moreover, there were no differences between those clients whose partners attended the sessions and those which were unaccompanied. Using only single clients with diverse sexual problems, Obler (1975) sought to test a low-cost package which included desensitization to slides and films, GSR feedback for anxiety, assertion and confidence training. With success determined via physiological, cognitive, and *in situ* behavioral measures, 80 percent of the clients treated overcame their disorders. That is, success occurred without co-therapist teams, partners in therapy, sensate focus exercises, and other components central to Masters and Johnson.

In another study assessing the components of therapy for orgasmic dysfunctional women, Robinson (1974) exposed clients to videotapes of models undergoing sex therapy. Robinson attempted to measure attitude and behavior change related to masturbatory practice. Both of Robinson's treatment groups viewed models receiving limited information concerning self-stimulatory practices as well as specific suggestions concerning self-exploration. In addition, one of Robinson's groups was first exposed to videotapes in which models were given a wide range of sexual information designed to initially modify attitudes.

Robinson's results indicate that both groups changed their attitudes regarding masturbation only after viewing the behavioral series of tapes (specific suggestions, limited information). Moreover, behavior change occurred without prior exposure to the tapes designed to elicit attitude change.

Behavioral Methods for Modification of Sexual Response

As Franks and Wilson (1974) are quick to point out, the individual components of the Masters and Johnson approach are not novel, but have been well documented in the behavioral literature since the early 1960's. Wolpe and Lazarus (1966) provided a detailed description of such procedures as the Seman's technique, graded sexual responses to ensure the dominance of sexual arousal over anxiety, non-demand procedures for coitus, *in vivo* desensitization, and the importance of partner participation in the treatment process. The following section summarizes the major traditional methods for treating sexual inadequacy and deviancy and includes a few promising ones of more recent origin. These procedures are organized into four functional categories: anxiety extinction techniques; reconditioning and counterconditioning procedures for increasing erotic attraction; methods for suppressing erotic attraction to deviant stimuli, and; modeling and prompting techniques for teaching novel sex behaviors.

Extinction of Competing Anxiety Responses

The function of anxiety as an inhibitor of sexual responding (the SAM), and the prominent role which the anxiety reduction paradigm has played in sex therapy have been mentioned previously. The sensate focus and non-demand caressing exercises leading to small and consistant increments in coital performance are construed behaviorally as *in vivo* desensitization (O'Leary & Wilson, 1975). Imaginal desensitization with relaxation training (Husted, 1975; Lazarus, 1963; Madsen & Ullmann, 1967; Obler, 1975; Wish, 1975; Wolpe & Lazarus, 1966) or with Brevital (Brady, 1966) are commonly applied to several types of dysfunctions and are often followed by specific skill training procedures.

Kraft (1971) provides an interesting example of desensitization used to treat heterophobia and urinal anxiety in a 22-year-old male homosexual patient. First hypnosis, and later Methohexitone sodium were used to relax the client. This was followed by the presentation of two hierarchies: one related to visiting a toilet at an Underground station in London as increasingly more people came in; the other consisted of a graded series of situations of increasing intimacy with girls, starting with kissing and finally leading to sexual intercourse in various positions. By the 14th session, the patient was able to use public urinals without difficulty and sometime after the 47th session he was enjoying intercourse with an older girl. Kraft reports that as his cient became increasingly heterosexual, he had a differential impact on two of his close gay friends: one began to show more interest in girls and the other began to show less interest in the patient.

Reconditioning Erotic Attraction

Counterconditioning or reconditioning of sexual responses has been implemented through pairing orgasm and other sexual UCSs with previously neutral stimuli. In an early study, Rachman (1967) paired slides of nude women with slides of knee-length women's boots to produce conditioned arousal. Thorpe, Schmidt, and Castell (1964) were the first to use orgasmic pairing clinically when they attempted to modify homosexual preferences through pairing masturbation with heterosexual pictures and fantasies. Later, Davison (1968), Marquis (1970) and Annon (1973) advanced similar methods for orgasmic reconditioning which other clinicians have been quick to employ (Lobitz & LoPiccolo, 1972; Sayner & Durrell, 1975, Wilson, 1973). Davison's article dealt with the elimination of a sadistic fantasy by having the client use the deviant fantasy to achieve arousal and then masturbate to orgasm while looking at *Playboy* pictures. To promote generalization, "real life" pictorial stimuli gradually replaced the magazine pictures, with Davison prompting his client to use heterosexual ideation. When the client failed to discard the sadistic fantasy, covert sensitization was used, with Davison articulating a scene involving a scatological incident.

Marquis (1970) suggests a procedure where a set of appropriate fantasies are developed first, followed by masturbation to the point of ejaculatory inevitability using whatever fantasy is most arousing. At this point, the appropriate fantasy is introduced and on subsequent trials these fantasies are gradually shifted backward in time. Sayner and Durrell (1975) suggest using this technique to pair arousal with disliked body parts; Wilson (1973) used it successfully to treat vaginismus by having the women imagine first minimal finger insertion prior to orgasm and then imagine increasing amounts of insertion progressively earlier in the arousal cycle.

Non-orgasmic UCSs have also been used in classical conditioning paradigms to increase heterosexual attraction. Barlow and his colleagues (Barlow & Agras, 1973; Herman, Barlow, & Agras, 1974) report two different procedures for conditioning arousal in homosexual clients to slides of nude females. In the first study, explicit controls were used to isolate the effects of conditioning. Slides and movies of nude males (UCS) were paired with nude female slides in a design that consisted of alternating backward pairing and classical conditioning procedures. Two of the three subjects showed sharp increases in heterosexual arousal during the classical conditioning phase only. In the second study, attempts were made to alter stimulus control of sexual arousal through a fading technique. Slides of nude females were faintly superimposed on colored slides of arousing nude males. Developing an erection from looking at the male nudes served to fade out the attractive slide and fade in the female. The clients advanced through sixteen graded exposure steps, contingent on maintaining erection, until they were able to achieve criterion arousal to the heterosexual slide alone. With these results, the authors suggest that aversion techniques may not be necessary for treating the homosexually-oriented.

Beech, Watts, & Poole (1971) treated a heterosexual pedophile using a method conceptually similar to the one just mentioned. Pictures of very young, prepubescent girls were used as the UCS, paired with pictures of progressively more mature girls. When the pictures of the older, more mature girls became arousing, these in turn became the UCS and were paired with pictures of still older girls until the pedophile was emitting proper arousal to pictures of appropriately mature and nubile women.

Paradoxically, an aversion paradigm has also been used to increase erotic attraction. It was reported that when the offset of a noxious condition was paired with the presentation of heterosexual stimuli, "relief" and "safe" responses could be conditioned to thse stimuli. Thorpe, Schmidt, Brown, and Castell (1964) were the first to initiate aversion relief in their treatment of sexual deviation. Twenty-three words connoting deviant experiences were projected up on the screen each followed by shock. The last word in the series described a "normal" activity, such as "heterosexual," and signified the end of the shocking experience.

Aversion-relief, as practiced by Feldman and MacCulloch (1965, 1971) has been applied to the largest number of cases in the literature. Although these authors claim that aversion-relief works to inhibit heterosexual anxiety, McConaghy (1969) in comparing electrical aversion therapy with relief pairing and chemical aversion without this element found no significant differences between the groups on subsequent heterosexual desire. Barlow (1973, 1974) registers dismay that in an empirical endeavour like behavior therapy, a therapeutic technique found ineffective in 150 cases would continue to be employed. Bancroft (1971), on the other hand, reports that the use of aversive stimuli in a punishment paradigm to extinguish inappropriate low-level erections paradoxically facilitates tumescence during non-aversive heterosexual trials. This "behavioral contrast" effect has been independently replicated by other investigators as well (Barlow, Leitenberg, & Agras, 1969; Gelder & Marks, 1969).

Suppression of Erotic Attraction

A number of clinicians operate on the assumption that once erotic responses to deviant stimuli are suppressed or counterconditioned, normal heterosexual outlets will develop (Bond & Evans, 1967). The fallacy of this hydraulic principle was noted earlier, yet aversion procedures continue to be used in the absence of complementary efforts to condition viable response alternatives (cf. Feldman, 1966).

Social Deviancy: Emetic drugs, electrical shock, and covert sensitization are popular methods employed by aversion therapists to reduce "deviant" arousal to same-sex partners. Max (1935) was the first to pair high levels of electric shock with the patient's homosexual fantasies to cause a "diminuition of the emotional value of the sexual stimulus." Freund (1960) and James (1962) followed with injections of apomorphine mixtures; nauseating emitics that were applied in conjunction with flashing slides of nude males. Both authors devised additional procedures for stimulating heterosexual desires. Freund administered testosterone propionate before showing films of nude women; James did likewise plus added a procedure where he woke his client every 2 hours to play a tape recording optimistically explaining the future consequences of not being homosexual.

Following these early examples, a host of fear conditioning studies involving homosexuals, fetishists, and pedophiles were performed in which shocks were contingently delivered for production of fantasies, erections, and affections to "inappropriate" pictorial stimuli (e.g., Birk, Huddleston, Miller, & Cohler, 1971; Evans, 1967, 1968, 1970; Feldman & MacCulloch, 1965; Fookes, 1969; Marks & Gelder, 1967; Marks, Gelder, & Bancroft, 1970; MacCulloch & Feldman, 1967; McGuire & Valance, 1964; Thorpe & Schmidt, 1964). The outcome of these studies indicate that shock punishment is more effective when it is (1) actually administered at some occasion during the avoidance procedure, (2) applied during the actual deviant act or a close representation of the act, and (3) delivered contingently upon clear evidence of arousal such as increases in penile tumescence (Callahan & Leitenberg, 1973). More recently, however, evidence from case presentations and well-designed control studies using covert sensitization (Barlow, et al., 1969; Barlow, et al., 1970; Callahan & Leitenberg, 1973; Davison, 1968) strongly challenges the necessity for nociceptive stimuli as used in aversion paradigms.

Criticisms of Anticipatory Avoidance: Feldman and MacCulloch's application of anticipatory avoidance learning to the treatment of homosexuality is an effort to translate learning principles derived from basic research into an applied strategy. Based on a desire to reproduce the unextinguishable avoidance learning prominently demonstrated by Solomon, Kamin, and Wynne (1953) with canines, Feldman and MacCulloch exposed their clients to a mixture of four trials including escape, pure avoidance, partial and delayed avoidance. An issue has arisen, however, as to whether this effort represents an extension of Solomon's laboratory procedures or whether it is perhaps purely metaphorical. Rachman and Teasdale (1969) cite the confounding of operant and classical conditioning paradigms as their major criticism of the procedure and maintain that the classical trials (non-avoidable shock) account for the outcome. MacDonough (1972) lists several additional problems with Feldman and MacCulloch's approach: (1) the un-avoidable shock trials and other prematurely introduced parameters actually impair the acquisition of avoidance responses to the male slides; (2) inappropriate terminology is used to describe the procedures—for example, the terms "reinforced" and "non-reinforced" trials as applied to the avoidance and non-avoidance conditions respectively, are inappropriate since no reinforcing stimuli are applied or withheld contingent upon the avoidance response; (3) the procedure represents a theoretical compendium which hinders a functional analysis of techniques and outcomes.

Perhaps the most damaging shortcoming of this method is noted by O'Leary and Wilson (1975). These authors point out that both avoidance conditioning and the intermittent schedules derive their high resistance to extinction from the inability of the animal to discriminate between the reinforcement contingencies operating during acquisition and extinction. Patients used in these studies differ from infrahumans, however, in that they are undoubtedly aware that shock contingencies are not present for homosexual behavior in the natural environment. Generalization of treatment effects cannot be accounted for, or logically predicted by Feldman and MacCulloch's procedural rationale.

Modeling Techniques

Although observational learning techniques, pioneered by Bandura (1969), have seen widespread usage in psychotherapeutic interventions, vicarious learning has only recently been applied as an ameliorative tool in cases of sexual dysfunction. One initial attempt to employ modeling procedures in a sex therapy format was reported by Wincze (1971), who treated a female client that reported anger towards her husband and a lack of sexual interest. Wincze desensitized the client and in separate sessions showed her films depicting various sexual behaviors. Although the desensitization was reportedly effective in reducing subjective anxiety, the vicarious extinction procedures were without therapeutic utility.

Wincze has recently reported that videotaped desensitization is more effective than systematic desensitization in decreasing scores on a fear survey schedule (Wincze & Caird, 1976). Neither method, however, was effective in producing behavioral change in orgasmic dysfunctional women.

Robinson (1974), in a study that was previously described, exclusively used video-taped models in the treatment of orgasmic dysfunctional women. Robinson found that attitude and behavior change could be achieved solely by the use of videotaped models (who were seen undergoing successful therapy which included specific instructions on masturbatory techniques).

TOWARDS AN INTEGRATED BEHAVIOR THERAPY FOR SEXUAL DISORDERS

Given this review of the engaging literature describing the methods, techniques and tactics of sex therapy, it is possible to develop an understanding of what behavioral sex therapy (in fact, behavior therapy in general) should and should not be. This presentation has depicted the current status of the field as an array of autonomous sex therapy programs; some represent eclectic grab-bags of unvalidated procedures derived from clinical intuition, while others which have theoretically deduced techniques are unduly narrow in their application or misapplied across clients. Writers like Kaplan, Ellis, Kraft and others, isolate and extract portions of behavior therapy and insert them pragmatically into their traditional psychotherapies to bolster outcome. Implicit reinforcement for this model of behavior therapy (which sees it as a cookbook collection of tactics) comes from leading behavior modifiers like Lazarus (1971), and Cautella and Upper (1975). These authors often emphasize technology over rationale, broad spectrum intervention with standardized packages versus individualized tailoring, and simplistic steps with "prescriptive formulae" as opposed to an intergration and creation of methods based on assessment and deductions from empirical principles.

The greatest hazard to following a Masters and Johnson, Hartman and Fithian, and Kaplan style of treatment is that their problem formulation and application of a general package to all cases constitutes a static and closed system of intervention. It is essentially devoid of evaluative appraisal, modifiability, and lacks the long range ability to deal with novel sexual dysfunctions.

In striking contrast, behavior therapy as practiced by scientist-professionals within the "empirical-evaluative" paradigm constitutes an open intervention system. The overarching strategy is to attain an integration of objective assessment methodologies with the principles of behavior change derived from empirical studies; an integration producing an individually formulated treatment program for the client with ongoing evaluation and feedback components incorporated. Relying on a set of nomothetic rationales rather than circumscribed formulae allows for flexibility and innovation when dealing with the exigencies of an individual case. In this respect, Wilson's (1973) case studies offer a model of behavior therapy. While treating a client with vaginismus, it was found that proven techniques like imaginal and *in vivo* desensitization were ineffective. Undaunted, Wilson demonstrated how behavior therapists have recourse to alternative procedures and creatively applied Davison's orgasmic reconditioning technique.

In essence, the key to an integrated behavior therapy for sexual dysfunction lies in the establishment of a predictive link between a comprehensive initial assessment and subsequent treatment approach. Clinicians require data for their moment-to-moment decisions in case management. From these data, strategies enabling them to make efficacious changes in their therapeutic procedure are derived. Both Barlow (1974), an applied researcher, and Annon (1974, 1975), a behavioral clinician, have gone the furthest toward conceptualizing schemas that introduce differential treatment based on initial client assessment. The theme cogently stressed by both authors is the necessity for deliberate sequencing of objectives in an ongoing process of behavioral assessment, modification, and feedback of intervention impact. Additionally, these writers emphasize the importance of multi-faceted and broad spectrum efforts, but carried out within a sound theoretically and empirically based plan which assists the clinician in ordering the selection of intervention techniques.

Barlow's (1974) approach to the treatment of sexual deviants is closely aligned with Kanfer and Saslow's (1969) dictum that factors in the patient's life, history, and environment dictate what treatment procedures will be used for which aspect of the patient's problem in a given social setting. Unlike the aversion therapists who choose to eliminate only an inappropriate or excessive arousal response, Barlow acknowledges that four other areas of surfeits and deficits in a client's behavior need assessment. There may be deficiencies in heterosexual arousal or in heterosexual skills; gender role deviation may be present with excesses in opposite gender motoric responses, interests, vocal characteristics and dressing patterns; moreover, there may be excesses and/or deficits in certain biochemical variables which serve a controlling function. Assessment outcome would yield which of the four factors is most relevant to the case and determine, for example, whether heterosexual responsiveness should be increased using systematic desensitization, masturbatory conditioning, or fading, if assertion and interpersonal competency training is required for increasing heterosexual skills, or whether hormones should be given and perhaps training in masculine/feminine role behaviors. Finally, the priority for initiating change in each of these behavioral components should be indicated by the assessment as well.

Annon's (1971) research has led him to develop, test, and refine the first comprehensive conceptual scheme for ordering sexual problems (dysfunctions as well as deviancy) and their treatment from within the learning theory framework. The approach presented by Annon attempts to handle simultaneously four functions: (1) assessment of the full range of circumstances related to the client's problem; (2) ordering priorities for intervention and providing guidelines for timing multiple interventions; (3) avoidance of proffering any particular behavioral technique, but rather developing appropriate procedures based on theoretical analysis; and (4) conducting ongoing evaluation. Annon offers a scheme for ordering sex problems into four levels based on the degree of treatment required for their amelioration. Annon terms this scheme the PLISSIT model, an acronym representing the four levels of treatment he has identified. The first three levels—Permission, Limited Information, Specific Suggestions—comprise the brief therapy approach for behavioral deficits which can be acquired with relative ease in most situations (Annon, 1974). The final level, Intensive Therapy, represents a highly individualized treatment primarily for behavioral excesses that becomes necessary when the briefer treatments are not successful in helping the client reach his/her goals (Annon, 1975). For those sexual problems with a long term duration requiring intensive therapy, Annon concludes that biphasic assessment is necessary: first, analysis of the client's sexual problem from within the A-R-D framework is made (Staats, 1975), that is, an analysis of the valences attached to the sexual stimuli and their hierarchical organization within the A-R-D system; second, a careful evaluation is conducted of relevant behavioral repertoires.

In brief, the strength of Barlow's approach and Annon's PLISSIT model rests on the tailored matching of problem with procedure, and the systematic introduction of graded increments of intervention using minimal influence to adequately alter the behavior in question. Adding levels of treatment complexity only as problem compiexity demands is an approach stimulated by ethical considerations as well. As it is unethical to involve all clients in an expensive, long term treatment program, first attempts should be made to resolve their problems from within a brief therapy format. Furthermore, it is ethically undesirable to continue requiring clients to undergo expensive multi-component brief therapy administered by therapist "teams" when there remains question as to whether or not many of the ingredients in the package are superfluous and could be abandoned.

In sum, we subscribe to Barlow's (1974) answer to these issues, in the investigative "empirical-evaluative" tradition: what is required is a precise delineation of the various behavioral components constituting sexual dysfunction and deviation, and further development of reliable and valid assessment devices. The acquisition of knowledge from these sources will stimulate research into treatments and determine which technique or combination of techniques are effective in ameliorating the various types of sexual dysfunctions.

ACKNOWLEDGMENTS

This chapter would not have been possible without the encouragement and assistance of Jack Annon, Ian Evans, and Ron Pion. We would also like to thank Larry Sine and Tony Lydgate for their helpful comments on an earlier version of the manuscript, and express appreciation as well to Georgia Niimoto for her fine administrative assistance. Finally, the authors take full responsibility for any errors contained herein.

REFERENCES

Annon, J.S. The extension of learning principles to the analysis and treatment of sexual problems (Doctoral dissertation, University of Hawaii, 1971). *Dissertation Abstracts International,* 1971, 32(6-B), 3627.

Annon, J.S. The therapeutic use of masturbation in the treatment of sexual disorders. In R.D. Rubin, J.P. Brady, & J.D. Henderson (Eds.), *Advances in behavior therapy* (Vol. 4). New York: Academic Press, 1973.

Annon, J.S. *The behavioral treatment of sexual problems: Vol 1.* Honolulu, Hawaii: Enabling Systems, Inc., 1974.

Annon, J.S. *The behavioral treatment of sexual problems: Vol 2.* Honolulu, Hawaii: Enabling Systems, Inc., 1975.

Bancroft, J. The application of psychophysiological measures to the assessment and modification of sexual behavior. *Behaviour Research and Therapy,* 1971, **9**, 119-130.

Bancroft, J., Jones, H.G., & Pullan, B.R. A simple transducer for measuring penile erection, with comments on its use in the treatment of sexual disorders. *Behaviour Research and Therapy*, 1966, **4**, 239-241.

Bancroft, J., & Mathews, A. Autonomic correlates of penile erection. *Journal of Psychosomatic Research,* 1971, **15**, 159-167.

Bandura, A. *Principles of behavior modification.* New York: Holt, Rinehart, & Winston, 1969.

Barlow, D.H. Aversive procedures. In W.S. Agras (Ed.), *Behavior modification: Principles and clinical applications.* Boston: Little, Brown, 1972.

Barlow, D.H. Increasing heterosexual responsiveness in the treatment of sexual deviation: A review of the clinical and experimental evidence. *Behavior Therapy,* 1973, **4**, 655-671.

Barlow, D.H. The treatment of sexual deviation: Toward a comprehensive behavioral approach. In K. Calhoun, H. Adams, & K. Mitchell (Eds.), *Innovative treatment methods in psychopathology.* New York: Wiley, 1974.

Barlow, D.H., & Agras, W.S. Fading to increase heterosexual responsiveness in homosexuals. *Journal of Applied Behavior Analysis,* 1973, **6**, 355-367.

Barlow, D.H., Becker, R., Leitenberg, H., & Agras, W.S. A mechanical strain gauge for recording penile circumference change. *Journal of Applied Behavior Analysis,* 1970, **3**, 73-76.

Barlow, D.H., Leitenberg, H., & Agras, W.S. The experimental control of sexual deviation through manipulation of the noxious scene in covert sensitization. *Journal of Abnormal Psychology*, 1969, **74**, 596-601.

Beach, F. Characteristics of masculine sex drive. *Nebraska Symposium on Motivation,* 1956, **4**, 1-32.

Beach, F., Westbrook, W., & Clemens, L. Comparisons of the ejaculatory response in men and animals. *Psychosomatic Medicine,* 1966, **28**, 749-763.

Beech, H.R., Watts, F., & Poole, A.D. Classical conditioning of sexual deviation: A preliminary note. *Behavior Therapy,* 1971, **2**, 400-402.

Bieber, I. A discussion of "Homosexuality: The ethical challenge." *Journal of Consulting and Clinical Psychology,* 1976, **44**, 163-166.

Belt, B. Some organic causes of impotence. *Medical Aspects of Human Sexuality*, 1973, **7**, 152-161.

Birk, L., Huddleston, W., Miller, E., & Cohler, B. Avoidance conditioning for homosexuality. *Archives of General Psychiatry*, 1971, **25**, 314-323.

Bond, I.K., & Evans, D.R. Avoidance therapy: Its use in two cases of underwear fetishism. *Canadian Medical Association Journal*, 1967, **96**, 1160-1162.

Brady, J.P. Brevital-relaxation treatment of frigidity. *Behaviour Research and Therapy*, 1966, **4**, 71-77.

Brady, J.P. Brevital-aided systematic desensitization. In R. Rubin, H. Fensterheim, A.A. Lazarus, & C.M. Franks (Eds.), *Advances in behavior therapy, 1969*. New York: Academic Press, 1969.

Callahan, E.J., & Leitenberg, H. Aversion therapy for sexual deviation: Contingent shock and covert sensitization. *Journal of Abnormal Psychology*, 1973, **81**, 60-73.

Cautella, J.R., & Upper, D. The process of individual behavior therapy. In M. Hersen, R. Eisler, & P. Miller (Eds.), *Progress in Behavior Modification*. New York: Academic Press, 1975.

Cohen, H.D., & Shapiro, A. A method for measuring sexual arousal in the female. *Psychophysiology*, 1971, **8**, 250-251. (Abstract)

Davison, G. Elimination of a sadistic fantasy by a client-controlled counter-conditioning technique. *Journal of Abnormal Psychology*, 1968, **73**, 84-90.

Davison, G. Homosexuality: The ethical challenge. Presidential Address to the Eighth Annual Convention of the Association for Advancement of Behavior Therapy, Chicago, November 2, 1974.

Davison, G.C. Homosexuality: The ethical challenge. *Journal of Consulting and Clinical Psychology*, 1976, **44**, 157-162.

Davison, G., & Wilson, G.T. Attitudes of behavior therapists toward homosexuality. *Behavior Therapy*, 1973, **4**, 686-689.

Deutch, R.M. *The key to feminine response in marriage*. New York: Random House, 1968.

Ellis, A. *Sex without guilt*. New York: Lyle Stuart, 1958.

Ellis, A. The rational-emotive approach to sex therapy. *The Counseling Psychologist*, 1975, **5**, 14-21.

Ellis, H. *The psychology of sex*. New York: Emerson, 1935.

Ellis, H. *Studies in the psychology of sex*. New York: Random House, 1936.

Evans, D.R. An exploratory study into the treatment of exhibitionism by means of emotive imagery and aversive conditioning. *Canadian Psychologist*, 1967, **8**, 162. (Abstract)

Evans, D.R. Masturbatory fantasy and sexual deviation. *Behaviour Research and Therapy*, 1968, **6**, 17-19.

Evans, D.R. Subjective variables and treatment effects in aversion therapy. *Behaviour Research and Therapy*, 1970, **8**, 147-152.

Evans, I.M. A conditioning model of a common neurotic pattern—fear of fear. *Psychotherapy: Theory, Research and Practice*, 1972, **9**, 238-241.

Evans, I.M. Sexual behavior: Normal and abnormal. In A.J. Marsella, *Abnormal psychology: Foundations, issues, disorders, therapies*. Monterey, California: Brooks/Cole, in press.

Evans, R.B. Physical and biochemical characteristics of homosexual men. *Journal of Consulting and Clinical Psychology*, 1972, **39**, 140-147.

Farkas, G.M. Sex Research: Laboratory analysis of human sexuality. Paper presented at the 1976 Convention of the Hawaii Psychological Association, Honolulu, Hawaii, May 1, 1976.

Farkas, G.M., & Rosen, R.C. Effect of alcohol on elicited male sexual response. *Journal of Studies on Alcohol*, 1976, **37**, 265-272.

Feldman, M.P. Aversion therapy for sexual deviation: A critical review. *Psychological Bulletin*, 1966, **65**, 65-79.

Feldman, M.P., & MacCulloch, M.J. The application of anticipatory avoidance learning to the treatment of homosexuality. I. Theory, technique, and preliminary results.

Behaviour Research and Therapy, 1965, **2**, 165-183.

Feldman, M.P., & MacCulloch, M.J. *Homosexual behavior: Theory and assessment.* Oxford: Pergamon Press, 1971.

Fensterheim, H. The initial interview. In A.A. Lazarus (Ed.), *Clinical behavior therapy.* New York: Brunner/Mazel, 1972.

Fisher, C., Gross, J., & Zuch, J. Cycle of penile erection synchronous with dreaming (REM) sleep. *Archives of General Psychiatry,* 1965, **12**, 29-45.

Fookes, B.H. Some experiences in the use of aversion therapy in male homosexuality, exhibitionism, and fetishism-transvestism. *British Journal of Psychiatry,* 1968, **115**, 339-341.

Freud, S. *Three contributions to the theory of sex.* New York: Dutton, 1962.

Freund, K. Some problems in the treatment of homosexuality. In H.J. Eysenck (Ed.), *Behavior therapy and the neuroses.* New York: Pergamon Press, 1960.

Freund, K. A laboratory method for diagnosing predominance of homo- or hetero-erotic Interest in the male. *Behaviour Research and Therapy,* 1963, **1**, 85-93.

Freund, K. Diagnosing heterosexual pedophilia by means of a test for sexual interest. *Behaviour Research and Therapy,* 1965, **3**, 229-235.

Freund, K. Diagnosing homo- or hetero-sexuality and erotic age preference by means of a psychophysiological test. *Behaviour Research and Therapy,* 1967, **5**, 209-228.

Freund, K., Sedlacek, F., & Knob, K. A simple transducer for mechanical plethysmography of the male genital. *Journal of the Experimental Analysis of Behavior,* 1965, **8**, 169-170.

Franks, C.M., & Wilson, G.T. *Behavior therapy, theory and practice. Vol. 2, 1974.* New York: Brunner/Mazel, 1974.

Gagnon, J.H. Sex research and social change. *Archives of Sexual Behavior,*1975, **4**, 111-142.

Geer, J.H., Morokoff, P., & Greenwood, P. Sexual arousal in women: The development of a measurement device for vaginal blood volume. *Archives of Sexual Behavior,* 1974, **3**, 559-564.

Gelder, M.G., & Marks, I.M. Aversion treatment in transvestism and transsexualism. In R. Green and J. Money (Eds.), *Transsexualism and sex reassignment.* Baltimore: Johns Hopkins Press, 1969.

Halleck, S. Another response to "Homosexuality: The ethical challenge." *Journal of Consulting and Clinical Psychology,* 1976, **44**, 167-170.

Hartman, W.E., & Fithian, M.A. *Treatment of sexual dysfunction: A bio-psycho-social approach.* Long Beach, Calif.: Center for Marital & Sexual Studies, 1973.

Haslam, M.T. The treatment of psychogenic dyspareunia by reciprocal inhibition. *British Journal of Psychiatry,* 1965, **111**, 280-282.

Heiman, J. Facilitating erotic arousal toward sex-positive sex research. Paper delivered at the 1974 American Psychological Association Convention, New Orleans, Louisiana.

Heiman, J. Use of the vaginal photoplethysmograph as a diagnostic and treatment aid in female sexual dysfunction. Paper delivered at the 1975 American Psychological Association Convention, Chicago, Illinois.

Henson, D., & Rubin, H. Voluntary control of eroticism. *Journal of Applied Behavioral Analysis,* 1971, **4**, 37-47.

Herman, S.H., Barlow, D.H., & Agras, W.S. An experimental analysis of classical conditioning as a method of increasing heterosexual arousal in homosexuals. *Behavior Therapy,* 1974, **5**, 33-47.

Holden, C. Sex therapy: Making it as a science and an industry. *Science,* 1974, **186**, 330-334.

Hoon, P.W., Wincze, J.P., & Hoon, E.F. Physiological assessment of sexual arousal in women. *Psychophysiology,* 1976, **13**, 196-204.

Hunt, M. *Sexual Behavior in the 1970's.* Chicago: Playboy Press, 1974.

Husted, J.R. Desensitization procedures in dealing with female sexual dysfunction. *The Counseling Psychologist,* 1975, **5**, 30-38.

Jacobs, M., & Whiteley, J.M. Approaches to sexual counseling. *The Counseling Psychologist,* 1975, **5**, 3-8.

James, B. Case of homosexuality treated by aversion therapy. *British Medical Journal,* 1962, **1**, 768-770.

Kanfer, F.H., & Saslow, G. Behavioral diagnosis. In C.M. Franks (Ed.), *Behavior therapy: Appraisal and status.* New York: McGraw-Hill, 1969.

Kaplan, H.S. *The new sex therapy.* New York: Brunner/Mazel, 1974.

Kegel, A.H. Sexual functions of the pubococcygeus muscle. *Western Journal of Surgery, Obstetrics and Gynecology,* 1952, **60**, 521.

Kiesler, D.J. Some myths of psychotherapy research and the search for a paradigm. *Psychological Bulletin,* 1966, **65**, 110-136.

Kinsey, A., Pomeroy, W., & Martin, C. *Sexual behavior in the human male.* Philadelphia: Saunders, 1948.

Kinsey, A., Pomeroy, W., Martin, C., & Gebhard, P. *Sexual behavior in the human female.* Philadelphia: Saunders, 1953.

Koch, J., & Koch, L. Sex therapy: Caveat emptor. *Psychology Today,* 1976, **9**, 37.

Kockott, G., Dittmar, F., & Nusselt, L. Systematic desensitization of erectile impotence: A controlled study. *Archives of Sexual Behavior,* 1975, **4**, 493-500.

Kohlenberg, R.J. Treatment of a homosexual pedophiliac using in vivo desensitization: A case study. *Journal of Abnormal Psychology,* 1974, **8**, 192-195.

Kraft, T. A case of homosexuality treated by systematic desensitization. *American Journal of Psychotherapy,* 1967, **21**, 815-821.

Kraft, T. Desensitization and the treatment of sexual disorders. *Journal of Sex Research,* 1969, **5**, 130-134.

Kraft, T. A case of homosexuality treated by combined behavior therapy and psychotherapy. *Psychotherapy and Psychosomatics,* 1971, **19**, 342-358.

Kraft, T., & Al-Issa, I. Behavior therapy and the treatment of frigidity. *American Journal of Psychotherapy,* 1967, **21**, 116-120.

Lang, P.J. The mechanics of desensitization and the laboratory study of human fear. In C. Franks (Ed.), *Behavior Therapy: Appraisal and Status.* New York: McGraw-Hill, 1969.

Lassen, C. Issues and dilemmas in sexual treatment. *Journal of Sex and Marital Therapy,* 1976, **2**, 32-39.

Laws, D., & Rubin, H. Instructional control of an autonomic sexual response. *Journal of Behavior Therapy and Experimental Psychiatry,* 1969, **2**, 93-99.

Lazarus, A. The Treatment of chronic frigidity by systematic desensitization. *The Journal of Nervous and Mental Disease,* 1963, **136**, 272-278.

Lazarus, A. Behavioral therapy for sexual problems. *Professional Psychology,* 1971, **121**, 349-353.

Lobitz, W.C., & LoPiccolo, J. New methods in the behavioral treatment of sexual dysfunction. *Journal of Behavior Therapy and Experimental Psychiatry,* 1972, **3**, 265-271.

LoPiccolo, J., & Miller, V.H. A program for enhancing the sexual relationship.of normal couples. *The Counseling Psychologist,* 1975, **5**, 41-45.

LoPiccolo, J., & Steger, J. The sexual interaction inventory: A new instrument for assessment of sexual dysfunction. *Archives of Sexual Behavior,* 1973, **3**, 585-595.

MacCulloch, M.J., & Feldman, M.P. Aversion therapy in management of 43 homosexuals. *British Medical Journal,* 1967, **2**, 594-597.

MacDonough, T. A critique of the first Feldman and MacCulloch avoidance conditioning treatment for homosexuals. *Behavior Therapy,* 1972, **3**, 104-111.

Madsen, C., & Ullmann, L.P. Innovations in the desensitization of frigidity. *Behaviour Research and Therapy,* 1967, **5**, 67-68.

Marks, I. Management of sexual disorders. In H. Leitenberg (Ed.), *Handbook of behavior modification and behavior therapy.* Englewood Cliffs, N.J.: Prentice-Hall, 1976.

Marks, I., & Gelder, M. Transvestism and fetishism: Clinical and psychological changes during faradic aversion. *British Journal of Psychiatry,* 1967, **113**, 711-729.

Marks, I., Gelder, M., & Bancroft, J. Sexual deviants two years after electric aversion. *British Journal of Psychiatry,* 1970, **117**, 73-85.

Marquis, J. Orgasmic reconditioning: Changing sexual object choice through controlling masturbation fantasies. *Journal of Behavior Therapy and Experimental Psychiatry,* 1970, **1**, 263-271.

Masters, W., & Johnson, V. *Human sexual response.* Boston: Little, Brown, 1966.

Masters, W., & Johnson, V. *Human sexual inadequacy.* Boston: Little, Brown, 1970.

Max, L. Breaking up a homosexual fixation by the conditioned reaction technique: A case study. *Psychological Bulletin,* 1935, **32**, 734. (Abstract)

McConaghy, N.A. Penile volume change to moving pictures of male and female nudes in heterosexual and homosexual males. *Behaviour Research and Therapy,* 1967, **5**, 43-48.

McConaghy, N.A. Subjective and penile plethysmograph responses following aversion relief and apomorphine aversion therapy for homosexual impulses. *British Journal of Psychiatry,* 1969, **115**, 723-730.

McConaghy, N.A. Measurements of change in penile dimensions. *Archives of Sexual Behavior,* 1974, **3**, 381-389.

McDowell, F.H. Sexual manifestations of neurologic disease. *Medical Aspects of Human Sexuality,* 1968, **2**, 13-21.

McGovern, K.B., Stewart, R.C., & LoPiccolo, J. Secondary orgasmic dysfunction. I. Analysis and strategies for treatment. *Archives of Sexual Behavior,* 1975, **4**, 265-276.

McGuire, R.J., Carlisle, J.M., & Young, B.G. Sexual deviation as a conditioned behavior: A hypothesis. *Behaviour Research and Therapy,* 1965, **2**, 185-190.

McGuire, R.J., & Vallance, M. Aversion therapy by electric shock: A simple technique. *British Medical Journal,* 1964, **1**, 151-153.

Medical World News, 1975, **15** (May 10), 17-18.

Meyer, J.K. Training and accreditation for the treatment of sexual disorders. *American Journal of Psychiatry,* 1976, **133**, 389-394.

Money, J. Strategy, ethics, behavior modification and homosexuality. *Archives of Sexual Behavior,* 1972, **2**, 78-81.

Obler, M. Multivariate approaches to psychotherapy with sexual dysfunction. *The Counseling Psychologist,* 1975, **5**, 55-63.

O'Leary, K.D., & Wilson, G.T. *Behavior therapy: Application and outcome.* Englewood Cliffs, N.J.: Prentice-Hall, 1975.

Pion, R.J. Diagnosis and treatment of inadequate sexual response. In J. Sciarra (Ed.), *Gynecology and Obstetrics* Vol. 2. Hagerstown, Maryland: Harper & Row, 1975.

Rachman, S. Sexual fetishism: An experimental analogue. *Psychological Record,* 1967, **16**, 293-296.

Rachman, S., & Teasdale, J. *Aversion therapy and behaviour disorders: An analysis.* London: Routledge & Kegan Paul, 1969.

Robbins, J., & Robbins, J. *An analysis of human sexual inadequacy.* New York: Signet, 1970.

Robinson, C.H. The effects of observational learning on sexual behaviors and attitudes in orgasmic dysfunctional women. Unpublished doctoral dissertation, University of Hawaii, 1974.

Rosen, R.C. Suppression of penile tumescence by instrumental conditioning. *Psychosomatic Medicine,* 1973, **35**, 509-514.

Rosen, R.C., Shapiro, D., & Schwartz, G.E. Voluntary control of penile tumescence. *Psychosomatic Medicine,* 1975, **37**, 479-483.

Runciman, A. Sexual therapy of Masters and Johnson. *The Counseling Psychologist,* 1975, **5**, 22-29.

Sayner, R., & Durrell, D. Multiple behavior therapy techniques in the treatment of sexual dysfunction. *The Counseling Psychologist,* 1975, **5**, 38-41.

Semans, J.H. Premature ejaculation: A new approach. *Southern Medical Journal,* 1956, **49**, 353-357.

Schachter, S., & Singer, J. Cognitive, social, and physiological determinants of emotional state. *Psychological Review,* 1962, **69**, 379-399.

Sintchak, G., & Geer, J. A vaginal plethysmograph system. *Psychophysiology,* 1975, **12**, 113-115.

Solomon, R.C., Kamin, L.J., & Wynne, L.C. Traumatic avoidance learning: The outcomes of several extinction procedures with dogs. *Journal of Abnormal Social Psychology*, 1953, **48**, 291-302.

Staats, A.W. *Social behaviorism.* Homewood, Ill.: Dorsey Press, 1975.

Thorpe, J.G., & Schmidt, E. Therapeutic failure in the case of aversion therapy. *Behaviour Research and Therapy*, 1964, **1**, 293-296.

Thorpe, J.G., Schmidt, E., Brown, P.T., & Castell, D. Aversion-relief therapy: A new method for general application. *Behaviour Research and Therapy*, 1964, **2**, 71-82.

Thorpe, J.G., Schmidt, E., & Castell, D. A comparison of positive and negative (aversive) conditioning in the treatment of homosexuality. *Behaviour Research and Therapy*, 1964, **1**, 357-362.

Ullmann, L.P., & Krasner, L. *A psychological approach to abnormal behavior.* Englewood Cliffs, N.J.: Prentice-Hall, 1975.

Weiss, H.D. The physiology of human penile erection. *Annals of Internal Medicine*, 1972, **76**, 793-799.

Wilson, G.T. Innovations in the modification of phobic behaviors in two clinical cases. *Behavior Therapy*, 1973, **4**, 426-430.

Wilson, G.T., & Davison, G.C. Behavior therapy and homosexuality: A critical perspective. *Behavior Therapy*, 1974, **5**, 16-28.

Wilson, G.T., & Evans, W.I.M. Behavior therapy and not the behavior "therapies." *Newsletter-Association for the Advancement of the Behavior Therapies*, 1967, **2**, 5-7.

Wincze, J.P. A comparison of systematic desensitization and "vicarious extinction" in a case of frigidity. *Journal of Behavior Therapy and Experimental Psychiatry*, 1971, **2**, 285-289.

Wincze, J.P., & Caird, W.K. The effects of systematic desensitization and video desensitization in the treatment of essential sexual dysfunction in women. *Behavior Therapy*, 1976, **7**, 335-358.

Wish, P.A. the use of imagery-based techniques in the treatment of sexual dysfunction. *The Counseling Psychologist*, 1975, **5**, 52-55.

Wolpe, J. *The practice of behavior therapy.* New York: Pergamon Press, 1969.

Wolpe, J., & Lazarus, A.A. *Behavior therapy techniques.* New York: Pergamon Press, 1966.

Zuckerman, M. Physiological measures of sexual arousal in the human. *Psychological Bulletin*, 1971, **75**, 347-356.

Appendix A
Sexual Response Inventory

RONALD J. PION

The goal of this questionnaire is to improve the quality and efficiency of your care. The information you provide is *confidential.* Please fill it out accurately and completely as you can. Feel free to ask for assistance. Thank you for your cooperation.

Today's Date _____

                            Month   Day   Year

REFERRED BY _____

Name _____

1. Physical health (circle the appropriate number that best describes your health)

   Poor 1 2 3 4 5 6 7 Good

2. Have children affected your health?_____Yes _____No (Not Applicable)_____

3. How would you describe your parents' relationship:

   Poor 1 2 3 4 5 6 7 Good

4. Communication about sex in parental home:

   _____ Questions answered freely   Never 1 2 3 4 5 6 7 Often

   _____ Questions answered with reservations Never 1 2 3 4 5 6 7 Often

   _____ No discussion of sex

5. Parental attitudes about sex

   _____ Sex O.K.

   _____ O.K. but not to be talked about

   _____ Not to be talked about because sex is not O.K.

6. How do you feel your parents got along sexually?

   Poorly 1 2 3 4 5 6 7 Well

7. Parental attitudes about nudity or partial nudity in the home

   Father — Modesty very unimportant 1 2 3 4 5 6 7 very important

   Mother — Modesty very unimportant 1 2 3 4 5 6 7 very important

8. Parent's attitudes about your sexual activity

   Parents discouraged   1 2 3 4 5 6 7 Parents encouraged

9. Where was your knowledge about reproduction acquired? (Put an **M** next to where you received Much information, an **L** next to where you received Little information

   Home_____ Friends _____ School_____ Church_____

   Other (specify)_____

10. Menstrual knowledge obtained from your parents

    Much information 1 2 3 4 5 6 7 No information

11. Did your parent(s) attempt to give you any information about:

    Sex and Reproduction_____ Yes_____ No_____

    Sex and Relationships_____ Yes_____ No_____

    Sex and Recreation _____ Yes_____ No_____

12. Religious attitudes and influences regarding sex

    ____ No sense of religious pressure

    My religion affected my attitudes regarding

    ____ Masturbation   ____ Oral-genital activities

    ____ Petting   ____ Contraception

    ____ Abortion   ____ Other sexual behaviors

    ____ Intercourse

13. Dating   Discouraged by parents 1 2 3 4 5 6 7 Encouraged

14. Petting on dates   No guilt 1 2 3 4 5 6 7 Much guilt

15. Were you satisfied with your dating?   No 1 2 3 4 5 6 7 Yes

16. Intercourse

    _____ No intercourse

    _____ With spouse only

    _____ With love relationship

    _____ With other — not necessarily in love relationship

17. Present feelings regarding past sex relationships

    Dissatisfied 1 2 3 4 5 6 7 Satisfied

18. Have you ever experienced orgasm? ____ Yes ___ No
19. Have you ever had orgasm with intercourse? ____ Yes ____ No
20. Is simultaneous orgasm necessary for you and partner for complete satisfaction?
    ____ Yes ____ No
21. Do you think it is acceptable for the *male* to initiate sex play? ____ Yes ____ No
22. Do you think it is acceptable for the *female* to initiate sex play? ___Yes ____ No
23. Do you think it is acceptable for *you* to initiate sex play? ____ Yes ____ No
24. Do you think that the size of the penis is important to your enjoyment of sex?
    ____ Yes ____ No
25. Do you think that orgasm should occur during vaginal intercourse? ___ Yes ___ No
26. Is it acceptable for you or your partner to have orgasm:
    before vaginal intercourse? ____ Yes ___No
    after vaginal intercourse? ____ Yes ___ No
27. How does your orgasm usually occur?
    ____ During vaginal intercourse   ____ By several of above means
    ____ By fantasy and daydreams   ____ Doesn't occur
    ____ By partner stimulation   ____ By other methods
    ____ By self-stimulation
28. How does your partner's orgasm usually occur?
    ____ During vaginal intercourse   ____ By several of above means
    ____ By fantasy and daydreams   ____ Doesn't occur
    ____ By my stimulation   ____ By other methods
    ____ By self-stimulation
29. Does your partner have orgasm when you are together sexually?
    Never   1 2 3 4 5 6 7   Always
30. Are you satisfied with the frequency of *your partner's* orgasm?
    Dissatisfied   1 2 3 4 5 6 7   Satisfied
31. Are you satisfied with the frequency of *your* orgasm?
    Dissatisfied   1 2 3 4 5 6 7   Satisfied
32. If your partner's orgasm does not occur with vaginal intercourse, are you
    Dissatisfied   1 2 3 4 5 6 7   Satisfied
33. If *your* orgasm does not occur with vaginal intercourse, are you
    Dissatisfied   1 2 3 4 5 6 7   Satisfied
34. Does *your* partner often desire sexual activity when *you* do not?
    Never   1 2 3 4 5 6 7   Always
35. Do *you* often desire sexual activity when *your partner* does not?
    Never   1 2 3 4 5 6 7   Always
36. When *you* are not sexually aroused do you act as if you are to please your parnter?
    Never   1 2 3 4 5 6 7   Always
37. When *your partner* does not desire intercourse, does he/she have intercourse any-
    way to please you?   Never   1 2 3 4 5 6 7   Always
38. Are you satisfied with your sexual relationship? ____ Yes ____ No
39. Do sexual fantasies or daydreams play a role in arousing you? ____ Yes ____ No
40. Do you have sexual dreams? ____ Yes ____ No
41. If yes, do you have orgasm with sexual dreams? _____ Yes ____ No
42. Do you often shower or bathe before (or after) intercourse? ____ Yes ____ No
43. Are you familar with the term douche? ____ Yes ____ No
44. What is your attitude concerning genital hygiene before and after intercourse or
    other sexual activity?   _____ Favorable ____ Unfavorable

45. Do you feel comfortable undressing in front of your partner?

    Never   1 2 3 4 5 6 7   Always

46. Does your partner feel comfortable undressing in front of you?

    Never   1 2 3 4 5 6 7   Always

47. What is your feeling about looking at your partner undressed?

    Uncomfortable   1 2 3 4 5 6 7   Comfortable

48. Do you find that your physical surroundings (e.g. lack of privacy) are a hindrance to having a satisfactory sexual relationship?

    Never   1 2 3 4 5 6 7   Often

49. Do you usually have intercourse at a particular time of the day (as in the evening before going to sleep)?   _____ Yes   _____ No

50. Which of the following situations are influencing (increasing or decreasing) your activity?

    _____ Separation   _____ Economic situation
    _____ Marital disturbance   _____ I have lost interest
    _____ Pregnancy   _____ Partner has lost interest
    _____ Health (yours or partner's) _____ Interest in another person
    _____ Lack of privacy   _____ Other (specify)

51. Which of the following feelings do you often have after intercourse?

    _____ Satisfaction   _____ Uneasiness or anxiety
    _____ Dissatisfaction   _____ Other (specify)_____
    _____ Guilt

52. Do you feel that orgasm is necessary for you to have satisfaction in your sexual relationship?   _____ Yes   _____ No

53. Do you have intercourse during menstrual periods?

    Never   1 2 3 4 5 6 7   Often

54. How do you feel about intercourse during menstrual periods?

    Not O.K.   1 2 3 4 5 6 7   O.K.

55. Do you and your partner differ in attitudes on any of the following:

    _____ Sexual matters   _____ Religion
    _____ Finances   _____ Leisure activity
    _____ Raising children   _____ Infidelity

56. Is there much disagreement between you and your partner on any of the above or other matters?

    _____ Yes, which one(s)_____
    _____ No

57. Are you and your partner using any method of contraception?

    _____ Condom   _____ Diaphragm
    _____ Pill   _____ Rhythm method
    _____ IUD   _____ Surgical method
    _____ Foam   _____ No method

58. How do you feel about your method or lack of a method of contraception?

    Dissatisfied   1 2 3 4 5 6 7   Satisfied

59. Do you and your partner communicate with each other about sexual matters?

    Seldom   1 2 3 4 5 6 7   Usually

60. Have you sought professional advice for problems relating to sexual adjustment
     previously?   ____ Yes ____ No
61. Are you familiar with the term masturbation (sexual self-stimulation)?
                                                          ____ Yes ____ No
62. What are your attitudes about masturbation (sexual self-stimulation)?
           Unnatural and should not be done 1 2 3 4 5 6 7 Natural and acceptable
63. What were your parents' attitudes about masturbation?
                              Discouraging 1 2 3 4 5 6 7 Encouraging
64. Have you ever masturbated? ____ Yes ____ No
65. Have you masturbated to orgasm? ____ Yes ____ No
66. Do you masturbate now? ____ Yes ____ No
67. Do you masturbate to orgasm now? ____ Yes ____ No
68. Do you have guilt feelings regarding masturbation?
                              Never 1 2 3 4 5 6 7 Always
69. Do you feel sexually attracted to a member of the *same* sex?
                              Never 1 2 3 4 5 6 7 Often
70. Have you all the children you plan to have? ____ Yes ____ No
71. How many children do you want? _____
72. How many children do you have? _____
73. If you have more (or fewer) children than you want, does this present a problem?
                                                  ____ Yes ____ No
74. Do you feel your partner is an adequate sexual companion? ____ Yes ____ No
75. Which aspects of your sex life would you change?
     ____ Increase frequency of intercourse   ____ Increase ability of partner to delay
     ____ Have more nearly the same sexual   orgasm
          desires as partner   ____ Variety (i.e. time of day, position, etc.)
     ____ Increase ability to achieve orgasm   ____ Other
     ____ Eliminate fears of pregnancy   ____ None
76. I find the following helpful to use in attaining sexual arousal.
     ____ Fantasies   ____ Alcohol
     ____ Books   ____ Drugs
     ____ Movies   ____ Verbal stimulation
     ____ Pictures   ____ Physical contact
     ____ Music   ____ Other _____
     ____ Cologne
77. Let the following be a scale of sexual DESIRE. Where do you think you fit
                              Little Desire 1 2 3 4 5 6 7 Much Desire
78. Let the following be a scale of sexual AROUSAL (without orgasm). In the past,
     practicing self-stimulation (masturbation) you have experienced
                              Little Arousal 1 2 3 4 5 6 7 Much Arousal
     In the past, with a partner you have experienced
                              Little Arousal 1 2 3 4 5 6 7 Much Arousal
79. Let the following be a scale of sexual ORGASM.
     In the past, while practicing self-stimulation (masturbation) your orgasms have been of
                              Minimum Intensity 1 2 3 4 5 6 7 Maximum Intensity
     In the past, with partner your orgasms have been of
                              Minimum Intensity 1 2 3 4 5 6 7 Maximum Intensity

80.   Let the following be a scale of SATISFACTION after sexual activity
       In the past, practicing self-stimulation (masturbation) you have experienced
                        Little Satisfaction   1 2 3 4 5 6 7 Much Satisfaction
       In the past with partner you have experienced
                        Little Satisfaction   1 2 3 4 5 6 7 Much Satisfaction

Your comments are welcome, feel free to continue them on the back of this form.

Additional Selected Readings

Annon, J.S. *The behavioral treatment of sexual problems.* Volume 1: *Brief Therapy.* Honolulu: Enabling Systems, 1974.

Annon, J.S. *The Behavioral Treatment of Sexual Problems. Volume 2. Intensive Therapy.* Honolulu: Enabling Systems, 1975.

Ard, B.N. *Treating Psychosexual Dysfunction.* New York: Jason Aronson, 1974.

Bancroft, J. The application of psychophysiological measures to the assessment and modification of sexual behavior. *Behavior Research and Therapy*, 1971, **9**, 119-130.

Bancroft, J. *Deviant Sexual Behavior.* London: Oxford University Press, 1974.

Barlow, D.H., Leitenberg, H. & Agras, W.S. Experimental control of sexual deviation through manipulation of the noxious scene in covert sensitization. *Journal of Abnormal Psychology*, 1969, **74**, 597-601.

Butterfield, W.H. Electric Shock — Safety Factors When Used for the Aversive Conditioning of Humans. *Behavior Therapy*, 1975, **6**, 98-110.

Danaher, B.G. & Lichtenstein, E. Aversion therapy issues: A note of clarification. *Behavior Therapy*, 1974, **5**, 112-116.

Feldman, M.P. Aversion therapy for sexual deviations. *Psychological Bulletin*, 1966, **65**, 65-79.

Freund, K. A note on the use of the phallometric method of measuring mild sexual arousal in the male. *Behavior Therapy*, 1971, **2**, 223-228.

Fordney-Settlage, D.S. Heterosexual dysfunction: Evaulation of treatment procedures, *Archives of Sexual Behavior.* 1975, **4**, 367-387.

Glick, B.S. Desensitization therapy in impotence and frigidity: Review of the literature, *American Journal of Psychiatry*, 1975, **132**, 169-171.

Hallam, R.S. & Rachman, S. Some effects of aversion therapy of patients with sexual disorders. *Behavior Research and Therapy*, 1972, **10**, 171-180.

Hallam, R.S. & Rachman, S. Theoretical problems of aversion therapy. *Behavior Research and Therapy*, 1972, **10**, 341-353.

Kaplan, H.S. *The New Sex Therapy.* New York: Brunner/Mazel, 1974.

Kaplan, H.S. *The Illustrated Manual of Sex Therapy.* New York: Quadrangle, 1975.

Kaplan, H.S. & Kohl, R.N. Adverse reactions to the rapid treatment of sexual problems. *Journal of Psychosomatics*, 1972, **13**, 185-190.

Kushner, M. & Sandler, J. Aversion therapy and the concept of punishment. *Behavior Research and Therapy*, 1966, **4**, 179-186.

Lansky, M.R. & Davenport, A.E. Difficulties in brief conjoint treatment of sexual dysfunction, *American Journal of Psychiatry*, 1975, **132**, 177-179.

Laws, D.R. & Pawlowski, A.V. A multi-purpose biofeedback device for penile plethys-mography. *Journal of Behavior Therapy and Experimental Psychiatry*, 1974, **4**, 339-341.

MacDonough, T.S. A critique of the first Feldman and MacCulloch avoidance condition-ing treatment for homosexuals. *Behavior Therapy*, 1972, **3**, 104-111.

Marks, I., Gelder, M. & Bancroft, J. Sexual deviants two years after electric aversion. *British Journal of Psychiatry*, 1970, **117**, 173-185.

Masters, W.H. & Johnson, V.E. *Human Sexual Inadequacy.* Boston: Little, Brown, 1970.

Masters, W.H. & Johnson, V.E. *Human Sexual Response.* Boston: Little, Brown, 1966.

McCarthy, B.W., Ryan, M., & Johnson, F. *Sexual Awareness: A Practical Approach.* San francisco: Boyd and Fraser, 1975.

McCullough, J.P. & Montgomery, L.E. A technique for measuring subjective arousal in clients. *Behavior Therapy*, 1972, **3**, 627-628.

McGuire, R.J. & Vallance, M. Aversion therapy by electric shock: A simple technique. *British Medical Journal*, 1964, **1**, 151-153.

Meyer, J.K., Schmidt, C.W., Lucas, M.J., & Smith, E. Short-term treatment of sexual problems: Interim report, *American Journal of Psychiatry*, Vol. 132, 1975, pp.172-176.

National Sex Forum. *SAR guide for a Better Sex Life,* New York: National Sex Forum, 1975.

Obler, M. Multivariate approaches to psychotherapy with sexual dysfunction. *Counseling Psychologist*, 1975, **5**, 55-63.

Prochaska, J.O. & Marzilli, R. Modifications of the Masters and Johnson approach to sexual problems. *Psychotherapy: Theory, Research and Practice*, 1973, **10**, 294-296.

Rachman, S.J. & Teasdale, J.D. *Aversion therapy and behavior disorders.* Coral Gables: University of Miami Press, 1969.

Tanner, B.A. Aversive shock issues: Physical danger, emotional harm, effectiveness and dehumanization. *Journal of Behavior Therapy and Experimental Psychiatry*, 1973, **4**, 113-115.

Thorpe, G.L. Learning paradigms in the anticipatory avoidance technique: A comment on the controversy between MacDonough and Feldman. *Behavior Therapy*, 1972, **3**, 614-618.

Thorpe, J.G., Schmidt, E., Brown, P.T. & Castell, D. Aversion-relief therapy: A new method for general application. *Behavior Research Therapy*, 1964, 2 71-82.

Werner, A. Sexual dysfunction in men and women. *American Journal of Psychiatry*, 1975, **132**, 164-168.

Wolpe, J. *The Practice of Behavior Therapy* (2nd ed.). New York: Pergamon Press, 1973.

Woody, R.H. Integrated aversion therapy and psychotherapy: Two sexual deviation case studies. *The Journal of Sex Research*, 1973, **9**, 313-324.

Zuckerman, M. Physiological measures of sexual arousal in the human. *Psychological Bulletin*, 1971, **75**, 347-356.

Name Index

This index includes authors referred to in both Volumes I and II of this Handbook. Volume I includes names on pages i to liii and 1-258. Volume II includes names on pages i to xxvi and 259-604. Roman numerals in bold type refer to Volume II.

Subject Index

This index includes subjects discussed in both Volumes I and II of this Handbook. Volume I includes subjects discussed on pages i to liii and pages 1-258. Volume II includes subjects discussed on pages i to xxvi and pages 259-604. Roman numerals in bold type refer to Volume II.